ALERT

to

God's Word

ALERT

to

GOD'S WORD

Ready-to-Read Scripture Guides for Weekday Masses

by

Reverend Cassian A. Miles, O.F.M.

with

James C. G. Conniff
Editorial Consultant

THE LITURGICAL PRESS

Collegeville, Minnesota

Nihil obstat: William G. Heidt, O.S.B., S.T.D., *Censor deputatus. Imprimatur*: † George H. Speltz, D.D., Bishop of St. Cloud.

To the Blessed Virgin Mary,
through whom all graces flow,
and to my parents,
my brother and my sister,
to whom I owe so much

CONTENTS

ACKNOWLEDGMENTS

The author gratefully acknowledges the following books as major sources in preparing the Scripture Guides. He assumes responsibility for his interpretation of this information in *Alert to God's Word.*

The Jerome Biblical Commentary, edited by Raymond E. Brown, S.S., Joseph A. Fitzmyer, S.J., and Roland E. Murphy, O.Carm. Englewood Cliffs, NJ, Prentice-Hall, Inc., 1968.

Peake's Commentary on the Bible, edited by Matthew Black and H. H. Rowley. London, Thomas Nelson and Sons, Ltd., 1962.

A New Catholic Commentary on Holy Scripture, edited by Reginald C. Fuller, Leonard Johnston, and Conleth Kearns, O.P. London, Thomas Nelson and Sons, Ltd., 1969.

The Interpreter's One-Volume Commentary on the Bible, edited by Charles M. Laymon. Nashville, TN, Abingdon Press, 1971.

Old Testament Reading Guide (30 booklets) and *New Testament Reading Guide* (14 booklets). Collegeville, MN, The Liturgical Press.

New Testament for Spiritual Reading (25 volumes), edited by John L. McKenzie, S.J. New York, Herder & Herder, Inc.

The Daily Study Bible (17 volumes), edited by William Barclay. Philadelphia, Westminster Press.

The Jerusalem Bible, General Editor, Alexander Jones, Garden City, NY, Doubleday & Co., Inc., 1966.

The Living Bible, Paraphrased. Wheaton, Il, Tyndale House, Publishers, 1971.

Dictionary of the Bible, John L. McKenzie, S.J. Milwaukee, Bruce Publishing Co., 1965.

Understanding the Old Testament, Bernhard W. Anderson. Englewood Cliffs, NJ, Prentice-Hall, Inc., 1957.

Rediscovering the Parables, Joachim Jeremias. New York, Charles Scribner's Sons, 1966.

Scripture texts in the Guides are from *The New American Bible.* Washington, DC, the Confraternity of Christian Doctrine, 1970.

PREFACE

Alert to God's Word has been written through a practical pastoral concern, namely, to help the faithful who attend weekday Mass to listen with greater understanding, and therefore more fruitfully, to the Scripture readings.

It is my experience as a priest — and I feel confident that others have observed this as well — that the weekday readings are often difficult to understand without some prior knowledge of their context. This is especially true for readings from the Old Testament, as well as for passages the understanding of which depends upon knowledge of the previous day's text.

Unless the congregation receives some orientation before hearing the text proclaimed, the sacred Word of God, in my judgment, will often fail to communicate all its riches to the people. To evaluate this judgment, one need only take a cursory sampling of the views of our people — religious and lay — who attend weekday Mass to determine how well they have understood the readings. It seems that our faithful simply do not reap the rich harvests that the Liturgy of the Word affords.

A homily certainly goes a long way toward remedying this unfortunate situation. But I believe the people need something more, even before they listen to the texts. Thus, *Alert to God's Word* offers a collection of brief ready-to-read commentaries designed to orient the faithful to the readings they hear at the weekday Masses throughout the Church year. An individual might also use this book to obtain a clearer insight into the readings and their relation to one another. To serve this additional purpose, Scripture citations for each Mass accompany the commentary for that day.

Each Scripture-Guide commentary is a complete and integrated unit, which the celebrant or a commentator should read to the congregation before the first reading — preferably right before the reading of the Scripture texts, rather than at the beginning of Mass. The orientation that the Scripture Guide provides will then be fresh in the people's minds as they listen to the readings.

Most of the commentaries deal in greater detail with the first Scripture readings than with the Gospels. I have adopted this imbalance deliberately, although reluctantly, because the texts of the first readings are, as a rule, less familiar to the average weekday churchgoer than the Gospels. The often difficult background of these first readings requires more explanation than do the familiar scenes of the Gospels.

Regrettably, because of space limitations, this choice prevents a more complete treatment of the Gospel for a particular day.

Another primary focus of each Scripture Guide is the relationship of the responsorial psalm to the first reading. While the foreword of the Lectionary recognizes this important aspect of the new arrangement for the Liturgy of the Word, it is nevertheless a relationship that unfortunately continues to be not widely understood. Whenever possible, I have quoted from psalm texts to show how they relate to the first reading.

However, I have been unable to locate guidelines — if indeed any such exist — to explain why the liturgy selects a particular psalm to accompany the text of a first reading. Thus, I have assumed the responsibility for determining this relationship — often a subtle one — that ties the psalm to a particular word, phrase, or theme of the first reading. Without the orientation of a commentary, the faithful may find this relationship of reading and responsory difficult to grasp. I have followed the same procedure in pointing out what appears to be a thematic reason for the choice of Scripture texts for the Advent and Lenten seasons.

In this book, the user will find commentaries for readings in the Lectionary for solemnities, feasts, and memorials of the Lord, the Blessed Virgin Mary, and the saints. There will be many occasions throughout the year when the celebrant may choose either (1) one of these Masses, or (2) the seasonal Mass of the day. Whichever he chooses will determine the commentary — either sanctoral or seasonal — for these days.

I leave to the celebrant's homily after the readings a more detailed comment on the texts and practical applications to the lives of those attending Mass beyond those I have suggested at times. I believe that the celebrant will find that the Scripture Guides will also stimulate ideas for a homily. With this in mind, I have incorporated, whenever the limits of the commentary permitted, points that the celebrant could elaborate on in a homily.

While I believe a commentary before the Scripture texts provides an invaluable aid for a better appreciation of God's Word, I do not thereby suggest that the commentary become a *substitute* for a homily. On the contrary, I agree wholeheartedly with the directive of the bishops at the Second Vatican Council, in the Constitution on the Sacred Liturgy, that "the homily is to be highly esteemed as part of the liturgy itself."

Whoever uses this book will also find an index of biblical passages that may prove helpful when he studies the Scriptures on his own. Although I do not offer these Scripture Guides as in any way scholarly commentaries on the texts, the reader may perhaps still find insights there that serve his spiritual growth.

In preparing the final text of this book, I have had the unusual and most gratifying experience of working closely with a demanding editorial consultant, Mr. James C. G. Conniff. In helping me revise the manuscript, Mr. Conniff taught me much about how to make the English language come alive for readers. If the commentaries do this, we will both be more than satisfied with this undertaking. We have prayed as well as toiled over this task. We leave the fruit of our labors to the Author of the Scriptures.

Finally, I would be very much amiss if I failed to acknowledge a number of others who played an important role in bringing these commentaries to a wider audience. I thank my fellow Franciscan friars for their encouragement when these commentaries first appeared in 1970 at St. Francis of Assisi, a busy service church in midtown Manhattan. I thank in particular Fr. Roy Gasnick, O.F.M., my colleague in the Franciscan Communications Office, and Mrs. Madeline Montague, our secretary, for their helpful criticisms; other friars who used the commentaries in parishes and shrine churches of our Holy Name Province, and several convents of sisters in Manhattan which also adopted the commentaries.

I recall, too, the response of Msgr. William K. Dolan, who discovered the commentaries on a visit to Manhattan and then used them at Marian Convent, Marywood, Scranton, PA., where he was chaplain; the encouraging approval to the idea for this book which I received from Fr. Stephen J. Hartdegen, O.F.M., Director of the U.S. Center for the Catholic Biblical Apostolate; the careful reading of the text by my brother Joseph, a professor of Scripture; the generous offer to type which Miss Margaret McDonald made at a critical juncture in completing the manuscript; all those who gave prayerful support to the task of revision; the inspiring articles I read years ago in the former *Orate Fratres* magazine (now *Worship*) by Fr. Clifford Howell, S.J. that nurtured my love for the Mass, and finally the insights into the subtle beauty of the liturgical texts that Dr. Pius Parsch taught me in his monumental *The Church's Year of Grace.*

It is my heartfelt wish that the use of these Scripture Guides may increasingly dispose believers everywhere to *be* alert to God's Word.

Feast of the Immaculate Conception   — Rev. Cassian A. Miles, O.F.M.
December 8, 1974   *New York City*

PROPER OF THE SEASON

176   MONDAY OF THE FIRST WEEK OF ADVENT — Cycle A

READING I   Is. 4:2-6   **RESP. Ps. 122:1-2, 3-4, (4-5, 6-7), 8-9**
GOSPEL   Matthew 8:5-11

Today's readings tell us about the age of the Messiah that the coming of Jesus into the world made a reality and which we recall in this Advent season. In the first passage, the prophet Isaiah looks forward to that age during which "the survivors of Israel" would live. These are the Jewish people who have survived a difficult time when God purified them because they had turned away from him. The prophet describes the blessings that the Jews enjoy in this age of the Messiah — rich harvests in the land, the favor of being God's holy people, and the protecting shelter of God's love over their lives. The responsorial psalm highlights these blessings in the verse, "May peace be within your walls, prosperity in your buildings." In the Gospel, Jesus also refers to the time when people from east and west will find a place at the banquet in God's kingdom.

176   MONDAY OF THE FIRST WEEK OF ADVENT — Cycles B & C

READING I   Is. 2:1-5   **RESP. Ps. 122:1-2, 3-4, (4-5, 6-7), 8-9**
GOSPEL   Matthew 8:5-11

At the weekday Masses of Advent, the liturgy selects Scripture readings that emphasize important themes of this season. Today's readings remind us that Jesus came as the promised Messiah to open the gates of God's kingdom to all men. The first passage looks forward to that day by describing how "all nations shall stream" toward "the mountain of the Lord's house." This mountain is the place where the Jews built the temple in Jerusalem. In this way, the liturgy teaches us that the Church is the new city of Jerusalem that welcomes all men into its fold. The responsorial psalm also portrays the people of all lands saying, "Let us go to the house of the Lord" in Jerusalem, which once again stands for God's kingdom. Then in the Gospel Jesus points out how not only the Jews but all men "will come from the east and the west" and find a place at the banquet in God's kingdom.

177   TUESDAY OF THE FIRST WEEK OF ADVENT

READING 1   Is. 11:1-10   **RESP. Ps. 72:1, 7-8, 12-13, 17**
GOSPEL   Luke 10:21-24

The first Scripture reading for today's Mass directs our attention to the theme of the Messiah as King of Israel. The prophet Isaiah explains

1

that once God has chastised the kingdom of Judah for its sins, the Lord will raise up a new king from the line of David. God will bestow on him all the qualities of the ideal king. His rule will begin the age of peace and justice when all nations will accept God. A reference near the end of this passage to the animals living in peace with one another suggests that the age of the Messiah will be a paradise restored. The responsorial psalm highlights this future messianic age in the refrain, "Justice shall flourish in his time, and fullness of peace forever." In the Gospel, Jesus tells his disciples that their knowledge of God's kingdom is what the prophets and kings of ages past looked forward to and spoke about.

178   WEDNESDAY OF THE FIRST WEEK OF ADVENT

Reading I   Is. 25:6-10   **RESP. Ps. 23:1-3, 3-4, 5, 6**
GOSPEL   Matthew 15:29-37

Today's Scripture readings present the theme of a feast that God will provide for all who have kept faith with him when his kingdom achieves its final victory at the end of time. This important message should offer hope to our hearts in this Advent season when we look forward to the final coming of Christ. The first reading tells us about a feast that God will give on his sacred mountain in Jerusalem for "all peoples" when sorrow and death will be no more. The responsorial psalm appropriately refers to God "spreading a table" for all who serve him faithfully. The Gospel describes how Jesus fed a crowd with only seven loaves and a few fish. This miracle suggests the bread of his own body that Jesus gave us at the Last Supper. Our Lord told his disciples then that he would share a banquet with them one day in the kingdom of his Father — a banquet we anticipate at this Mass.

179   THURSDAY OF THE FIRST WEEK OF ADVENT

READING I   Is. 26:1-6   **RESP. Ps. 118:1, 8-9, 19-21, 25-27**
GOSPEL   Matthew 7:21, 24-27

The Scripture readings for today's Mass ask us to consider to what extent we really place our trust in God and make him the firm foundation of our lives. In the first passage, the prophet Isaiah reveals that God is someone whom we can rely on with complete confidence. Isaiah's opening words depict God as setting up the walls of the city he loves and afterwards protecting it. But the prophet reminds us that God does this because the people who live in the city are faithful to him. On the other hand, God is like a rock who crushes those people who are proud and who trust in material riches rather than in him. The responsorial psalm accents the theme of the Mass by pointing out the rewards that come to the man who trusts in the Lord. The Gospel completes this theme by showing us a man who builds his life on the firm foundation of God's sacred words.

180 FRIDAY OF THE FIRST WEEK OF ADVENT

READING I   Is. 29:17-24   **RESP. Ps. 27:1, 4, 13-14**
GOSPEL   Matthew 9:27-31

Restoring sight to the blind is the theme that unifies the Scripture readings for today's Mass. However, this theme doesn't emphasize just the physical fact of being able to see again. The liturgy uses this wondrous change from blindness to sight to teach us, instead, about our faith and the way it ties us personally to Jesus. The Bible often treats blindness as a symbol for a person's lack of faith. In the first Scripture reading, the prophet Isaiah promises the cure of those who are physically and spiritually blind in the future age of the Messiah. Through the public ministry of Jesus, that longed-for age became a reality and is still with us. The responsorial psalm emphasizes this theme by proclaiming, "The Lord is my light," and by stating our desire to "gaze on the loveliness of the Lord." The Gospel story of the two blind men reminds us that faith delivers us from spiritual blindness.

181 SATURDAY OF THE FIRST WEEK OF ADVENT

READING I   Is. 30:19-21, 23-26   **RESP. Ps. 147:1-2, 3-4, 5-6**
GOSPEL   Matthew 9:35—10:1, 6-8

The Scripture readings for today's Mass focus on the theme of God taking care of his people. In the first passage, we hear God promising that he will not abandon them. He indicates through vivid word-pictures how he will give them prosperity. He will relieve their sufferings, their hunger, their want. He will grant abundant crops and cattle. Through such heart-warming images of the messianic times, the prophet Isaiah tries to bring hope and encouragement to the people to sustain them in times of trial. The responsorial psalm echoes this theme by referring to various ways that God will care for his people through his power and wisdom. The Gospel completes this theme by showing how the heart of Jesus was moved with pity at the sight of all the sick who came to have him heal them.

182 MONDAY OF THE SECOND WEEK OF ADVENT

READING I   Is. 35:1-10   RESP. Ps. 85:9-10, 11-12, 13-14
GOSPEL   Luke 5:17-26

Today's readings apply to the Advent theme of Jesus as the long-awaited Messiah. We discover in the first passage the kind of blessings that God will give to his people in the age of the Messiah. Among these, God will "make firm the knees that are weak," and then "the lame will leap like a stag." In the Gospel, we find Jesus performing a miracle for a crippled man that makes those blessings a reality for the people of his time. After forgiving the man's sins, our Lord heals the paralytic's weak limbs so that he can take up his mat and walk home, giving thanks to God. The first reading also promises that in the age of the Messiah the people "will see the glory of the Lord." We note in the Gospel that after our Lord's miracle, the crowd praises God for the wonder they have seen. The responsorial psalm echoes another theme of the reading, that "our God will come to save us."

183 TUESDAY OF THE SECOND WEEK OF ADVENT

READING I   Is. 40:1-11   RESP. Ps. 96:1-2, 3, 10, 11-12, 13
GOSPEL   Matthew 18:12-14

The first Scripture reading tells how God called the prophet Isaiah to bring comfort to God's people. This passage mentions a voice that cries out, "In the desert prepare the way of the Lord." This same expression occurs frequently in the prayers throughout the Advent season. It describes the mission of John the Baptist to prepare the way for the Messiah. Near the end of this reading, the prophet tells of a shepherd-king who "feeds his flock." It is a theme that calls to mind the image of Jesus as a shepherd which we find in today's Gospel. Our Lord uses the image of one sheep that has gone astray to teach us God's compassion for sinners. The responsorial psalm that we pray between these readings proclaims God's coming to us in all his strength and majesty — another important Advent theme.

184 WEDNESDAY OF THE SECOND WEEK OF ADVENT

READING I   Is. 40:25-31   RESP. Ps. 103:1-2, 3-4, 8, 10
GOSPEL   Matthew 11:28-30

The Scripture readings for today's Mass teach us that God gives us the strength we need to face difficult situations, discouragement, and loneliness. The first passage describes a period of discouragement for the Jewish people — the sixth century before Christ when the Babylonians had taken them into exile. The Jews fell into despair, thinking that God had abandoned them. That was why God sent a prophet to remind his beloved people that the Lord is the creator of all things and will not abandon those he loves. The responsorial psalm describes various ways that God bestows benefits upon his people. In thanksgiving, we pray, "O bless the Lord, my soul." The Gospel also deals with the theme of God comforting his people in time of trial. Jesus invites us to come to him with all our problems and he will refresh us.

185 THURSDAY OF THE SECOND WEEK OF ADVENT

READING I Is. 41:13-20   RESP. Ps. 145:1, 9, 10-11, 12-13
GOSPEL   Matthew 11:11-15

Today's Scripture readings present two themes of the Advent season — first, the blessings of the future age of the Messiah which the Jews looked forward to, and second, John the Baptist's preaching to prepare men for the Messiah's coming. In the first passage, God speaks as the Holy One of Israel to his chosen people in their Babylonian exile. God tells them not to fear because he will restore their land to them. In images familiar to the agricultural society of that time, the Lord describes the many ways he will enrich Israel. Today's liturgy suggests that we apply these images to the spiritual blessings we have experienced in our life of faith and be grateful for them. The responsorial psalm is a prayer thanking God for his kindness to us. In the Gospel, Jesus praises John the Baptist but teaches that the least member of God's kingdom is greater than this saint.

186 FRIDAY OF THE SECOND WEEK OF ADVENT

READING I Is. 48:17-19   RESP. Ps. 1:1-2, 3, 4, 6
GOSPEL   Matthew 11:16-19

Today's Scripture readings present two quite different ways in which men relate to God. The first passage shows us the way of the faithful and the blessings that come to them. God promises to give prosperity to the Jewish people if they remain true to him. The Gospel indicates the way of the faithless and their punishment. Our Lord tells a parable in which the Jews are like domineering children at play in the marketplace of life. They are angry because John the Baptist and Jesus — their

5

playmates — will not play their game of easy living and looking down on sinners. As a result, the Jews fail to realize that this is the very last chance that God will give them to reform their lives. The responsorial psalm between these readings is another contrasting picture of two men — one who is faithful to God's ways and one who is not.

187 SATURDAY OF THE SECOND WEEK OF ADVENT

READING I   Sirach 48:1-4, 9-11   RESP. Ps. 80:2-3, 15-16, 18-19
GOSPEL   Matthew 17:10-13

In today's readings we discover the relationship between the prophet Elijah and John the Baptist, the last in the line of the prophets, who prepared the way for Christ. The first passage declares that Elijah would return to soften the hearts of the people to welcome the Messiah. That was why the Jews at the time of Christ looked forward to Elijah's return as a sign that the Messiah would shortly deliver them from their Roman oppressors. As the Gospel begins, the disciples of Jesus have just witnessed his transfiguration on Mount Tabor. Moses and Elijah had appeared, talking with Jesus. The disciples then ask when Elijah will return. Jesus indicates that Elijah had already come to them through John the Baptist. The responsorial psalm proclaims the familiar cry of the Advent season, "Rouse your power, and come to save us."

188 MONDAY OF THE THIRD WEEK OF ADVENT

If today is December 17 or 18, omit these readings and use those for the weekdays of Advent, Nos. 194 or 195.

READING I   Num. 24:2-7, 15-17   RESP. Ps. 25:4-5, 6-7, 8-9
GOSPEL   Matthew 21:23-27

Today's first Scripture reading presents a figure from the days of the Old Testament, a man named Baalim. The Spirit of the Lord inspires Baalim to utter oracles or prophecies about the future of the Jewish people and the age of the Messiah. We hear Baalim declare that "a star shall advance from Jacob, and a staff shall rise from Israel." The terms "star" and "staff" are symbols for the royal power of a king. From very early times, both Jewish and Christian commentators on this passage have applied this prophecy to the Messiah. We may regard the responsorial psalm refrain as Baalim's prayer that God might prepare his heart to speak to the people. He pleads, "Teach me your ways, O Lord." In the Gospel, the chief priests question Jesus about his right to teach the way he does. Like Baalim, our Lord speaks on the authority of another, his Father, and not on his own.

189   TUESDAY OF THE THIRD WEEK OF ADVENT

If today is December 17 or 18, omit these readings and use those for the weekdays of Advent, Nos. 194 or 195.

READING I   Zeph. 3:1-2, 9-13   RESP. Ps. 34:2-3, 6-7, 17-18, 19, 23
GOSPEL   Matthew 21:28-32

Both Scripture readings for today's Mass reveal how God rebukes the Jewish people of the Old and New Testaments for not cooperating with his grace. The first passage begins with the prophet Zephaniah's reproach to the city of Jerusalem — a symbol for the whole nation. At that time, tyranny ruled the city and a religious outlook had practically disappeared in the wake of gross injustices. Zephaniah then promises that God will spare a small number of people who were faithful to him. The responsorial psalm refers to two themes of the reading in the verses "the Lord hears the cry of the poor" and "the Lord destroys the remembrance of evildoers." In the Gospel, Jesus rebukes the chief priests and elders of the people for not believing in him and for failing to repent their evil ways.

190   WEDNESDAY OF THE THIRD WEEK OF ADVENT

If today is December 17 or 18, omit these readings and use those for the weekdays of Advent, Nos. 194 or 195.

READING I   Is. 45:6-8, 18, 21-25   RESP. Ps. 85:9-10, 11-12, 13-14
GOSPEL   Luke 7:18-23

In today's first Scripture reading you will hear the words, "Let justice descend, O heavens, like dew from above . . . let the earth open and salvation bud forth." The liturgy uses these verses frequently during the Advent season. They express the ancient longing of the Jewish people for their Messiah as well, as our own longing for the final coming of Christ. In the responsorial psalm refrain, we once again plead for the coming of Jesus by praying, "Let the clouds rain down the Just One, and the earth bring forth a savior." In the Gospel, Jesus answers the questions from John the Baptist's disciples about whether our Lord is the Messiah they have so long awaited. Instead of giving a direct answer, Jesus describes the things the Old Testament prophets had foretold the

Messiah would do. Our Lord then declares that these are the very same things he is doing for the people.

191 THURSDAY OF THE THIRD WEEK OF ADVENT

If today is December 17 or 18, omit these readings and use those for the weekdays of Advent, Nos. 194 or 195.

READING I   Is. 54:1-10   RESP. Ps. 30:2 and 4, 5-6, 11-12 and 13
GOSPEL   Luke 7:24-30

The first reading for today's Mass takes us back to the closing years of the sixth century before Christ. At this time, the Jews were returning to their homeland in Palestine after a long forced exile in Babylonia. Their land's smaller size and enormous problems had discouraged the Jews. God's prophet consoles them with hope for the future. He assures them that their numbers will increase and that God, who may appear to have abandoned them, will take pity on them and bless them. The Gospel shows us how God's promise ripened in the preaching of John the Baptist that prepared for the saving ministry of Jesus. The responsorial psalm praises God for rescuing his chosen people and changing "my mourning into dancing."

192 FRIDAY OF THE THIRD WEEK OF ADVENT

If today is December 17 or 18, omit these readings and use those for the weekdays of Advent, Nos. 194 or 195.

READING I   Is. 56:1-3, 6-8   RESP. Ps. 67:2-3, 5, 7-8
GOSPEL   John 5:33-36

The first Scripture reading for today's Mass emphasizes the Advent theme that God calls all men to salvation. At the time of Israel's return from the Babylonian exile, the Jews allowed foreigners living within Palestine certain rights and privileges in their community. Today's passage shows that God would extend these benefits even to those outside the promised land — that is, to all who believe in the Lord and keep his commandments. The responsorial psalm refrain also accents this theme of universal salvation as we pray, "O God, let all the nations praise you." In the Gospel, you will hear Jesus referring to the way John the Baptist spoke publicly in our Lord's behalf. Jesus then points out that his miracles are even greater evidence than John's word that he is truly the long-awaited Messiah.

READING I   Gen. 49:2, 8-10   RESP. Ps. 72:3-4, 7-8, 17
GOSPEL   Matthew 1:1-17

In today's Mass the Scripture readings remind us that Jesus was a member of King David's royal family as God promised the Messiah would be. In the first passage, we meet Jacob, an ancestor of Jesus, who tells his sons, "The scepter shall never depart from Judah." A scepter was a staff that a ruler carried as a symbol of authority. In this way, Jacob indicates the supremacy of the tribe of Judah over all other tribes of Israel. Since King David was a member of the tribe of Judah, the passage shows God choosing David's family for the Messiah. In the Gospel, we hear St. Matthew's account of the ancestry of Christ. Matthew establishes the two requirements for the Messiah. First, he must be a true Israelite who can trace his lineage to Abraham. Second, his family line must descend from King David. The responsorial psalm describes the blessings in the age of the Messiah.

195 DECEMBER 18 — WEEKDAY OF ADVENT

READING I   Jer. 23:5-8   RESP. Ps. 72:1, 12-13, 18-19
GOSPEL   Matthew 1:18-24

Today's readings teach us how our Lord fulfilled the prophecies that the Messiah would come from King David's family. The first passage tells about this in the imagery of a family tree that is common even today. God promises through his prophet Jeremiah that he will raise up "a righteous shoot" (or branch) from the family tree of David. This future king, the Messiah, "shall reign and govern wisely." The responsorial psalm accents this theme by saying of God's king, "He shall govern your people with justice." The Gospel also shows how Jeremiah's prophecy about David's royal line came true. In Matthew's account of our Lord's birth, an angel refers to Joseph as "the son of David." Thus the Son of God has become man legally in the family of David through Joseph his foster-father, and naturally through Mary — as Luke's Gospel indicates.

196 DECEMBER 19 — WEEKDAY OF ADVENT

READING I   Judg. 13:2-7, 24-25   RESP. Ps. 71:3-4, 5-6, 16-17
GOSPEL   Luke 1:5-25

The Scripture readings today tell matching stories about the births of two important people involved in saving mankind from its sinfulness. The first reading tells the story of the birth of Samson, and the Gospel describes the birth of John the Baptist. You will notice a number of strikingly similar events in each of these stories. An angel comes to announce the news of each child's birth as someone whom God has set apart for a special mission to the Jewish people. Since each mother had previously been unable to have children, her pregnancy is evidence of God's special favor and purpose at work in her life. God invites each child to live a life of total dedication to his special calling. We may regard the responsorial psalm as a prayer from Samson and John, asking the Lord to help them carry out the assignments he has destined them for.

197 DECEMBER 20 — WEEKDAY OF ADVENT

READING I   Is. 7:10-14   RESP. Ps. 24:1-2, 3-4, 5-6
GOSPEL   Luke 1:26-38

Today's readings focus on an underlying theme of this season — how the Messiah was born of a virgin. In the first passage, God assures the Jewish King Ahaz that the throne of Judah will not go vacant because God has promised to continue the royal family of David forever. God gives the sign of a child whose name Immanuel means "God is with us." St. Matthew in his Gospel relates this prophecy to the birth of Jesus from the Virgin Mary. The responsorial psalm is one that the Jews sang during processions into the temple. In the words, "Let the Lord enter," the liturgy discovers a plea for the coming of Christ into our hearts through the graces of Christmas. The Gospel tells how God invited Mary to become the Mother of the Messiah. Some scholars find in the angel's greeting, "The Lord is with you," a reference to the Immanuel who God said would one day come to his people.

198 DECEMBER 21 — WEEKDAY OF ADVENT

READING I   Song. 2:8-14   RESP. Ps. 33:2-3, 11-12, 20-21
GOSPEL   Luke 1:39-45

The theme of joy runs through the Scripture readings for today's Mass. By continually sounding this note of joy, the liturgy encourages us to anticipate eagerly the joys of the Christmas season just a few days away. These joys are primarily spiritual, as we recall the way God showed his great love for us by becoming man. To develop this theme, the liturgy selects for the first reading one of the many love songs in the lyrical Song of Songs in the Old Testament. The girl talking in this passage symbolizes the Jewish people, and her lover represents God. The season of springtime is a further symbol that God expects to renew Israel when he comes as Messiah. The responsorial psalm accents this theme of joy in saying, "Cry out with joy in the Lord." In the Gospel, we share the joy Elizabeth experienced when Mary visited her.

OR:

READING I   Zeph. 3:14-18   RESP. Ps. 33:2-3, 11-12, 20-21
GOSPEL   Luke 1:39-45

The theme of joy runs through the Scripture readings for today's Mass. By continually sounding this note of joy, the liturgy encourages us to anticipate eagerly the joys of the Christmas season just a few days away. These joys are primarily spiritual, as we recall the way God showed his great love for us by becoming man. To develop this theme, the liturgy invites us to listen to a joyful message from the prophet Zephaniah in the first reading. He calls the Jewish people to proclaim their joy because the Lord has forgiven them. Especially appropriate for this season is what the prophet says about the Lord God being in the midst of his people as a mighty savior who renews them by his love. The responsorial psalm accents this theme of joy by inviting us to "cry out with joy in the Lord." In the Gospel, we share Elizabeth's joy when Mary visited her.

199   DECEMBER 22 — WEEKDAY OF ADVENT

READING I   1 Sam. 1:24-28   RESP. Ps. 1 Sam. 2:1, 4-5, 6-7, 8
GOSPEL   Luke 1:46-56

The responsorial psalm and the Gospel for today's Mass present two inspiring prayers of praise to God by women who were important figures in the history of man's salvation. The first prayer is that of Hannah, the mother of Samuel. He was the man who anointed David as king of Israel. We will respond to the first reading by saying Hannah's prayer. The reading itself tells us what prompted Hannah to pray this way. She had brought her baby Samuel to the temple and dedicated him to the service of God. She did this to thank God for allowing her to have a child. The Gospel passage contains the prayer of praise Mary spoke when she arrived at the house of her cousin Elizabeth. The liturgy uses this hymn, which we call the Magnificat, in her evening prayer of Vespers.

READING I Mal. 3:1-4, 23-24   RESP. Ps. 25:4-5, 8-9, 10, 14
GOSPEL   Luke 1:57-66

The first Scripture reading for today's Mass calls our attention to a special messenger who will prepare the Jewish people for the coming of the Messiah. We hear the prophet Malachi identify this person as the prophet Elijah. This passage apparently had a strong influence in creating the people's expectation at the time of Jesus that Elijah would return one day to announce the coming of the Messiah. The Gospel tells us about the birth of John the Baptist. We know he was the messenger that Malachi spoke about because Jesus told his disciples that John had fulfilled the destiny of Elijah. John's mission was to proclaim repentance — a reminder for us today to prepare our own hearts for the graces of the Christmas season. The responsorial psalm also anticipates the approaching feast of Christ's birth in the refrain, "Your redemption is near at hand."

201 DECEMBER 24 — WEEKDAY OF ADVENT

READING I 2 Sam. 7:1-5, 8-12, 14, 16   RESP. Ps. 89:2-3, 4-5, 27, 29
GOSPEL   Luke 1:67-79

The Scripture readings for today's final Mass of the Advent season focus our attention on God's promise to send a Messiah for his people from the family line of King David. The first passage takes us back to the time when David had overcome many of his enemies. The king began to think of building a temple where his people could worship God. The Lord indicated to David through the king's friend, the prophet Nathan, his own wishes about this project. God then promised to continue the house of David forever. Our response to this reading highlights this theme with the words, "Forever will I confirm your posterity." The Gospel contains the hymn of praise that Zechariah, the father of John the Baptist, prayed when the boy received the name John at his circumcision. In the opening lines, you will hear Zechariah refer to God's promise to bring salvation to his people through David.

696 DECEMBER 26 — ST. STEPHEN, First Martyr

READING I Acts 6:8-10; 7:54-59   RESP. Ps. 31:3-4, 6, 7, 8, 17, 21
GOSPEL   Matthew 10:17-22

The special Scripture readings for today's Mass direct our attention to St. Stephen, the first Christian martyr. He was one of the seven deacons the apostles appointed to assist them in caring for the needs of the Christian community. The first passage tells of the "great wonders and signs" Stephen performed in his witness to the risen Christ, before the supreme court of the Jews arrested him. We then learn about the tragic outcome of his trial as the Jews rise up in blind hatred and drag Stephen to his death by stoning. The responsorial psalm refrain echoes the last words Stephen spoke as he died. In the Gospel, Jesus warns his disciples that they will undergo many sufferings in preaching his message to the world. We find our Lord's words fulfilled in Stephen's violent death because he preached about Jesus so fearlessly.

697 DECEMBER 27 — ST. JOHN, Apostle and Evangelist

READING I   1 John 1:1-4   RESP. Ps. 97:1-2, 5-6, 11-12
GOSPEL   John 20:2-8

The first Scripture readings for the Masses during the next two weeks are from the first letter of St. John the Apostle, whose feast we celebrate today. In this opening passage of his letter, John explains that he has every right to talk about the Christian life because he personally knew Jesus and was an eyewitness to his life. He wishes to share with others his own joyful friendship with God. The responsorial psalm refrain after this reading captures the special joy we feel in our hearts at Christmas, in the words, "Let good men rejoice in the Lord." The Gospel directs our attention to the morning of the resurrection. Scripture commentators believe that the apostle John is the "other disciple" who runs with Peter to the tomb in search of Jesus.

698 DECEMBER 28 — HOLY INNOCENTS, Martyrs

READING I   1 John 1:5—2:2   RESP. Ps. 124:2-3, 4-5, 7-8
GOSPEL   Matthew 2:13-18

We find the main themes of today's feast in the responsorial psalm and the Gospel reading. We may regard the psalm as Joseph's and Mary's reflection on how God allowed them to escape with the child Jesus from King Herod's wrath. Especially appropriate is the refrain, "Our soul has escaped like a bird from the hunter's net." In the Gospel, St. Matthew regards the Holy Family's flight into Egypt and Herod's massacre of the innocent children as fulfilling two Old Testament prophecies. The first reading continues St. John's first letter that the liturgy assigns to this season when we celebrate his feast. We hear John explain his view of the world as divided into "light" and "darkness" — two words that appear frequently throughout his Gospel. Although a Christian tries to walk "in light," he may turn to Christ for forgiveness if he sins.

203 DECEMBER 29 — FIFTH DAY IN THE OCTAVE OF CHRISTMAS

READING I 1 John 2:3-11   RESP. Ps. 96:1-2, 2-3, 5-6
GOSPEL Luke 2:22-35

In the first Scripture reading, the apostle John emphasizes that we must keep God's commandments to achieve a loving intimacy with him. John points out the self-sacrificing love that Christians must have for one another, based on the love Jesus has for them. A man or woman's failure to keep this new commandment of love removes that individual from the light of Christ, so that he walks as much in the darkness as the blind. The verses of the responsorial psalm emphasize the joy in heaven and on earth over the birth of Jesus because it has brought salvation to all nations. The Gospel tells how Joseph and Mary presented the child Jesus in the temple as the Law of Moses required. After the Holy Spirit gave the old man Simeon the privilege of recognizing the child, Simeon proclaimed that the birth of Jesus heralded the age of the Messiah.

204 DECEMBER 30 — SIXTH DAY IN THE OCTAVE OF CHRISTMAS

READING I 1 John 2:12-17   RESP. Ps. 96:7-8, 8-9, 10
GOSPEL Luke 2:36-40

In today's first reading, St. John challenges the Christians of his day to resist the temptations that the world puts in their path. His message offers a powerful antidote to the poisons that corrupt our own society. We hear John address two groups in the community as his "little children." These are the fathers or older members and the young people. John urges them to free their hearts from lust, greed, and self-importance. The responsorial psalm emphasizes the joy in heaven and on earth over the birth of Jesus. The Gospel continues yesterday's account of how Joseph and Mary, obeying Jewish law, presented the child Jesus in the temple. The Holy Spirit had guided the old man Simeon to recognize the promised Messiah in the infant Jesus cradled in his arms. Today we learn that God gives the holy woman Anna an experience that is almost as overwhelming as Simeon's.

205 DECEMBER 31 — THE SEVENTH DAY IN THE OCTAVE OF CHRISTMAS

READING I   1 John 2:18-21   RESP. Ps. 96:1-2, 11-12, 13
GOSPEL   John 1:1-18

In the first Scripture reading, we continue the apostle John's first letter to the Christian communities in what is now Turkey. You will hear John rebuking those who have deserted the faith. He views this as a sign of the coming of the antichrist, a term that means those who oppose Christ. John concludes that the failure of these people to remain true to the faith indicates they were not really believers to start with. The verses of the responsorial psalm emphasize the joy in heaven and on earth over the birth of Jesus. The Gospel reading is also appropriate for this Christmas season. It is the famous prologue or introduction to St. John's Gospel. He reveals that Jesus Christ, the Word of God, has existed from all eternity with God. In the fullness of time, the Word became flesh and made his dwelling among us.

18 JANUARY 1 — OCTAVE OF CHRISTMAS, SOLEMNITY OF MARY, MOTHER OF GOD

READING 1   Num. 6:22-27   RESP. Ps. 67:2-3, 5, 6, 8
READING II   Gal. 4:4-7
GOSPEL   Luke 2:16-21

The Scripture readings for today's Mass draw our attention to the birth of Jesus and his sacred name. The first passage tells how God gave Moses and his brother Aaron a special formula for blessing the people of Israel in God's name. This blessing, widely used through the centuries, was also the one which St. Francis of Assisi chose to bless his little brothers. The responsorial psalm takes up this theme as we pray, "May God bless us in his mercy." In the special second reading today, St. Paul refers to the birth of Jesus while reminding the Galatians that God has freed them from the bonds of the Law of Moses. In the Gospel, the shepherds adore the baby Jesus. Eight days later he receives his name — which means "Savior."

206 JANUARY 2

READING I   1 John 2:22-28   RESP. Ps. 98:1, 2-3, 3-4
GOSPEL   John 1:19-28

In the first Scripture reading for today's Mass, the apostle John warns the Christian communities in Asia Minor about false teachers who deny that Jesus is the promised Messiah. We hear John explain that the anointing of the Holy Spirit enables each Christian to adhere to the truth of what the Church teaches about Jesus. The responsorial psalm praises the Lord for making his offer of salvation known to all nations. The liturgy then chooses a Gospel scene from the beginning of our Lord's public ministry, for a special reason. Through this reading we realize that the birth of Jesus we recall in this season was God's first step toward revealing his Son as the Messiah thirty years later. And so in the Gospel we hear John the Baptist explain to those who question him that he is simply preparing the way for the Messiah.

In countries where Epiphany is celebrated on the Sunday between January 2 and January 8, the readings assigned to the days January 7 to January 12 are used after Epiphany and the following readings are omitted (see nos. 213-218).

207 JANUARY 3

READING I   1 John 2:29—3:6   RESP. Ps. 98:1, 3-4, 5-6
GOSPEL   John 1:29-34

Today's first Scripture reading returns to a basic teaching of St. John that Christians are children of God. This is why John exhorts the Christian communities in Asia Minor to behave the way sons of God should behave by responding to God's love and avoiding sin. The responsorial psalm praises the Lord for making his offer of salvation known to all nations. The liturgy then chooses a Gospel scene from the beginning of our Lord's public ministry, for a special reason. By this reading we come to realize that the birth of Jesus we recall this season was God's first step toward revealing his Son as the Messiah thirty years later. And so in the Gospel John the Baptist gives public witness to Jesus. John declares that he recognized Jesus as the one whom God had chosen when John baptized Jesus in the Jordan.

208 JANUARY 4

READING I   1 John 3:7-10   RESP. Ps. 98:1, 7-8, 9
GOSPEL   John 1:35-42

In the first Scripture reading for today's Mass, the apostle John teaches the Christian communities in Asia Minor that a sinful way of life is not in keeping with God's love for them. We hear John explain that no one begotten of God should act sinfully, because "he remains of God's stock," that is, he belongs to the same family as God himself by adoption. The responsorial psalm praises the Lord for making his offer of salvation known to all nations. The liturgy then chooses a Gospel scene from the beginning of our Lord's public ministry, for a special reason. By this reading we come to realize that the birth of Jesus we recall in this season was God's first step toward revealing his Son as the Messiah thirty years later. And so in the Gospel we learn how Jesus called Simon Peter and his brother Andrew to be his disciples.

209   JANUARY 5

READING I   1 John 3:11-21   **RESP.** Ps. 100:1-2, 3, 4, 5
GOSPEL   John 1:43-51

In today's first reading, the apostle of love, St. John, explains what it really means to love others. He begins by showing the opposite of brotherly love — Cain's murder of his brother Abel. John uses this incident to develop his Christian insight that when we show hatred toward a person we are committing very much the same thing as murder. He insists that we must prove our love by actions and not merely by words. The responsorial psalm invites all the earth to cry out with joy because God has become man and made us his special people. The liturgy chooses a Gospel scene from the beginning of our Lord's public ministry, for a special reason. Through this reading we realize that the birth of Jesus we recall in this season was God's first step toward revealing his Son as the Messiah thirty years later. And so, in the Gospel, Jesus calls Philip and Nathanael to be his disciples.

210   JANUARY 6

These readings are used in countries where Epiphany is celebrated on January 7 or 8.

READING I   1 John 5:5-13   **RESP.** Ps. 147:12-13, 14-15, 19-20
GOSPEL   Mark 1:7-11

In the first Scripture reading for today's Mass, the apostle John teaches the Christian communities in Asia Minor that God has given them eternal life in his Son Jesus. You will hear John explain that Jesus came "through water and blood," that is, the water of his baptism in the Jordan River and the blood he shed for mankind's redemption. John

17

then declares that what God said in support of his Son should convince our hearts more than what any mere man might say. The responsorial psalm invites the Church, the new Jerusalem, to praise God for sending his Son to bring peace to the world, to fill our hearts with the saving wheat of the Eucharist, and to proclaim his salvation to all men. The liturgy selects a Gospel reading that applies to John's mention of our Lord's coming "in water." We will hear St. Mark's account of the baptism of Jesus.

211 JANUARY 7

These readings are used in countries where Epiphany is celebrated on January 8.

READING I 1 John 5:14-21	RESP. Ps. 149:1-2, 3-4, 5, 6, 9
GOSPEL John 2:1-12	

Today's Scripture reading concludes the first letter of the apostle John. He declares that a Christian may turn in confident prayer to God for all his needs, as long as he is striving to be faithful to God's will. John then sketches some of the basic ideas he has previously emphasized in his letter. The responsorial psalm refrain reminds us of God's great love for us which we celebrate in this season. We joyfully proclaim, "The Lord takes delight in his people." The liturgy chooses the Gospel about the wedding feast in Cana today, for a special reason. Through this reading we realize that the birth of Jesus we recall this season was God's first step toward revealing his Son as the Messiah thirty years later, when our Lord turned the water into wine.

The readings assigned from January 7 to January 12 are used on the days which follow Epiphany, even if this is transferred to Sunday, up to the following Saturday.
Nevertheless on Monday after the Sunday on which the Baptism of the Lord is celebrated (i.e., the Sunday after January 6), the readings of the season of the year begin, and any readings left over from those assigned for January 7 to January 12 are omitted.

213 JANUARY 7 — OR MONDAY AFTER EPIPHANY

READING I 1 John 3:22—4:6	RESP. Ps. 2:7-8, 10-11
GOSPEL Matthew 4:12-17, 23-25	

In today's first Scripture reading, the apostle John warns the Christians in Asia Minor not to delude or deceive themselves about spiritual matters. He had in mind the dangers the communities faced from the false teachings of those who were trying to pollute what Christ taught. John declares that if anyone "acknowledges Jesus Christ come in the flesh," that is, the incarnation of God's Son, then he truly belongs to God. The responsorial psalm recalls the adoration of the Magi in the verse, "And now, O kings . . . with trembling, pay homage to him." The liturgy also selects a Gospel reading that is appropriate for this week after Epiphany, a Greek word that means an appearance. St. Matthew tells of the first *appearance* of Jesus in Galilee, preaching repentance and healing the sick.

214 JANUARY 8 — OR TUESDAY AFTER EPIPHANY

READING I 1 John 4:7-10   RESP. Ps. 72:1-2, 3-4, 7-8
GOSPEL   Mark 6:34-44

In the first Scripture reading for today's Mass, the apostle John returns to the theme of love for one another in his letter to the Christians in Asia Minor. He tells them that God is love, and love characterizes all of God's dealings with men. God has given his love freely, and the most perfect way he has to show his love is through his Son's offering of himself for our sins. The responsorial psalm refrain recalls the adoration of the Magi in the words, "Lord, every nation on earth will adore you." The liturgy also selects a Gospel reading that is appropriate for this week after Epiphany, a Greek word for a manifestation or showing. St. Mark tells how Jesus *manifested* his miraculous powers by feeding a crowd of five thousand.

215 JANUARY 9 — OR WEDNESDAY AFTER EPIPHANY

READING I 1 John 4:11-18   RESP. Ps. 72:1-2, 10, 12-13
GOSPEL   Mark 6:45-52

In today's first Scripture reading, the apostle John continues to discuss God's love for us, and our duty in turn to share this love with others. John declares that the Holy Spirit we received at baptism guarantees our union with God. Our awareness of God living in our hearts will help us not to be afraid of God. Love has no room for fear. This same theme of freedom from fear occurs in the Gospel. The passage is also appropriate for this special week after the feast of the Epiphany, a Greek word that means an appearance. Jesus *appears* to the apostles as they battle a fierce storm on the Sea of Galilee. Our Lord tells them not to be afraid, but to have faith in him. The responsorial psalm recalls the adoration of the Magi in the verse, "The kings of Tarshish and the Isles shall offer gifts."

READING I   1 John 4:19—5:4   RESP. Ps. 72:1-2, 14-15, 17
GOSPEL   Luke 4:14-22

The first Scripture reading for today's Mass continues St. John's reflections on how much God loves us and our responsibility for loving one another. You will hear the apostle warn the Christian communities in Asia Minor how easy it is for them to deceive themselves about this. No one can pretend to love God who does not love his brothers. In the final chapter of his letter, John reminds us how faith and love relate to each other. The responsorial psalm refrain recalls the adoration of the Magi in the words, "Lord, every nation on earth will adore you." The liturgy also selects a Gospel reading that is appropriate for this week after Epiphany, a Greek word for a manifestation or showing. St. Luke points out that our Lord's preaching of glad tidings to the poor has fulfilled the prophet Isaiah's words and *manifested* God's saving presence among men.

217   JANUARY 11 — OR FRIDAY AFTER EPIPHANY

READING I   1 John 5:5-13   RESP. Ps. 147:12-13, 14-15, 19-20
GOSPEL   Luke 5:12-16

In today's first reading, we hear the apostle John teaching about the incarnation of the Son of God. He points out that Jesus has come through water and blood. By water John means our Lord's baptism by John the Baptist in the River Jordan. The blood refers to the redeeming death of Jesus on the cross. Commentators find in this passage a symbolic reference to the water and blood in the sacraments of baptism and the Eucharist. The responsorial psalm recalls the adoration of the Magi by inviting the Church, symbolized by the city of Jerusalem, to "praise the Lord." The liturgy also selects a Gospel reading that is appropriate for this week after Epiphany, a Greek word for a manifestation or showing. After telling how Jesus healed a leper, St. Luke discloses that our Lord *manifested* himself increasingly among men because "his reputation spread more and more."

218   JANUARY 12 — OR SATURDAY AFTER EPIPHANY

READING I   1 John 5:14-21   RESP. Ps. 149:1-2, 3-4, 5-6, 9
GOSPEL   John 3:22-30

Today's first Scripture reading concludes the first letter of the apostle John. We hear John remind the Christians in Asia Minor to approach God in confident prayer, especially for sinners. He then stresses one of the main themes of his letter, that sin should have no place in the life of a Christian. The responsorial psalm is a joyful song of praise to God as we recall how "the Lord takes delight in his people." The liturgy selects a Gospel reading that is appropriate for this week after Epiphany, a Greek word for a manifestation or showing. John the Baptist tells his disciples that the time is ripe for Jesus to *manifest* himself to the people. Our Lord must increase, and John must decrease. John's words also prepare our hearts to reflect on St. Mark's account of the public ministry of Jesus when the Season of the Year begins on Monday.

220 ASH WEDNESDAY

READING I   Joel 2:12-18   **RESP.** Ps. 51:3-4, 5-6, 12-13, 14, 17
GOSPEL   Matthew 6:1-6, 16-18

In today's first Scripture reading we hear a sermon about the need to repent that the prophet Joel preached to the Jewish people centuries ago. The way he called his fellow men to fast and renew their interior lives applies also to our lives today. But we must realize that when Joel summons us to repent he is not talking about it as a step for the individual to take. He sees this as a social concern for the whole community — a step toward God by a people the Lord has chosen for himself. In this way, the liturgy reminds us that we begin Lent not only as individuals but with our hearts joined with those of all God's people throughout the world. The responsorial psalm allows us to acknowledge our sinfulness before the Lord. The Gospel also emphasizes the need for an inner conversion of heart that is basic to the life of a Christian.

221 THURSDAY AFTER ASH WEDNESDAY

READING I   Deut. 30:15-20   **RESP.** Ps. 1:1-2, 3, 4, 6
GOSPEL   Luke 9:22-25

As we listen to the Lenten Scripture readings, we must keep in mind that the Church is interested not so much in the original meaning and context of the passages, but how we apply them to our lives. These readings become in this way an opportunity for the Church to instruct us each day about certain attitudes of heart and the way to practice virtue. For that reason we must go beyond what Moses says to the Jews in the first reading about being true to God's commandments. Instead, the Church is telling us why we must be faithful to God's laws every day of our lives. The liturgy stresses this point again in the responsorial psalm. It says that a man achieves happiness when he does what God wants him to do in his life. The Gospel presents another important Lenten theme as Jesus tells his disciples that he will have to endure many sufferings and then go to his death.

222 FRIDAY AFTER ASH WEDNESDAY

READING I Is. 58:1-9   **RESP.** Ps. 51:3-4, 5-6, 18-19
GOSPEL Matthew 9:14-15

In today's first reading, the liturgy reminds us not to make the Lenten season just a matter of fasting from food. The prophet Isaiah teaches us what the real spirit of fasting should be. He tells us first that a certain hypocrisy marked those Jewish people who fasted for show on holy days but displeased God by mistreating their fellow human beings. Isaiah then spells out practical works of mercy that do please God. We might imitate these in a variety of ways in our own lives during this penitential season. After this reading, we pray several verses from Psalm 51. These emphasize another important Lenten theme — contrition for our sins. The Gospel also suggests that at times a particular situation may take priority over fasting. For instance, our Lord's disciples cannot fast as long as they enjoy the presence of God's own Son among them.

223 SATURDAY AFTER ASH WEDNESDAY

READING I Is. 58:9-14   **RESP.** Ps. 86:1-2, 3-4, 5-6
GOSPEL Luke 5:27-32

The liturgy uses the words of the prophet Isaiah in the first reading to teach us the blessings that will come to us if we practice kindness and show compassion to others. The passage reminds us that selfish concentration on things, instead of people, separates us from God and from all his other children. As we listen, we will notice that the prophet insists on how important it is for us to worship God on his holy day instead of getting involved in things that take us away from him. At the end of the reading, we will pray from Psalm 86, which tells us the way we should regard Lent. That way means to open up our hearts so that

God can teach us what he wants us to do. In the Gospel, Jesus explains that he has come to call sinners to change their hearts. This theme will appear often in the prayers and readings throughout this season.

225 MONDAY OF THE FIRST WEEK OF LENT

READING I   Lev. 19:1-2, 11-18   **RESP.** Ps. 19:8, 9, 10, 15
GOSPEL   Matthew 25:31-46

The Scripture readings today show us how to make our lives more holy during Lent by treating other people the way we should. To teach us what God expects of us in this matter, the first passage contains many practical reminders of how to act toward members of our family, our friends and neighbors, and the people we work with. The closing words of God to Moses — "you shall love your neighbor as yourself" — find concrete application again in the familiar Gospel scene of the last judgment. We learn that Jesus will reward us or punish us by the way we have responded to people's needs. Even more so, what we do for others — or neglect to do — directly relates to Christ, who identifies himself with the needy. Since the first reading contains God's commands on right conduct, the responsorial psalm emphasizes how God's laws "give wisdom" and "refresh the soul."

226 TUESDAY OF THE FIRST WEEK OF LENT

READING I   Is. 55:10-11   **RESP.** Ps. 34:4-5, 6-7, 16-17, 18-19
GOSPEL   Matthew 6:7-15

Today's Scripture readings give us an insight into what we ask for so often in the "Our Father" when we pray, "Thy will be done on earth as it is in heaven." The prophet Isaiah helps us to understand first of all how perfectly God's will is done in heaven. Every word that proceeds from God's mouth serves God without fail. This word accomplishes whatever plan God has ordained, just as surely as the rain and snow bring fertility to the soil. On earth, however, it is possible that men do not carry out God's plans for their happiness because they have a free will. For this reason, Jesus asks us to pray that God's will "be done" — that is, that men will not keep on blocking God's purposes for the world. This Lenten season gives us opportunities to change whatever in our lives prevents God's will from governing here on earth as it does in heaven.

227 WEDNESDAY OF THE FIRST WEEK OF LENT

READING I Jonah 3:1-10   RESP. Ps. 51:3-4, 12-13, 18-19
GOSPEL   Luke 11:29-32

The lesson of the Scripture readings in today's Mass is that penance pleases God and wins his mercy and forgiveness. The first passage shows God telling the prophet Jonah to go to Nineveh and preach repentance to its people. Their response to Jonah made God set aside the punishment he had in store for these sinful men and women. Instead, God thought of them as friends. In the Gospel, we will hear Jesus refer to Jonah by pointing out to the sinful Jewish people that someone greater than Jonah is living among them. Our Lord is talking about his mission from the Father to make people realize they have a lot to be sorry for. This repentance is at bottom an honest acknowledgment that we are selfish by nature, and it's about time we admitted it and turned to God for forgiveness. The responsorial psalm allows us to express our feelings of regret for our sins.

228 THURSDAY OF THE FIRST WEEK OF LENT

READING I Esther C:12, 14-16, 23-25   RESP. Ps. 138:1-2, 2-3, 7-8
GOSPEL   Matthew 7:7-12

In today's Mass, we continue to develop the pattern of teaching that lies behind the Scripture readings the liturgy has chosen for this Lenten season. So far we have listened to passages that impress on us God's call to repent and make our peace with him. Today's readings deal with our life of prayer so that we may realize how important this is and cultivate prayer again during Lent if we have been neglecting it in the past. The first passage presents an inspiring model of prayer in the story of Esther. This heroic woman of the Old Testament went before God to plead for her people. The responsorial psalm encourages us to pray for God's help at every turn in our lives and assures us that the Lord will always answer us. In the Gospel, Jesus reminds us never to give up on prayer because God is always anxious to help us.

229 FRIDAY OF THE FIRST WEEK OF LENT

READING I Ezek. 18:21-28   RESP. Ps. 130:1-2, 3-4, 4-6, 7-8
GOSPEL   Matthew 5:20-26

The Scripture readings for today's Mass remind us to convert our hearts to the ways of God. As we listen to the readings, we should think of them as a practical message that the Church is teaching us and not as words that someone wrote centuries ago that do not apply to us. In this way, the liturgy shows us today in the first passage how pleasing it is to God when a man turns away from his bad habits and how displeasing it is when a good person falls into a life of serious sin. In the Gospel, Jesus also stresses the need to convert our hearts. Our Lord warns that we must restore good relations with our brothers before coming to the altar to offer our gifts to God. Jesus is referring to those cases where we are at fault and can do something to make amends. The responsorial psalm is an opportunity for us to pray that God may forgive our sins.

230   SATURDAY OF THE FIRST WEEK OF LENT

READING I   Deut. 26:16-19   RESP. Ps. 119:1-2, 4-5, 7-8
GOSPEL   Matthew 5:43-48

Today's readings continue to focus our attention on important virtues for us to practice during the Lenten season. We have heard much already about prayer, fasting, and sorrow for sin. Today the readings stress how important it is for us to keep God's commandments. In the first passage, we hear God impressing on the Jewish people why they should be faithful to his commandments. The liturgy intends this as a reminder for us to obey them also today. Then, in the Gospel reading, we hear Jesus extend the scope of the commandments to embrace the total love of all men — enemy and friend alike. The responsorial psalm between these readings is our way of saying that we accept God's laws and want to fulfill them in our lives every day. In doing so, we realize that "happy are they who follow the law of the Lord."

231   MONDAY OF THE SECOND WEEK OF LENT

READING I   Dan. 9:4-10   RESP. Ps. 79:8, 9, 11, 13
GOSPEL   Luke 6:36-38

The readings from Scripture for today's Mass remind us that we must show compassion for the faults of others because God has been so understanding of our own failings. In the first passage, the prophet Daniel makes a public act of contrition for the sins of the Jewish nation. You will hear Daniel mention that God showed compassion and forgiveness toward his children even though they were so rebellious. The liturgy suggests to us today that if God can be willing to forgive the sins of his beloved people who so often hurt and disappointed him, how much more should we be willing to find ways to reconcile ourselves with others, despite the many times they have hurt us. The responsorial psalm accents this theme in the verse, "May your compassion quickly come to us, for we are brought very low." In the Gospel we also hear Jesus asking us to imitate the compassion of his Father.

232 TUESDAY OF THE SECOND WEEK OF LENT

READING I Is. 1:10, 16-20   **RESP.** Ps. 50:8-9, 16-17, 21, 23
GOSPEL   Matthew 23:1-12

The Scripture readings for today's Mass teach us another important lesson for the Lenten season — we must practice what we preach. In the first passage, the prophet Isaiah speaks in God's name and warns the Jewish people that they must "cease doing evil" and "learn to do good." The Church urges us today to take his message to heart in our own lives. In the Gospel, Jesus teaches the crowds and his disciples to avoid the insincere, hypocritical deeds of the Pharisees. They perform their works only to be pleasing in the sight of men. The responsorial psalm between these readings also accents this theme in the Lord's question, "Why do you profess my covenant with your mouth . . . and then cast my words behind you?"

233 WEDNESDAY OF THE SECOND WEEK OF LENT

READING I Jer. 18:18-20   **RESP.** Ps. 31:5-6, 14, 15-16
GOSPEL   Matthew 20:17-28

The Scripture readings for the Lenten Masses usually emphasize a spiritual outlook for us to put into practice during this penitential season. At times, however, the liturgy departs from this plan to remind us of the climax of Lent — the suffering and death of Jesus that we recall in the final days of Holy Week. We find an example of this in the readings for today's Mass. In the first passage, we hear how the Jewish leaders of his time plotted against Jeremiah and how this prophet prayed that God would deliver him from his enemies. What these people did to Jeremiah foreshadowed what Christ would undergo at the hands of the Jewish leaders centuries later. In the Gospel, Jesus refers to his arrest, his sufferings, and his divine destiny to ransom the world. We may regard the responsorial psalm as a prayer of both Jeremiah and Jesus when their enemies surrounded them.

234 THURSDAY OF THE SECOND WEEK OF LENT

READING I   Jer. 17:5-10   RESP. Ps. 1:1-2, 3, 4, 6
GOSPEL   Luke 16:19-31

In the Scripture readings for today's Mass, we find three examples of a figure who often appears in the books of the Bible for us to imitate. He is the man who places his trust in God and not just in human beings. In each case, we discover the contrast between the man who clings fast to God in spite of everything and the man who relies only on human resources. In the first reading, we hear the prophet Jeremiah sketch the details of these contrasting portraits in images familiar to the farm people of his time. Then we will pray several verses from Psalm 1 that develop a similar picture of the good man and the wicked man. Finally, in the Gospel reading, our Lord provides a memorable story about a beggar and a rich man. Here, too, we find a man who suffers but trusts in God and another man who realizes too late his need for God.

235 FRIDAY OF THE SECOND WEEK OF LENT

READING I   Gen. 37:3-4, 12-13, 17-28   RESP. Ps. 105:16-17, 18-19, 20-21
GOSPEL   Matthew 21:33-43, 45-46

Today's Scripture readings remind us that many of his own people first rejected Jesus and then arrested, tortured and killed him. The first passage develops this key Lenten theme by telling the story of Joseph, the beloved son of a man named Israel. As we learn of the attempt that Joseph's brothers made to kill him, we should recall that Jesus suffered this same fate centuries later at the hands of his brother Jews. The responsorial psalm also points to "Joseph, sold as a slave." In the Gospel, Jesus relates a parable about a property owner's son who also became a victim of hatred. In the way the tenant farmers kill the son outside the vineyard, we discover an image of how the soldiers crucified Jesus outside the city of Jerusalem. At the end of this story, Jesus also refers to himself as the stone that the builders — that is, the religious leaders — have rejected.

236 SATURDAY OF THE SECOND WEEK OF LENT

READING I   Micah 7:14-15, 18-20   RESP. Ps. 103:1-2, 3-4, 9-10, 11-12
GOSPEL   Luke 15:1-3, 11-32

The consoling picture of God as a Father who delights in showing mercy to his children and removing guilt from their hearts is the subject of the Scripture readings for our Mass today. In the opening words of the first passage, we hear the prophet Micah praying to God, the Good Shepherd who shows a loving concern for his flock. The responsorial psalm verses echo the prophet's assurance that God will pardon sins, that he does not persist in anger forever, and that he will cast our sins far away from him. The Gospel reading tells us one of the most moving of all the parables of Jesus — the story of the Prodigal Son. Too often we concentrate on the wayward young man in the parable and forget that his father is a central figure. Our Lord reminds us that the way the father extends loving forgiveness to his son is an image of how much more God our Father offers pardon to us.

237 OPTIONAL MASS FOR THE THIRD WEEK OF LENT

READING I   Exod. 17:1-7   RESP. Ps. 95:1-2, 6-7, 8-9
GOSPEL   John 4:5-42

Today's readings focus on the sacrament of baptism which is at the heart of the approaching Easter season. In the first passage, we learn that the Jewish people become angry with Moses because they have no water left to drink during their journey through the desert from Egypt. God tells Moses to strike a rock so that water can flow forth for the people's needs. The liturgy today regards the glorified body of Jesus as this rock. From his body, which we first contact in baptism, Jesus pours out the graces of redemption that quench our thirst for eternal life. Baptism is also the theme of the Gospel story of our Lord's meeting with the Samaritan woman at the well. Jesus promises to give her living water, that is, the water of divine life. The responsorial psalm recalls the incident in the first reading when the Jews hardened their hearts against God.

238 MONDAY OF THE THIRD WEEK OF LENT

READING I   2 Kings 5:1-15   RESP. Pss. 42:2, 3; 43:3, 4
GOSPEL   Luke 4:24-30

Today's readings reveal that God makes his offer of salvation to all men — Jew and Gentile alike. The first passage teaches us about this in the way God's prophet heals a pagan soldier named Naaman, who was a leper. In the Gospel, we hear Jesus refer to this cure of Naaman, as well as to God's favor for a poor widow from another pagan land.

God blessed their lives — a symbol of salvation — even though they were not members of the chosen Jewish people. The story of Naaman also reminds us about the Easter sacrament of baptism. The liturgy discovers in the waters of the Jordan River that cleanse Naaman's body of his leprosy a symbol of the baptismal waters that unite us to our Lord's risen body. The responsorial psalm also uses the imagery of water to describe how all men thirst for union with the living God.

239 TUESDAY OF THE THIRD WEEK OF LENT

READING I Dan. 3:25, 34-43   **RESP. Ps.** 25:4-5, 6-7, 8-9
GOSPEL Matthew 18:21-35

The Scripture readings for today's Mass give us two different views of the important Lenten theme of forgiveness. In the first passage, the liturgy teaches us that forgiveness is a matter of seeking pardon from God for our own personal faults. We discover this through the story of a Jew named Azariah, who lived at the time of the Babylonian captivity. The pagan king had thrown Azariah and two others into a roaring furnace because they refused to worship idols. You will hear Azariah pleading with God to forgive the sins of his beloved people. Then in the Gospel Jesus teaches us another aspect of forgiveness — that we must pardon others when they offend us. His parable emphasizes that God forgives us to the extent that we forgive others. The responsorial psalm allows us to pray for God's mercy because we know we are sinners.

240 WEDNESDAY OF THE THIRD WEEK OF LENT

READING I Deut. 4:1, 5-9   **RESP. Ps.** 147:12-13, 15-16, 19-20
GOSPEL Matthew 5:17-19

In today's Mass the liturgy draws our attention once again to how important God's commandments are in our lives and how much we need to obey them. The first reading is from a book in the Old Testament that deals with the laws God proclaimed on Mount Sinai. As we listen, we hear Moses exhorting the Jewish people in the desert to be faithful to God's commands. The liturgy intends his words to preach a message for our lives as well during this Lenten season. Then in the Gospel we find Jesus stressing the importance of the Law of Moses and how our Lord came not to abolish the Law but to fulfill it. The responsorial psalm between these readings mentions the laws that God gave to Israel. We may also use this psalm to praise God for revealing his ways to us through Jesus and the guidance of his Church.

241 THURSDAY OF THE THIRD WEEK OF LENT

READING I Jer. 7:23-28   RESP. Ps. 95:1-2, 6-7, 8-9
GOSPEL Luke 11:14-23

Conversion of heart is a theme we frequently hear in the Scripture readings at the Lenten Masses. Today, however, the Church warns us about the opposite attitude — a hardness of heart that refuses to listen to the voice of God. The Church hopes that the lesson of today's readings may keep us alert to avoid falling into such a state in our spiritual lives. In the first passage we learn how God's beloved people hardened their hearts to his kindness and mercy to them in the past. They rejected God's messengers, the prophets, who tried to call the people to repentance. Then in the Gospel we find another example of hardness of heart. Some people in the crowd he was talking to accused Jesus of being possessed by evil spirits. They refused to see God at work in his miracles. The responsorial psalm refrain also implores us to "harden not your hearts."

242 FRIDAY OF THE THIRD WEEK OF LENT

READING I Hos. 14:2-10   RESP. Ps. 81:6-8, 8-9, 10-11, 14, 17
GOSPEL Mark 12:28-34

Today's Scripture readings focus on the quality and depth of our love for God. In the first passage, we hear God invite his beloved Jewish people to return to a sincere worship of him. God assures them that he will love them freely and bestow many blessings on them despite their failings. In this way, the liturgy calls on us to deepen our love for God during the Lenten season. The same theme appears in the Gospel as Jesus teaches a scribe the two great commandments of the love of God and neighbor. We should make our Lord's exhortation to love God with all our heart, soul, mind, and strength a matter of serious concern in our lives today. Since the prophet Hosea says in the first reading that "straight are the paths of the Lord, in them the just walk," the responsorial psalm accents this theme in the verse, "If only Israel would walk in my ways."

243 SATURDAY OF THE THIRD WEEK OF LENT

READING I Hos. 6:1-6   RESP. Ps. 51:3-4, 18-19, 20-21
GOSPEL Luke 18:9-14

The readings for today's Mass teach that God wants us to come to him in prayer with humble and sincere hearts and not in a mere pious show of religion. The liturgy makes this point in the first reading. We hear the Jewish people declaring that they intend to repent and reform their lives. But God does not grant them pardon because their repentance is insincere and as quickly fading as the morning dew. We hear God insist that we love him with our heart and not the external display of empty sacrificial offerings. The responsorial psalm also takes up this theme in the verse, "A heart contrite and humbled, O God, you will not spurn." In the Gospel, Jesus tells the story of a self-righteous Pharisee and a sinful but repentant tax collector who pray to God in the temple. The lesson again is that true love of God is genuine and humble.

244   OPTIONAL MASS FOR THE FOURTH WEEK OF LENT

READING I   Micah 7:7-9   RESP. Ps. 27:1, 7-8, 8-9, 13-14
GOSPEL   John 9:1-41

Today's readings center on Jesus as the Light of the world who heals our blindness when we believe in him. The first passage develops the theme of light in two verses about a right-living man who places his confidence in God. We hear him say, "Though I sit in darkness, the Lord is my light," and "God will bring me forth to the light." His words suggest the man we meet in the Gospel. Although from birth he had sat in the dark world of the blind, yet he believed that our Lord could lead him forth to the light. Jesus responded to his faith by healing him. We learn from our Lord's closing words that the man who in foolish pride closes his eyes to the light of grace that Jesus gives is the man who is really blind. The responsorial psalm underscores this theme in the words, "The Lord is my light and my salvation."

245   MONDAY OF THE FOURTH WEEK OF LENT

READING I   Is. 65:17-21   RESP. Ps. 30:2, 4, 5-6, 11-13
GOSPEL   John 4:43-54

Today's readings show us how Jesus fulfilled the promised blessings in the age of the Messiah far beyond what the Old Testament writers expected. In the first passage, God reveals those blessings in his intention to create a new heaven and a new earth. Especially appropriate are the verses, "No longer shall the sound of weeping be heard," and "no longer shall there be an infant who lives but a few days." The Gospel then tells how Jesus more than satisfied these particular messianic blessings. Our Lord cures a child near death from a fever, and the sound of weeping vanishes from the home of a royal official. Then we learn that the cure was really a path toward salvation for the official and his household. We may regard the responsorial psalm as the official's prayer of gratitude. It was his experience that "at nightfall, weeping enters in, but with the dawn, rejoicing."

246 TUESDAY OF THE FOURTH WEEK OF LENT

READING I   Ezek. 47:1-9, 12   **RESP. Ps.** 46:2-3, 5-6, 8-9
GOSPEL   John 5:1-3, 5-16

Today's Scripture readings demonstrate through the imagery of water that God's own life has flowed into our hearts through the sacramental waters of baptism and brought us the promise of a life filled with blessings. In the first passage, the prophet Ezekiel beholds in a vision a wonderful stream flowing from the sacred temple in Jerusalem. Wherever the water flows, it brings growth and life. This account reminds us that the waters of baptism bring new life to the dry, sinful soul of man. The responsorial psalm also accents this theme in the verse, "There is a stream whose runlets gladden the city of God." The Gospel tells how a crippled man's act of faith in bathing in a pool not only cures him but earns him forgiveness of his sins. In the same way baptism cures our spiritual sickness by washing away original sin and adopting us in Christ as children of God.

247 WEDNESDAY OF THE FOURTH WEEK OF LENT

READING I   Is. 49:8-15   **RESP. Ps.** 145:8-9, 13-14, 17-18
GOSPEL   John 5:17-30

The theme of today's Lenten Mass comes to us in this verse from the first reading, "The Lord comforts his people and shows mercy to his afflicted." The entire passage is rich in practical examples of God's mercy, which restores life to the land and men's hearts. A closing verse reminds us that God's love is more tender than a mother's natural love for her child. We find a parallel thought in the Gospel where Jesus reveals the Father to us. Throughout our Lord's words, we hear him refer often to life — the new life of grace that God in his merciful love gives us at baptism. The responsorial psalm accents this theme in the refrain, "The Lord is kind and merciful."

248 THURSDAY OF THE FOURTH WEEK OF LENT

READING I   Exod. 32:7-14   RESP. Ps. 106:19-20, 21-22, 23
GOSPEL   John 5:31-47

The figure of Moses appears in today's Scripture readings as a man who assumes two different attitudes toward the Jewish people concerning their relationship with God. In the first passage, Moses is the leader of the Jewish people in the desert who pleads with God not to condemn them even though they have failed to keep his commandments. We hear Moses appeal to God's mercy in the light of the promises God made to Abraham, Isaac, and Israel. The responsorial psalm recalls this same incident in the verse, "Then God spoke of exterminating them, but Moses withstood God to turn back his destructive wrath." On the other hand, we find Jesus in the Gospel telling the Jews that "the one to accuse you is Moses." In this case, Moses reminds the Jews that the whole Old Testament revelation they believe in points the way to Jesus as the promised Messiah.

249 FRIDAY OF THE FOURTH WEEK OF LENT

READING I   Wis. 2:1, 12-22   RESP. Ps. 34:17-18, 19-20, 21 and 23
GOSPEL   John 7:1-2, 10, 25-30

At the Lenten Masses on the two Fridays before Good Friday, the liturgy selects Scripture readings about the sufferings and death of Jesus. In today's first passage, you will hear a group of wicked men plotting harm against a just man. The liturgy suggests that we listen to the words as if the enemies of Jesus were talking about plans to put him to death. In this way we will discover many points in the conversation of these wicked men that apply to events in the final days of our Lord's life. The Gospel reading shows us how the enemies of Jesus were looking for a chance to kill him. The responsorial psalm between these readings describes God's concern for the just man who is undergoing troubles at the hands of evildoers. We discover in these verses still another image of Jesus, who became a victim of the Jewish leaders and the Roman soldiers.

250 SATURDAY OF THE FOURTH WEEK OF LENT

READING I   Jer. 11:18-20   RESP. Ps. 7:2-3, 9-10, 11-12
GOSPEL   John 7:40-53

As we conclude this fourth week of Lent and the days of Holy Week draw nearer, the liturgy invites us to meditate today on the growing opposition to Jesus that will climax in his violent death for our sins. For this purpose, the liturgy chooses for the first reading a passage from the prophet Jeremiah. He shares his fears about the plots his enemies are concocting to destroy him and then expresses his confidence in God's protection. We should listen to his words as if Jesus were talking about the enemies plotting against his own life. The responsorial psalm is the prayer of a man under threat of harm from evil men. Again, we may regard this as a prayer of Jesus to his Father. In the Gospel, the Jewish people seek to learn whether Jesus is truly the promised Messiah. We then learn that the chief priests and Pharisees are striving to have Jesus arrested.

251 OPTIONAL MASS FOR THE FIFTH WEEK OF LENT

READING I 2 Kings 4:18-21, 32-37   RESP. Ps. 17:1, 6-7, 8 and 15
GOSPEL   John 11:1-45

In today's readings we discover a theme of resurrection that invites us to look forward to the approaching joys of the Easter season. The readings tell how two people — a young boy and a man — receive the gift of life again from the hands of God's holy men. In the first passage, the prophet Elisha restores life to the child of a woman from Shunem, a town in northern Palestine. In the Gospel, Jesus raises his friend Lazarus to life. We hear Jesus teaching Martha that whoever believes in him shall never die. Our Lord's words should bring comfort to our own hearts today. Our sharing in his divine life at Holy Communion in this Mass also assures us that we too will rise to a new life with Jesus. The responsorial psalm declares that God answers the prayers of all who call upon him, even as he heard the requests of Martha and Mary, and the woman from Shunem.

252 MONDAY OF THE FIFTH WEEK OF LENT — Cycles A & B

READING I Dan. 13:1-9, 15-17, 19-30, 33-62 OR Dan. 13:41-62
                                             RESP. Ps. 23:1-3, 3-4, 5, 6
GOSPEL   John 8:1-11

Today's Scripture readings illustrate two important Lenten themes — the compassionate love that God shows for people in trouble and how we should avoid judging the actions of others. Both readings concern women — one innocent, one guilty — who have to face public charges of sexual wrongdoing. In the first passage, God acts through the prophet Daniel to rescue from death an innocent woman named Susanna. We hear Daniel reexamine the charge against Susanna that leads to the conviction of two lustful men. The Gospel tells the story of a woman caught in adultery whom the Pharisees accuse before Jesus. Instead of condemning her, our Lord tells the woman to go and sin no more. The responsorial psalm allows us to express our confidence that God will protect us against the troubles and dangers that threaten our lives.

252 MONDAY OF THE FIFTH WEEK OF LENT — Cycle C

READING I   Dan. 13:1-9, 15-17, 19-30, 33-62 OR Dan. 13:41-62

RESP. Ps. 23:1-3, 3-4, 5, 6

GOSPEL   John 8:12-20

Today's readings teach us the important lesson that when innocent people are wrongly accused, God defends them — in his own way and in his own time. We meet two people — an innocent woman named Susanna and Jesus, the Holy One of God. Both have to face false accusations from their enemies, and they cannot defend themselves. In the first passage, God sends the prophet Daniel to rescue Susanna from death. We hear Daniel reexamine the charge against Susanna that leads to the conviction of two lustful men. In the Gospel, the Pharisees claim that Jesus cannot really prove that God has sent him simply by saying so. But our Lord insists that the Father bears witness to the truth of everything Jesus says. The time has not yet come for the Father to defend Jesus as the Pharisees demand, but the Father will vindicate his Son one day by raising Jesus from the dead.

253 TUESDAY OF THE FIFTH WEEK OF LENT

READING I   Num. 21:4-9   **RESP. Ps.** 102:2-3, 16-18, 19-21
GOSPEL   John 8:21-30

Today's Scripture readings direct our attention to the wounded body of Jesus hanging from the cross as a sign of salvation for all mankind. For this reason, the first passage takes us back to the days of the Old Testament when the Jews rebelled against God during their journey to the promised land. Then God told Moses to put a serpent made of bronze on a pole so that God might spare from punishment all those who looked at the serpent. This ancient sign of salvation foreshadowed the raising of the cross on Calvary which saved all mankind from eternal punishment. The responsorial psalm also leads us to the scene of our redemption in the words, "The Lord looked down from his holy height . . . to release those doomed to die." In the Gospel, we hear Jesus tell the Pharisees that one day they will recognize who he is "when you lift up the Son of Man" — a reference to his death.

254   WEDNESDAY OF THE FIFTH WEEK OF LENT

READING I   Dan. 3:14-20, 91-92, 95   RESP. Ps. Dan. 3:52, 53, 54, 55, 56
GOSPEL   John 8:31-42

Today the Scripture readings remind us that when we are free from the slavery of sin, we are really free in our hearts no matter what other trials come into our lives to imprison us. The first reading teaches us the story of the three Jews who were willing to sacrifice their lives rather than worship a pagan statue. Although the Babylonian soldiers had thrown them into a roaring furnace, the men were still free from the slavery of false worship. The responsorial psalm is the prayer of praise that the men offered when God delivered them from the furnace. In the Gospel, we learn how attachment to their sinful lives kept many Jews from responding freely in faith to Jesus. Our Lord's words ring out to challenge our own lives today in this penitential season, as he warns, "Everyone who lives in sin is the slave of sin."

255   THURSDAY OF THE FIFTH WEEK OF LENT

READING I   Gen. 17:3-9   RESP. Ps. 105:4-5, 6-7, 8-9
GOSPEL   John 8:51-59

As the days of Holy Week draw nearer, today's Scripture readings remind us that Jesus fulfilled through his death and resurrection God's first covenant or solemn promise of friendship with mankind at the dawn of history. The first passage tells us about that ancient agreement God made with Abraham. We hear God promising to bless Abraham and his descendants in return for their faithful love and service of the Lord. The responsorial psalm also touches on this covenant with Abraham. In the Gospel, Jesus tells the Jews that Abraham rejoiced that he might see the day when the Messiah would come, and that he himself is this promised Messiah. But the Jews, unable to accept this message, try to kill Jesus. How our own hearts should rejoice with Abraham as we realize today that God has given us the privilege of knowing his Son through faith.

256 FRIDAY OF THE FIFTH WEEK OF LENT

READING I   Jer. 20:10-13   RESP. Ps. 18:2-3, 3-4, 5-6, 7
GOSPEL   John 10:31-42

On this Friday before Good Friday, the liturgy selects Scripture readings that refer to the approaching arrest and death of Jesus. In the first passage, we hear the prophet Jeremiah describing the threats of the evil men in his time who wished to kill him. He then utters a prayer of confidence that God will protect him. The liturgy suggests that we listen to Jeremiah's words as if Jesus were speaking about the threats against his own life and then entrusting himself into his Father's care. In the Gospel, St. John tells how the enemies of Jesus threatened his life and attempted to arrest him. The responsorial psalm between these readings also emphasizes this theme. The psalm is the prayer of a man who has confidence in God despite the dangers that threaten him from his enemies.

257 SATURDAY OF THE FIFTH WEEK OF LENT

READING I   Ezek. 37:21-28   RESP. Ps. Jer. 31:10, 11-12, 13
GOSPEL   John 11:45-57

Today's Scripture readings emphasize that the day will come when all God's children will gather into one redeemed nation. In the first passage, the prophet Ezekiel looks forward to a brighter day for the Jewish people when a new David will unite and shepherd them and when God alone will rule as King. The psalm verses after this reading develop this theme, as we acknowledge how well God protects and cares for us, like a shepherd guarding his flock. Then the Gospel shows St. John interpreting a statement that the high priest Caiaphas made about Jesus. John says Caiaphas prophesied that Jesus would die not only for the nation "but to gather into one all the dispersed children of God." The sacrament of the Eucharist that we receive today is itself a sign that God's people have become one in Christ and with one another. We must do all we can to preserve that unity.

258 MONDAY OF HOLY WEEK

READING I   Is. 42:1-7   RESP. Ps. 27:1, 2, 3, 13-14
GOSPEL   John 12:1-11

The Scripture readings for this final week of the Lenten season focus our attention on the mystery of our Lord's Passion and death. The liturgy chooses for the first passage today a "Song of the Servant of God" from the prophet Isaiah. The New Testament identifies this mysterious servant of God with Jesus. For this reason, we may listen to the first reading as if God the Father were dedicating his Son for his mission to redeem mankind. We may regard the responsorial psalm as a confident prayer of Jesus to his Father, although our Lord knows the dangers before him. The Gospel shows Jesus taking a meal with his friends, and in this scene Judas has a prominent part. The reading thus prepares us for the betrayal and arrest of Jesus, which the final days of this week commemorate.

259 TUESDAY OF HOLY WEEK

READING I Is. 49:1-6 **RESP. Ps. 71:1-2, 3-4, 5-6, 15, 17**
GOSPEL John 13:21-33, 36-38

Today's Scripture readings help us to reflect on the mystery of our Lord's Passion and death. The liturgy chooses for the first passage another "Song of the Servant of God" from the prophet Isaiah. The New Testament identifies this mysterious servant of God with Jesus. For this reason, we may listen to this reading as if Jesus were speaking about his destiny to become redeemer of the world, so that "salvation may reach to the ends of the earth." The responsorial psalm is the prayer of a man persecuted by his enemies. He seeks help from the God who has protected him since his infancy. We may consider this psalm a prayer of Jesus as he faces his enemies in his Passion. The Gospel shows Jesus at the Last Supper with his disciples. Judas leaves the meal to prepare for his betrayal of our Lord, which the final days of this week commemorate.

260 WEDNESDAY OF HOLY WEEK

READING I Is. 50:4-9 **RESP. Ps. 69:8-10, 21-22, 31 and 33-34**
GOSPEL Matthew 26:14-25

Today's Scripture readings emphasize the mystery of our Lord's Passion and death. The liturgy chooses for the first passage a "Song of the Servant of God" from the prophet Isaiah. The New Testament identifies this mysterious servant of God with Jesus. For this reason, we may listen to this reading as if Jesus were describing his sufferings during his trial and at the hands of the Roman soldiers. The responsorial psalm is the prayer of a man in great distress who prays to God for help against his enemies. We may regard this psalm as a prayer of Jesus when his enemies thronged around him during his Passion. The Gospel shows Jesus at the Passover meal with his disciples after Judas had arranged to betray him. Jesus warns them about his betrayal, and his words prepare our hearts for the tragic events of the next three days of Holy Week.

261 MONDAY OF THE OCTAVE OF EASTER

READING I   Acts 2:14, 22-32   **RESP.** Ps. 16:1-2 and 5, 7-8, 9-10, 11
GOSPEL   Matthew 28:8-15

Today's first Scripture reading is an account of part of the first Christian sermon ever preached. When we read the full texts of Peter's sermons in this chapter of the Acts of the Apostles and elsewhere in the Acts, we discover the main points the apostles emphasized in preaching about Jesus. This preaching involved a personal witness to the death and resurrection of Jesus, certain details about his public ministry, an appeal to the past to show how Jesus fulfilled the prophecies in the Old Testament about the Messiah, and an invitation to repent and believe in Jesus. Since Peter draws his argument for our Lord's resurrection from David's remarks about the Messiah in Psalm 16, the liturgy uses this same psalm for our response after the reading. The Gospel gives St. Matthew's account of an appearance of our Lord to the women who had come to the tomb.

262 TUESDAY OF THE OCTAVE OF EASTER

READING I   Acts 2:36-41   **RESP.** Ps. 33:4-5, 18-19, 20, 22
GOSPEL   John 20:11-18

In today's reading, we learn how three thousand people became the first converts to Christianity shortly after the Holy Spirit had descended on the disciples of Jesus in Jerusalem. As this dramatic story begins, we hear St. Peter accuse the crowds of putting to death the very Messiah they were longing for. We can imagine how grief-stricken the people felt when they heard this. After Peter finished preaching, the first converts expressed their new-found faith and sorrow for their sins by submitting to baptism in the name of Jesus. In the responsorial psalm, the liturgy finds an allusion to the resurrection of Jesus. A just man declares that "the eyes of the Lord are upon those" who hope that God may "deliver them from death." The Gospel narrates how Jesus appeared to Mary Magdalene at the tomb. In our Lord's words to her, we find one meaning of the resurrection for us — that Jesus' Father is also our own.

263 WEDNESDAY OF THE OCTAVE OF EASTER

READING I   Acts 3:1-10   RESP. Ps. 105:1-2, 3-4, 6-7, 8-9
GOSPEL   Luke 24:13-35

In the first Scripture reading, we begin the important story that tells how Peter and John cured a man who was lame. This event marks the first conflict with the Jewish religious leaders after the resurrection of Jesus. It also provides the apostles with an opportunity to give witness before all the people that they believe Jesus is the promised Messiah — now risen and glorified. The responsorial psalm after this reading refers to the covenant, or solemn promise of friendship, that God once made with Abraham and Isaac. The liturgy reminds us that this covenant finds its fulfillment in the death and resurrection of Jesus which we commemorate at today's Mass. The Gospel reading from St. Luke narrates how our Lord revealed himself to two disciples along the road to Emmaus on the morning of the resurrection.

264 THURSDAY OF THE OCTAVE OF EASTER

READING I   Acts 3:11-26   RESP. Ps. 8:2 and 5, 6-7, 8-9
GOSPEL   Luke 24:35-48

In today's first reading, the cure of a lame man prompts Peter to give to the people his second sermon about the risen Jesus. Into this sermon Peter weaves many of the strands of early Christian teaching. Peter draws attention to the vision of the prophet Isaiah, who foresaw the Messiah as a suffering servant. Peter also refers to an Old Testament passage in which Moses promised the Israelites a prophet like himself as his successor. Peter teaches that this prophet is Jesus, and the Jews now have a right to share in the great blessings of the age of the Messiah. Since Peter insists that trust in the name of Jesus cured the lame man, the responsorial psalm declares, "O Lord, how wonderful your name in all the earth." In the Gospel, Jesus appears to his disciples and teaches them that the Old Testament prophecies foretold that the Messiah must suffer.

265   FRIDAY OF THE OCTAVE OF EASTER

READING I   Acts 4:1-12   **RESP. Ps. 118:1-2 and 4, 22-24, 25-27**
GOSPEL   John 21:1-14

Today's first Scripture reading begins with the arrest of the apostles Peter and John because they had healed a lame man in the name of Jesus risen from the dead. During the trial before the priests and scribes, Peter bears witness that these religious leaders — the very men God had chosen to build the house of Israel — have rejected its most important stone, the cornerstone, who is Jesus. We have to admire the courage of Peter, a former fisherman in Galilee, who now stands before the most powerful Jews in the land as their judge. We hear Peter refer to a text from Psalm 118 about the rejection of the cornerstone. That is the reason why the liturgy selects verses from this psalm for our response after the reading. The Gospel describes how Jesus appeared to his disciples at the Sea of Tiberias.

266   SATURDAY OF THE OCTAVE OF EASTER

READING I   Acts 4:13-21   **RESP. Ps. 118:1 and 14-15, 16-18, 19-21**
GOSPEL   Mark 16:9-15

Today's first Scripture reading tells us more about the trial of the apostles Peter and John before the Jewish priests and scribes. Some members of the Sanhedrin comment on the self-assurance and boldness of the apostles in addressing them. Because the Jewish religious leaders are afraid of the crowd's enthusiastic reception of the apostles' preaching, they can do no more than threaten Peter and John and then dismiss them. We may regard the responsorial psalm after this reading as a prayer of Christ to his Father. If we listen to the psalm in this way, we will note several verses appropriate to the circumstances of our Lord's resurrection. In the Gospel, St. Mark mentions several appearances of Jesus after his resurrection. Our Lord rebukes his followers for their lack of faith.

267   MONDAY OF THE SECOND WEEK OF EASTER

READING I   Acts 4:23-31   **RESP. Ps. 2:1-3, 4-6, 7-9**
GOSPEL   John 3:1-8

During the weeks between Easter and Pentecost, the liturgy assigns passages from the Acts of the Apostles for our meditation in the first reading at Mass. The readings last week told us how the Jews arrested the apostles Peter and John because they had preached about the risen Christ. In today's passage, we learn how the Christian community reacted to the release of the apostles. Instead of being depressed about the troubles that surely lay ahead of them, the Christians met this challenge with a fearless prayer of trust in God's protection. Since this prayer includes verses from Psalm 2, this psalm also becomes our response after the reading and accents this theme of trust. The Gospel reading throughout this Easter season will be from St. John. Today's passage begins the third chapter, which tells us the story of Nicodemus and his visit to Jesus at night.

268 TUESDAY OF THE SECOND WEEK OF EASTER

READING I   Acts 4:32-37   RESP. Ps. 93:1, 1-2, 5
GOSPEL   John 3:7-15

Today's Mass concludes the fourth chapter of the Acts of the Apostles. St. Luke describes the common life of the early Christians. We note how they feel responsible for one another and how they desire to share everything they have. This strong community life enabled them to give bold and fearless witness to the risen Jesus. When people challenged their loyalty to Jesus, they responded confidently because they knew they possessed the power of the Holy Spirit in their hearts. This is one reason why we sometimes call the Acts of the Apostles the "Gospel of the Holy Spirit." The responsorial psalm is a prayer of praise to the risen and glorified Christ, our King. The Gospel continues the story of Nicodemus. Jesus declares that he has the right to speak about God, since he has come from heaven.

269 WEDNESDAY OF THE SECOND WEEK OF EASTER

READING I   Acts 5:17-26   RESP. Ps. 34:2-3, 4-5, 6-7, 8-9
GOSPEL   John 3:16-21

As we begin the fifth chapter of the Acts of the Apostles today, we learn that the growing popularity of the apostles created jealousy among the Jewish priests. They seized a number of apostles and imprisoned them. During the night, however, a messenger of God freed them. The apostles continued to preach even in the very precincts of the temple until eventually the Jews arrested them again. As this passage concludes, Peter gives witness before the Jewish supreme court to the resurrection of Jesus. The responsorial psalm refers to the miraculous release of the apostles from prison in the verse, "The angel of the Lord encamps around those who fear him, and delivers them." The Gospel continues the conversation of Jesus with Nicodemus. This passage includes the key words "light" and "darkness" that are so prominent throughout John's Gospel.

270   THURSDAY OF THE SECOND WEEK OF EASTER

READING I   Acts 5:27-33   RESP. Ps. 34:2 and 9, 17-18, 19-20
GOSPEL   John 3:31-36

Today's first Scripture reading continues the trial of the apostles before the Jewish Sanhedrin. The Jews accuse the apostles of ignoring their command to stop preaching about Jesus. Peter's answer to this charge covers the basic points about our Lord's redemption of mankind. The apostle's words so enrage the members of the Jewish supreme court that they are tempted to condemn the apostles to death. The responsorial psalm accents how God protected the apostles in the verse, "Many are the troubles of the just man, but out of them all the Lord delivers him." The Gospel reading from St. John concludes the discourse of Jesus with Nicodemus. In our Lord's words we discover that what really matters in life is how a man responds to Christ — the eternal choice we too must make in our lives today.

271   FRIDAY OF THE SECOND WEEK OF EASTER

READING I   Acts 5:34-42   RESP. Ps. 27:1, 4, 13-14
GOSPEL   John 6:1-15

The first Scripture reading for today's Mass concludes the account of the trial that the apostles had to face in the Jewish supreme court. The apostles receive unexpected help from a noted rabbi Gamaliel, who had been the teacher of Paul. The sincerity of the apostles and the miracles they performed must have made a deep impression on Gamaliel. We hear him recall for the Jewish priests two previous cases of fraud. He concludes that if the apostles are frauds as well, their preaching will come to nothing. As a result of his remarks, the Sanhedrin decides only to chastise the apostles and then release them. The responsorial psalm accents the determined effort the apostles made to proclaim Jesus as the Messiah. They sought only "to dwell in the house of the Lord" rather than seek their own safety by not preaching about Jesus. In the Gospel, Jesus miraculously feeds a crowd of five thousand.

272 SATURDAY OF THE SECOND WEEK OF EASTER

READING I   Acts 6:1-7   RESP. Ps. 33:1-2, 4-5, 18-19
GOSPEL   John 6:16-21

Today's first reading tells about a conflict between two Jewish-Christian groups that led to the ordination of the first deacons. One group was the Hellenists or Greeks. These were foreigners — Jews born outside Palestine — but who had their own synagogues in Jerusalem. The other group was the Hebrews or Jews from Palestine. Bad feelings arose between these groups and found their way into the practical matter of distributing money and food each day to the needy in the community. The widows of the Greek-speaking Jews were being neglected, and the apostles did not want to get involved in petty quarrels and serving at the tables. As a result, the first deacons enter the Christian community for a special ministry of service. The responsorial psalm is a prayer of trust in God's mercy. In the Gospel, Jesus appears to his disciples during a storm on the Sea of Galilee.

273 MONDAY OF THE THIRD WEEK OF EASTER

READING I   Acts 6:8-15   RESP. Ps. 119:23-24, 26-27, 29-30
GOSPEL   John 6:22-29

The first Scripture reading for today's Mass continues the sixth chapter of the Acts of the Apostles. Today we learn about the activities of Stephen, one of the seven deacons. Eventually, the Jews arrested him on charges that he spoke against all the important things they believed in — the temple, the Law, and Moses. Stephen's defense will be the subject of tomorrow's Scripture reading. We may consider the responsorial psalm as a prayer of Stephen in which he expresses his confidence that God will protect him against his enemies. The liturgy also selects portions of St. John's Gospel during this Easter season. Today we continue the events following our Lord's feeding of the five thousand. The people continue to look for miraculous signs, but Jesus invites them to believe in *him*, not his works.

274 TUESDAY OF THE THIRD WEEK OF EASTER

READING I   Acts 7:51—8:1   RESP. Ps. 31:3-4, 6, 7, 8, 17, 21
GOSPEL   John 6:30-35

In today's Mass, we hear more about the trial of the deacon Stephen before the Jewish supreme court. We find anger in Stephen's words to his accusers because they are responsible for the death of the long-awaited Messiah. We also find sadness because Stephen realizes the Jews have rejected God's special choice of them. The court condemns Stephen to death, but in his final hour he finds strength in the welcome of Jesus that awaits him. The responsorial psalm echoes the words of the dying Stephen. In St. John's Gospel we hear the people ask for bread. In reply, Jesus begins his important instruction on the Bread of Life. Our Lord will teach the Jews that in the bread of his words and the sacramental bread of the Eucharist men will find completely satisfied the hunger of their restless hearts.

275 WEDNESDAY OF THE THIRD WEEK OF EASTER

READING I   Acts 8:1-8   RESP. Ps. 66:1-3, 4-5, 6-7
GOSPEL   John 6:35-40

In the first Scripture reading for today's Mass, we learn about a persecution against the Church in Jerusalem. This forces the Christians to scatter and seek safety in the remoter parts of Palestine and in other pagan lands of the Roman empire. In the readings over the next few weeks, we will see how this presence of the Christians among their pagan neighbors led to the critical question of admitting the Gentiles into God's kingdom. This concern for the salvation of all men appears in the verses of Psalm 66 which we pray after the reading. We beseech God, "Let all on earth worship and sing praise to you." St. John's Gospel continues the discourse of Jesus on the Bread of Life. Our Lord explains that the heavenly bread of his teachings nourishes man for eternal life.

276 THURSDAY OF THE THIRD WEEK OF EASTER

READING I   Acts 8:26-40   RESP. Ps. 66:8-9, 16-17, 20
GOSPEL   John 6:44-51

Today's first Scripture reading concludes the eighth chapter of the Acts of the Apostles. We hear an incident in the missionary work of the apostle Philip. The Holy Spirit prompts him to approach an Ethiopian court official who is returning home from a pilgrimage to Jerusalem. On this occasion, Philip preaches that Jesus is the suffering servant who the prophet Isaiah foretold lays down his life for the sins of his people. The responsorial psalm echoes the court official's joy over the grace of salvation that he received through baptism. St. John's Gospel continues our Lord's discourse on the Bread of Life. We hear Jesus remind the Jews that the interior gift of faith in him is a gift that comes from his Father. Our Lord then begins his promise of the Eucharist.

277 FRIDAY OF THE THIRD WEEK OF EASTER

READING I Acts 9:1-20   **RESP. Ps. 117:1, 2**
GOSPEL John 6:52-59

The conversion of Saul on the road to Damascus — an event of supreme significance for the Church and the world — is the subject of the first Scripture reading for today's Mass. The words of Jesus, "Saul, Saul, why do you persecute me?" made a profound and lasting impact on Saul — who would become the fearless apostle Paul. Through his reflection on this experience of the risen Lord present in his disciples, Paul eventually developed the doctrine that Christians are the body of Christ, and Jesus is the head of this body. The responsorial psalm accents Paul's vocation as the apostle of the Gentiles in the refrain, "Go out to all the world, and tell the Good News." In St. John's Gospel, Jesus reveals the mystery of the Eucharist. The sacrament of his body and blood will be the source of new life for all who believe in him.

278 SATURDAY OF THE THIRD WEEK OF EASTER

READING I Acts 9:31-42   **RESP. Ps. 116:12-13, 14-15, 16-17**
GOSPEL John 6:60-69

The first Scripture reading for today's Mass concludes the ninth chapter of the Acts of the Apostles. We learn how the Church in Palestine grew beyond the regions of Jerusalem and Samaria, and that Peter made several visits to the Christian communities. He healed a crippled man who was bedridden for eight years and raised a dead woman to life. We may regard the responsorial psalm as a prayer of gratitude that these people offered for God's kindness to them through Peter. We may also pray this psalm in thanksgiving for all the good things God has done for us. In St. John's Gospel, we discover that our Lord's promise to give his own flesh and blood to eat as spiritual food causes many of his disciples to reject him. But Jesus challenges them to accept his words and to have faith in him.

279 MONDAY OF THE FOURTH WEEK OF EASTER — Cycle A

READING I   Acts 11:1-18   **RESP.** Pss. 42:2-3, 43:3, 4
GOSPEL   John 10:11-18

We continue our reading from the Acts of the Apostles today with the eleventh chapter, which presents a very important incident in the early Church. A report had reached the Jewish converts to Christianity in Jerusalem that the apostle Peter had permitted the baptism of uncircumcised Gentiles. Such an action was unthinkable to the Jewish religious mentality at that time. We then hear Peter defend himself by explaining a vision he had received from God. The Lord indicated clearly that salvation was not only for the Jews but for all men. The responsorial psalm after this reading expresses our yearning for union with God. We then continue our reading of St. John's Gospel for this season as we turn today to Chapter 10. Our Lord describes himself as the Good Shepherd who lays down his life for the sheep.

279 MONDAY OF THE FOURTH WEEK OF EASTER — Cycles B & C

READING I   Acts 11:1-18   **RESP.** Pss. 42:2-3, 43:3, 4
GOSPEL   John 10:1-10

We continue our reading from the Acts of the Apostles today with the eleventh chapter, which presents a very important incident in the early Church. A report had reached the Jewish converts to Christianity in Jerusalem that the apostle Peter had permitted the baptism of uncircumcised Gentiles. Such an action was unthinkable to the Jewish religious mentality at that time. We then hear Peter defend himself by explaining a vision he had received from God. The Lord indicated clearly that salvation was not only for the Jews but for all men. The responsorial psalm after this reading expresses our yearning for union with God. We then continue our reading of St. John's Gospel for this season as we turn today to Chapter 10. Our Lord speaks of himself as the Good Shepherd and as the gate to eternal life.

280 TUESDAY OF THE FOURTH WEEK OF EASTER

READING I   Acts 11:19-26   RESP. Ps. 87:1-3, 4-5, 6-7
GOSPEL   John 10:22-30

The first Scripture reading for today's Mass describes in restrained language one of the great events in history — the deliberate preaching of the Good News of salvation to the Gentiles for the first time. Two steps had paved the way for this moment — the mission of Philip to the Samaritans and Peter's acceptance of the Roman centurion, Cornelius. The grace of God now shows itself in power, and a large number of Gentiles accept conversion in Antioch. This city, the third largest in the world at that time, will occupy our attention at other points in the Acts of the Apostles from now on. The responsorial psalm refrain accents the theme of God's call of the Gentiles in the words, "All you nations, praise the Lord." In the Gospel, we hear Jesus identify himself with his Father. He calls attention to the works he has performed which bear witness to his divinity.

281 WEDNESDAY OF THE FOURTH WEEK OF EASTER

READING I   Acts 12:24—13:5   RESP. Ps. 67:2-3, 5, 6 and 8
GOSPEL   John 12:44-50

At this point in our reading of the Acts of the Apostles, we rejoin Paul and Barnabas as they return to the city of Antioch from Jerusalem. We learn first about the prophets and teachers in the Church at Antioch. Then the Holy Spirit selects Paul and Barnabas for the first missionary journey to the Gentiles on the island of Cyprus and in the area that is present-day southern Turkey. The responsorial psalm accents their mission to preach the Good News of salvation in Christ to all men. In the Gospel, St. John records the last talk that Jesus gave to the crowds. The remainder of his Gospel concerns the words Jesus spoke to his disciples at the Last Supper, as well as the Passion and resurrection narrative. We hear Jesus emphasize a message that lies at the heart of his whole redeeming mission — he has come not to condemn men but to save them.

282 THURSDAY OF THE FOURTH WEEK OF EASTER

READING I   Acts 13:13-25   RESP. Ps. 89:2-3, 21-22, 25 and 27
GOSPEL   John 13:16-20

Our reading from the Acts of the Apostles today continues the first missionary journey of St. Paul and his companions. They have arrived at another city named Antioch — located in present-day southern Turkey. They follow their usual custom of preaching about Christ to the Jews in the synagogue. St. Luke then presents a model missionary sermon that he says Paul delivered on that occasion. The apostle gives a digest of God's dealings with his chosen people through the Old Testament right up to the preaching of John the Baptist. Since Paul refers to God's choice of King David, the responsorial psalm accents this point in the verse, "I have found David, my servant." In the Gospel, we find Jesus washing the feet of his disciples. He asks that they follow his example through their service and love of others.

283   FRIDAY OF THE FOURTH WEEK OF EASTER

READING I   Acts 13:26-33   RESP. Ps. 2:6-7, 8-9, 10-11
GOSPEL   John 14:1-6

Today's liturgy continues St. Paul's sermon in the Jewish synagogue at Antioch in present-day southern Turkey. Paul says that the promises of the Messiah have been fulfilled in the present generation with the coming of Christ. Paul tells how the Jews and their leaders rejected Jesus, and then he preaches the Good News of the resurrection of our Lord. Since the apostle quotes from Psalm 2 at the end of this reading, the liturgy selects this same psalm for our response. In St. John's Gospel, Jesus takes three basic ideas of the Jewish religion and shows that they find their full expression in him — he is "the way, the truth, and the life." Our Lord not only gives advice, he walks with us along the *way* of our lives. He embodies the *truth* of everything he teaches us. He gives his very self to us as our Eucharistic *life* and makes our lives worth living.

284   SATURDAY OF THE FOURTH WEEK OF EASTER

READING I   Acts 13:44-52   RESP. Ps. 98:1, 2-3, 3-4
GOSPEL   John 14:7-14

Over the past two days, the first Scripture readings have given us part of St. Paul's sermon to the Jews in Antioch during his first missionary journey to the Gentiles. However, we should not think Paul always preached to the kind of well-disposed audience that a modern priest finds in his congregation. Many of the Jews refused to listen to the idea that the uncircumcised Gentiles could share in any of their privileges. These Jews often violently showed that they resented this notion. Today's first reading gives us an example. A persecution forces Paul and Barnabas to leave the city and continue on their way. The responsorial psalm refrain accents the theme that salvation is available to all men. St. John's Gospel continues our Lord's discourse at the Last Supper. Jesus reveals the union of divine life that he shares with the Father. Whoever knows Jesus, also knows the Father.

285 MONDAY OF THE FIFTH WEEK OF EASTER

READING I   Acts 14:5-18   RESP. Ps. 115:1-2, 3-4, 15-16
GOSPEL   John 14:21-26

Today's first reading tells us more about the activities of Paul and his companion Barnabas during their first missionary journey. In the city of Lystra, a Roman colony in the area of present-day southern Turkey, the people worship the apostles as gods after Paul heals a crippled man. In explaining this action, some scriptural commentators recall a legend popular in that area. The Greek gods Zeus and Hermes had once visited the land in disguise and then destroyed the population when no one gave them hospitality. Apparently fearful that the gods have returned, the people honor Paul and Barnabas and give them the names of the Greek gods. The responsorial psalm refrain relates to Paul's rejection of this idolatrous worship by saying, "Not to us, O Lord, but to your name give the glory." In the Gospel, Jesus promises to send the Holy Spirit to guide the apostles.

286 TUESDAY OF THE FIFTH WEEK OF EASTER

READING I   Acts 14:19-28   RESP. Ps. 145:10-11, 12-13, 21
GOSPEL   John 14:27-31

The first Scripture reading for today's Mass continues the account of St. Paul's stay at the city of Lystra. We learn how the Jews persecute Paul there and how he sets off to preach the good news to other towns in what is present-day Turkey. The passage gives us a practical insight into the missionary activity of the apostles. We note Paul's reminder to his converts that they must be willing to suffer hardships for their new-found faith in Christ. The responsorial psalm sums up the work of Paul and his companions in the verse, "Your friends tell the glory of your

50

kingship, Lord." In the Gospel, Jesus extends peace to his disciples as his farewell gift to them during his discourse at the Last Supper. Our Lord's words appear at Mass each day in the celebrant's prayer before the Sign of Peace.

287 WEDNESDAY OF THE FIFTH WEEK OF EASTER

READING I   **Acts 15:1-6**   **RESP. Ps. 122:1-2, 3-4, 4-5**
GOSPEL   **John 15:1-8**

At this point in our reading of the Acts of the Apostles, Paul and Barnabas have returned to the city of Antioch in Syria from their first missionary journey to the Gentiles. We then learn about the visit of some Pharisees from Jerusalem. They create a disturbance in the community by insisting that all converts must be circumcised according to the Law of Moses. Paul and Barnabas then decide to visit Jerusalem to obtain official guidance on this critical issue from the apostles. This decision to travel to Jerusalem lies behind the liturgy's choice of the responsorial psalm. The psalm was one that the Jews sang while they went on pilgrimage to the holy city — much as pilgrims sing hymns to Mary on their way to Lourdes today. In the Gospel, Jesus describes our union with him through grace in the rich imagery of a vine and its branches.

288 THURSDAY OF THE FIFTH WEEK OF EASTER

READING I   **Acts 15:7-21**   **RESP. Ps. 96:1-2, 2-3, 10**
GOSPEL   **John 15:9-11**

In today's first reading we reach the middle of the Acts of the Apostles. The event that St. Luke tells us about marks a turning point in the story of the early Church. The apostles hold a special council in Jerusalem. We hear them officially approve the practice of preaching the Gospel to the Gentiles without requiring them to be circumcised and to follow the Law of Moses. In this way, the Christian Church finally breaks out of the Jewish mold. This will be the last act that Luke records about Peter or the other apostles. He concentrates instead on the outward thrust of the Church to the Gentiles, which is the special task of St. Paul and his companions. The responsorial psalm accents this mission of the Church to "proclaim God's marvelous deeds to all nations." In the Gospel, Jesus reminds his disciples at the Last Supper how much he loves them.

289 FRIDAY OF THE FIFTH WEEK OF EASTER

READING I Acts 15:22-31   RESP. Ps. 57:8-9, 10-12
GOSPEL John 15:12-17

Today's first Scripture reading tells us a further development in the important decision of the Council of Jerusalem that Gentile converts did not have to be circumcised. We learn about a letter that the apostles composed for the benefit of other communities in the Church to explain this difficult question. We see in this letter the forerunner of all the official statements of the popes and councils of the Church through the centuries, down to the encyclicals of the Holy Father in our time. The responsorial psalm emphasizes this mission the Church has to preach redemption in Christ to all nations. In the Gospel reading, we find the new commandment and standard of love — that we are to love one another as Jesus has loved us.

290 SATURDAY OF THE FIFTH WEEK OF EASTER

READING I Acts 16:1-10   RESP. Ps. 100:1-2, 3, 5
GOSPEL John 15:18-21

In today's first reading, we discover St. Paul on his second missionary journey to the Gentiles. He is visiting cities in what is now southern Turkey on a trip that will take him as far as Corinth in Greece before he returns home. We learn that God favors Paul with a vision which indicates to him that he should concentrate his apostolic labors in the area of Greece. St. Luke, the author of this passage, apparently joined Paul at this point in the journey. We hear him say, "We immediately made efforts to get across to Macedonia." Elsewhere in his book, St. Luke will inject such a comment to indicate that he was an eyewitness to the event he tells about. The responsorial psalm also reminds us that God has called all men to salvation. In the Gospel, Jesus warns his disciples that men will persecute them, just as they had mistreated him.

291 MONDAY OF THE SIXTH WEEK OF EASTER

READING I Acts 16:11-15   RESP. Ps. 149:1-2, 3-4, 5-6 and 9
GOSPEL John 15:26—16:4

The first reading takes up again St. Paul's second missionary journey to the Gentiles. The Holy Spirit has directed Paul to visit the area of Macedonia, part of present-day Greece. Today we see Paul arrive at

Philippi, the first European city that he preached in. A woman merchant named Lydia becomes Europe's first convert. She then offers hospitality to Paul — the first of many kindnesses that the Christians of Philippi extended to the apostle over the following years. Since the reading tells how Paul increased the ranks of the people of God in the city, the responsorial psalm expresses God's pleasure in this growth of the early Church by declaring, "The Lord takes delight in his people." In the Gospel, Jesus tells his disciples to bear witness to him, just as the Holy Spirit will do when he comes. Our Lord then shows how this witness will demand suffering and even death.

292 TUESDAY OF THE SIXTH WEEK OF EASTER

READING I   Acts 16:22-34   RESP. Ps. 138:1-2, 2-3, 7-8
GOSPEL   John 16:5-11

As today's first Scripture reading begins, St. Paul and his co-worker Silas have become victims of an angry mob in the city of Philippi in northern Greece. They had freed a slave girl from an evil spirit that enabled her to tell fortunes and earn much money for her masters. As a result, these men incited the Philippians against Paul and Silas and had them arrested. We then learn how Paul opens the door of salvation to the Roman soldier who shut the prison door on him. Since God delivered Paul from jail in a great display of power, the responsorial psalm accents this theme in the refrain, "Your right hand has saved me, O Lord." In the Bible, the right hand is a symbol of God's power because it is usually our stronger hand. In the Gospel, Jesus declares that he must leave the world so that he can send the Holy Spirit to work in men's hearts.

293 WEDNESDAY OF THE SIXTH WEEK OF EASTER

READING I   Acts 17:15, 22—18:1   RESP. Ps. 148:1-2, 11-12, 12-14, 14
GOSPEL   John 16:12-15

In today's first reading we learn that Paul has arrived in Athens, the intellectual and artistic center of the Greek world, during his second missionary journey to the Gentiles. His first impression of the city is not a happy one. The worship of pagan gods is everywhere. Paul then goes to a public forum, the Areopagus, to speak about the one true God. Unlike his other sermons to the Jews, in this one Paul uses a philosophical approach and quotes the Greek poets. The Greeks had dedicated an altar "to a God Unknown" that they might have overlooked, and Paul uses this idea as a basis for his talk. The responsorial psalm echoes the apostle's attempt to reveal the glory of God to the Greeks. In the Gospel, our Lord promises that he will send the Holy Spirit, the Spirit of Truth, fo guide his Church.

294 THURSDAY OF THE SIXTH WEEK OF EASTER

In countries where the celebration of the Ascension is transferred to the seventh Sunday of Easter, these readings are used on this Thursday.

READING I   Acts 18:1-8   RESP. Ps. 98:1, 2-3, 3-4
GOSPEL   John 16:16-20

The first Scripture reading for today's Mass tells us more about St. Paul's second missionary journey to the Gentiles. We learn that Paul has arrived in Corinth, the capital of the Roman province of Achaia in southern Greece and a city with a notorious reputation for sexual immorality. Paul goes often to the synagogue and tries to convince the Jews that Jesus is truly the Messiah. However, when they reject his preaching, he turns instead to the Gentiles. The responsorial psalm also develops this theme that God has revealed his saving power not only to the Jews but to all the nations. In the Gospel, we continue the discourse of Jesus to his disciples at the Last Supper. Our Lord promises that they will see him again, and then their sad hearts will rejoice.

59 ASCENSION THURSDAY — Cycle A

READING I   Acts 1:1-11   RESP. Ps. 47:2-3, 6-7, 8-9
READING II   Eph. 1:17-23
GOSPEL   Matthew 28:16-20

In a special second reading, St. Paul helps us to understand what the mystery of the ascension really means. He points out that Jesus, now ruling in heaven, governs the hearts of all people as the exalted Lord of the world and as Head of the Church. The responsorial psalm also teaches us that because Jesus has ascended to heaven he is "the Lord, the great king over all the earth." In the Gospel, Jesus reveals to his apostles that "full authority has been given to me both in heaven and on earth." Now it is up to men to recognize Jesus as Lord, and find happiness by *living* that fact in their daily lives. This is why as Christians we must heed the advice Jesus gives the apostles in the first reading when he says, "You are to be my witnesses, yes, even to the ends of the earth." To follow the Lord Jesus, we must strive to plant justice and peace in the heart of everyone we meet.

59 ASCENSION THURSDAY — Cycle B

READING I Acts 1:1-11   **RESP.** Ps. 47:2-3, 6-7, 8-9
READING II Eph. 1:17-23
GOSPEL   Mark 16:15-20

In a special second reading, St. Paul helps us to understand what the mystery of the ascension really means. He points out that Jesus, now ruling in heaven, governs the hearts of all people as the exalted Lord of the world and as Head of the Church. The responsorial psalm also teaches us that because Jesus has ascended to heaven he is "the Lord, the great king over all the earth." In the Gospel, St. Mark notes that Jesus "took his seat at God's right hand," a symbol of his authority over creation. Now it is up to men to recognize Jesus as Lord and find happiness by *living* that fact in their daily lives. This is why as Christians we must heed the advice Jesus gives the apostles in the first reading when he says, "You are to be my witnesses, yes, even to the ends of the earth." To follow the Lord Jesus, we must strive to plant justice and peace in the heart of everyone we meet.

59 ASCENSION THURSDAY — Cycle C

READING I Acts 1:1-11   **RESP.** Ps. 47:2-3, 6-7, 8-9
READING II Eph. 1:17-23
GOSPEL   Luke 24:46-53

In a special second reading, St. Paul helps us to understand what the mystery of the ascension really means. He points out that Jesus, now ruling in heaven, governs the hearts of all people as the exalted Lord of the world and as Head of the Church. The responsorial psalm also teaches us that because Jesus has ascended to heaven he is "the Lord, the great king over all the earth." In the Gospel, Jesus shows his supreme authority over men because he is the one who will send the promised Holy Spirit. Now it is up to men to recognize Jesus as Lord and find happiness by *living* that fact in their daily lives. This is why as Christians we must heed the advice Jesus gives the apostles in the first reading when he says, "You are to be my witnesses, yes, even to the ends of the earth." To follow the Lord Jesus, we must strive to plant justice and peace in the heart of everyone we meet.

295 FRIDAY OF THE SIXTH WEEK OF EASTER

READING I Acts 18:9-18 **RESP. Ps.** 47:2-3, 4-5, 6-7
GOSPEL John 16:20-23

In today's reading we find Paul in the Greek city of Corinth during his second missionary journey to the Gentiles. Paul's preaching upsets a group of Jews, and they bring the apostle before the civil court. However, the proconsul Gallio refuses to get involved in the religious debate and lets Paul go. The apostle heads homeward to Antioch. We hear St. Luke mention that Paul shaved his head because of a vow. This was the way a pious Jew showed his gratitude to God for a particular blessing. Some scriptural commentators believe that Paul may have done this in return for God's goodness to him in Corinth. The responsorial psalm accents the theme of universal salvation. In the Gospel, Jesus teaches his disciples about true Christian joy. The world can never take this joy away, and it will be so perfect that we will even forget our past sorrows.

296 SATURDAY OF THE SIXTH WEEK OF EASTER

READING I Acts 18:23-28 **RESP. Ps.** 47:2-3, 8-9, 10
GOSPEL John 16:23-28

As the first Scripture reading begins today, St. Paul has just completed his visit to the Christian community in Antioch. He had returned and spent some time there following his second missionary journey to the Gentiles. Now he is off on a third trip, heading northwest this time into the region of Galatia — in what is present-day Turkey. The reading introduces us to a Jew named Apollos and describes his efforts to preach about Jesus. The responsorial psalm proclaims God as the King of all the earth. In this way, we recall the sacrifices Paul made to tell the men of his age about the kingdom of God made manifest to them in Christ. In the Gospel, Jesus urges us to offer our requests to his Father with full confidence that he will hear us. However, we must ask in the name of Jesus, that is, aware that we are one with our Lord through grace.

297 MONDAY OF THE SEVENTH WEEK OF EASTER

READING I Acts 19:1-8 **RESP. Ps.** 68:2-3, 4-5, 6-7
GOSPEL John 16:29-33

As we begin Chapter 19 of the Acts of the Apostles today, we find

St. Paul on his third missionary journey to the Gentiles in the area of present-day Turkey. He arrives at the seaport of Ephesus, an important center of trade in the Roman world. Paul would work in this city for almost three years — longer than he stayed anywhere else. We discover an important truth in Paul's baptism of a group of disciples who had not yet received the Holy Spirit. The Christian life is not complete without the gift of the Spirit. The verses of Psalm 68 after this reading draw our attention to our Lord's call of salvation to all the kingdoms of the earth. In the Gospel, Jesus challenges the apostles to persevere in their faith despite trials and difficulties. Our Lord's final words offer encouragement to us also, as he says, "I have overcome the world."

298 TUESDAY OF THE SEVENTH WEEK OF EASTER

READING I Acts 20:17-27   **RESP. Ps. 68:10-11, 20-21**
GOSPEL   John 17:1-11

In today's first reading we find Paul at the end of his third missionary journey. He reveals his deep affection for the Church in Ephesus in a sad farewell to the Church leaders before sailing back to Jerusalem. Paul's words are charged with emotion as he recalls the trials he has been through and the dangers he knows he will face. Here is a man who has given his whole heart to the special work of preaching Jesus to the Gentiles. The responsorial psalm after this reading reminds us of Paul's vocation in the words, "Sing to God, O kingdoms of the earth." The Gospel continues our Lord's discourse to his apostles at the Last Supper. We hear Jesus talk about the glory that awaits him after his death, the work he has done on earth to glorify his Father, and the gift of eternal life for those who believe in him. He then begins a prayer for his disciples.

299 WEDNESDAY OF THE SEVENTH WEEK OF EASTER

READING I Acts 20:28-38   **RESP. Ps. 68:29-30, 33-35, 35-36**
GOSPEL   John 17:11-19

Today's first reading continues St. Paul's farewell remarks to the Church leaders in the city of Ephesus at the end of his third missionary journey. After warning the elders to be watchful for dangers to the faith of the community, Paul prepares to leave for Jerusalem. This touching farewell scene reveals the deep affection the people felt for Paul. The verses of the responsorial psalm focus our attention on the theme of

Paul's preaching — that the grace of salvation is now available to all nations. The Gospel reading continues the prayer of Jesus at the Last Supper for his disciples and the Church. Because our Lord must soon leave them alone in the world, he asks the Father to guard them and keep them united. Jesus then summons his disciples to dedicate themselves to their missionary task with the same dedication that he himself has given to his redemptive work.

300   THURSDAY OF THE SEVENTH WEEK OF EASTER

READING I   Acts 22:30; 23:6-11   **RESP. Ps.** 16:1-2 and 5, 7-8, 9-10, 11
GOSPEL   John 17:20-26

To understand today's first reading, we must recall that St. Paul has returned to Jerusalem after twelve years of preaching to the Gentiles. He is an unpopular man with the Jews because he has associated with the Gentiles and has denied the value of the Law of Moses for a man's salvation. Shortly after Paul arrived in Jerusalem, the Jews accused him of bringing a Gentile into a forbidden area of the temple. They seized Paul and tried to kill him, but Roman soldiers rescued the apostle by placing him under arrest. It is at this point that the reading begins today with Paul's trial before the Jewish supreme court. Since the passage mentions a threat on Paul's life, the liturgy selects a responsorial psalm that refers in several verses to the way God protects the right-living man. In the Gospel, Jesus prays for unity in the Church, and that the world may believe that the Father has sent him.

301   FRIDAY OF THE SEVENTH WEEK OF EASTER

READING I   Acts 25:13-21   **RESP. Ps.** 103:1-2, 11-12, 19-20
GOSPEL   John 21:15-19

Today we learn of further developments in the story of St. Paul's difficulties with the Jews upon his return to Jerusalem from his third missionary journey. Paul's trial before the Jewish supreme court had erupted into violence. To safeguard the apostle's life, the Roman officials had placed him in protective custody and sent him to the city of Caesaria, the seat of the Roman government in Palestine. The scene of today's reading is two years later, and Paul is still in prison. We hear a conversation between the Roman governor, Festus, and a Jewish ruler of Palestine, King Agrippa II. Festus gives a summary of his involvement in Paul's case. The presence of a king in this reading suggests the choice of Psalm 103 as the response, with its appropriate refrain, "The Lord has set his throne in heaven." In the Gospel, Jesus makes Peter the shepherd of his flock.

302 SATURDAY OF THE SEVENTH WEEK OF EASTER
(Mass in the Early Morning)

READING I Acts 28:16-20, 30-31   **RESP. Ps. 11:4, 5, 7**
GOSPEL   John 21:20-25

The first Scripture reading for today's Mass concludes the Acts of the Apostles. Our story has recently dealt with the arrest of the apostle Paul by the Roman officials. They have protected him from the threats of a faction of Jews in Jerusalem who wish to kill him. Since Paul is a Roman citizen, he has appealed his case to Rome. Today we learn of his arrival in that capital of the world. Perhaps St. Luke ends his account of the early Church at this point to dramatize how the followers of Christ have spread out from Jerusalem to embrace the world — symbolized here by Rome. The just merits of Paul's case suggest the responsorial psalm which declares, "The just will gaze on your face, O Lord." We also conclude our reading of St. John's Gospel today. The apostle describes himself as "the disciple whom Jesus loved" and as a credible witness to the events of our Lord's life.

WEEKDAYS OF
ORDINARY TIME

305 MONDAY OF THE FIRST WEEK OF THE YEAR

YEAR I

READING I   Heb. 1:1-6   RESP. Ps. 97:1-2, 6-7, 9
GOSPEL   Mark 1:14-20

The first reading begins the letter to the Hebrews, one of the twenty-one letters in the New Testament. We do not know who the author is nor the letter's specific destination, although some scholars today believe it must have been one of the large communities of Christians in Rome. We now hear the author demonstrate that Jesus was eminently superior to the prophets and angels who heralded his coming because he came as God's own Son to teach us and redeem us. Since the passage refers to angels worshiping God, the responsorial psalm refrain declares, "Let all his angels worship him." From now until the Lenten season, the Gospel readings are from St. Mark, probably the earliest Gospel that we possess. An early Church tradition claims he was a disciple of St. Peter. Today Mark describes how Jesus called his first apostles while they were fishing.

YEAR II

READING I   1 Sam. 1:1-8   RESP. Ps. 116:12-13, 14-17, 18-19
GOSPEL   Mark 1:14-20

In today's first reading, we begin the story of Samuel, a gifted prophet and last of the military leaders the Jews called judges in the eleventh century B.C. The setting for today's story is the hill country in central Palestine where Samuel's father Elkanah lives with his two wives. Hannah, his favorite, has to bear the double agony of constant ridicule from the other wife because Hannah can have no children. Now Elkanah and his wives prepare to make the annual pilgrimage to the central religious shrine at Shiloh, about twenty miles north of Jerusalem, where all the Jewish tribes honored God's sacred presence in the ark of the covenant. The liturgy suggests that in the responsorial psalm we hear Elkanah praying to God in the sanctuary at Shiloh. Today we begin reading from St. Mark, probably the earliest Gospel that we possess. He tells us how Jesus called his first apostles.

306 TUESDAY OF THE FIRST WEEK OF THE YEAR

YEAR I

READING I   Heb. 2:5-12   RESP. Ps. 8:2 and 5, 6-7, 8-9
GOSPEL   Mark 1:21-28

The first reading emphasizes the supreme place that Jesus holds in the universe. The author quotes from Psalm 8, which refers to the dignity God gave to "the son of man." Because Jesus identifies himself as "the Son of Man," the author finds that this psalm applies to our Lord. For a time during his life on earth, Jesus was "lower than the angels." But the way Christ humbled himself by suffering and dying was precisely what brought him his crown of glory. The death of Jesus has given all men the opportunity to become his brothers. A concluding verse from Psalm 22 accents this point. The responsorial psalm also highlights verses from Psalm 8 to show that God gave his Son authority over all his creation. In the Gospel, Jesus begins his public career by displaying personal authority in his teaching that is quite different from the way the Scribes taught.

YEAR II

READING I   1 Sam. 1:9-20   **RESP. Ps.**   1 Sam. 2:1, 4-5, 6-7, 8
GOSPEL   Mark 1:21-28

Today's first reading helps us grasp Hannah's deep devotion to God as she comes to pray in the Jewish religious shrine at Shiloh in central Palestine. We hear her vow to the "Lord of hosts" to dedicate a son to the Lord's service if God ever favors her with a child. The priest Eli believes at first that Hannah has been celebrating the harvest festival at this time with too much wine, but then he realizes his error. His blessing is not a mere formula but a heartfelt prayer for all that would serve Hannah's best interests in God's sight. As the passage ends, we learn how God has answered her prayer by giving her a son. In the responsorial psalm, we join our hearts to Hannah's song of praise to God for his gift of a child. The Gospel shows Jesus beginning his public ministry with a display of personal authority in teaching and healing unlike that of the Scribes and Pharisees.

307   WEDNESDAY OF THE FIRST WEEK OF THE YEAR

YEAR I

READING I   Heb. 2:14-18   **RESP. Ps.**   105:1-2, 3-4, 6-7, 8-9
GOSPEL   Mark 1:29-39

The first reading emphasizes that the Son of God shared in our human nature to the extent that he endured temptation, suffering, and death. Only in this way could Jesus be the merciful and faithful high priest whom we need to represent us before God the Father. This role of Jesus as mankind's high priest will soon become a major theme of this letter. Since the reading says that Jesus came to help "the children of Abraham," the responsorial psalm refers to the descendants of Abraham — "his servants, sons of Jacob, his chosen ones" — and God's covenant with them. In the Gospel, we discover that people quickly learned — as we also should — that they could take their troubles to Jesus and he was never too tired or busy to help them. Yet we also learn that our Lord did not neglect to spend time alone with his Father in prayer — the source of his healing power.

YEAR II

READING I 1 Sam. 3:1-10, 19-20   RESP. Ps. 40:2 and 5, 7-8, 8-9, 10
GOSPEL Mark 1:29-39

The first reading describes God's dramatic summons to the young man Samuel to become the Lord's servant as a prophet and military leader of the Jewish people in the eleventh century B.C. A lamp burned through the night in the pilgrimage shrine at Shiloh where the Jews kept the ark of the covenant, the sign of God's saving presence among his people. Today a sanctuary lamp burns continuously in every place where the Church reserves the Blessed Sacrament. Samuel shows that he had the heart of a prophet because he listened to God's words and then obeyed them promptly. The liturgy suggests that in the words of the responsorial psalm we hear Samuel placing himself completely at God's service. In the Gospel, people learned quickly — as we should, too — that Jesus was never too tired or too busy when they took their troubles to him. Yet he always had time for prayer.

308 THURSDAY OF THE FIRST WEEK OF THE YEAR

YEAR I

READING I Heb. 3:7-14   RESP. Ps. 95:6-7, 8-9, 10-11
GOSPEL Mark 1:40-45

In today's Mass, the author of the letter to the Hebrews begins by quoting from Psalm 95 as the voice of the Holy Spirit. This psalm tells the sad experience the Jews had during their wandering in the desert to the promised land, when they proved unfaithful to God. The writer urges the Christian community to be faithful on their own journey to heaven, lest they too become weary and discouraged. Our response to this reading also uses verses from Psalm 95 — such as, "If today you hear his voice, harden not your hearts" — to direct our attention again to the theme of keeping faith. The Gospel describes how Jesus showed pity toward a man with the dread disease of leprosy. At the same time, our Lord respects what the Jewish law required by telling the leper, "Go off and present yourself to the priest."

YEAR II

READING I 1 Sam. 4:1-11   RESP. 44:10-11, 14-15, 25-26
GOSPEL Mark 1:40-45

In today's first reading, we learn that the Philistines — a people who lived along the coastal plain of Palestine — captured the ark of the covenant, a symbol of God's presence among his chosen people, and crushed the forces of Israel. The Philistines went on from this incident to burn to the ground the central place of Jewish worship at Shiloh, leaving Israel in a state of shock and despair. The need for a more stable government was evident, and we shall discover tomorrow that the answer came in Israel's first king. We hear in the responsorial psalm the anguish of the people because the Lord had delivered them over to their enemies. The Gospel tells how Jesus showed pity toward a man with the dread disease of leprosy. At the same time, our Lord respects the requirements of Jewish law by telling the leper, "Go off and present yourself to the priest."

309 FRIDAY OF THE FIRST WEEK OF THE YEAR

YEAR I

READING I   Heb. 4:1-5, 11   RESP. Ps. 78:3 and 4, 6-7, 8
GOSPEL   Mark 2:1-12

In the first reading, we hear the author refer to "the promise of entrance into his rest." This statement refers to God's promise that the Jews would occupy the land of Canaan without trouble and in this way achieve a peaceful rest at the end of their long journey from Egypt. Because the Jews were then not faithful to God, he did not give them this rest. The author explains that this rest is still available to the new chosen people of the Church at the end of their spiritual journey to heaven. God has been waiting since his own rest on the seventh day of creation to give eternal rest to all who keep faith with him. The responsorial psalm refrain emphasizes this theme of fidelity by urging us, "Do not forget the works of the Lord!" In the Gospel, resourceful friends of a crippled man get him into our Lord's presence within a crowded home. Jesus forgives the man's sins and then heals him.

YEAR II

READING I   1 Sam. 8:4-7, 10-22   RESP. Ps. 89:16-17, 18-19
GOSPEL   Mark 2:1-12

Today's reading unfolds the need in Israel about 1020 B.C. for a king to lead the Jewish people against their enemy the Philistines, who threatened to conquer the land of Palestine. We learn that a group of respected men in the community come to the home of Samuel, then the military leader of Israel, and ask him to give them a king as the neighboring pagan city states have. Samuel fears that the people will reject the rule of God if they have an earthly king. For this reason he explains the severe demands a king would surely make on Israel. God decides nonetheless to let Samuel grant their request. The responsorial psalm emphasizes that "the Holy One of Israel, our king," is the sole ruler of his people. In the Gospel, resourceful friends of a crippled man get him into our Lord's presence within a crowded home. Jesus forgives the man's sins and then heals him.

310   SATURDAY OF THE FIRST WEEK OF THE YEAR

YEAR I

READING I   Heb. 4:12-16   RESP. Ps. 19:8, 9, 10, 15
GOSPEL   Mark 2:13-17

The first reading opens with a reminder that man cannot hide from the word of God, which penetrates his heart like a two-edged sword. This word forces a man to recognize the masks of self-deception that he wears and to evaluate his motives for living the way he does because one day "at the judgment" he will meet the eyes of his Maker. The author then returns to his major theme of Jesus as our high priest who has compassion for us. The responsorial psalm refrain highlights the theme of God's saving word by assuring us, "Your words, Lord, are spirit and life." In the Gospel, Jesus comes upon one of the tax collectors at work — Levi, another name of Matthew — and invites him to become his disciple. Levi's decision reflects a risk greater than the other apostles took because he could never have gotten his job back. Sometimes God also calls us to risk all for him.

YEAR II

READING I   1 Sam. 9:1-4, 17-19; 10:1   RESP. Ps. 21:2-3, 4-5, 6-7
GOSPEL   Mark 2:13-17

In today's first reading, we meet the handsome and striking figure of Saul — a man who went off in search of his father's lost donkeys and found instead a royal crown, the kingship of Israel. In a ceremony common among other peoples of that time, about 1020 B.C., Samuel anoints Saul with oil to show that he is now a new man set apart with God-given authority and strength to serve the people. For the same reason, a bishop anoints the hands of a newly ordained priest to show that he is now another Christ, whom the Church appoints in God's name to serve all men. The responsorial psalm hails God's choice of Israel's first king. In the Gospel, Jesus comes upon one of the tax collectors at work — Levi, another name of Matthew — and invites him to risk himself as the Lord's disciple. Sometimes God also calls us to risk all for him.

MONDAY OF THE SECOND WEEK OF THE YEAR

YEAR I

READING I   Heb. 5:1-10   RESP. Ps. 110:1, 2, 3, 4
GOSPEL   Mark 2:18-22

In today's reading, the author of the letter to the Hebrews describes the qualifications that a man aspiring to serve as a priest in any society must fulfill. He then shows that the priesthood Jesus received from his Father met these requirements. The author points out that a priest named Melchizedek, who lived at the time of Abraham, was an image of Jesus as a priest. We will learn more about this relationship between Jesus and Melchizedek in Wednesday's reading. The responsorial psalm reminds us again that Melchizedek was a figure of the unique kind of priesthood that Jesus enjoyed. In the Gospel, our Lord replies to a question about fasting. He explains that he is not against fasting, but the limited period he has to spend with his apostles is a time of joy for them. They will fast once he leaves them.

YEAR II

READING I   1 Sam. 15:16-23   RESP. Ps. 50:8-9, 16-17, 21 and 23
GOSPEL   Mark 2:18-22

As the first reading begins, Saul has enjoyed success as the first king of Israel by driving the Philistines from the central hill country of Palestine into their own territory along the coast. But we discover today that a conflict develops between the king and God's prophet Samuel — a conflict that will arise on several other occasions in Israel's history between civil and religious authority. In this case, Samuel tells Saul that the king has lost favor with God because in his holy war against the Amalekites he spared from slaughter their sheep and oxen to use for sacrifices to God. Instead, the Lord had commanded that the king kill not only all the people but every living thing — and so Saul had disobeyed God's orders. The responsorial psalm also stresses that God desires an obedient heart and not ritual sacrifices. In the Gospel, Jesus replies to a question about fasting.

TUESDAY OF THE SECOND WEEK OF THE YEAR

YEAR I

READING I   Heb. 6:10-20   RESP. Ps. 111:1-2, 4-5, 9 and 10
GOSPEL   Mark 2:23-28

The first reading discusses God's promise to give salvation to all who serve him with strong faith and patience in suffering. As an example of how God keeps his promises, the author points to the life of

Abraham. God promised he would give Abraham a son in spite of his old age, and he did. The author then stresses that God, in a sense, even took an oath to fulfill his promises to Abraham — and what more solid basis can one find to swear on than the divine nature itself. This hope we have that God will save us, the author says, is like an anchor that we can throw — not into the sea — but up to heaven where Christ eagerly waits to greet us when we die. The responsorial psalm underscores God's promise to keep faith with his covenant. In the Gospel, some Pharisees accuse our Lord's disciples of violating the law that prohibited farm work of any kind on the Sabbath.

YEAR II

READING I   1 Sam. 16:1-13   RESP. Ps. 89:20, 21-22, 27-28
GOSPEL   Mark 2:23-28

The first reading reveals that although Samuel had deposed Saul as king of Israel, because Saul had not proved himself obedient to God, this act had no practical result. The people were not willing to lose the man who had so far successfully routed their enemies. We then learn how God sends his prophet Samuel to Bethlehem to find the man who will replace Saul as king. At a banquet in the home of Jesse, God reveals his choice of the young shepherd, David — a name unique in the Old Testament. The closing statement that the "spirit of the Lord rushed upon David" shows that he had received the God-given power to rule when the right time came. The responsorial psalm accents this theme in the refrain, "I have found David, my servant." In the Gospel, the Pharisees accuse our Lord's disciples of violating the Sabbath law against farm work by eating grain as they walk in a field.

313   WEDNESDAY OF THE SECOND WEEK OF THE YEAR

YEAR I

READING I   Heb. 7:1-3, 15-17   RESP. Ps. 110:1, 2, 3, 4
GOSPEL   Mark 3:1-6

In today's reading, the author of the letter to the Hebrews teaches that the priesthood of Jesus is distinct from that of the Jewish priests. Christ, he explains, is a priest of the rank of the Old Testament priest-king, Melchizedek. We learn that Melchizedek was evidently superior to Levi — who centuries later founded the Jewish priesthood — because Levi's distinguished ancestor Abraham made a religious offering to the priest-king and received his blessing. Melchizedek also foreshadowed Christ the eternal priest, since he himself was "eternal" in the sense that Scripture records no family history for him. From these arguments, the author concludes that Jesus enjoys a superior and eternal priesthood that does not depend on descent from a human family. In the Gospel, Jesus provokes the Pharisees by curing a man with a crippled hand on the Sabbath.

YEAR II
READING I   1 Sam. 17:32-33, 37, 40-51   RESP. Ps. 144:1, 2, 9-10
GOSPEL   Mark 3:1-6

In the first reading we hear the famous story of David and Goliath — the memorable conflict that took place while the Israelites were at war with the Philistines in the eleventh century B.C. The setting was the hill country in Judah about fourteen miles west of Bethlehem. Because David wears no armor and carries only a sling as his weapon, he makes clear his role as an instrument in God's hands. When the giant mocks David's youth, the shepherd boy replies that he is fighting in God's name — another sign that victory comes to Israel because God defends his people. We may regard the responsorial psalm as David's prayer of gratitude to God for his victory. Appropriately, the refrain reminds us that the stone which stunned the giant was "the Lord, my Rock." In the Gospel, Jesus provokes the Pharisees by curing a man with a crippled hand on the Sabbath.

314   THURSDAY OF THE SECOND WEEK OF THE YEAR

YEAR I
READING I   Heb. 7:25—8:6   RESP. Ps. 40:7-8, 8-9, 10, 17
GOSPEL   Mark 3:7-12

We learn in the first reading that thoughts of Jesus as high priest still preoccupy the writer of the letter to the Hebrews. He points out that Jesus is precisely the high priest whom mankind needs — holy, sinless, and interceding for us at the right hand of God. Our Lord had no need to offer his sacrifice daily for the sins of men as the Jewish priests did. He made a single offering of himself on the cross once and for all. The responsorial psalm is the prayer of an obedient servant of the Lord. The verses remind us how willing Jesus was as our high priest to offer himself for our sins. We may also pray this psalm to express our own readiness to do God's will. In the Gospel, we hear Jesus forbidding the unclean spirits to reveal who he is. Our Lord still has to convince the people that the Messiah is not a king who will lead the Jews to world power.

YEAR II
READING I   1 Sam. 18:6-9; 19:1-7   RESP. Ps. 56:2-3, 9-10, 10-12, 13-14
GOSPEL   Mark 3:7-12

The first reading presents — as a scene typical after successful battle — the women rejoicing with singing and dancing because David has conquered the Philistine giant and routed Israel's enemies. This incident helps us see that jealousy has taken hold of King Saul's heart at the rising popularity of the young David. When Saul plots to take David's life, the king's son Jonathan intercedes for his dear friend. Saul finally agrees to let David continue serving as a harp player in his court. The liturgy regards the responsorial psalm as David's confident prayer for God to protect him from his enemies. In the Gospel, we hear Jesus forbidding the unclean spirits to reveal who he is. Our Lord still has to convince the people that the Messiah is not a king who will lead the Jews to world power.

315   FRIDAY OF THE SECOND WEEK OF THE YEAR

YEAR I

READING I   Heb. 8:6-13   RESP. Ps. 85:8 and 10, 11-12, 13-14
GOSPEL   Mark 3:13-19

The first reading informs us that God found fault with the Jews because they did not keep their part of the covenant or agreement he made with them through Moses. Nevertheless, God promised a new covenant in the words of the prophet Jeremiah, whom the author quotes in this passage. Jeremiah sees a covenant written not on stone like the Ten Commandments but one that God will write on men's hearts. This new covenant will bring into existence a new community — the people of God. We realize in gratitude today that we are this community of the new covenant. We proclaim our covenant-relationship to God through Jesus every day in the Mass. The responsorial psalm points to the blessings in the age of the new covenant in the words, "The Lord himself will give his benefits." In the Gospel, Jesus appoints his apostles to the task of preaching the Good News.

YEAR II

READING I   1 Sam. 24:3-21   RESP. Ps. 57:2, 3-4, 6 and 11
GOSPEL   Mark 3:13-19

Today's first Scripture reading demonstrates that it was just a matter of time before David would succeed Saul as king of Israel. As this dramatic narrative opens, David has taken refuge from the king's anger in the harsh desert hill country of Judah overlooking the Dead Sea. There we learn how David has an opportunity to kill Saul in a cave but spares him because David respects the king as a servant of the Lord. After David assures Saul that he means him no harm, the king admits he himself is guilty of having a murderous heart. He blesses David, and they go their separate ways. The liturgy chooses for our response to the reading a prayer that tradition says David offered to the Lord, asking God to deliver him from Saul. In the Gospel, Jesus appoints his apostles to the task of preaching the Good News.

316 SATURDAY OF THE SECOND WEEK OF THE YEAR

YEAR I

READING I   Heb. 9:2-3, 11-14   RESP. Ps. 47:2-3, 6-7, 8-9
GOSPEL   Mark 3:20-21

Today's first reading begins by recalling the sacred tent for worship that the Jews carried with them during their journey through the Sinai Desert to the promised land. We hear the author of this letter describe the holy place and the holy of holies in which the Jewish priests worshiped God in their tabernacle-tent. The author then explains how Jesus as the superior high priest passed through the heavenly region — the holy place — to the very dwelling of God himself — the Holy of Holies — when he offered up his own blood on the cross for mankind's redemption. The responsorial psalm refrain also describes how Christ our new high priest "mounts his throne" in heaven. In the Gospel, we learn how our Lord's relatives and friends believe Jesus has lost his mind in getting so involved with helping people whom everyone else despises.

YEAR II

READING 1   2 Sam. 1:1-4, 11-12, 19, 23-27   RESP. Ps. 80:2-3, 5-7
GOSPEL   Mark 3:20-21

In today's reading, the anguished voice of David, soon to be king, crosses twenty-nine centuries into our own times as we hear the very words that poured from his heart when he learned that the Philistines had killed Saul and Jonathan. These two men — the king who had hated David and the king's son who had loved David as a brother — had died in a battle at Mount Gilboa that gave Israel's enemies an important victory. David learned the tragic news after he returned to a city in Judah from his own victory over the Amalekites. The responsorial psalm underscores David's grief in the verse, "You have fed them with the bread of tears and given them tears to drink in ample measure." In the Gospel, we learn how our Lord's relatives and friends believe Jesus has lost his mind in getting so involved with helping people whom everyone else despises.

317 MONDAY OF THE THIRD WEEK OF THE YEAR

YEAR I

READING I Heb. 9:15, 24-28   RESP. Ps. 98:1, 2-3, 3-4, 5-6
GOSPEL   Mark 3:22-30

The first reading tells us more today about the priesthood of Christ. The author compares the many sacrifices the Jewish priests offered for sins with the one offering Jesus made of his own self to redeem the world. There remains now only one thing more — the coming of our Lord at the final judgment "to bring salvation to those who eagerly await him." The responsorial psalm recalls this theme in the verse, "All the ends of the earth have seen the salvation by our God." In the Gospel, Jesus answers the accusation that he has power over the demons because Satan has taken charge of his life. Our Lord also refers to blasphemy against the Holy Spirit as the unforgivable sin. This means that the power of the Holy Spirit at work in Jesus to forgive sins cannot flow into a heart that deliberately blocks out that forgiveness and credits our Lord's work to demons instead of to God.

YEAR II

READING I 2 Sam. 5:1-7, 10   RESP. Ps. 89:20, 21-22, 25-26
GOSPEL   Mark 3:22-30

As the first reading begins, David has just put down a brief revolt that King Saul's sons staged in northern Israel following their father's death. David now takes a critical step toward forging into a nation all the loosely organized Palestinian tribes who accept him as their king. David needs for his capital city a neutral area on the border between the tribes of north and south to make it clear that his rule will not favor any special claims by a particular tribe. And so he sets his sights on the fortress of Jerusalem — a city so difficult to conquer that its rulers boasted even the blind and the lame could defend it. But with God's help, the city falls into David's hands. The responsorial psalm accents the theme of David as supreme ruler of Israel. In the Gospel, Jesus answers his critics' false charge that our Lord has command over demons because Satan has power over him.

318 TUESDAY OF THE THIRD WEEK OF THE YEAR

YEAR I

READING I Heb. 10:1-10   RESP. Ps. 40:2 and 4, 7-8, 10, 11
GOSPEL   Mark 3:31-35

In today's Mass, the writer of the letter to the Hebrews discusses the difference between the worship the Jews gave to God in the days of the old covenant and the one perfect sacrifice that Jesus offered on the cross. The writer teaches that the former sacrifices of animals could not move God to forgive mankind's guilt. For this reason, the Son of God himself came into the world to offer his own life to sanctify all men. Since the author quotes from Psalm 40 in explaining the sacrifice of Jesus, the liturgy selects verses from this psalm as our response to the reading. They remind us how willing Jesus was to offer himself for our sins, particularly in the refrain, "Here am I, Lord; I come to do your will." In the Gospel, Jesus tells us what it means to be a brother or sister to him — we must rededicate ourselves each day to doing God's will in our lives.

YEAR II

READING I   2 Sam. 6:12-15, 17-19   RESP. Ps. 24:7, 8, 9, 10
GOSPEL   Mark 3:31-35

Today's first reading tells how King David brought the sacred ark of the covenant into Jerusalem amid dancing and celebration. This festive religious ceremony also achieved a political purpose. It would pave the way for the union of the northern kingdom of Israel and the southern kingdom of Judah under David's rule because the Jews of both territories shared a reverence for the ark as God's dwelling place among all his people. Jerusalem would in this way become their common center for worship. In the responsorial psalm, a procession of Jewish pilgrims carries the "king of glory" — that is, the ark of the covenant — up to the gates of the temple where worshipers inside wait for them. In the Gospel, Jesus teaches us what it means to be a brother or sister to him — we must rededicate ourselves each day to doing God's will in our lives.

319   WEDNESDAY OF THE THIRD WEEK OF THE YEAR

YEAR I

READING I   Heb. 10:11-18   RESP. Ps. 110:1, 2, 3, 4
GOSPEL   Mark 4:1-20

Today's first Scripture reading offers further observations from the letter to the Hebrews about the one perfect sacrifice of Christ. Whereas the Jewish priests offered daily sacrifices that failed to remit sins, Jesus offered the one sacrifice of himself on the cross that obtained God's forgiveness for the sins of all mankind. It is this sacrifice that the Church offers to God each day in the Mass. The responsorial psalm underscores this theme of the superior priesthood of Jesus when it says, "You are a priest forever." St. Mark's Gospel tells the parable of the sower and the seed — a story from the everyday life of a Jew.

Our Lord's point is that we should leave the rich harvest to God. Our job is to sow seed patiently and not let failure or wasted effort discourage us.

YEAR II

READING I 2 Sam. 7:4-17
GOSPEL Mark 4:1-20

In the first Scripture reading, David proposes to bui... Lord to dwell in, but God promises instead to build a ho... king — a royal family that will endure forever. This divine assura... comes through the lips of Nathan, the prophet who served in David's court. As we listen to Nathan's words, we discover how God reminds David of the things the Lord has done for the king and for the Jewish people in the past and what he will do for them as their God in the future. The whole structure of the prophecy makes it clear that God, not man, always makes the first move in the drama of salvation and that no one can frustrate God's plans. The responsorial psalm asks that God fulfill in his mercy the promise he once made "to David my servant." St. Mark's Gospel tells the parable of the sower and the seed — a story from the everyday life of a Jew.

320 THURSDAY OF THE THIRD WEEK OF THE YEAR

YEAR I

READNG I Heb. 10:19-25   **RESP. Ps.** 24:1-2, 3-4, 5-6
GOSPEL Mark 4:21-25

The author of the letter to the Hebrews gives us today several practical insights that come to him from reflecting on the priesthood of Christ. He urges his readers to draw near to God with confidence, since they now understand how their high priest has brought forgiveness of their sins. He exhorts them to remember that they are Christians not for their own sake but to inspire the lives of others. Because the reading tells how "the blood of Jesus assures our entrance into the sanctuary" of heaven, the responsorial psalm reminds us to prepare our hearts for that day. The psalm asks, "Who can ascend the mountain of the Lord? or who may stand in his holy place?" In the Gospel, we find four sayings of Jesus that St. Mark groups together in a single passage. In one verse, Jesus stresses that we must let men see the light of our faithful Christian life.

YEAR II

READING I 2 Sam. 7:18-19, 24-29   **RESP. Ps.** 132:1-2, 3-5, 11, 12, 13-14
GOSPEL Mark 4:21-25

Today's first reading takes us into the stillness of a sacred room in

Jerusalem where we find a king at prayer. The solitary figure of David sits in the sanctuary before the ark of the covenant — the symbol of God's awesome presence among his people. David's thoughts turn from this gift of the Lord to everyone in the nation to the Lord's most recent personal gift to him — God's promise to be with the king's family for all time to come. We then hear David pour out his grateful praise to the Lord for this blessing. The responsorial psalm dramatizes David's desire to build a temple for God and the Lord's promise of an everlasting royal family for him. In the Gospel, we find four sayings of Jesus that St. Mark groups together in a single passage. In one verse, Jesus stresses that we must let men see the light of our faithful Christian life.

321 FRIDAY OF THE THIRD WEEK OF THE YEAR

YEAR I

READING I Heb. 10:32-39   **RESP.** Ps. 37:3-4, 5-6, 23-24, 39-40
GOSPEL   Mark 4:26-34

The first Scripture reading concludes the tenth chapter of the letter to the Hebrews. The author strives to encourage the members of the Christian community to be more heroic and steadfast in their life of faith. He recalls the sufferings they willingly endured for their faith in the past, and he urges them to have confidence in God's promises to them in Christ. The responsorial psalm emphasizes this theme of trust in God in such verses as, "Commit to the Lord your way; trust in him, and he will act." In the Gospel we find a parable of Jesus that Mark alone relates — the seed that grows while man sleeps. This story teaches us that God's kingdom is secretly yet constantly growing in the world toward the final day of judgment. Taking part in daily Mass will help us to prepare for that day.

YEAR II

READING I 2 Sam. 11:1-4, 5-10, 13-17   **RESP.** Ps. 51:3-4, 5-6, 6-7, 10-11
GOSPEL   Mark 4:26-34

Today's first reading unfolds the tragic events that led King David — an ancestor of the Messiah and one of Israel's most illustrious rulers — to commit adultery and murder. When Bathsheba becomes pregnant after her sin with David, the king tries to make it appear that her soldier husband Uriah is the father by bringing him home from battle so he can stay with his wife. When the scheme fails, David saves Bathsheba from death for her adultery by sending Uriah to his own certain death in a fierce battle against Israel's enemies. But man cannot mock God. This incident will trigger a series of tragedies for David's own family as well as his kingdom. The responsorial psalm is the prayer that tradition tells us David poured out to God in repentance for his sins. The Gospel parable teaches that God's kingdom is secretly growing in the world toward the day of judgment.

322 SATURDAY OF THE THIRD WEEK OF THE YEAR

YEAR I

READING I   Heb. 11:1-2, 8-19   **RESP.** Ps. Luke 1:69-70, 71-72, 73-75
GOSPEL   Mark 4:35-41

In today's first reading, we begin the eleventh chapter of the letter to the Hebrews. We hear in the opening sentence a classic description of faith. The author then recalls people and events from the days of the Old Testament to portray an inspiring picture of a religious faith that obeys God without questioning. He singles out the heroic faith of Abraham as an important example for all in the community to follow. The responsorial psalm highlights God's sacred promise to Abraham that he would be faithful to his covenant in return for Abraham's obedient service of the one true God. In the Gospel, Jesus calms one of those storms which are notorious on the Sea of Galilee for their frightening suddenness. Jesus brings peace to the troubled hearts of his disciples, as he does for us today if only we go to him in faith.

YEAR II

READING I   2 Sam. 12:1-7, 10-17   **RESP.** Ps. 51:12-13, 14-15, 16-17
GOSPEL   Mark 4:35-41

In today's first reading we find one of the most dramatic encounters in the Bible — the meeting of King David with the prophet Nathan after David has committed adultery and murder. Nathan tells a parable of obvious injustice closely paralleling the king's own sins, which contradict his role as minister of justice in Israel. The way David reacts to the story proves he knows he is guilty. He reveals his true character, however, by an immediate act of repentance. In the end, the anguish David must endure reconciles him with God. As Uriah's body died by the sword, so David's spirit will die daily from the sword-thrusts of constant problems with his sons. The responsorial psalm takes up again David's prayer of sorrow for his sins. In the Gospel, Jesus calms one of those storms notorious on the Sea of Galilee for their frightening suddenness. His presence brings peace to our hearts, too.

323 MONDAY OF THE FOURTH WEEK OF THE YEAR

YEAR I

READING I   Heb. 11:32-40   **RESP.** Ps. 31:20, 21, 22, 23, 24
GOSPEL   Mark 5:1-20

Today's Mass continues our reading of the letter to the Hebrews, one of the twenty-one letters in the New Testament. We hear the author describe how the faith of various people in the days of the Old Testament inspired them to overcome enormous hardships. He points out, however, that although God was pleased with their faith, these people could not attain the "better plan" of God. This plan was the life of eternal happiness in heaven which man could attain only after the death and resurrection of Jesus. The responsorial psalm refrain accents the theme of hope in the words, "Let your hearts take comfort, all who hope in the Lord." The Gospel tells how Jesus heals a demon-possessed man — a savage and naked madman who becomes "perfectly sane." The incident upsets the people in the town, and they urge our Lord to leave.

YEAR II

READING I   2 Sam. 15:13-14, 30; 16:5-13   RESP. Ps. 3:2-3, 4-5, 6-7
GOSPEL   Mark 5:1-20

In the first reading, we continue the story of the Jewish people under King David in the tenth century before Christ. Quarrels have now divided the king's household, and the people themselves are discontent with David's rule and his lack of concern for their problems. The time was ripe for a rebellion, and it came at the hands of David's own son Absalom, who proclaimed himself king in the city of Hebron. This is the setting for today's story of David's flight with his troops from Jerusalem northward toward Jericho. On the way, a relative of the former King Saul curses David as a murderer. The responsorial psalm is one that tradition says David prayed when he fled from Absalom. The Gospel tells how Jesus heals a demon-possessed man — a savage and naked madman who becomes "perfectly sane." The incident upsets the people in the town, and they urge our Lord to leave.

324   TUESDAY OF THE FOURTH WEEK OF THE YEAR

YEAR I

READING I   Heb. 12:1-4   RESP. Ps. 22:26-27, 28 and 30, 31-32
GOSPEL   Mark 5:21-43

In today's passage from the letter to the Hebrews, we hear the author compare the Christian life to a long-distance race. He urges his readers to stay in this race despite trials and difficulties. They should follow the inspiration of Christ, who courageously endured his own sufferings. Since the reading invites us "to keep our eyes fixed on Jesus," the responsorial psalm expresses our longing for God and declares that "all the ends of the earth shall remember and turn to the Lord." In the Gospel, Jesus performs two miracles in response to deep faith.

78

A ruler of a synagogue forgets his pride and prejudices, and as a result his faith in Jesus brings the cure of his daughter. When as a last resort a sick woman approaches our Lord, she finds that merely touching his robe heals her.

YEAR II

READING I 2 Sam. 18:9-10, 14, 24-25, 30—19:3   RESP. Ps. 86:1-2, 3-4, 5-6
GOSPEL   Mark 5:21-43

To understand today's first Scripture reading, we need to realize that King David has easily defeated the rebellious forces of his own son Absalom in a thick forest east of the Jordan River. As the passage begins, we discover Absalom fleeing for his life on his terrified mule because he had set himself up as king against his father — and lost the gamble. Fate then brings Absalom to a violent death. The news breaks David's heart in one of the Bible's most memorable scenes of grief. The liturgy places the responsorial psalm on David's lips as he calls out to God, "Incline your ear, O Lord . . . for I am afflicted and poor." The Gospel tells how a ruler of a synagogue forgets his pride and prejudices, and as a result his faith in Jesus brings the cure of his daughter. We also learn how a sick woman approaches our Lord in faith, and merely touching his robe heals her.

325 WEDNESDAY OF THE FOURTH WEEK OF THE YEAR

YEAR I

READING I Heb. 12:4-7, 11-15   RESP. Ps. 103:1-2, 13-14, 17-18
GOSPEL   Mark 6:1-6

In today's reading, the author of the letter to the Hebrews applies a principle of family life to God's dealings with his children. He explains that a certain amount of discipline is a sign of God's fatherly love — a proof that God is taking a firm but loving hand in the spiritual education of his children. He quotes a passage from the Book of Proverbs to support his view. The writer then exhorts the early Christians to live in peace with others and to strive for holiness. The responsorial psalm after this reading also draws our attention to the consoling thought of God's fatherly compassion for his children. In the Gospel, we learn how important faith is. Because the people of his own village did not believe in him, Jesus could not perform any miracles there to help them — and this deeply distressed the divine physician.

YEAR II

READING I 2 Sam. 24:2, 9-17   RESP. Ps. 32:1-2, 5, 6, 7
GOSPEL   Mark 6:1-6

In today's first reading, we learn how King David offended God by taking a census of the people to determine how many men were fit for military service. No clear reason appears why the Lord became angry. Some Scripture commentators believe the census revealed that David relied on human resources to protect the country instead of God's help. The incident where the prophet offers David a choice of three calamities as punishment reflects the simplistic religious outlook of this time that saw famines, plagues, and other natural disasters as signs of God's punishment for sin. We may regard the responsorial psalm as David's prayer of repentance. In the Gospel, we learn how important faith is. Because the people of his own village did not believe in him, Jesus could perform no miracles there to help them — and this deeply distressed the divine physician.

326 THURSDAY OF THE FOURTH WEEK OF THE YEAR

YEAR I

READING I   Heb. 12:18-19, 21-24   RESP. Ps. 48:2-3, 3-4, 9, 10-11
GOSPEL   Mark 6:7-13

Today's first reading contrasts the former covenant of friendship that God made with the Jews through Moses and the new covenant God made through Christ. We hear the author refer first to the events that took place on Mount Sinai, when God gave his Law to Moses. Then the author explains how the Christian people have drawn near to God through Jesus, "the mediator of a new covenant." Since the reading refers to Mount Zion, one of the two hills where the Jews built Jerusalem, the liturgy chooses a responsorial psalm which praises God for his presence in the temple on "Mount Zion, the city of the great King." In the Gospel, Jesus sends his apostles to the towns and country villages in Galilee to prepare them for the coming of God's kingdom. The apostles must live simply, trust in God, and preach "the need of repentance."

YEAR II

READING I   1 Kings 2:1-4, 10-12
                                  RESP. Ps. 1 Chr. 29:10, 11, 11-12, 12
GOSPEL   Mark 6:7-13

The first reading takes us to King David's deathbed about the year 971 B.C. We hear David give his son Solomon, who has succeeded him as Israel's third king, practical advice on following God's ways. David wants to make certain that the Lord will bless Solomon in ruling the chosen people. The text declares that David ruled Israel for forty years — a round number meaning a full career — and describes Jerusalem for the first time as the "City of David." Later historians of Israel tended to forget the king's weaknesses and painted glowing pictures of David as the ideal servant of God — the way we tend to idealize great figures of our own history. The responsorial psalm includes portions of a hymn of thanksgiving that tradition says David prayed on the day before he died. In the Gospel, Jesus sends his apostles to towns in Galilee to prepare them for God's kingdom.

327   FRIDAY OF THE FOURTH WEEK OF THE YEAR

YEAR I

READING I   Heb. 13:1-8   RESP. Ps. 27:1, 3, 5, 8-9
GOSPEL   Mark 6:14-29

Today's first reading from the letter to the Hebrews outlines five practical ways of living as a Christian. In regard to showing hospitality, the author refers indirectly to the times when Abraham and Tobiah showed kindness to strangers who turned out to be angels in disguise. The author's observation to "be content with what you have" seems to offer a Christian response to the modern spirit of "keeping up with the Joneses." His comment on the dignity of marriage contains a timely reminder for Christian couples today that their sacrament is a lived-out daily relationship of total love for each other. Because the author quotes from Psalm 27 to support his counsel to have confidence in God, the liturgy selects verses from this psalm for us to pray after the reading. The Gospel explains the dramatic events that led to the beheading of John the Baptist.

YEAR II

READING I   Sirach 47:2-11   RESP. Ps. 18:31, 47 and 50, 51
GOSPEL   Mark 6:14-29

In the first reading, we survey the basically God-oriented yet sorrow-laden life of King David eight centuries after his death through the eyes of a Jewish wisdom teacher. About the year 180 B.C., Ben Sirach included David among the illustrious heroes of Israel's past whom he offered as examples to his students of wisdom. We hear Sirach recall David's military exploits, his concern for the proper worship of God, and the divine promise that David's royal family would continue forever. The responsorial psalm highlights today's praise of David to whom God gave "great victories" and "showed kindness." The Gospel explains the dramatic events that led to the beheading of John the Baptist. With his death, the career of Jesus takes a new turn. John has fulfilled the role of the prophet Elijah in preparing the way for the Messiah, and now Jesus will fulfill his own destiny.

328 SATURDAY OF THE FOURTH WEEK OF THE YEAR

YEAR I

READING I   Heb. 13:15-17, 20-21   RESP. Ps. 23:1-3, 3-4, 5, 6
GOSPEL   Mark 6:30-34

In the first reading, the author begins by exhorting the community to praise God "through Jesus," a reminder that we always come before God our Father as brothers and sisters of Christ. Everywhere in the prayers at Mass we note this same approach to God through Christ. The author also reminds the Christians not to neglect "good deeds" and "generosity" because these are some of the practical ways we live the sacrifice of the Mass in our daily lives. The responsorial psalm highlights the author's reference to Jesus as "the Great Shepherd" by declaring in the refrain, "The Lord is my shepherd." The Gospel also has a shepherd theme. St. Mark points out that Jesus felt pity for the crowds. He saw that so many of them did not know which way to turn in life, while others lacked the strength to go on. They were like sheep without a shepherd.

YEAR II

READING I   1 Kings 3:4-13   RESP. Ps. 119:9, 10, 11, 12, 13, 14
GOSPEL   Mark 6:30-34

Today's reading begins the story of King Solomon. He bore a name that became a symbol of worldly splendor, as Jesus indicated when he spoke about the lilies of the field. We do not know how old Solomon was when he took over the throne from David and had the legendary dream in today's passage, but the Jewish historian Josephus hints he may have been barely out of his teens. Religious leaders of that time regarded dreams as an important way in which God communicated with men. Solomon would lose no time in applying the practical wisdom God gave him. Not long after, he made his famous decision in the case of the two mothers who claimed the same baby. The liturgy suggests that we hear Solomon praying again for wisdom in the verses of the responsorial psalm. In the Gospel, we find Mark pointing out how Jesus felt pity for the crowds, who were like sheep without a shepherd.

329 MONDAY OF THE FIFTH WEEK OF THE YEAR

YEAR I

READING I   Gen. 1:1-19   RESP. Ps. 104:1-2, 5-6, 10 and 12, 24 and 35
GOSPEL   Mark 6:53-56

Today we begin a special section in the first book of the Old Testament, the Book of Genesis — a word that means "beginning." As we listen to these first eleven chapters over the coming weeks, we must keep in mind that the author is not presenting an exact scientific explanation of how the world began. Instead, these chapters relate, in what the Biblical Commission called "simple and figurative language," the truths underlying God's plan for our salvation, and "a popular description of the origin of the human race and of the chosen people." Today's passage tells about the first four days of the creation of the world. The responsorial psalm echoes this theme in rich images of God creating the earth, the ocean, and all living things. St. Mark ends the sixth chapter of his Gospel by summarizing the healing ministry of Jesus in many towns and villages of Galilee.

YEAR II

READING I   1 Kings 8:1-7, 9-13   RESP. Ps. 132:6-7, 8-10
GOSPEL   Mark 6:53-56

Today we join the thousands of people jammed into the courtyard for the dedication of the magnificent stone temple King Solomon has completed on Mount Zion about 953 B.C. after seven years of labor. As we watch, a procession of Jewish priests — carrying the sacred ark of the covenant — moves solemnly up the ten front steps of the temple into the vestibule. They pass through the large cedar-paneled room called the Holy Place and then up another stairway into a windowless inner room — the pitch-dark Holy of Holies. God then shows he accepts his new dwelling place by filling the temple with the cloud of his presence. The responsorial psalm appropriately recalls when David first brought the ark into a simple sanctuary in Jerusalem — its home until Solomon built the temple. In the Gospel, St. Mark summarizes the healing ministry of Jesus in many towns of Galilee.

330   TUESDAY OF THE FIFTH WEEK OF THE YEAR

YEAR I

READING I   Gen. 1:20—2:4   RESP. Ps. 8:4-5, 6-7, 8-9
GOSPEL   Mark 7:1-13

The first reading from the Book of Genesis teaches us important religious truths about God's role in creating the world. The climax of God's creation is man, who shares God's image by the way he rules over all other creatures. The author divides God's creative activity into six days to emphasize how sacred in the Jewish religion is the Sabbath rest on the seventh day. The responsorial psalm recalls God's wondrous love in creating man. Today's Gospel is important in helping us to understand the basic disagreement between Jesus and some orthodox Jews of his day. They tended to emphasize external rituals and ceremonies as what really mattered in worshiping God. We hear Jesus rebuke some Pharisees for distorting the traditions they have received from Moses. Our Lord insists that the Pharisees must not neglect caring for human needs and serving God with a sincere heart.

YEAR II

READING I   1 Kings 8:22-23, 27-30   RESP. Ps. 84:3, 4, 5 and 10, 11
GOSPEL   Mark 7:1-13

The first reading takes us again to the dedication ceremony for the temple that King Solomon has built in Jerusalem as part of his palace complex. We see the king come out of the temple into the crowded courtyard and walk to the altar of sacrifice. He raises his arms in prayer to thank God for bringing this day to pass. We hear him recall that God has always been faithful to his covenant promise to Israel, and he exhorts the people to keep faith in turn with the Lord. Solomon then asks God to answer the requests that his people will make when they come to worship in front of the temple. The responsorial psalm is appropriately one that a pilgrim would sing on visiting the temple. In the Gospel, Jesus challenges the outlook of many Jewish religious leaders who put their ceremonial laws ahead of human needs and the interior service of God.

331   WEDNESDAY OF THE FIFTH WEEK OF THE YEAR

YEAR I

READING I   Gen. 2:5-9, 15-17   RESP. Ps. 104:1-2, 27-28, 29-30
GOSPEL   Mark 7:14-23

Today's reading reminds us that the Book of Genesis is a complex work containing stories from various literary sources. Up to this point we have heard one account of the story of creation. Now we hear a second version that emphasizes how God created the first man and placed him in the garden of Eden. For the responsorial psalm, the liturgy selects Psalm 104 — a hymn of praise to God as creator of the universe. The Gospel passage reveals a revolutionary teaching of Jesus that casts new light on the whole Jewish outlook of insisting on certain foods and things as unclean. It is hard for us to appreciate today how shattering our Lord's words must have sounded to the Jews — especially when we consider that St. Peter himself needed a revelation from God later on to teach him the same lesson.

YEAR II

READING I   1 Kings 10:1-10   RESP. Ps. 37:5-6, 30-31, 39-40
GOSPEL   Mark 7:14-23

In today's first reading, we discover that the wealthy and prosperous kingdom of Solomon attracted a visit to his court from the queen of

Sheba, a neighboring monarchy in northern Arabia. The excavations of modern archeologists at the ancient seaport Solomon built on the Gulf of Aqaba help us to read between the lines of today's passage. Because this seaport enabled Solomon to do business with merchants in distant ports, the queen of Sheba was probably visiting Israel to expand her own trade. This incident reveals how God fulfilled his promise to give Solomon wealth as well as wisdom. The responsorial psalm highlights this wisdom theme in the refrain, "The mouth of the just man murmurs wisdom." The Gospel passage reveals a revolutionary teaching of Jesus that casts a new light on the Jewish outlook of insisting on certain foods and things as unclean.

332 THURSDAY OF THE FIFTH WEEK OF THE YEAR

YEAR I

READING I   Gen. 2:18-25   RESP. Ps. 128:1-2, 3, 4-5
GOSPEL   Mark 7:24-30

In today's first reading, God's creation of the first woman teaches basic religious truths about her relationship to man. The author's description of how the Lord formed woman from man reveals that as equals they share the same nature and the same rights and privileges. This fact contradicted the Near East view of woman as someone inferior to man whom he could treat as his property. The author also sees the union of one man and one woman in marriage as God's ideal for their happy relationship. Their nakedness suggests an open and honest giving of themselves to each other. The responsorial psalm stresses today's marital theme in an image of the joys of married life. The Gospel informs us that a Gentile woman comes to Jesus seeking a cure for her daughter. The miracle Jesus works for her discloses that the Gentiles, too, are to have a share in God's kingdom.

YEAR II

READING I   1 Kings 11:4-13   RESP. Ps. 106:3-4, 35-36, 37, 40
GOSPEL   Mark 7:24-30

Today's reading foreshadows how Solomon's kingdom will lose its glory because he compromised the faith of Israel by letting the people worship false gods. This evil situation built up over many years of Solomon's reign. The king provided special shrines — called "high places" — where his foreign wives could practice their own religions and which attracted others to worship there, too. God had warned Solomon in dreams about this idolatry, but the king continued to disobey. As a result, we learn that God will divide the kingdom after Solomon's death. The responsorial psalm finds a parallel to this worship of false gods in the period when the Jews first settled in the promised land. There "they mingled with the nations . . . and served their idols." The Gospel tells the story of a Gentile woman who comes to Jesus seeking a cure for her daughter.

333 FRIDAY OF THE FIFTH WEEK OF THE YEAR

YEAR I

READING I Gen. 3:1-8
RESP. Ps. 32:1-2, 5, 6, 7
GOSPEL Mark 7:31-37

The first reading tells how our first parents lost their friendship with God — the fatal event that spelled tragedy for the human race. The author probably showed that a serpent was responsible for the downfall of man so that the Jews would not find attractive the serpent worship of their pagan neighbors. The teaching of the Church about origina sin derives from this story of man's fall from grace. We know for certain that man disobeyed God's command, but precisely how he did this we do not know. In the responsorial psalm we seem to hear Adam and Eve admitting their guilt to God and acknowledging the Lord's mercy to them. In the Gospel, Jesus calls a deaf man away from the embarrassing presence of the crowd before healing him. This miracle reveals our Lord's concern for each person as an individual — just as he treats our problems today.

YEAR II

READING I 1 Kings 11:29-32; 12:19
RESP. Ps. 81:10-11, 12-13, 14-15
GOSPEL Mark 7:31-37

In today's first reading, the prophet Ahijah dramatizes the revolution that will rip Solomon's kingdom apart soon after his death. Ahijah tears his cloak into twelve pieces and gives ten to a man named Jeroboam to symbolize that he will become king of the ten northern tribes. This is another instance in the Old Testament where a prophet performs an act that not only symbolizes something that will happen but actually *guarantees* it will come true. After this incident, Solomon learned about the plot to take over his domain, and Jeroboam had to flee to Egypt for political asylum. Because the reading closes on the note of Israel's rebellion, the responsorial psalm points to the people's worship of false gods as its cause. St. Mark's Gospel shows Jesus giving special consideration to a deaf man while healing him, which reveals our Lord's concern for each person as an individual.

334 SATURDAY OF THE FIFTH WEEK OF THE YEAR

YEAR I

READING I Gen. 3:9-24 RESP. Ps. 90:2, 3-4, 5-6, 12-13
GOSPEL Mark 8:1-10

Today's first Scripture reading tells us more about the fall of our first parents. Sin has destroyed the divine friendship that man once enjoyed with God. The author now gives us, in the way God condemns the serpent, a prophecy of Satan's defeat. Later ages understood this passage as God's first promise to fallen mankind of a Redeemer who would overcome Satan. Since God says to Adam, "For you are dirt, and to dirt you shall return," the responsorial psalm recalls this theme in the words, "You turn man back to dust." In the Gospel, Jesus feeds a crowd of four thousand with only seven loaves of bread and a few fish. We might learn a lesson here. From the little we have, God also asks us to help others in trouble at the moment of need — rather than wait for a better opportunity later on.

YEAR II

READING I 1 Kings 12:26-32; 13:33-34 RESP. Ps. 106:6-7, 19-20, 21-22
GOSPEL Mark 8:1-10

The first reading illustrates how King Jeroboam tried for political purposes to keep the attention of the ten tribes of northern Israel fixed on their own kingdom. He set up more convenient religious shrines for the people at Dan in the far north and at Bethel in the south to offset the attraction to worship at Jerusalem in the rival southern kingdom of Judah. Unfortunately, Jeroboam's use of golden calves as images of Israel's God at these shrines provided a dangerous temptation for the people to fall into idolatry. For this reason, as well as for setting up his own priesthood, the author of this passage condemns Jeroboam. The responsorial psalm accents the theme of idolatry by recalling the worship of the golden calf in the days of Moses. In the Gospel, Jesus feeds a crowd of four thousand with only seven loaves of bread and a few fish.

335 MONDAY OF THE SIXTH WEEK OF THE YEAR

YEAR I

READING I Gen. 4:1-15, 25 RESP. Ps. 50:1, 8, 16-17, 20-21
GOSPEL Mark 8:11-13

In our reading thus far from the Book of Genesis, we have learned about the creation of the world, the creation of man and woman, their rebellion against God, and their dismissal from paradise. Today's story of

Cain and Abel teaches us that man's revolt against God leads to his revolt against his fellowman and that we must worship God with the right spirit. In the responsorial psalm we seem to hear God's reprimand of Cain in the verses, "When you do these things, shall I be deaf to it? . . . I will correct you by drawing them up before your eyes." Other verses in the psalm also apply to the story of Cain. In the Gospel, the Pharisees seek a special sign from Jesus — over and above his miracles — that he is truly the Messiah. They are repeating the blindness and distrust that the Jews showed toward God during their journey to the promised land.

YEAR II

READING I   James 1:1-11   RESP. Ps. 119:67, 68, 71, 72, 75, 76
GOSPEL   Mark 8:11-13

In the first reading, we begin the letter of St. James, leader of the Jewish community in Jerusalem. He met a martyr's death in the year 62. Unlike St. Paul in his letters to particular communities, James directed his reflections on the Christian life to the whole Church. We hear James comment today on how to handle situations that test how strong our faith really is. He stresses our need to ask God for help in solving problems without ever doubting that the help will come. He notes the risk that people run in counting too much on having a lot of money. Unlike faith in God, money doesn't last. The responsorial psalm reinforces this idea by underscoring the value of trials in the Christian life. In the Gospel, the Pharisees seek a special sign from Jesus — over and above his miracles — to show that he is truly the Messiah.

336   TUESDAY OF THE SIXTH WEEK OF THE YEAR

YEAR I

READING I   Gen. 6:5-8; 7:1-5, 10   RESP. Ps. 29:1-2, 3-4, 3 and 9-10
GOSPEL   Mark 8:14-21

Today's first reading tells how the overwhelming weight of mankind's sins led God to destroy his creation by unleashing a flood. This story emphasizes that man brings grief to God's heart when he turns his back on his Creator to follow his own selfish ways. We meet here for the first time in the Bible the idea of a small group of people — Noah and his household — who remain faithful to God and make possible a new beginning after a time of disaster. This theme will appear again at critical points in Jewish history. The responsorial psalm accents the flood theme in the verses, "The voice of the Lord is over the waters" and "The Lord is enthroned above the flood." The Gospel reveals that false ideas about what the Messiah would do for the Jewish people prevented our Lord's disciples for a time from understanding what his miracles really meant — and this disappointed Jesus.

YEAR II

READING I   James 1:12-18   RESP. Ps. 94:12-13, 14-15, 18-19
GOSPEL   Mark 8:14-21

The first reading deals with the temptations we all experience to do things that go against our Christian way of life. In pointing to the "crown" that awaits all who overcome temptations, St. James uses the familiar image of the garland of laurel leaves the winner received in Roman games. James then stresses that the lure to commit sin comes not from God but from a man's own selfish impulse to do wrong. He says that God, whose children we are, not only does not tempt us, but, good Father that he is, he at all times wants what is best for us. The responsorial psalm suggests that God in fact helps us cope with temptation in the verse, "When cares abound within me, your comfort gladdens my soul." The Gospel reveals how disappointed Jesus was with his disciples for failing to understand his miracles when he multiplied bread to feed the crowds.

337   WEDNESDAY OF THE SIXTH WEEK OF THE YEAR

YEAR I

READING I   Gen. 8:6-13, 20-22   RESP. Ps. 116:12-13, 14-15, 18-19
GOSPEL   Mark 8:22-26

The first reading concludes the account of Noah and the flood. After Noah offers a sacrifice to God, the Lord promises not to destroy the world again. The word "ark" that occurs in this story will appear later in the Bible to describe the basket that carried the baby Moses to safety over the waters of a river. In each case, God in his mercy saves important men who will bring new hope to the world. On the walls of the catacombs and in contemporary art, Noah's ark is a popular symbol for baptism and for the Church because they save us from sin. St. Peter in one of his letters discovers an image of baptism in the story of the flood. The responsorial psalm refrain expresses Noah's gratitude in the words, "To you, Lord, I will offer a sacrifice of praise." The Gospel tells how a blind man gradually regained his sight — a miracle that St. Mark alone records.

YEAR II

READING I   James 1:19-27   RESP. Ps. 15:2-3, 3-4, 5
GOSPEL   Mark 8:22-26

In the first reading, St. James continues to teach the early Christians the practical side of their way of life. He warns them first to be especially careful in situations when their first impulse would be to lash out in anger at others. James then emphasizes that a Christian cannot settle for merely listening to God's message about how he should live. James selects as concrete examples the effort we must all make to curb our tongues, to take care of needy fellow human beings, and to guard against falling into worldly ways of thinking. The responsorial psalm gives further examples of people who live their faith. The Gospel tells how the blind man in the town of Bethsaida gradually regained his sight at the healing touch of Jesus — a miracle that St. Mark alone records.

338 THURSDAY OF THE SIXTH WEEK OF THE YEAR

YEAR I

READING I   Gen. 9:1-13   RESP. Ps. 102:16-18, 19-21, 29 and 22-23
GOSPEL   Mark 8:27-33

In today's Mass, God gives his solemn promise to Noah, after the flood, that he will maintain friendship with man. This is another stage in God's Old Testament strategy to draw men and women closer to his heart after the fall of our first parents. We hear God assure Noah that he will never again destroy the earth by a flood. Every time that a man sees a rainbow after a storm he can recall that promise. In God's command that Noah may eat only bloodless meat, we find the origin of the Jewish kosher laws. The responsorial psalm refrain, "From heaven the Lord looks down on the earth," reminds us of God's covenant with Noah and its sign of the rainbow. In the Gospel, our Lord's public career up to this time reaches a climax when St. Mark says that Peter recognized Jesus as the Messiah. Mark also shows our Lord teaching for the first time that the Messiah would have to suffer.

YEAR II

READING I   James 2:1-9   RESP. Ps. 34:2-3, 4-5, 6-7
GOSPEL   Mark 8:27-33

The first reading warns the early Christians not to neglect the poor by unduly cultivating the rich. St. James illustrates how a Christian might fall into this trap by treating a poor man and a rich man differently at a church service. Such discrimination, James explains, violates God's special concern for the poor that the Old Testament and the teachings of Jesus clearly point out. James follows here a fundamental insight of Christianity that God values the inner dispositions of a man's heart and not the clothes he wears or other externals of his life. As

God's children, we must reflect that outlook by treating all men as our brothers in the Lord. The responsorial psalm takes up today's theme in the refrain, "The Lord hears the cry of the poor." Mark's Gospel tells us that Peter acknowledged Jesus as the Messiah. Our Lord then reveals his suffering, death, and resurrection that Peter fails to understand.

339 FRIDAY OF THE SIXTH WEEK OF THE YEAR

YEAR I

READING I Gen. 11:1-9   RESP. Ps. 33:10-11, 12-13, 14-15
GOSPEL Mark 8:34—9:1

The first reading brings to a climax the whole history of mankind before the time of Abraham. The author has previously shown that man's efforts to be like God have only separated him from his Creator and his fellowman. The story of the tower of Babel deals with this same theme. The author suggests that when man's attempt to build a civilization turns into an end in itself the project detours him from God. The breakdown in communications among men results when they become proud and self-sufficient — as it does to this day. The responsorial psalm recalls that theme in the verse, "The Lord brings to nought the plans of nations." In the Gospel, St. Mark gives us several sayings of Jesus that go to the heart of our Christian life. Taking up our cross daily, overcoming selfishness, putting God first in our life — all these values challenge us today, too.

YEAR II

READING I James 2:14-24, 26   RESP. Ps. 112:1-2, 3-4, 5-6
GOSPEL Mark 8:34—9:1

Today's first Scripture reading on "faith without works" is probably the most famous passage in the letter of St. James. He appears to deal with a self-righteous person who claims that it is sufficient to believe in God without necessarily putting forth that faith into practice. James uses several arguments to prove that such an outlook is completely contrary to the Christian way of life. Pious wishes will never clothe the naked or feed the hungry, James insists, for even the devils believe in God — but not by that will they ever gain heaven. He also points to the example of Abraham who was willing to sacrifice his own son to prove his faith. The responsorial psalm emphasizes this practical faith, too, in the refrain, "Happy are those who do what the Lord commands." In the Gospel, St. Mark gives us several sayings of Jesus that go to the heart of our Christian life.

YEAR I

READING I Heb. 11:1-7   RESP. Ps. 145:2-3, 4-5, 10-11
GOSPEL   Mark 9:2-13

Over the past two weeks, we have been reading important passages from the first eleven chapters of Genesis. We heard about the creation of man and woman, their fall, the stories of Cain and Abel, and Noah and the flood. As if to sum up, the liturgy presents today an appropriate passage from the New Testament. The author looks back to these ancient figures in the history of salvation and offers their inspiring faith as an example for our own lives. The responsorial psalm emphasizes this theme in the verse, "Let your faithful ones bless you." St. Mark's Gospel describes how Jesus appeared in all his dazzling glory on a mountain before three of his apostles. Mark apparently sees in the presence of Moses and Elijah a sign that Jesus is the Messiah. The Father's voice confirms his mission. Afterwards, our Lord indicates that John the Baptist had fulfilled Elijah's destiny.

YEAR II

READING I James 3:1-10   RESP. Ps. 12:2-3, 4-5, 7-8
GOSPEL   Mark 9:2-13

In today's reading, St. James studies how difficult it is for a person to control his tongue and the harm that results from failing to do so. He reminds us that rumors and gossip, lies and name-calling, and all other mischief of the tongue can rage out of control like a forest fire to destroy people's lives. James suggests that the same tongue that praises God in our private prayers and receives the Lord in Holy Communion must not become a weapon to wound the hearts of our brothers and sisters in Christ. He follows here the wisdom of the Old Testament which held that loose, irresponsible talk was the mark of a fool. The responsorial psalm also points out what harm a man can do by misusing his God-given gift of speech. The Gospel story of the transfiguration reveals that Jesus, the Son of Man, even before his resurrection was really the glorious Son of God.

341 MONDAY OF THE SEVENTH WEEK OF THE YEAR

YEAR I

READING I Sirach 1:1-10   RESP. Ps. 93:1, 1-2, 5
GOSPEL   Mark 9:14-29

Over the next two weeks, the first readings deal with the writings of Ben Sirach, a respected Jewish wisdom-teacher who lived in the second century before Christ. Sirach conducted a school in Jerusalem where he taught his knowledge of the Scriptures, as well as the practical wisdom he had learned in his lifetime. In today's passage, Sirach explains how God shared his wisdom with the world in varying degrees. In some measure, God reflected his wisdom in "all his works" and in "every living thing," but on Israel — "upon his friends" — God bestowed his wisdom in abundance by means of his wise laws. Since Sirach describes God, the source of all wisdom, as "awe-inspiring, seated upon his throne," the responsorial psalm also reveals God "in splendor robed" whose "throne stands firm from of old." The Gospel shows in the cure of a demon-possessed boy that prayer is the power that works miracles.

YEAR II

READING I   James 3:13-18   RESP. Ps. 19:8, 9, 10, 15
GOSPEL   Mark 9:14-29

In the first reading, St. James talks about the virtue of wisdom — an important theme in the Bible. When Biblical writers deal with wisdom, they usually contrast the false wisdom of the worldly man with the true wisdom that God alone can give to the man who loves him. We note today that James also follows this pattern by contrasting true and false wisdom. James closes by setting in a gardening image the special quality of peace that characterizes Christian wisdom. The harvest of a life pleasing to God, James says, can sprout only from the soil of a man's effort to live at peace with himself and others. The responsorial psalm highlights this wisdom theme by reminding us that "the decree of the Lord is trustworthy, giving wisdom to the simple." The Gospel shows in the cure of a demon-possessed boy that prayer is the power that works miracles.

342   TUESDAY OF THE SEVENTH WEEK OF THE YEAR

YEAR I

READING I   Sirach 2:1-11   RESP. Ps. 37:3-4, 18-19, 27-28, 39-40
GOSPEL   Mark 9:30-37

In the first reading, the Jewish wisdom-teacher Sirach speaks about serving God in times of trial — a favorite Old Testament theme, especially in the Psalms. He explains that all affliction in life is really under the control of God and his providential concern for us. Sirach recommends standing firm through the difficulties of life. He assures his students that God will reward patience. Because Sirach advises his pupils, "Trust God and he will help you," the responsorial psalm refrain declares, "Commit your life to the Lord, and he will help you." Today's

Gospel reveals how human were the disciples of Jesus — they do not understand that he must suffer, and they argue about who is the most important among men. Our Lord then teaches them that they must seek to serve others who, in their need, are as helpless as a child.

YEAR II

READING I   James 4:1-10   RESP. Ps. 55:7-8, 9-10, 10-11, 23
GOSPEL   Mark 9:30-37

Today's first Scripture reading reveals that the early Christians were just as human as we are. We hear St. James rebuke the local communities in the Church for their "conflicts" and "disputes." He then digs into the roots of these difficulties — the same evil desires, jealousies, greedy attitudes that trouble our hearts, too. James compares these evil-doers to "unfaithful ones" — an image from married life that the prophets sometimes used in condemning the Jewish people for turning away from God. The passage concludes with a call to the Christians to repent their sins and approach God with humble hearts. The liturgy suggests that we hear the voice of James cry out again in the responsorial psalm verse, "In the city I see violence and strife." The Gospel shows how human our Lord's disciples were, too, as we hear them argue about who is the most important among them.

343 WEDNESDAY OF THE SEVENTH WEEK OF THE YEAR

YEAR I

READING I   Sirach 4:11-19   RESP. Ps. 119:165, 168, 171, 172, 174, 175
GOSPEL   Mark 9:38-40

In today's first reading, the Jewish wisdom-teacher Sirach compares wisdom to a mother instructing her children in the ways of life. He then describes the various blessings that come to those who love, serve, and obey the wise ways of God. He concludes that the secrets of wisdom bring a happiness that is well worth the effort to achieve them. In this way, Sirach hoped to encourage his readers to follow the wisdom of God and not the false wisdom of the Greeks in his day. Because Sirach affirms that "with her precepts" wisdom puts her disciples "to the proof," the responsorial psalm shows us a faithful disciple of wisdom. He proclaims to God, the author of wisdom, "I keep your precepts . . . for all my ways are before you." In the Gospel, Jesus warns the apostle John not to be jealous or intolerant of those who perform good works because "Anyone who is not against us is with us."

READING I   James 4:13-17   RESP. Ps. 49:2-3, 6-7, 8-10, 11
GOSPEL   Mark 9:38-40

In today's reading, St. James teaches the early Christians the out-look they should have about the future of their lives. He begins by por-traying a merchant of his day confidently planning to launch a new business. James uses this scene to demonstrate that the future is in God's hands, not ours. James suggests we acknowledge this by saying of whatever we attempt, "If the Lord wills it." He is Christianizing a similar expression the Romans used to place any new venture in the hands of their gods. James ends with a warning. To continue seeking to arrange one's life by leaving God out of the picture, he says, is just as much a sin as doing something wrong. The theme of a rich man who lives without thought for God appears in the responsorial psalm. In the Gospel, Jesus warns the apostle John not to be jealous or intolerant of those who perform good works.

344   THURSDAY OF THE SEVENTH WEEK OF THE YEAR

READING I   Sirach 5:1-8   RESP. Ps. 1:1-2, 3, 4 and 6
GOSPEL   Mark 9:41-50

In today's first reading, Ben Sirach points out the dangers for an in-dividual's spiritual life when he relies on the amount of money he has instead of on God. Sirach does not condemn riches as such, but he condemns the false sense of power and security that people feel when they have a lot of money. He also teaches that a sinner cannot rashly presume on God's mercy if he makes no attempt to reform his life. Be-cause Sirach claims that "upon the wicked alights God's wrath," the responsorial psalm emphasizes this verdict in the verse, "but the way of the wicked vanishes." In the Gospel, Jesus warns his disciples about the danger of giving scandal. Instead, they should allow the goodness of their lives to flavor the lives of other people, just as salt flavors food. Our Lord also reminds his disciples that God's kingdom is worth any sacrifice they have to make for it.

READING I   James 5:1-6   RESP. Ps. 49:14-15, 15-16, 17-18, 19-20
GOSPEL   Mark 9:41-50

The first reading reveals once again in dramatic words that the Bible exhibits a passionate concern for the cause of social justice and a serious awareness that rich people bear a heavy responsibility to relieve the needs of those who are poor. In this matter, St. James adds his own ringing condemnation of wealthy people who acquired their money by dishonest or selfish means. James says that on the day of judgment there will stand in witness against greedy rich people the wealth that they have hoarded away instead of sharing it with their less fortunate fellow men. He closes on the grim note of how the rich in the ancient world exploited farm workers who had no way to protect themselves. The responsorial psalm also centers on the challenging theme of rich and poor. In the Gospel, Jesus warns us to avoid giving scandal and whatever will keep us away from our union with God.

345 FRIDAY OF THE SEVENTH WEEK OF THE YEAR

YEAR I

READING I Sirach 6:5-17   RESP. Ps. 119:12, 16, 18, 27, 34, 35
GOSPEL   Mark 10:1-12

Today's reading examines the qualities of true and false friends. The Jewish teacher of wisdom Ben Sirach treats this theme of friendship more extensively than any other biblical writer. First, we hear Sirach discussing the various types of what we would call "fair weather" friends. He then goes on to point out the characteristics of a true friend. Since Sirach suggests we be careful about whom we allow to be our friends, we pray in the responsorial psalm that God may "open my eyes" and "give me discernment" in this matter. In the Gospel, some Pharisees approach Jesus with a question about divorce — a burning issue in his day as well as ours. Our Lord goes back to God's ideal of marriage in the opening pages of the Bible.

YEAR II

READING I James 5:9-12   RESP. Ps. 103:1-2, 3-4, 8-9, 11-12
GOSPEL   Mark 10:1-12

In today's first reading, St. James turns to the early Christians who were eagerly looking forward to Christ's Second Coming and advises them on how to prepare their hearts for that event. His observation "See! The judge stands at the gate" reveals that James probably wrote at a period when the Church believed that the coming of our Lord was near at hand. The delay of this event apparently caused many Christians to become impatient with the sufferings they had to bear. For this reason, we hear James counsel them to imitate the patience with which Job accepted his many misfortunes before God rewarded him. James says finally that the lives of Christians should bear witness to the truth of everything they say. The responsorial psalm refrain accents the theme that God is "kind and merciful." In the Gospel, Jesus gives his teaching on marriage and divorce.

346 SATURDAY OF THE SEVENTH WEEK OF THE YEAR

YEAR I

READING I   Sirach 17:1-15   RESP. Ps. 103:13-14, 15-16, 17-18
GOSPEL   Mark 10:13-16

The wisdom-teacher Sirach describes in today's first reading the great gifts that God gave to man in creating him. Sirach tells how God endowed man with wisdom, knowledge, and freedom so that man might reflect his Creator's wisdom in ruling the earth, praising God's name, and obeying his laws. The responsorial psalm highlights several themes in the reading by saying that God "knows how we are formed." He gives us a heart to show "compassion on our children," he blesses those "who keep his covenant," and he receives us when we return to "dust." The Gospel shows our Lord blessing the children. He teaches that the kingdom of God belongs to those people who cultivate a child-like relationship to God — who are humble, obedient, and trusting.

YEAR II

READING I   James 5:13-20   RESP. Ps. 141:1-2, 3 and 8
GOSPEL   Mark 10:13-16

Today's reading shows how St. James reminded the early Christians to call in "the elders of the Church" to anoint with oil the sick in the community and pray over them. For centuries, the Church has seen in this ritual evidence that the Sacrament of the Sick — as we call it to-day — existed in the first days of the Christian community. The back-ground of this ceremony is our Lord's own concern to heal the sick that the Gospels reveal on almost every page. James then empha-sizes how powerful is the prayer of a holy man and the great reward that awaits anyone who gets a sinner to give up whatever he was doing wrong. The responsorial psalm reminds us again how pleased God is by our prayers that "come like incense" before him. In the Gospel, Jesus says flatly that the kingdom of God belongs only to those who cultivate a childlike relationship to God.

347 MONDAY OF THE EIGHTH WEEK OF THE YEAR

YEAR I

READING I   Sirach 17:19-27   RESP. Ps. 32:1-2, 5, 6, 7
GOSPEL   Mark 10:17-27

At this season of the year, we are reading from the Book of Sirach for the first Scripture passage at the weekday Masses. Ben Sirach was a respected Jewish wisdom-teacher who wrote this work about the year 180 B.C. We are presently up to Chapter 17, where Sirach has already described man's great dignity as a creature of God. In today's passage, he exhorts his students of wisdom to serve God and forsake sin. In keeping with this theme, the liturgy chooses for our responsorial psalm the prayer of a repentant sinner. In St. Mark's Gospel, Jesus challenges a rich young man not to be satisfied with his present respectable life but to dedicate himself to helping others. The man's many possessions — as our own at times — keep him from this once-in-a-lifetime opportunity for his happiness.

YEAR II

READING I   1 Peter 1:3-9   **RESP. Ps. 111:1-2, 5-6, 9, 10**
GOSPEL   Mark 10:17-27

In the first reading we begin another of the twenty-one divinely inspired letters in the New Testament. The apostle Peter accents the "new birth" we undergo in Christ at baptism that makes us children of God and heirs of an "imperishable inheritance." In using this term "inheritance," Peter takes a word that the Jews traditionally applied to Palestine because God gave them this land as their inheritance after delivering them from Egypt. In this way, Peter teaches that heaven is the new promised land all Christians can look forward to with hope in their hearts and that no enemies can ever take away. The responsorial psalm underlines this theme by reminding us how God gave his chosen people "the inheritance of the nations." In the Gospel, Jesus challenges a rich young man not to be satisfied with his present respectable life but to dedicate himself to helping others.

348   TUESDAY OF THE EIGHTH WEEK OF THE YEAR

YEAR I

READING I   Sirach 35:1-12   **RESP. Ps. 50:5-6, 7-8, 14 and 23**
GOSPEL   Mark 10:28-31

In the first reading, the Jewish wisdom-teacher Sirach discusses the kind of worship that is most acceptable to God. He explains that observing the Law of Moses by keeping the commandments, avoiding injustice, and practicing charity are ways of pleasing God equally as important as external rituals of sacrifice — and more so when a worshiper of God performs these rituals only for an outside show of piety. The responsorial psalm after this reading also centers our attention on the real meaning of sacrificial worship in such words as "Offer to God praise as your sacrifice" and "Fulfill your vows to the Most High." In the Gospel, Jesus points out the rewards that God will give those who follow him at some personal cost.

YEAR II
READING I 1 Peter 1:10-16   RESP. Ps. 98:1, 2-3, 3-4
GOSPEL Mark 10:28-31

In today's first reading, St. Peter points out how the prophets had looked forward to the day when God would reveal his love for all men by sending his Son to redeem them. Peter then sounds a call to live a life that imitates the very holiness of God himself. This call will be as demanding on us in our present age of "anything goes" morality as it was in the pagan Roman society of first century Christendom. Peter asks his readers to "gird the loins" in meeting this challenge to holiness. In modern terms, he would say that we had better "roll up our sleeves" and get to work *today* on whatever is keeping us from growing closer to God. The responsorial psalm accents this theme by referring to our Lord's "holy arm" which "has won victory for him" over the world of sin. In the Gospel, Jesus explains the rewards that God will give those who follow him at some personal cost.

349 WEDNESDAY OF THE EIGHTH WEEK OF THE YEAR

YEAR I
READING I Sirach 36:1, 5-6, 10-17   RESP. Ps. 79:8, 9, 11 and 13
GOSPEL Mark 10:32-45

The Jewish teacher of wisdom Ben Sirach prays in today's reading that God may deliver his chosen people from the rule of pagan nations. Palestine at this time in the second century before Christ had just come under the rule of a Greek dynasty. Sirach recalls God's past acts of power for his people, and he then asks God to perform new wonders for Israel. He prays that in this way Israel may achieve its destiny, and all nations serve the one true God. The responsorial psalm after this reading also asks that God may have pity on his beloved people struggling under foreign rulers who oppress them. In the Gospel, Jesus makes another prediction of his sufferings˙and death. He then teaches the apostles his revolutionary idea that authority is for *service*, not power, since our Lord himself "has not come to be served but to serve."

YEAR II
READING I 1 Peter 1:18-25   RESP. Ps. 147:12-13, 14-15, 19-20
GOSPEL Mark 10:32-45

Today we hear St. Peter urge his readers never to forget the ransom

Jesus paid — "his blood beyond all price" — to deliver them from the foolish lives they had been leading. Peter describes our Lord as a "spotless lamb," an image that appears in Christian art in the catacombs as well as in our churches today. He then borrows a passage from the prophet Isaiah about "the word of the Lord" which "endures forever." Peter uses it to remind the Christians that they received this word through the preaching of the apostles, which not only prepared their hearts for baptism but continues to nourish their spiritual life in the Church. The responsorial psalm also stresses how God "has proclaimed his word to Jacob" and all his spiritual descendants. In the Gospel, Jesus teaches the apostles his revolutionary idea that authority in the Church is for *service*, not power.

350 THURSDAY OF THE EIGHTH WEEK OF THE YEAR

YEAR I

READING I   Sirach 42:15-25   RESP. Ps. 33:2-3, 4-5, 6-7, 8-9
GOSPEL   Mark 10:46-52

The first reading begins the final section of Ben Sirach's book of wisdom with a hymn of praise to God's works in nature. Sirach hoped in this way to impress his readers with God's superior power and knowledge to prevent the Jews from turning to the attractions of Greek culture all around them at this time in the second century before Christ. We find in the verse, "At God's words were his works brought into being," one of the earliest biblical references to the idea of the creative word of God. St. John developed this idea in the opening chapter of his Gospel and elsewhere in his writings. To highlight this theme, the liturgy chooses Psalm 33 — a hymn of praise to God for his creative word — as the responsorial psalm. The Gospel tells the story of the blind man on the road to Jericho. Jesus will heal the blindness of our faults if we also respond with faith in him.

YEAR II

READING I   1 Peter 2:2-5, 9-12   RESP. Ps. 100:2, 3, 4, 5
GOSPEL   Mark 10:46-52

Today's first reading abounds with ideas to help us understand what the Christian life really means. St. Peter reminds us first that we must be "newborn babies" in the sense that we never stop hungering for the food that will help us grow up spiritually. Then he says we are "living stones" built into a "holy priesthood." These images reveal the union we share with our brothers and sisters in Christ. Peter also declares that we are "strangers and in exile" in pagan society. We have to show this society by the way we act what it means to follow Jesus. In the responsorial psalm, Peter's image of ourselves as "God's people" appears again in the verse, "His we are; his people, the flock he tends." The Gospel tells the story of the blind man on the road to Jericho. Jesus will heal the blindness of our faults if we also respond with faith in him.

351 FRIDAY OF THE EIGHTH WEEK OF THE YEAR

YEAR I

READING I   Sirach 44:1, 9-13   RESP. Ps. 149:1-2, 3-4, 5-6 and 9
GOSPEL   Mark 11:11-26

Today's first reading praises the outstanding men of Israel's past. The author hoped to show in this way that these men attained wisdom as Jews by virtue of their God-fearing lives. They did not need the wisdom of foreign cultures, such as Greece, that held out many enticements to Jewish young people at this time, about the year 180 B.C. The responsorial psalm refrain highlights this hymn to the past by affirming, "The Lord takes delight in his people." In the Gospel, St. Mark discloses how Jesus told parables by what he *did* as well as by what he said. Our Lord's command to a fruitless fig tree along the roadside — "Never again shall anyone eat of your fruit" — dramatically reveals God's judgment on Israel for its lack of faith. Jesus then drives the money changers from the temple and gives lessons on faith and prayer.

YEAR II

READING I   1 Peter 4:7-13   RESP. Ps. 96:10, 11-12, 13
GOSPEL   Mark 11:11-26

Against a background of widespread belief that the Second Coming of Christ was near at hand, St. Peter sketches in the first reading some reminders about practical aspects of the Christian life. Peter interrupts the flow of his message with a brief prayer praising God the Father. This formula appears in different styles twenty-six times throughout the New Testament. We then hear Peter refer to a "trial by fire occurring in your midst" that may indicate he wrote his letter during persecution. The responsorial psalm also deals with the theme of the Second Coming in the refrain, "The Lord comes to judge the earth." In the Gospel, St. Mark discloses how Jesus told parables by what he *did* as well as by what he said. Our Lord's command to a fruitless fig tree along the roadside dramatically reveals God's judgment on Israel for its lack of faith.

352 SATURDAY OF THE EIGHTH WEEK OF THE YEAR

YEAR I

READING I   Sirach 51:12-20
GOSPEL   Mark 11:27-33

RESP. Ps. 19:8, 9, 10, 11

In today's reading, the Book of Sirach concludes with a poetical description of a man's intense pursuit of wisdom from his early youth. In the original Hebrew, this text took the form of an alphabetical poem where each verse began with a successive letter of the Hebrew alphabet. The responsorial psalm echoes the theme of this passage by declaring, "The decree of the Lord is trustworthy, giving wisdom to the simple." The refrain teaches us that we find true wisdom by following the precepts of the Lord, for they "give joy to the heart." In the Gospel, the chief priests and the experts on the Law of Moses challenge our Lord's authority to teach and to act the way he does. Because they are not willing to face the truth, Jesus does not answer their insincere question.

YEAR II

READING I   Jude 17, 20-25
GOSPEL   Mark 11:27-33

RESP. Ps. 63:2, 3-4, 5-6

The first Scripture reading is from the brief letter of Jude, who may be the relative of Jesus whom St. Mark and St. Matthew mention in their Gospels. The liturgy selects this letter today because its purpose and many of its ideas relate closely to the second letter of St. Peter that we will begin at Monday's Mass. Both Peter and Jude were anxious to combat false teachings about the Christian faith and way of life that were endangering several communities in the early Church. For this reason, we find Jude in this passage advising his readers on how to deal with the "confused" men who pretend to instruct them. The responsorial psalm accents the ideas of "glory" and "power" from Jude's closing praise of God. In the Gospel, the chief priests and the experts on the Law of Moses challenge our Lord's authority to teach and to act the way he does.

353 MONDAY OF THE NINTH WEEK OF THE YEAR

YEAR I

READING I   Tobit 1:1, 2; 2:1-9
GOSPEL   Mark 12:1-12

RESP. Ps. 112:1-2, 3-4, 5-6

The Book of Tobit that we begin today emphasizes a basic teaching of the Jewish religion — men and women should persevere in faith in God even when it seems that God has abandoned them. The following passage shows how a devout and wealthy man named Tobit keeps faith with the customs of his religion even while living in exile in the pagan land of Assyria. Since Tobit found happiness in showing reverential fear of God, the liturgy chooses an appropriate responsorial psalm refrain, "Happy the man who fears the Lord." In the Gospel, Jesus tells a parable about the punishment that waits for the wicked men who take care of a vineyard. The Jewish religious leaders realize that the vineyard is God's kingdom and that Jesus is aiming the story at them. They want to arrest him immediately but do not because they fear the crowd's reaction.

YEAR II

READING I   2 Peter 1:1-7   RESP. Ps. 91:1-2, 14-15, 15-16
GOSPEL   Mark 12:1-12

The reading for today's Mass is from what is probably the last writing that we have by an inspired author in the New Testament. The author, who writes in the name of Peter the apostle, begins by pointing out how God has given us everything we need to live a life that will please him. To guarantee that we will get the blessings God promises, the author then mentions key virtues that we should practice in the Christian life. We note how they reinforce one another like links in a chain. Since the author declares that through God's love for us we have become "sharers of the divine nature," the responsorial psalm also reminds us that we "dwell in the shelter of the Most High, and abide in the shadow of the Almighty." In the Gospel, Jesus tells a parable about the punishment that awaits the wicked men who take care of a vineyard. The Pharisees realize Jesus aims the story at them.

354 TUESDAY OF THE NINTH WEEK OF THE YEAR

YEAR I

READING I   Tobit 2:9-14   RESP. Ps. 112:1-2, 7-8, 9
GOSPEL   Mark 12:13-17

Today's first reading continues the story of Tobit, a pious man who lived among the Jews in exile in Assyria. Almost as if in response to Tobit's faith, God permits him to fall victim to an accident which blinds him. We hear his wife point out how foolish it is to be virtuous and hope in God when Tobit has met with such misfortune. In this way, the inspired author of this story tried to show that there is no real connection between virtue and happiness. The sinless man who suffers must still cling to his hope in God's love for him. Tobit's trust in God is the theme of the responsorial psalm we will pray after this reading. In the Gospel, the enemies of Jesus pose a shrewd question about giving tribute to Caesar. Our Lord's famous reply distinguishes unerringly between the rights of the State and the lawful claims of God.

YEAR II

READING I   2 Peter 3:12-15, 17-18   RESP. Ps. 90:2, 3-4, 10, 14, 16
GOSPEL   Mark 12:13-17

The opening verse of today's reading aims at combating an early false teaching that denied the Second Coming of Christ. We hear the author suggest that his readers should even "try to hasten" that event by the holiness of their lives, because the only thing that delays this day is the period God gives for sinners to repent. He urges that the Lord find them at his final coming "without stain or defilement" — a reference to the spotless sacrificial victims the Jews offered to God. The author concludes with a warning not to allow false teachers to lead the community astray, since this would forfeit everything the Christians have gained so far in their lives. The responsorial psalm recalls the theme of the Second Coming by referring to the timeless presence of God to man "in every age." In the Gospel, the enemies of Jesus pose a shrewd question about giving tribute to Caesar.

355   WEDNESDAY OF THE NINTH WEEK OF THE YEAR

YEAR I

READING I   Tobit 3:1-11, 16   RESP. Ps. 25:2-4, 4-5, 6-7, 8-9
GOSPEL   Mark 12:18-27

The first reading begins with the prayer of a pious Jew named Tobit. He tells how God has exiled the Jews in Assyria to punish them for violating his laws. Tobit then prays that death may deliver him from the misery of his blindness. The reading then tells the story of a Persian woman Sarah who has also suffered great misfortune. She, too, prays for death as a relief from her trials. In response to their prayers, God sends his archangel Raphael to help them. The responsorial psalm echoes many thoughts from the prayers of Tobit and Sarah. In the Gospel, the Sadducees propose a difficult question to Jesus about the resurrection of the dead. It shows they have the wrong idea about the life to come. Their story about seven brothers involves a situation similar to that of Sarah's seven husbands in the first reading.

YEAR II

READING I   2 Tim. 1:1-3, 6-12   RESP. Ps. 123:1-2, 2
GOSPEL   Mark 12:18-27

St. Paul must have felt very frustrated as he wrote today's first reading from his prison cell in Rome to his friend Timothy, whom he had appointed bishop of Ephesus. Like some contemporary missionary imprisoned behind the Iron Curtain, Paul had to while away fruitless hours, no longer able to preach about Jesus to the Gentiles. Now he can work only through Timothy's hands. Perhaps for this reason we find Paul urging Timothy to "stir into flame" the graces he received as a priest when the apostle ordained him and to bear all the hardships that preaching salvation will cost him. In the responsorial psalm, Paul lifts his eyes in confident prayer that God may "have pity" on him in his sufferings. In the Gospel, the Sadducees question Jesus about the resurrection of the dead. Since they quote Moses, Jesus also refers to a passage from Moses to prove that the Father is a God of the living.

356 THURSDAY OF THE NINTH WEEK OF THE YEAR

YEAR I

READING I   Tobit 6:10-11; 7:1, 9-14; 8:4-7   RESP. Ps. 128:1-2, 3, 4-5
GOSPEL   Mark 12:28-34

In today's reading, the pious Jew Tobit, who has gone blind, has sent his son Tobiah to Persia to obtain a sum of money for him. Tobiah goes with a friend Raphael, an angel in disguise, who guides Tobiah to the unfamiliar land. When they arrive there, Tobiah expresses his desire to marry his kinswoman, Sarah. Her father warns Tobiah that each of his daughter's seven husbands had died on their wedding night. Nevertheless, Tobiah marries Sarah, and the passage concludes with the touching scene of the couple praying that God may spare their lives. The responsorial psalm accents this marital theme by praising a God-fearing husband who rejoices in his wife and children. In the Gospel, Jesus gives a unique moral principle for our lives. He combines two separate passages from the Old Testament to teach us about love for God and love for men.

YEAR II

READING I   2 Tim. 2:8-15   RESP. Ps. 25:4-5, 8-9, 10 and 14
GOSPEL   Mark 12:28-34

In today's first Scripture reading, St. Paul reveals his awareness that although a prisoner in Rome he can still carry out his vocation as an apostle to the Gentiles by offering his sufferings for their salvation. Paul also finds comfort in knowing that the enemies of God cannot chain the Good News of man's redemption to the walls of a cell and that his dear friend Timothy is busy preaching that Good News as a bishop in the Church. Paul includes in his letter part of a baptismal hymn emphasizing that a Christian who perseveres faithfully through all his trials will surely reign in heaven with Jesus. Since Paul tells Timothy to avoid arguments with false teachers and preach "the truth" instead, the responsorial psalm highlights this theme in the verse, "Guide me in your truth and teach me." In the Gospel, Jesus gives us the great commandments about God and neighbor.

357 FRIDAY OF THE NINTH WEEK OF THE YEAR

YEAR I

READING I   Tobit 11:5-15   RESP. Ps. 146:2, 7, 8-9, 9-10
GOSPEL   Mark 12:35-37

As today's reading begins, Tobit's son Tobiah and his wife return to the Jewish community living in exile in Assyria. An angel of God, Raphael, accompanies them, but they still do not know who he really is. We then learn how Tobiah restores his father's sight by following Raphael's advice. Joy fills Tobit's heart, and he praises God for his kindness. The responsorial psalm refrain echoes Tobit's joy. Another verse of the psalm appropriately declares, "The Lord gives sight to the blind." In the Gospel, Jesus tries to teach the Jews that the Messiah is not someone who will satisfy their political hopes. He reveals that the Messiah will be far more than a mere natural descendant of King David, since even David calls him his "Lord."

YEAR II

READING I   2 Tim. 3:10-17   RESP. Ps. 119:157, 160, 161, 165, 166, 168
GOSPEL   Mark 12:35-37

In today's reading, St. Paul describes from his prison cell in Rome how he has suffered in preaching salvation to the Gentiles, particularly the dangers he faced in three cities during his missionary journey. We also learn Paul's deep reverence for the Scriptures. He points out that Timothy learned God's word from his childhood, and those inspired writings have been valuable for nourishing all the rest of Timothy's spiritual life. The tradition of the Church has always understood this passage as teaching that the Scriptures are the word of God in the words of men. The liturgy finds a parallel to Paul's outlook on his sufferings in the responsorial psalm verse, "Though my persecutors and my foes are many, I turn not away from your decrees." The Gospel reveals that the Messiah will be more than a mere natural descendant of King David, who calls him Lord.

106

358 SATURDAY OF THE NINTH WEEK OF THE YEAR

YEAR I

READING I Tobit 12:1, 5-15, 20   RESP. Ps. Tobit 13:2, 6
GOSPEL   Mark 12:38-44

In today's first reading, the angel Raphael discloses who he really is to Tobit and his son Tobiah. In the way of a teacher of wisdom, Raphael points out the consistent thread of God's providential design in all the seemingly chance events that have led to this happy outcome of Tobit's life. The angel's remarks cover the areas of prayer, fasting, almsgiving, righteousness, and the proper attitude toward wealth. The liturgy selects the responsorial psalm from Tobit's beautiful song of thanksgiving which he prayed after the angel left. One verse seems to sum up the story of this God-fearing man in the words, "God scourges and then has mercy." In the Gospel, Jesus points to a poor widow giving to the temple from the little she has. Our Lord says that she is an example of what loving God is all about.

YEAR II

READING I 2 Tim. 4:1-8   RESP. Ps. 71:8-9, 14-15, 16-17, 22
GOSPEL   Mark 12:38-44

In today's first reading, St. Paul, writing from prison in Rome, tells his co-worker Timothy in solemn tones that he must take seriously his vocation to preach about Jesus to all men. The apostle then refers to his approaching death in two images. He declares that he is "being poured out like a libation." Pious Romans poured out the libation of wine in their pagan temples as a gesture of reverence to their gods. Paul sees his own shedding of blood in martyrdom as this same kind of act — and, as such, pleasing to God. Paul also uses figures from the world of sports to express his joy at having come to the end of his life prepared to meet his "just judge." In the responsorial psalm we also hear Paul's voice beseeching God, "As my strength fails, forsake me not." In the Gospel, Jesus points to a poor widow donating to the temple as an example of what loving God is all about.

359 MONDAY OF THE TENTH WEEK OF THE YEAR

YEAR I

READING I 2 Cor. 1:1-7   RESP. Ps. 34:2-3, 4-5, 6-7, 8-9
GOSPEL   Matthew 5:1-12

Today we begin the second letter that St. Paul wrote to the Christians in the Greek city of Corinth while en route there late in the year 57 during his third missionary journey to the Gentiles. Paul thanks God for letting him find consolation from the Lord in all his troubles. Now he can console the Corinthians in their trials. The responsorial psalm accents this theme in the words, "When the afflicted man called out, the Lord heard." As we begin St. Matthew's Gospel, we recall that he has previously told us about the preaching of John the Baptist, the baptism of Jesus, and the call of the apostles. Now we turn to the Sermon on the Mount. Matthew sees Jesus as the successor of Moses who announces the new covenant's law of love on another "Mount Sinai." The Beatitudes are his guidelines for finding happiness in our lives as Christians.

YEAR II

READING I   1 Kings 17:1-6   RESP. Ps. 121:1-2, 3-4, 5-6, 7-8
GOSPEL   Matthew 5:1-12

At the time of today's first reading, about 850 B.C., the ruler of the northern kingdom of Israel, King Ahab, had provoked a religious crisis by letting his pagan wife worship her false god right in Palestine. The queen then stirred up persecution of the Jews so vigorously that it threatened to stamp out their worship of Israel's one true God. That is why we find the Lord's prophet Elijah warning the king that Israel's God will prove he is master over the land by sending a severe drought. Elijah then flees the king's wrath to a safer place across the Jordan River. In such verses as, "The Lord will guard you from all evil," the responsorial psalm emphasizes how God provided for Elijah during the famine. In the Gospel account of the Sermon on the Mount, Matthew sees Jesus as the successor of Moses who announces the new covenant's law of love, such as the Beatitudes that we hear today.

360   TUESDAY OF THE TENTH WEEK OF THE YEAR

YEAR I

READING I   2 Cor. 1:18-22   RESP. Ps. 119:129, 130, 131, 132, 133, 135
GOSPEL   Matthew 5:13-16

In today's first reading, we hear Paul defending himself against those who accused him of saying "Yes" and "No" about visiting the community at Corinth again. He emphasizes that Christ himself "was never anything but 'yes.'" At this time, internal troubles had split the Church at Corinth into sects and parties that attached themselves to individual leaders. For that reason Paul had postponed his visit until this time rather than cause more heartache. Since Paul says, "Whatever promises God has made have been fulfilled in Christ," the responsorial psalm accents this theme by saying, "Steady my footsteps according to your promise." St. Matthew's Gospel continues our Lord's Sermon on the Mount. Jesus teaches us that we as Christians are to the world what salt is to food. We must flavor the lives of others with our joy and our thoughtfulness.

YEAR II
READING I 1 Kings 17:7-16   RESP. Ps. 4:2-3, 4-5, 7-8
GOSPEL Matthew 5:13-16

The first reading reveals that about 850 B.C. a famine had spread throughout Palestine and into a neighboring land called Phoenicia. It was a punishment God visited on the Jewish king and his people because the king had yielded to the demands of his queen, Jezebel, a Phoenician woman, and permitted her to worship her pagan god in Palestine. Today's story tells how God furnished enough flour and oil to feed a widow in Phoenicia and the Lord's prophet Elijah, whom she cared for during the famine. This miracle demonstrates how superior God was to Phoenicia's pagan god — the one Jezebel worshiped — because the Lord provided food for his friends in the god's pagan famine-devastated territory. The responsorial psalm sums up today's reading in the verse, "The Lord works wonders for those he loves." In the Gospel, Jesus urges us to let the light of our good example shine forth before men.

361 WEDNESDAY OF THE TENTH WEEK OF THE YEAR

YEAR I
READING I 2 Cor. 3:4-11   RESP. Ps. 99:5, 6, 7, 8, 9
GOSPEL Matthew 5:17-19

In today's reading, St. Paul contrasts the former legal covenant of friendship God made with the Jews through Moses on Mount Sinai — what he calls "the ministry of death" — and the living covenant God made with all mankind through the death of Jesus — that is, "the ministry of the Spirit." Paul then refers to Moses leaving the mountaintop after receiving the Ten Commandments, his face reflecting the glory of God. That glory quickly faded, Paul says, but the glory we receive through our new relationship to God in Jesus will last forever. The responsorial psalm recalls God's revelation to Moses in the pillar of cloud in the Sinai Desert. In the Gospel, Jesus explains that his teachings will bring out the deeper meaning of the Old Testament laws, which aimed at fostering respect for God and man.

YEAR II
READING I I Kings 18:20-39   RESP. Ps. 16:1-2, 4, 5 and 8, 11
GOSPEL Matthew 5:17-19

As the first reading begins, three years of severe famine have devastated Palestine by about 847 B.C. God has sent this punishment on Israel because King Ahab had permitted his queen to worship a false god in his land. This god had the name "Baal," meaning "the lord," because his worshipers believed he controlled the power to make the ground produce good crops. Now we learn in today's dramatic story how Israel's prophet Elijah challenged the pagan prophets of Baal to a showdown on Mount Carmel before the Jewish people to prove which deity really was more powerful and deserved their worship. The responsorial psalm underscores the cause of the famine in the verse, "They multiply their sorrows who court other gods." In the Gospel, Jesus explains that his teachings will bring out the deeper meaning of the Old Testament laws which fostered respect for God and man.

362 THURSDAY OF THE TENTH WEEK OF THE YEAR

YEAR I

READING I   2 Cor. 3:15—4:1, 3-6   RESP. Ps. 85:9-10, 11-12, 13-14
GOSPEL   Matthew 5:20-26

In today's reading, St. Paul deals first with the blindness of those Jews who insist on following the Law of Moses as the way to find salvation. To Paul it seems that those unfortunate people have a veil over their faces that keeps them from seeing the glory of the risen Christ. Paul claims further that a veil of blindness covers the minds of those who will not accept "the splendor of the gospel" that he is preaching. He concludes by urging the Corinthians to lead others to the joy of knowing the glorified Christ. The responsorial psalm refrain echoes today's theme in the words, "The glory of the Lord will dwell in our land." In the Gospel, Jesus teaches his new ideal of justice that forbids not only murder but unreasonable anger and a critical tongue as well. Our Lord then stresses that we must strive to reconcile ourselves with others before coming to worship God.

YEAR II

READING I   1 Kings 18:41-46   RESP. Ps. 65:10, 10-11, 12-13
GOSPEL   Matthew 5:20-26

The first reading takes us to the heights of Mount Carmel on the coast of Palestine overlooking the blue Mediterranean Sea. A small storm cloud appears on the horizon, signaling to the prophet Elijah that God has answered his prayers. Heavy rains are on the way to relieve the three-year drought and prove that Israel's God alone controls the forces of nature. We hear Elijah warn Israel's King Ahab to hurry toward his palace in the valley of Jezreel before the rain comes. The prophet himself then receives special strength from God to run ahead of the king's chariot so he can announce to the people that the drought is over. The responsorial psalm accents this theme in the verse, "You have visited the land and watered it." In the Gospel, Jesus teaches that his new ideal of justice forbids anger as well as murder. We must also strive to reconcile ourselves with others.

363 FRIDAY OF THE TENTH WEEK OF THE YEAR

YEAR I

READING I   2 Cor. 4:7-15   RESP. Ps. 116:10-11, 15-16, 17-18
GOSPEL   Matthew 5:27-32

St. Paul begins today's reading by pointing out the real source of the power that wins men to salvation. It is not the dull earthenware jar of himself and his talents, Paul insists, but the treasure inside the jar — the power of God at work in his preaching. Paul then declares that sufferings and dangers never discourage him. He reminds the community at Corinth that he sees his salvation as joined to theirs, and for this reason his sufferings become beneficial for their own lives. Paul quotes from Psalm 116 in regard to the faith that sustains his preaching, and so the liturgy chooses this psalm as our response to the reading. In the Gospel, Jesus condemns deliberate use of the eyes to stimulate sexual desire and warns his followers to remove all other obstacles to growth in the Christian life. He then gives his teaching on marriage and divorce.

YEAR II

READING I   1 Kings 19:9, 11-16   RESP. Ps. 27:7-8, 8-9, 13-14
GOSPEL   Matthew 5:27-32

Today's reading reveals how the prophet Elijah has fled for his life from the threats of Israel's pagan queen, Jezebel, whose false god Elijah had vanquished. He makes a three-hundred-mile pilgrimage to a cave on Mount Horeb — another name for Mount Sinai — where centuries ago God had revealed himself in a wondrous way to Moses. In much the same way, God now manifests himself to Elijah and then reminds him that the prophet still has an important role to play in Israel's history — and he cannot run away from it. The passage closes as God gives Elijah three orders to execute on returning to Palestine that are tantamount to stirring up a revolution. The responsorial psalm appropriately refers to Elijah in the verse, "Your presence, O Lord, I seek. Hide not your face from me." In the Gospel, Jesus forbids sexual misbehavior and gives his teaching about marriage and divorce.

111

YEAR I

READING I 2 Cor. 5:14-21   RESP. Ps. 103:1-2, 3-4, 8-9, 11-12
GOSPEL   Matthew 5:33-37

In today's reading we first hear St. Paul mention the basic motivating force behind his whole life — awareness of the love that Christ has for him. This spurs him on in turn to proclaim God's love to all men. The apostle has a new set of standards. Where once he persecuted the Church, he now works to get men back into God's good graces. Paul says that Jesus sent him as his "ambassador" to bring sinners into God's kingdom the way the Roman emperor sent a civil ambassador to bring a newly conquered country into the empire. The responsorial psalm highlights this theme of reconciliation by reminding us that God "pardons all your iniquities, he heals all your ills." In the Gospel, Jesus teaches an outlook on telling the truth that taking oaths cannot provide. When we strengthen our character by cultivating honesty in our hearts, then all oaths become unnecessary.

YEAR II

READING I 1 Kings 19:19-21   RESP. Ps. 16:1-2 and 5, 7-8, 9-10
GOSPEL   Matthew 5:33-37

In today's first reading, the prophet Elijah sets out to fulfill God's command to find a man named Elisha to serve as his assistant and eventually to succeed him. The prophet travels into central Palestine and finds Elisha plowing a field on his farm near the Jordan River. Elijah places his cloak over the shoulders of the young well-to-do farmer, who immediately recognizes this gesture as a sign that God is calling him to serve the prophet. Elisha demonstrates how willing he is to dedicate himself completely to this vocation by saying farewell to his parents and then breaking off from his former life by slaughtering his oxen. The responsorial psalm also highlights Elisha's response to the Lord's call in the verse, "I say to the Lord, 'My Lord are you.'" In the Gospel, Jesus suggests that when we strengthen our character by cultivating honesty, then all oaths become unnecessary.

365 MONDAY OF THE ELEVENTH WEEK OF THE YEAR

YEAR I

READING I 2 Cor. 6:1-10   RESP. Ps. 98:1, 2-3, 3-4
GOSPEL   Matthew 5:38-42

As today's first reading begins, we hear the apostle Paul urging the community at Corinth not to put off to a tomorrow which may never come opportunities for growth in their Christian lives. He then begins a lyrical statement of the various trials he has endured in preaching the Good News. Not in a boastful spirit but to answer some who have slandered him, Paul's statement reveals how faithful an apostle he has been. In facing a challenging world, Paul carries "the weapons of righteousness with right hand and left" that enable him to win the victory for Christ. To highlight this theme, the responsorial psalm asserts, "His right hand has won victory for him, his holy arm." In St. Matthew's Gospel, we hear Jesus set aside the old law permitting retaliation for evil in favor of his new spirit of non-violence and extending ourselves for others.

YEAR II

READING I 1 Kings 21:1-16   RESP. Ps. 5:2-3, 5-6, 7
GOSPEL   Matthew 5:38-42

Today's first reading narrates how the Jewish King Ahab tried to acquire from a man named Naboth a vineyard that adjoined the royal palace in the valley of Jezreel. We note that Naboth refuses to sell his vineyard because it was his "ancestral heritage." Naboth's words tell us that the Jews in those days believed that no family owning land which had come down from the first Jewish settlers in Palestine should dispose of the property to those outside the family. Even though Ahab acknowledges this right, we learn that his treacherous Queen Jezebel has a plan to get hold of the vineyard anyway — a plot that will cost Naboth his life. The responsorial psalm forecasts God's just punishment of the king and queen in such verses as "You hate all evildoers. You destroy all who speak falsehood." In the Gospel, Jesus reminds us to be generous to others who need our help.

366 TUESDAY OF THE ELEVENTH WEEK OF THE YEAR

YEAR I

READING I 2 Cor. 8:1-9   RESP. Ps. 146:2, 5-6, 7, 8-9
GOSPEL   Matthew 5:43-48

The reading for today's Mass concerns an important collection Paul was organizing to support the needy Church in Jerusalem. The apostle would not allow the Christians converted from paganism to forget that Jerusalem was the cradle of their salvation. In the hope that his words may spark a warm response from the Corinthians, Paul points to the sacrifices the Churches in Macedonia made for this charity, as well as the example of Christ's own self-surrender to enrich their lives. The responsorial psalm echoes this theme by praising God for his many practical acts of charity to his children. The Gospel reading presents our Lord's revolutionary teaching that Christian love must embrace all men — even our enemies. Jesus reminds us that only in loving people that way can we express God's own totally selfless love.

YEAR II

READING I   1 Kings 21:17-29   **RESP. Ps. 51:3-4, 5-6, 11 and 16**
GOSPEL   Matthew 5:43-48

In the first reading, the prophet Elijah encounters the Jewish King Ahab face-to-face in the vineyard of the king's neighbor Naboth. The ruler of Israel has just taken over the vineyard after learning of Naboth's death — a brutal murder that Ahab's wife was responsible for. In a tone revealing God's righteous anger over this savage injustice, Elijah paints a graphic picture of the violent deaths that await the king, his wicked Queen Jezebel, and their descendants. The passage closes by telling how the king repented his involvement in the crime — a confession of guilt that recalls King David's own confession after his sin of adultery. For this reason, the liturgy chooses for the responsorial psalm the prayer David made to God to express his guilt when he realized he had done wrong. In the Gospel, Jesus tells us that our love, like his, must embrace everyone — even our enemies.

367   WEDNESDAY OF THE ELEVENTH WEEK OF THE YEAR

YEAR I

READING I   2 Cor. 9:6-11   **RESP. Ps. 112:1-2, 3-4, 9**
GOSPEL   Matthew 6:1-6, 16-18

The first Scripture reading concerns a special collection for the benefit of the Church in Jerusalem. We hear Paul develop a convincing argument for a generous response to this charity from the Church at Corinth. Paul follows here the spirituality of the Old Testament, since the Jews looked on helping others as something God told them to do in return for his blessings. Because Paul strengthens his appeal to generosity with a quotation from Psalm 112 — "He scattered abroad and gave to the poor, his justice endures forever" — the liturgy chooses several more verses from this psalm for our response to the reading. In the Gospel, our Lord's advice in his Sermon on the Mount also applies to today's theme. Jesus points out the right attitude we should have toward three important areas of Christian life — contributing to charities, prayer, and fasting.

READING I   2 Kings 2:1, 6-14   RESP. Ps. 31:20, 21, 24
GOSPEL   Matthew 6:1-6, 16-18

In the first reading, we hear one of the most breathtaking stories in the Old Testament. Along the bank of the Jordan River, the young man Elisha is walking with the prophet Elijah. Suddenly, from out of the sky, flaming horses appear. They swoop up Elijah in their fiery chariot and take him off into the heavens. This legendary account stamped itself vividly on the imagination of Israel. The Jewish people eventually looked with hopeful hearts for the day when Elijah would return to announce the coming of the Messiah. As this drama ends, Elisha takes up his master's mantle — symbol of the prophet's authority — and goes forth to speak to the people as Elijah's successor. The responsorial psalm accents how Elijah departed from the world "in the sight of men" at the Jordan. In the Gospel, Jesus talks about our outlook on contributing to charities, prayer, and fasting.

368   THURSDAY OF THE ELEVENTH WEEK OF THE YEAR

READING I   2 Cor. 11:1-11   RESP. Ps. 111:1-2, 3-4, 7-8
GOSPEL   Matthew 6:7-15

In today's first reading, St. Paul asks the Corinthians to be patient with his boasting about his accomplishments for them as an apostle. Paul does not find it easy to keep talking about himself, but he believes he must do so to defend his reputation against the slanders of his opponents at Corinth — the "super apostles," as he calls them. Paul finally points out how the generous support he received from the other Churches freed the community in Corinth from the burden of supporting him. The apostle's works in behalf of the Corinthian community inspire us to praise in the responsorial psalm God's own works of justice and truth toward all mankind. In the Gospel, Jesus teaches his apostles the model for all prayer that we call the Our Father. He also stresses that God forgives us to the extent we forgive others.

READING I   Sirach 48:1-14   RESP. Ps. 97:1-2, 3-4, 5-6, 7
GOSPEL   Matthew 6:7-15

The first reading gives a poetic account of highlights in the careers of the two prophets Elijah and Elisha. A Jewish wisdom teacher, centuries after the prophets died, emphasizes how fearlessly Elijah and Elisha upheld the faith of Israel in times of crisis. This teacher was trying to impress a lesson on young Jewish people living in a society where

Greek culture tempted them to forsake their heritage. If Elijah and Elisha were men who never compromised their religious ideals, the author says in effect, then neither should their spiritual children in the faith of Israel. The responsorial psalm verse — "Fire goes before him and consumes his foes round about" — reminds us of the several occasions when God revealed himself to Elijah in forms of fire. In the Gospel, Jesus teaches his apostles the model for all prayer that we call the Our Father.

369 FRIDAY OF THE ELEVENTH WEEK OF THE YEAR

YEAR I

READING I   2 Cor. 11:18, 21-30   RESP. Ps. 34:2-3, 4-5, 6-7
GOSPEL   Matthew 6:19-23

In the first reading for today's Mass, St. Paul describes the danger and discouragement he experienced while preaching the Good News of salvation to the Gentiles. The background for what Paul has to say is the criticism he received from certain proud religious leaders and teachers in Corinth, intent on furthering their own glory at Paul's expense. If these people could boast of what they did and how they suffered, Paul could do the same, although he did not really wish to do so. The responsorial psalm refrain takes up this theme of Paul's sufferings and reminds us that "from all their afflictions God will deliver the just," even as he helped Paul. In the Gospel, Jesus tells us to give priority to those things in life that will help us get to heaven and not to take our sights off this heavenly goal.

YEAR II

READING I   2 Kings 11:1-4, 9-18, 20   RESP. Ps. 132:11, 12, 13-14, 17-18
GOSPEL   Matthew 6:19-23

Today we learn how a seven-year-old boy named Jehoash became ruler of the land of Judah about 835 B.C. We learn further how his grandmother Athaliah met a violent death when the people rose up to overthrow her tyrannical rule. She had usurped the throne by killing off all her grandsons — all, that is, except Jehoash, whom his aunt had rescued. This revolt came in protest against the way Athaliah promoted worship of her pagan god Baal, even building a temple to him — a temple the Jews destroy at the end of the reading. The Jewish high priest Jehoiada, who led the revolt, then restored God's covenant with the boy-king and his people. The responsorial psalm recalls how God continued King David's line by setting Jehoash on his throne. In the Gospel, Jesus urges us to live in such a way that we store up for ourselves rich treasures in heaven.

370 SATURDAY OF THE ELEVENTH WEEK OF THE YEAR

YEAR I

READING I 2 Cor. 12:1-10   RESP. Ps. 34:8-9, 10-11, 12-13
GOSPEL   Matthew 6:24-34

Today's reading concludes the second letter of St. Paul to the Christian community at Corinth. The apostle gives us a rare opportunity to look into his heart and discover there the special graces God had given him. We hear Paul, in the wonder he feels over God's love for him, describe a past mystical experience as if it had happened to someone else. He adds that God also disciplined him with suffering lest he become proud through his special graces. The responsorial psalm refrain invites us to "taste and see the goodness of the Lord" — a reference to Paul's tasting of deep union with God despite the apostle's weaknesses and trials. In his Sermon on the Mount, Jesus gives his reasons why we should avoid those fearful and needless worries that take the joy out of life. God will get us through them all — one day at a time.

YEAR II

READING I 2 Chr. 24:17-25   RESP. Ps. 89:4-5, 29-30, 31-32, 33-34
GOSPEL   Matthew 6:24-34

Today's reading tells about the cold-blooded murder of the prophet Zechariah in the courtyard of the temple in Jerusalem about the year 796 B.C. To make this story even more tragic, the prophet's father, the Jewish high priest Jehoiada, had years before saved the life of the man responsible for this crime and even paved the road to royalty for him — because the murderer was none other than the king of Judah himself, a man named Joash. At the end of this reading, we learn how God allowed a small force of warriors from Syria to stage a raid on Judah in order to punish the king and his people for turning away from the Lord. The responsorial psalm also stresses how God punished Judah for abandoning him in the verse, "If they keep not my commands, I will punish their crime with a rod." In the Gospel, Jesus teaches us to trust in the loving care of God our Father.

371 MONDAY OF THE TWELFTH WEEK OF THE YEAR

YEAR I

READING I Gen. 12:1-9   RESP. Ps. 33:12-13, 18-19, 20, 22
GOSPEL   Matthew 7:1-5

During the next three weeks, the liturgy chooses the first Scripture reading at the weekday Masses from Genesis, the first book in the

Bible. Earlier this year, we read the first eleven chapters of Genesis that told how God created the world and man, how man rebelled against his Maker, and the subsequent religious history of mankind up to the account of Noah and the flood. Today we meet a man named Abram. When God called this man of faith to leave his homeland, the story of our salvation began. This drama tells how God reached out to men through the Jewish people down through the centuries to prepare the world for its redemption. The responsorial psalm also reminds us that God chose a special people "to be his own." In St. Matthew's Gospel, we again take up our Lord's Sermon on the Mount. Jesus warns us to avoid judging the reasons why people act the way they do.

YEAR II

READING I 2 Kings 17:5-8, 13-15, 18   RESP. Ps. 60:3, 4-5, 12-13
GOSPEL   Matthew 7:1-5

In the first reading we learn how the northern kingdom of Israel — which had endured for about two hundred years after the death of King Solomon — fell to the Assyrian empire in the year 721 B.C. History tells us that the conquerors took captive into Assyria some twenty-seven thousand Israelites and turned over the northern part of Palestine for peoples from neighboring countries to colonize. Today's passage then explains that this terrible tragedy came to Israel because the people had turned away from the Lord to worship false gods — despite warnings from God's prophets. The responsorial psalm becomes the terrified voice of the Jewish people in Samaria crying out to God — but too late — as the Assyrians besiege their city. The Gospel continues our Lord's Sermon on the Mount. Jesus warns us to avoid judging why people act the way they do.

372 TUESDAY OF THE TWELFTH WEEK OF THE YEAR

YEAR I

READING I Gen. 13:2, 5-18   RESP. Ps. 15:2-3, 3-4, 5
GOSPEL   Matthew 7:6, 12-14

Today we continue the story of Abram, whose name God would later change to Abraham as a mark of his new vocation to become the father of God's people. We learn how Abram finds it necessary to separate from his nephew Lot because their combined livestock overtaxes the land they share. Lot decides to settle in the area south of the Dead Sea, while the less attractive land to the north falls to Abram. Nevertheless, God reassures Abram that he will keep his promise to give him many descendants. Abram's "justice" — that is, his unselfish consideration for his nephew — appears again as the theme of the responsorial psalm. In the Gospel, Jesus teaches the golden rule — his positive code for living that men of all faiths have admired and respected. The compelling force for our Lord's new guideline to life can only be a selfless love that reflects God's own way of loving.

YEAR II

READING I   2 Kings 19:9-11, 14-21, 31-35, 36   RESP. Ps. 48:2-3, 3-4, 10-11
GOSPEL   Matthew 7:6, 12-14

The first reading deals with a time of grave danger that the Jewish people in the southern kingdom of Judah faced during the reign of King Hezekiah nearly seven centuries before Christ. The powerful forces of Assyria — recent conquerors of northern Israel — had now captured all the principal fortified cities in the south, except Jerusalem. Today we learn how the Assyrians laid siege to that terrified city, demanding unconditional surrender. However, King Hezekiah had one trump card to play — his firm confidence that prayer to God would not go unanswered. We finally learn how God sends what some think was a plague among the Assyrian troops that lays waste their ranks and saves Israel. The responsorial psalm underlines this theme in the refrain, "God upholds his city forever." In the Gospel, Jesus teaches us to treat others as we would want them to treat us.

373   WEDNESDAY OF THE TWELFTH WEEK OF THE YEAR

YEAR I

READING I   Gen. 15:1-12, 17-18   RESP. Ps. 105:1-2, 3-4, 6-7, 8-9
GOSPEL   Matthew 7:15-20

In the first reading, God promises Abram that he will have numerous descendants through a child of his own despite his advanced years. We then learn about a special covenant or agreement between God and Abram. It was the practice in those ancient times for parties to a covenant to carry out some special ceremony to show that they really meant to keep their word — just as the ring ceremony at a wedding today is a sign of marriage vows. God and Abram would have to walk between the split bodies of animals to show they were willing to suffer the fate of the animals if they broke the agreement. God fulfills his part of the ceremony through a mysterious flaming torch in the dead of night. The responsorial psalm echoes this covenant theme. In the Gospel, Jesus reminds us that the way a person acts shows clearly what kind of person he is in his heart.

YEAR II

READING I   2 Kings 22:8-13; 23:1-3   RESP. Ps. 119:33, 34, 35, 36, 37, 40
GOSPEL   Matthew 7:15-20

In today's first Scripture reading, we learn about an important discovery that had a strong influence on reforming the lives of the people in the southern kingdom of Judah late in the seventh century B.C. At this time, the worship of false gods had once again turned the people's hearts from the God of Israel. But then a Jewish high priest found in the temple one day a scroll containing the Law of Moses and brought it to King Josiah. When the king realized how far his people had drifted from their religious heritage, he summoned everyone to the temple and there renewed Israel's covenant with God. The responsorial psalm also recalls how important God's laws are for guiding our lives. In the Gospel, Jesus reminds us that a person shows his true character by the way he acts.

374   THURSDAY OF THE TWELFTH WEEK OF THE YEAR

YEAR I

READING I   Gen. 16:1-12, 15-16 or 16:6-12, 15-16   RESP. Ps. 106:1-2, 3-4, 4-5
GOSPEL   Matthew 7:21-29

Today's Mass continues the story of Abram to whom God had promised a great family. It was difficult for Abram's wife Sara to believe this promise because she was beyond the age for bearing children. Instead of placing her faith in God, Sara took matters into her own hands and urged Abram to have a child by her Egyptian maid Hagar. In today's passage, we learn about the events preceding the birth of Ishmael, the maid's child. Because Sara failed in faith, Ishmael would not be the child God promised. However, God did bless Ishmael with many descendants. The responsorial psalm praises God for his "mighty deeds" throughout the history of mankind's salvation. The Gospel brings to a close our Lord's Sermon on the Mount. Jesus teaches that a man can really call himself a Christian only if he does God's will and proves his love by the way he behaves.

YEAR II

READING I   2 Kings 24:8-17   RESP. Ps. 79:1-2, 3-5, 8, 9
GOSPEL   Matthew 7:21-29

Today's first reading tells of the tragic events that led to the Babylonian captivity in 597 B.C. About 125 years before, the powerful forces of Assyria had conquered the ten northern tribes of Israel and led them off into captivity. Now the southern kingdom of Judah would suffer the same cruel fate at the hands of the new world power, Babylonia. We learn how the Babylonian soldiers not only stripped the magnificent temple of Solomon, but they also left destitute the Jewish population as well. Only the poor and unskilled remained behind under a new king, Zedekiah. A yet more dire fate awaited the city of Jerusalem itself, however, as we will learn tomorrow. The responsorial psalm becomes a prayer of the Jewish people in which they acknowledge guilt for the sins that have brought ruin to their land. In the Gospel, Jesus emphasizes that his real disciples obey God's will and keep his word.

375   FRIDAY OF THE TWELFTH WEEK OF THE YEAR

YEAR I

READING I   Gen. 17:1, 9-10, 15-22   RESP. Ps. 128:1-2, 3, 4-5
GOSPEL   Matthew 8:1-4

In today's first reading, we learn about another important detail of God's covenant with Abraham. A religious covenant or contract was incomplete without some sign of the agreement — that is, a visible pledge of the commitment between God and his people, a sacred reminder of their obligations. For Noah, God gave the sign of a rainbow in the sky. For Abraham, the sign was the ritual of circumcision, a practice common among the people of that time. As a religious sign of God's special call of the Jewish people, circumcision prevailed until the dawn of Christianity. Baptism is the sign of our new covenant with the Father in Christ. Since God promises a son to Abraham's wife, the responsorial psalm underscores this theme in the verse, "Your wife shall be like a fruitful vine in the recesses of your home." The Gospel shows Jesus healing a victim of leprosy.

YEAR II

READING I   2 Kings 25:1-12   RESP. Ps. 137:1-2, 3, 4-5, 6
GOSPEL   Matthew 8:1-4

The first reading discloses the tragic price the Jewish people paid for not listening to God's prophets and persisting in their sinful lives. The once impregnable fortress of Jerusalem glows from the fires that marauding Babylonian soldiers have set, and the city walls lie in rubble. The magnificent temple of Solomon is in ruins, a pile of stones and charred wood. This proud people, dragged off in chains to a foreign land, now watch their enemies mocking the one true God. The lush countryside fades into barren wasteland, where a few poor peasants tend what is left of the vineyards. Echoing all this pain and loss, the responsorial psalm comes down to us from the days of the Babylonian captivity, as the exiles weep to recall their past glories. In the Gospel, we learn how Jesus heals a man afflicted with leprosy.

376 SATURDAY OF THE TWELFTH WEEK OF THE YEAR

YEAR I

READING I   Gen. 18:1-15   RESP. Ps. Luke 1:46-47, 48-49, 50, 53, 54-55
GOSPEL   Matthew 8:5-17

Today's selection from the Book of Genesis reveals that the first Scripture readings at the weekday Masses sometimes give us two versions of the same story. This happens because many books in the Bible are not the work of a single writer but a composite of several sources woven into one text. These sources combine to give us an overview, from various vantage points, of events in the history of God's people. Yesterday, we heard the story — from what scholars call the Priestly Tradition — of how God promised a son to Abraham. Today we hear another account of this promise from the Yahwist Tradition — so called from its use of "Yahweh" as the word for God throughout its material. God's promise to Abraham is also the theme of the responsorial psalm. The Gospel tells of a Roman centurion's strong faith in our Lord's healing power. Jesus also cures Peter's sick mother-in-law.

YEAR II

READING I   Lam. 2:2, 10-14, 18-19   RESP. Ps. 74:1-2, 3-5, 5-7, 20-21
GOSPEL   Matthew 8:5-17

The first reading gives us a frightful picture of the terrors the Jewish people experienced during the siege of Jerusalem by Babylonian troops in the year 586 B.C. The scenes are not pleasant — but they etch on our minds what tragedies people bring on themselves when they simply refuse to listen to God's voice. The passage is from a poem in the Book of Lamentations that weeps for this day when the land of Judah all but perished from the earth and Jerusalem lay in ruins. A final glimmer of hope appears, however, in the author's call for tears of repentance so that God may show mercy toward his people — as the Lord did do after they had spent nearly fifty years of exile in a foreign land. The responsorial psalm describes the Babylonian soldiers desecrating the temple of Solomon. In the Gospel, Jesus heals a centurion's son and Peter's mother-in-law.

377 MONDAY OF THE THIRTEENTH WEEK OF THE YEAR

YEAR I

READING I   Gen. 18:16-33   RESP. Ps. 103:1-2, 3-4, 8-9, 10-11
GOSPEL   Matthew 8:18-22

In today's reading, Abraham bargains with God to spare Sodom and Gomorrah, the cities which he in his divine anger has doomed for their immorality. This scene suggests the give-and-take of a business transaction. Abraham asks God to consider the lives of the innocent who will suffer, too. The responsorial psalm echoes Abraham's plea for mercy in the refrain, as well as in the verse, "He redeems your life from destruction." We are also currently reading the Gospel of St. Matthew. One of his purposes is to show how the words Jesus spoke and the things he did are all aimed at setting up God's kingdom in the hearts of men. In today's passage Jesus makes a scribe and a disciple face the hard facts that following him won't be easy — as it won't be for us today either.

YEAR II

READING I   Amos 2:6-10, 13-16   RESP. Ps. 50:16-17, 18-19, 20-21, 22-23
GOSPEL   Matthew 8:18-22

In the first reading we meet a shepherd named Amos who at God's call left his flocks on a hillside in Bethlehem about 760 B.C. to travel to the northern kingdom of Israel and there denounce the evils of his times. Amos was the pioneer in a long line of prophets in Israel who left us written accounts of the sermons they fearlessly delivered in the name of God himself. We grasp in the vivid images of today's passage the kind of social injustices Amos denounced, as well as the doom he so typically foretold that no one in Israel would escape — neither the fleet of foot nor the strongest of warriors. The responsorial psalm also emphasizes the sins of the people that kindled God's wrath. In the Gospel, Jesus makes a scribe and a disciple face the hard facts that following him won't be easy — as it won't be for us today either.

378 TUESDAY OF THE THIRTEENTH WEEK OF THE YEAR

YEAR I

READING I   Gen. 19:15-29   RESP. Ps. 26:2-3, 9-10, 11-12
GOSPEL   Matthew 8:23-27

The first reading tells how God destroyed the cities of Sodom and Gomorrah south of the Dead Sea. Scripture commentators suggest that God may have used a natural disaster in the area, such as an earthquake, to serve his purpose. God's judgment on Sodom came when

Abraham could not find even ten righteous men in this city of sexual depravity. The tragic story dramatically reveals the mercy God showed to Lot and his family in sparing their lives. The liturgy suggests that we regard the responsorial psalm as Lot's prayer that God may always find him a man of integrity. In the Gospel, Jesus calms a storm on the Sea of Galilee. The miracle should mean more to us than our Lord's conquest of the angry waters and raging winds. Jesus would want us to realize that we too may turn to him whenever a storm threatens the peace of our lives today.

YEAR II

READING I   Amos 3:1-8; 4:11-12   RESP. Ps. 5:4-6, 6-7, 8
GOSPEL   Matthew 8:23-27

The first reading begins with the prophet Amos sternly reminding the Jewish people that because God had shown special love for them their failure to return that love will bring a punishment all the more severe. We then hear Amos ask a series of questions. Each one clearly demonstrates that nothing happens without a reason. In this way, Amos warns that the grievous sins of the people are the reason God's punishment awaits them. Amos carefully points out that God in his mercy reveals to the prophets his plans to punish the nation so that the people may have fair warning. The responsorial psalm underlines God's just anger with his people in the verse, "You hate all evildoers; you destroy all who speak falsehood." In the Gospel, Jesus calms a storm on the Sea of Galilee. We too may turn to him whenever a storm threatens the peace of our lives today.

379 WEDNESDAY OF THE THIRTEENTH WEEK OF THE YEAR

YEAR I
READING I   Gen. 21:5, 8-20   RESP. Ps. 34:7-8, 10-11, 12-13
GOSPEL   Matthew 8:28-34

In the first reading, grief troubles Abraham's heart when God tells him to send away his son Ishmael, born of Hagar, an Egyptian slave girl. Abraham finally agrees when God assures him the Lord will also bless Ishmael with many descendants. Then we learn how God "heard the boy's cry" when Hagar and her child were in distress in the desert after leaving Abraham's home. The responsorial psalm echoes this concern of God in the verse, "The Lord hears the cry of the poor." In the Gospel, when Jesus drives demons out of two men, the devils scream, "Have you come to torture us before the *appointed time?*" Matthew in this way reveals that our Lord has now begun his attack on Satan's realm —

with the final victory at the appointed time of his *final hour* on the cross of our redemption.

YEAR II

READING I   Amos 5:14-15, 21-24   RESP. Ps. 50:7, 8-9, 10-11, 12-13, 16-17
GOSPEL   Matthew 8:28-34

Today's reading contains a powerful statement to show God's concern for social justice among the people of Israel about seven hundred years before Christ. We hear the prophet Amos warn first that justice should "prevail at the gate" — that is, let fair dealings replace corruption in courts of law. However, the prophet's most dramatic message comes when he portrays God as completely undeceived by the people's outward show of piety at religious festivals and their "noisy songs." The Lord will accept their worship only when justice and goodness flow in the people's lives like the bountiful water in their streams. The responsorial psalm echoes this theme as God declares, "Not for your sacrifices do I rebuke you," but because you "profess my covenant" only "with your mouth." In the Gospel, Jesus displays his power over evil by driving out demons from two possessed men.

380   THURSDAY OF THE THIRTEENTH WEEK OF THE YEAR

YEAR I

READING I   Gen. 22:1-19   RESP. Ps. 115:1-2, 3-4, 5-6, 8-9
GOSPEL   Matthew 9:1-8

We hear in the first reading the climax of the story of Abraham, as God commands him to offer his son Isaac as a sacrifice. In this way, God tested just how firm was Abraham's faith in the promise that through his son Isaac God would bless all the nations of the earth. Other passages in the Bible, notably the letters of St. Paul, praise and hold up for imitation Abraham's obedient faith on this occasion. The image of Isaac carrying the wood for the sacrifice, in a gesture of total submission to his father, foreshadows how Jesus submitted in complete obedience to his Father's will in his death on the wood of the cross. The responsorial psalm refrain expresses Abraham's act of faith as walking "in the presence of the Lord, in the land of the living." In the Gospel, Jesus confirms his divine authority to heal a man's sinful heart by healing his crippled legs as well.

YEAR II

READING I   Amos 7:10-17   RESP. Ps. 19:8, 9, 10, 11
GOSPEL   Matthew 9:1-8

The first reading takes us to the sacred halls of the Jewish king's religious shrine at Bethel, fourteen miles above Jerusalem, about 755

ა.C. In a face-to-face encounter, Amos, the former shepherd, proclaims God's message to Amaziah, the royal priest, and to his sinful people. We hear Amaziah banish Amos from the northern kingdom of Israel for his treason in daring to predict the king's death and the exile of his nation. Undaunted, Amos testifies that he is not a court prophet who earns his living by predictions. The Lord himself has called Amos to warn his people of impending doom — including tragedies in Amaziah's own family. The responsorial psalm emphasizes that "the judgments of the Lord" which Amos proclaimed "are true, and all of them just." In the Gospel, Jesus confirms his divine authority to heal a man's sinful heart by healing his crippled legs as well.

381 FRIDAY OF THE THIRTEENTH WEEK OF THE YEAR

YEAR I

READING I Gen. 23:1-4, 19; 24:1-8, 62-67   **RESP. Ps.** 106:1-2, 3-4, 4-5
GOSPEL Matthew 9:9-13

In today's reading we learn of the death of Abraham's wife Sarah and his search for a wife for Isaac. According to God's plan, Isaac could not marry a girl from the area of Canaan because that would contaminate the line of Abraham and bring God's promise to naught. So Abraham's servant went to the ancestral homeland in Mesopotamia with instructions to have the prospective wife brought back to the land of promise. In today's passage we also hear the outcome of this search as Isaac meets Rebekah and takes her as his wife. The responsorial psalm sees in this marriage another example of "the mighty deeds of the Lord" in behalf of his chosen people, and it thanks God "for he is good." The Gospel tells how Jesus invited the tax collector Matthew to become one of his disciples. Later, while dining at Matthew's home, our Lord reveals that his mission is to heal sinners.

YEAR II

READING I Amos 8:4-6, 9-12   **RESP. Ps.** 119:2, 10, 20, 30, 40, 131
GOSPEL Matthew 9:9-13

Today's reading describes some of the dishonest tricks that the rich Jewish merchants pulled on the poor people, which would bring down God's wrath on Israel. The prophet Amos criticizes the traders for "diminishing the ephah," the bushel measure for grain, so that a customer didn't get all he paid for, and "adding to the shekel," the stone used to weigh a customer's money, so he had to pay more than he needed to. For these and other crimes, the prophet warns, the people will soon be following their funeral customs because God's day of vengeance is at hand. On this day, Amos predicts, there will be a famine of prophets as the people seek a word of hope that their troubles are over — but "they shall not find it." The responsorial psalm refrain accents how important is the word of God. The Gospel tells how Jesus invited the tax collector Matthew to become one of his apostles.

382   SATURDAY OF THE THIRTEENTH WEEK OF THE YEAR

YEAR I

READING I   Gen. 27:1-5, 15-29   **RESP. Ps. 135:1-2, 3-4, 5-6**
GOSPEL   Matthew 9:14-17

Today's reading introduces us to one of Isaac's sons, Jacob, who will become another important figure in the history of the Jewish people. We learn how Jacob deceitfully obtains his aged father's blessing that rightfully belongs to his brother Esau. Scripture commentators explain that God's free choice of Jacob despite his fraud is but another example of the Lord's inscrutable ways that we find throughout the story of mankind's salvation. The responsorial psalm underscores today's theme in the verse, "For the Lord has chosen Jacob for himself." In the Gospel, our Lord's reply to a question about fasting, as well as two brief illustrations he gives from daily life, suggest his new vision of our relationship with God. The old cloak and old wineskins symbolize the traditional Jewish ideas that Jesus has come to fulfill.

YEAR II

READING I   Amos 9:11-15   **RESP. Ps. 85:9, 11-12, 13-14**
GOSPEL   Matthew 9:14-17

In today's readings we find what most modern scholars consider an appendix to the prophecy of Amos that a writer of a later period probably added to inject a note of hope for Israel's future. The passage appears to originate at the time of the Babylonian exile about 587 B.C. because God promises that he will one day "raise up the fallen hut of David" — a reference to the city of Jerusalem that the Babylonians destroyed. The author reveals that a day is coming when Israel will conquer her enemies in Edom south of the Dead Sea, and the land will produce such incredible harvests that planters and reapers will toil in a joyful round of work. The responsorial psalm underscores this theme in the verse, "The Lord himself will give his benefits; our land shall yield its increase." In the Gospel, Jesus tells two brief parables that suggest the new vision his teachings offer mankind.

127

383 MONDAY OF THE FOURTEENTH WEEK OF THE YEAR

YEAR I

READING I Gen. 28:10-22   RESP. Ps. 91:1-2, 3-4, 14-15
GOSPEL Matthew 9:18-26

The first reading describes Jacob's dream while on his journey to Haran, the land of his mother's family, to escape the wrath of his brother Esau. Jacob sees angels going up and down on a ladder that reaches into heaven — that is, they are communicating between God and man. Jesus had this vision in mind when he suggested to Nathanael that the Father would henceforth communicate with men not through the "ladder" of human or angelic go-betweens but through his own Son. The responsorial psalm recalls Jacob's trust in God's protection during his journey. In the Gospel, Jesus raises to life the daughter of a synagogue leader — a story that teaches us how the Gospel writers used a miracle to serve different purposes. St. Mark's account is a healing story. Matthew's version that we hear today is a resurrection story that suggests our Lord's own victory over death.

YEAR II

READING I Hos. 2:16, 17-18, 21-22   RESP. Ps. 145:2-3, 4-5, 6-7, 8-9
GOSPEL Matthew 9:18-26

In today's first reading, we hear the Lord speak as a husband who will win his unfaithful wife back to him in the desert, where God first espoused Israel to himself — a reference to God's covenant with Moses in the Sinai Desert. The prophet Hosea, writing about 755 B.C., then reminds Israel that she must bring as her dowry to the Lord the gifts of right living, justice, love, mercy, and fidelity. If Israel does so, she will "know the Lord" — that is, she will experience the joys of intimate union with her divine lover. Hosea was the first prophet to use a marriage image to describe God's covenant relationship with the Jewish people. Later prophets adopted it, as did St. Paul, who applied it to Christ and his Church. The responsorial psalm recalls Israel's bridal gifts of "justice" and "mercy." In the Gospel, Jesus performs two miracles as the reward for great faith.

384 TUESDAY OF THE FOURTEENTH WEEK OF THE YEAR

YEAR I

READING I Gen. 32:23-33   RESP. Ps. 17:1, 2-3, 6-7, 8, 15
GOSPEL Matthew 9:32-38

As today's first reading begins, many years have passed since Jacob fled from his homeland after obtaining by fraud God's blessing from his father Isaac. Now we learn that Jacob has decided to return home together with his family. The central event of this passage is the fierce all-night struggle that Jacob has with a messenger of God. As a result God changes Jacob's name to Israel, which means "one who struggles with God." This name Israel will later become the identifying mark of the Jewish nation itself. The test that Jacob underwent and his seeing God face-to-face are two themes which the responsorial psalm highlights. In the Gospel, we hear Jesus point to the harvest that awaits the reapers. In our Lord's words we discover a challenge for ourselves to harvest for Christ someone we can have a good influence on today.

YEAR II

READING I Hos. 8:4-7, 11-13   **RESP. Ps.** 115:3-4, 5-6, 7-8, 9-10
GOSPEL Matthew 9:32-38

Today's reading spells out two reasons why northern Israel would suffer destruction in 721 B.C. The prophet Hosea suggests first that Israel often chose rulers who did not uphold God's laws. Second, these rulers tolerated the worship of false gods that turned the people's hearts away from the Lord. In this regard, Hosea refers to the "calf in Samaria" — that is, replicas of a golden image of God. These images, on display at several shrines in the kingdom, eventually led to idolatry. Hosea also tells how Ephraim, a poetic name for Israel, abused its many altars by sacrificing to false gods. Finally, the prophet threatens that the days of slavery in Egypt will return. The responsorial psalm stresses how much God rejects pagan gods. The Gospel sums up the work of Jesus as teaching, preaching — and healing the needs of men because they moved his heart to pity.

385 WEDNESDAY OF THE FOURTEENTH WEEK OF THE YEAR

YEAR I

READING I Gen. 41:55-57; 42:5-7, 17-24   **RESP. Ps.** 33:2-3, 10-11, 18-19
GOSPEL Matthew 10:1-7

In today's Mass, we take up an acknowledged biblical masterpiece — the story of Joseph, next-to-youngest of Jacob's twelve sons. Joseph had aroused the jealousy of his brothers by the interpretation he gave to dreams. His brothers betrayed him and sold him into slavery in Egypt. There, through the grace of God, Joseph's ability to interpret dreams gained him a prominent position in the service of the pharaoh. As today's reading opens, famine has ravaged the lands of the Near East. Joseph's wise storage of grain during the seven previous years of plentiful crops has spared Egypt. His brothers come to Egypt seeking grain from him, but they do not realize who he is. This theme of the famine appears again in the responsorial psalm, which explains how God watches over his children to "preserve them in spite of famine." In the Gospel, Jesus chooses his twelve apostles.

YEAR II

READING I   Hos. 10:1-3, 7-8, 12   RESP. Ps. 105:2-3, 4-5, 6-7
GOSPEL   Matthew 10:1-7

The first reading condemns the rulers of Israel for multiplying altars and shrines to pagan gods in the northern kingdom about 750 B.C. The prophet Hosea then describes how Israel's enemies will soon devastate the land and inflict such suffering that the people will cry out for the mountains to bury their agonies. Centuries later, Jesus, in referring to the destruction of Jerusalem, quoted this verse to the women who met him along his way of the cross. Hosea finally pleads with the people to break up the field of their hardened hearts by repenting their sins, so the rain of God's salvation can water their lives. The responsorial psalm refrain accents Hosea's plea for Israel to "seek always the face of the Lord." In the Gospel, Jesus calls his twelve apostles. In the New Testament lists of the apostles, no two agree on the exact order of names, but Peter's name always heads each group.

386 THURSDAY OF THE FOURTEENTH WEEK OF THE YEAR

YEAR I

READING I   Gen. 44:18-21, 23-29; 45:1-5   RESP. Ps. 105:16-17, 18-19, 20-21
GOSPEL   Matthew 10:7-15

As today's reading begins, Joseph's brothers have come to Egypt seeking food at a time of famine. They do not realize that the man selling them grain is their brother Joseph, whom they sold into slavery years before. Joseph then pretends to keep the youngest brother as his slave for allegedly stealing his drinking cup. At this point, we hear Joseph's brother Judah striving to convince Joseph how deeply this loss of the younger brother will grieve their father Jacob. He already bears a heavy sorrow because he thinks Joseph is dead. Judah's speech finally touches Joseph's heart, and in a deeply moving scene he reveals to his brothers who he really is. The responsorial psalm provides a thumbnail sketch of Joseph's life in Egypt. In the Gospel, Jesus instructs his apostles before sending them out to heal the sick and preach repentance to the towns of Galilee.

READING I   Hosea 11:1, 3-4, 8-9   RESP. Ps. 80:2, 3, 15-16
GOSPEL   Matthew 10:7-15

In today's first reading, the prophet Hosea compares God's care for Israel to a father's continuing love for an ungrateful son who rejects him. This comparison reinforces Hosea's previous image of Israel as the beloved but unfaithful wife. Hosea assures the people that even though God may have to discipline his son, he will not destroy him. Hosea's comment — "Out of Egypt I called my son" — recalls the time when God rescued his beloved people from slavery in Egypt. St. Matthew's Gospel applies this verse to the return of the child Jesus from Egypt, when God began through his own Son the world's delivery from bondage. The responsorial psalm underscores God's love for "the son of man whom you yourself made strong." In the Gospel, Jesus gives practical advice to his apostles before sending them out on a preaching tour of the towns and villages of Galilee.

387   FRIDAY OF THE FOURTEENTH WEEK OF THE YEAR

YEAR I

READING I   Gen. 46:1-7, 28-30   RESP. Ps. 37:3-4, 18-19, 27-28, 39-40
GOSPEL   Matthew 10:16-23

The first reading narrates the touching story of Joseph's reunion with his father Israel. Joseph, who served the pharaoh in Egypt, wanted his father to come and settle there with his entire family. We learn how God assured Israel that he need not be afraid to live in Egypt. This would launch a period of peace that the Jews would enjoy in the region of Goshen in lower Egypt sometime between 1700 and 1500 B.C. The responsorial psalm accents this theme in the words, "Trust in the Lord . . . that you may dwell in the land and enjoy security." The Gospel continues our Lord's instruction to his apostles before sending them through Galilee to prepare the people for the coming of God's kingdom. Jesus then looks ahead to the early days of his Church. He warns the apostles that they will face opposition later on in preaching his message of repentance to all men.

YEAR II

READING I   Hos. 14:2-10   RESP. Ps. 51:3-4, 8-9, 12-13, 14, 17
GOSPEL   Matthew 10:16-23

In the first reading, the prophet Hosea begins by inviting Israel to repent her sins and "return to the Lord." He then calls on Israel's rulers to abandon their former ways of relying on the human resources of foreign nations like Assyria and Egypt or on the false security of pagan gods. The prophet describes God's blessings for the land in images that suggest only the Lord can grant the gifts which the people have previously sought by worshiping idols. In the verse, "Let him who is wise understand these things," we discover a brief section added to this prophecy centuries later that shows how other generations found Hosea's words instructive for their lives. The responsorial psalm emphasizes the prophet's theme of repentance and the wisdom we find in his writings. In the Gospel, Jesus points out the opposition the apostles will have to endure in preaching his message to men.

388 SATURDAY OF THE FOURTEENTH WEEK OF THE YEAR

YEAR I

READING I   Gen. 49:29-33; 50:15-24   RESP. Ps. 105:1-2, 3-4, 6-7
GOSPEL   Matthew 10:24-33

In the first reading, Jacob asks his sons to bury him in Canaan, the land of promise, and not in Egypt, the place of temporary sojourn. We then learn how Jacob's sons fear that their brother Joseph will take revenge on them for selling him into slavery — but Joseph graciously forgives them. The passage concludes with Joseph's words before his death which point to God's promise to give the Jews a land of their own. Years of peace would yield to the yoke of oppression under native Egyptian rulers, paving the way for the drama of the Exodus which we will consider next week. The responsorial psalm calls our attention again to Jacob and his sons. In the Gospel, St. Matthew has collected a group of our Lord's sayings that apply to the missionary efforts of the apostles. We hear Jesus remind them not to fear since the Father will protect them.

YEAR II

READING I   Is. 6:1-8   RESP. Ps. 93:1, 1-2, 5
GOSPEL   Matthew 10:24-33

The first reading allows us to stand at the side of a young married man named Isaiah during his religious experience at Solomon's temple in Jerusalem about 742 B.C. Amid the chanting of priestly choirs, Isaiah gazes at the Holy of Holies where stands the throne of God's glory. Suddenly he beholds the breathtaking vision he describes today — a scene of other-worldly majesty. It fills him with a deep sense of how unworthy he is to be in the presence of Israel's God. An angel then purifies his lips, and Isaiah agrees to walk in the footsteps of the

Lord's prophets. The echo of this vision rings out in the "Holy, Holy, Holy" praises immediately before the Eucharistic Prayer at every Mass. The responsorial psalm recalls the scene of "The Lord . . . in splendor-robed." In the Gospel, Jesus instructs his apostles that God cares about the least thing that happens to them.

389   MONDAY OF THE FIFTEENTH WEEK OF THE YEAR

YEAR I

READING I   Exod. 1:8-14, 22   RESP. Ps. 124:1-3, 4-6, 7-8
GOSPEL   Matthew 10:34—11:1

As we begin the first reading today, we need to realize that the Jewish people had enjoyed for more than two hundred years a period of prosperity and peace in lower Egypt. They had gone there from Palestine sometime before the year 1500 B.C. to avoid the ravages of a famine. Then came a change in the dynasty of the pharaohs. Before long, the new ruler had forced the Jews into slavery and started killing off their little boys as a way of controlling the Jewish population. The responsorial psalm underscores the Egyptian persecution "when men rose up against us." As we listen to St. Matthew's Gospel, it may help us to realize that he arranged the teaching and good works of Jesus into five sections of material so that the first Christians could learn it more easily. The final part of our Lord's missionary talk to his disciples that we now hear ends the second of those sections.

YEAR II

READING I   Is. 1:10-17   RESP. Ps. 50:8-9, 16-17, 21, 23
GOSPEL   Matthew 10:34—11:1

The scene of today's first reading is very likely the courtyard of the temple in Jerusalem where crowds of Jews have gathered to celebrate a feast day. We hear the prophet Isaiah's voice cry out over the noisy festivities. He addresses the rulers and people of Jerusalem in God's name, as if they were the wicked sinners who once lived in Sodom and Gomorrah. Because the people fail to respond to the needs of their fellowmen, Isaiah reminds them that God does not find acceptable the many sacrifices they are offering. Isaiah's criticisms of religion that divorces itself from morality shows how important social justice was in the eyes of the prophets. The responsorial psalm also highlights the theme of what religion really means. In the Gospel, Jesus warns that those who take literally his way of life may find even members of their own family turning against them.

133

YEAR I

READING I   Exod. 2:1-15   RESP. Ps. 69:3, 14, 30-31, 33-34
GOSPEL   Matthew 11:20-24

As today's reading begins, the Egyptians have enslaved the Jews and are killing all their male children to force the people into extinction. We learn in this passage how God spares Moses from this fate. Ironically, the child who will grow up to deliver Israel from bondage finds safety in the arms of the pharaoh's daughter. Henceforth Moses will dominate our attention as we reflect on this period of Jewish history. The responsorial psalm affirms God's care for his people with the words, "His own who are in bonds he spurns not." Today's Gospel message indicates that Jesus attracted large crowds throughout Galilee by his miracles and preaching, but the people did not reform their lives. Our Lord's reference to the works he performed in certain lake towns — works which none of the Gospels record — remind us how little we really know about his life on earth.

YEAR II

READING I   Is. 7:1-9   RESP. Ps. 48:2-3, 3-4, 5-6, 7-8
GOSPEL   Matthew 11:20-24

Today's first reading concerns a time of national crisis for the southern kingdom of Judah about 733 B.C. The kings of two nations to the north — Israel and Aram (or Syria) — had formed an alliance to march against Jerusalem, where they hoped to set up their own puppet king. We meet the ruler of Judah, King Ahaz, as he inspects the water supplies while preparing for the siege of the city. The prophet Isaiah comes out to meet the king with a hopeful message that if Ahaz puts his trust in God, instead of foreign allies, all will go well. Instead, the king will turn to Assyria for help and thereby pave the way for future disasters in Palestine. The responsorial psalm also portrays the threat facing Jerusalem at this time. Today's Gospel passage indicates that Jesus attracted large crowds in Galilee by his miracles and preaching, but the people made little response in faith and repentance.

391 WEDNESDAY OF THE FIFTEENTH WEEK OF THE YEAR

YEAR I

READING I   Exod. 3:1-6, 9-12   RESP. Ps. 103:1-2, 3-4, 6-7
GOSPEL   Matthew 11:25-27

Today's first Scripture reading from the Book of Exodus describes God's dramatic appearance to Moses in the burning bush. God gave this shepherd the responsibility of leading the Hebrew flock out of slavery in Egypt. We hear God assure Moses, "I will be with you." This promise of divine help to his chosen servants will continue to echo through the pages of the Old Testament. It found expression at last on the lips of Jesus when he spoke to his apostles before leaving the world. The responsorial psalm accents today's theme by recalling that God "has made known his ways to Moses." The Gospel passage presents in our Lord's words a key insight into Christian faith. God reveals himself not through natural wisdom and understanding but through his own Son. A childlike heart disposes us for the gifts that God wishes to shower on us — if only we will let him.

YEAR II

READING I   **Is. 10:5-7, 13-16**   **RESP. Ps. 94:5-6, 7-8, 9-10, 14-15**
GOSPEL   **Matthew 11:25-27**

Today the prophet Isaiah reveals that toward the end of the eighth century B.C. God will use the empire of Assyria as a "rod" to discipline the southern kingdom of Judah for its sins. The prophet then explains that the ruler of Assyria does not realize he is an instrument in the Lord's hands. As a result, Isaiah portrays the king as foolishly boasting that his success is due completely to his own power and wisdom. Isaiah replies that an axe, a saw, and a rod cannot boast of what they do because they only serve the one who uses them, just as Assyria serves God's purposes. For this pride, Assyria, too, in time will taste defeat. The responsorial psalm accents today's theme by asking, "Shall he who instructs nations not chastise?" In the Gospel, Jesus teaches us that a childlike heart disposes men to know God as their Father — a truth that our Lord alone can reveal.

392   THURSDAY OF THE FIFTEENTH WEEK OF THE YEAR

YEAR I

READING I   **Exod. 3:11-20**   **RESP. Ps. 105:1, 5, 8-9, 24-25, 26-27**
GOSPEL   **Matthew 11:28-30**

Today's Mass describes how God revealed to Moses in the burning bush on Mount Horeb his sacred name — "I am who am." In contrast to the idols of the pagan nations, the God of Abraham, Isaac, and Jacob is a living God. For this reason, the faith of the Jewish people takes root not in pious imagination but in the events of history through which God works out his loving purposes for mankind. This God now hears his people's cry for deliverance from slavery in Egypt and sends Moses to lead them into the land of promise. The liturgy chooses the historical Psalm 105 as the response to the reading because the verses relate to today's events. In the Gospel, we hear Jesus invite those who are all tired out from trying to shoulder the yoke of the Law of Moses to try on for size his easy-to-carry yoke of love.

YEAR II

READING I   Is. 26:7-9, 12, 16-19   RESP. Ps. 102:13-14, 15, 16-18, 19-21
GOSPEL   Matthew 11:28-30

As the first reading begins, we hear the people from the land of Judah sing how they want to remain loyal to God's will and to honor his name. They long for the day of God's judgment to dawn so that all peoples of the world will live the way the Lord wants them to. Then the people confess that the nation has been like a woman in childbirth, but nothing has come of her suffering since the earth has not yet achieved salvation. The passage concludes with the earliest mention in the Bible of the idea of resurrection. Because the reading tells how the nation suffered in God's presence, the responsorial psalm declares, "From heaven God beheld the earth, To hear the groaning of the prisoners." In the Gospel, we hear Jesus invite those who are all tired out from trying to shoulder the yoke of the Law of Moses to try on for size his easy-to-carry yoke of love.

393   FRIDAY OF THE FIFTEENTH WEEK OF THE YEAR

YEAR I

READING I   Exod. 11:10—12:14
                                           RESP. Ps. 116:12-13, 15-16, 17-18

GOSPEL   Matthew 12:1-8

The first reading continues the story of Moses, as God prepares a tenth and final plague for Egypt — the death of every firstborn man and beast. We hear God give detailed instructions to Moses and his brother Aaron about the Passover meal they are to prepare. This meal will become an annual way of remembering the night when God delivered his people — just as our Mass recalls daily how Jesus delivered not one nation but the world itself from sin. The responsorial psalm is one of several psalms of thanksgiving that the Jews in time came to pray after the Passover supper. The twelfth chapter of St. Matthew's Gospel that we begin today records the growing opposition to Jesus among the Scribes and Pharisees. It will climax in our Lord's death. We discover one of the reasons why the Pharisees came to hate Jesus — his different attitude toward the sacred Sabbath.

READING I   Is. 38:1-6, 21-22, 7-8   RESP. Ps.   Is. 38:10, 11, 12, 16
GOSPEL   Matthew 12:1-8

In today's reading, God hears the prayer of King Hezekiah, ruler of the southern kingdom of Judah, and grants added years to his life. To assure the king that he will get well, the prophet Isaiah gives a special sign that probably symbolizes God's holding back the shadow of death from Hezekiah's sickbed. This incident took place sometime before the forces of Assyria invaded Judah in 701 B.C. After this stormy period, we know nothing further about the rest of Isaiah's life because he no longer appears in Israel's history. The liturgy suggests that we regard the responsorial psalm as King Hezekiah's prayer that God might spare his life. The Gospel reveals the growing opposition to Jesus among the Scribes and ·Pharisees. It will climax in our Lord's death. We discover that the Pharisees came to hate Jesus because he had a different attitude toward the sacred Sabbath.

394   SATURDAY OF THE FIFTEENTH WEEK OF THE YEAR

YEAR I

READING I   Exod. 12:37-42   RESP. Ps. 136:1, 23-24, 10-12, 13-15
GOSPEL   Matthew 12:14-21

In today's first reading, we learn how the captive Jews fled for their lives from Egypt under Moses' leadership. They headed south for the wilderness area that today borders the Suez Canal. The Jews still recall this landmark event in their history every year when they celebrate the Passover feast. Several of the psalms also recall this epic journey. We find an example in today's responsorial psalm. As in a litany, the first line of each verse tells the story of the Exodus, while the second line repeatedly proclaims God's love in the words, "For his mercy endures forever." In the Gospel, Jesus avoids publicity in healing the sick. St. Matthew regards this as fulfilling the words of Isaiah about the Servant of God — whom Matthew identifies with Jesus — when the prophet wrote, "He will not contend or cry out, nor will his voice be heard in the streets."

YEAR II

READING I   Micah 2:1-5   RESP. Ps. 10:1-2, 3-4, 7-8, 14
GOSPEL   Matthew 12:14-21

In today's reading, the prophet Micah — like his eighth-century contemporary Isaiah — warns Judah's king and people about the punishment God would send to them because thy oppressed the poor and unfortunate. Micah begins by pointing out that many people in Jerusalem are so wicked that they even lie awake at night planning how to deprive others of their human rights. For these crimes, Micah says, foreign armies will soon invade the land and devastate it so thoroughly that the wicked will hear a funeral dirge, "Our ruin is complete." The responsorial psalm also recalls the crimes of "the wicked man who glories in his greed," as well as God's concern for the "misery and sorrow" of the poor. In the Gospel, Jesus avoids publicity in healing the sick. St. Matthew regards this as fulfilling the words of Isaiah about the Servant of God — whom Matthew identifies with Jesus.

395 MONDAY OF THE SIXTEENTH WEEK OF THE YEAR

YEAR I

READING I   Exod. 14:5-18   RESP. Ps. Exod. 15:1-2, 3-4, 5-6
GOSPEL   Matthew 12:38-42

This week in the first Scripture readings at Mass we will continue the story of the Exodus, that is, how the Jewish people escaped from slavery in Egypt. As today's passage opens, a report has reached the king of Egypt that the Jews have fled. The pharaoh and his army then pursue the Israelites and catch up with them in the desert. The Jews are justifiably in terror and regret that they have so hastily followed Moses on a path of certain death. Then God promises Moses that he will give victory to his people. The liturgy chooses for an appropriate response to this reading a passage from the ancient Song of Moses that recalls the Exodus. In St. Matthew's Gospel, we hear the Jews asking Jesus to give them some extraordinary sign that he is the Messiah. Matthew then points to the three days Jonah spent in the belly of a whale as a sign of our Lord's future death and resurrection.

YEAR II

READING I   Micah 6:1-4, 6-8   RESP. Ps. 50:5-6, 8-9, 16-17, 21, 23
GOSPEL   Matthew 12:38-42

In the first reading, the eighth century prophet Micah creates an imaginary courtroom drama in which God presents a lawsuit against his chosen people, Israel, for failing to keep faith with the solemn promise of his covenant with them. The Lord summons as his witnesses the mountains that have looked down on the history of Israel and seen how generously God has provided for the people in keeping his part of the covenant. When the people ask Micah whether they can make up for their offenses by simply offering more sacrifices to God, the prophet stresses instead that they show sincere worship by leading good lives. The responsorial psalm also presents a courtroom theme in the verses, "Gather my faithful ones before me . . . for God himself is the judge." In the Gospel, St. Matthew points to the three days Jonah spent in a whale's belly as a sign of Jesus' resurrection.

396 TUESDAY OF THE SIXTEENTH WEEK OF THE YEAR

YEAR I

READING I   Exod. 14:21—15:1   RESP. Ps. Exod. 15:8-9, 10, 12, 17
GOSPEL   Matthew 12:46-50

We hear in today's Mass how God demonstrates his power, his love, his protection of the chosen people. God alone brings his holy war with Egypt to a successful outcome by annihilating the pharaoh's army. God fights for Israel so that he may fulfill his ancient promise to give a homeland to Abraham, Isaac, and Jacob, and their descendants. At the end of this passage, we discover the reaction of the Jewish people to this awesome miracle that God has worked in their behalf. The two verses we hear of the Israelites' song are part of the Song of Moses that recalls God's delivery of the Jews. The liturgy chooses other verses from this song as the responsorial psalm. In the Gospel, the visit of his mother and his relatives gives Jesus an opportunity to explain the value of doing God's will. In this way we become his true brothers and sisters beyond mere blood relationship.

YEAR II

READING I   Micah 7:14-15, 18-20   RESP. Ps. 85:2-4, 5-6, 7-8
GOSPEL   Matthew 12:46-50

The first reading unfolds a tender prayer of the Jewish nation for God to forgive their sins and bestow his blessings as in days gone by. The prayer begins by describing the people as wayward sheep lost in the hills of Mount Carmel to the north because their enemies have driven them away from Judah. The people ask that the Lord may shepherd his flock to the rich pasture lands of Bashan and Gilead east of the Jordan River that Judah lost because she had sinned. The prayer closes by praising God for the way he has always shown compassion and pardon in fulfilling his ancient promises to Abraham and his descendants. The responsorial psalm underscores the theme of the prayer in the verse, "Restore us, O God our savior, and abandon your displeasure against us." In the Gospel, the visit of his mother and his relatives gives Jesus an occasion to explain the value of doing God's will.

YEAR I

READING I Exod. 16:1-5, 9-15   RESP. Ps. 78:18-19, 23-24, 25-26, 27-28
GOSPEL   Matthew 13:1-9

Today's reading tells of a shortage of food during the journey through the Sinai Desert two months after the Jews escaped from Egypt. The people grumble against God and Moses — a reaction that would occur again and again in the history of Israel because the faith of the Israelites was weak and their hearts rebellious. We then learn how God fed the people with a bread-like food from heaven called manna. Jesus referred to this event when he told the Jews that he was the new bread come down from heaven to nourish their hearts for eternal life. The responsorial psalm retells God's miraculous feeding of the people. In the Gospel, we begin a collection of parables explaining how the kingdom of God begins, grows and develops, and then reaches full maturity. Today's account assures us the grain of God's kingdom will grow despite obstacles to an abundant harvest on the last day.

YEAR II

READING I Jer. 1:1, 4-10   RESP. Ps. 71:1-2, 3-4, 5-6, 15, 17
GOSPEL   Matthew 13:1-9

In today's first reading, a young man named Jeremiah — barely out of his teens — unfolds the inner workings of God's grace in his heart as the Lord calls him to become a prophet to the Jewish people, as well as to all nations, about 626 B.C. Like Moses before him, Jeremiah at first shrinks from this awesome responsibility. But God extends his hand and touches the lips of the trembling youth to assure him that he now has the power to speak in the Lord's own name. Even so, more than fifteen years would pass before the people recognized the voice of Jeremiah as one of the major forces shaping the destiny of that period. The liturgy suggests that in the responsorial psalm Jeremiah thanks the Lord for his vocation by praying, "O God, you have taught me from my youth." Today's Gospel assures us the grain of God's kingdom will grow to an abundant harvest on the last day.

398 THURSDAY OF THE SIXTEENTH WEEK OF THE YEAR

YEAR I

READING I Exod. 19:1-2, 9-11, 16-20   RESP. Ps. Dan. 3:52, 53, 54, 55, 56
GOSPEL   Matthew 13:10-17

The first Scripture reading reveals that the Jewish people, wandering in the desert, have finally arrived at Mount Sinai. It was God's purpose that these many loosely joined tribes should become a united community, a special nation bound to him by a religious agreement or covenant. This initiative on God's part demanded a response. And so in this passage we hear God instructing Moses to gather the people at the foot of the mountain to prepare them for their covenant with the Lord — he would be their God and they would be his people. The responsorial psalm takes up the theme of God's glory as he revealed it on Mount Sinai and praises the Lord for his holiness. In the Gospel, Jesus explains to his disciples why he teaches in parables. Our Lord's words suggest that he really can do little to help those Jews who refuse to accept him as the Messiah.

YEAR II

READING I Jer. 2:1-3, 7-8, 12-13   RESP. Ps. 36:6-7, 8-9, 10-11
GOSPEL Matthew 13:10-17

In today's reading, Jeremiah addresses the city of Jerusalem as a symbol for the land of Judah. The prophet considers first how she once kept faith with the Lord during her wandering in the desert after God had delivered her from Egypt. Then, in the promised land, the rulers led the people astray, and they fell to worshiping false gods. Even now Judah has preferred the "broken cisterns" of alliances with foreign countries to relying on God, "the source of living waters." We hear Jeremiah voice his horror that the people could ever have done such a thing. The responsorial psalm also emphasizes how God alone is the real source of Judah's salvation in the verse, "For with you is the fountain of life." In the Gospel, Jesus suggests that his parables can really do little to help those Jews who refuse to accept him as the Messiah.

399 FRIDAY OF THE SIXTEENTH WEEK OF THE YEAR

YEAR I

READING I Exod. 20:1-17   RESP. Ps. 19:8, 9, 10, 11
GOSPEL Matthew 13:18-23

Today's reading presents the Ten Commandments God gave to Moses on Mount Sinai. They were the most noble code of morality known to the world until the time of Christ. In the form of these sacred words God expressed his covenant relationship with the Jewish people. This awesome event marks a high-point in the life of the indomitable Moses. Here in the Sinai Desert he assumes a new role as the one who speaks for the Israelite people to their God and receives his holy laws. The liturgy accents today's theme by selecting verses from Psalm 19, which praises the Law of God. In the Gospel, Jesus explains the parable of the sower and the seed. Our Lord points out how people respond in different ways to the word of God which invites them into the kingdom.

YEAR II

READING I   Jer. 3:14-17   RESP. Ps. Jer. 31:10, 11-12, 13
GOSPEL   Matthew 13:18-23

In the first reading, we see why some commentators describe the writings of the prophet Jeremiah as a sort of scrapbook or anthology of passages from various periods in his life, rather than the orderly, chronological collection we might expect. Here at the beginning of his work, for instance, where he deals mainly with prophecies from his early career, we find a passage that apparently relates to a period nearly forty years later — the Babylonian exile in 587 B.C. We hear the Lord call the exiles to a glorious reunion at Jerusalem, which will become the religious center of the nation once again — indeed, for all nations. This theme also appears in the responsorial psalm verse, "He who scattered Israel, now gathers them together." In the Gospel parable of the sower and the seed, Jesus explains how people respond in different ways to the word of God which invites them into the kingdom.

400 SATURDAY OF THE SIXTEENTH WEEK OF THE YEAR

YEAR I

READING I   Exod. 24:3-8   RESP. Ps. 50:1-2, 5-6, 14-15
GOSPEL   Matthew 13:24-30

In today's first Scripture reading, we hear one version of the sacred ceremony that confirmed the covenant or agreement God made with the Jews in the Sinai Desert. Moses acts as the agent of this agreement by using the blood of bulls. Ancient belief held that sacrificial blood had the power to bind parties to a solemn contract. The Letter to the Hebrews in the New Testament quotes this event to demonstrate the superior value of the blood of Jesus for his new covenant with mankind. The liturgy chooses Psalm 50 for the response because it appropriately declares, "Gather my faithful ones before me, those who have made a covenant with me by sacrifice." In the Gospel, we have a parable that Matthew alone tells us about — the weeds and the wheat. Jesus warns against a false zeal that is impatient with evil and does not allow time for repentance.

READING I Jer. 7:1-11   RESP. Ps. 84:3, 4, 5-6, 8, 11
GOSPEL Matthew 13:24-30

The first reading reveals how Jeremiah — after remaining an obscure prophet in the land of Judah for nearly twenty years — suddenly claimed public attention as a vigorous spokesman for God's cause. We find him in the temple courtyard in Jerusalem in 609 B.C. warning the people who come to worship to repent their crimes of social injustice and worshiping false gods. Jeremiah specifically attacks the warped idea that Judah's enemies could never destroy Jerusalem because God's temple was there. This false security prevented the people from recognizing how perilous their situation was. To underscore the temple theme, the responsorial psalm celebrates how joyful it was to worship in "the courts of the Lord." In the Gospel parable of the weeds and the wheat, Jesus warns against a false zeal that is impatient with evil and does not allow time for repentance.

401 MONDAY OF THE SEVENTEENTH WEEK OF THE YEAR

YEAR I

READING I Exod. 32:15-24, 30-34   RESP. Ps. 106:19-20, 21-22, 23
GOSPEL Matthew 13:31-35

This week we continue the story of the Jewish people as they journey to the promised land. So far, we have learned how God miraculously delivered the Jews from the slavery of the Egyptians. He then began to fashion them into a united community during their desert experience. On Mount Sinai, he gave his Ten Commandments as the expression in words of his covenant with them. Now, in today's story, we find Moses smashing the stone tablets of the commandments in anger as a sign that the people have broken their agreement by worshiping a golden calf. The responsorial psalm retells this story of the golden calf. In St. Matthew's Gospel, we take up again the thirteenth chapter with its parables about the kingdom of God. Today's stories about the mustard seed and yeast show how God's worldwide kingdom will grow from small beginnings.

YEAR II

READING I Jer. 13:1-11   RESP. Ps. Deut. 32:18-19, 20, 21
GOSPEL Matthew 13:31-35

The first reading tells how God directed his prophet Jeremiah to hide a piece of linen cloth among some rocks of a riverbank until the cloth finally decayed. We do not know for certain whether this incident actually happened in Jeremiah's life, or if it was a vision he had, or even a brief play he may have acted out in the temple courtyard at Jerusalem to dramatize God's warning to the people. As for the meaning of this event, the linen cloth probably stands for the land of Judah that God would hide in exile near the rocks of the Parah, that is, the Euphrates River — a river signifying Judah's conqueror, Babylonia. There the Jewish people would decay as a nation in punishment for worshiping false gods. The responsorial psalm also accents the theme of Judah's infidelity to God. The Gospel stories of the mustard seed and yeast show how God's worldwide kingdom will grow from small beginnings.

402 TUESDAY OF THE SEVENTEENTH WEEK OF THE YEAR

YEAR I

READING I   Exod. 33:7-11; 34:5-9, 28   RESP. Ps. 103:6-7, 8-9, 10-11, 12-13
GOSPEL   Matthew 13:35-43

At the time of today's first reading, the Jews had settled at a desert oasis not far from Mount Sinai called Kadesh. This passage tells us about a special meeting tent or tabernacle — as we now call the miniature form of it in our churches — where Moses would go on occasion to meet the Lord and bring the needs of the people to him. This scene suggests our own practice of "making a visit" to meet God in the Eucharist and place our needs before his heart. We also hear a consoling passage about the mercy God has for sinners. The responsorial psalm underscores the kindness and mercy of God toward his people. In the Gospel, Jesus explains the parable of the weeds growing with the wheat. We learn the lesson here that we live in a human Church of saints and sinners, where we recognize our own responsibility to build up the Body of Christ by avoiding sin.

YEAR II

READING I   Jer. 14:17-22   RESP. Ps. 79:8, 9, 11, 13
GOSPEL   Matthew 13:35-43

The first reading takes us back six centuries before the birth of Christ to the time of a severe drought in the southern kingdom of Judah. The Jewish people assemble at the temple in Jerusalem to take part in a penitential service. First, the people listen — as we do today — to the prophet Jeremiah describe in a poetic way the ravages that the drought has caused. Then we hear the people acknowledge how guilty they feel about their past sins, which they see as responsible for the drought. Their prayer closes with an appeal for God to send rain and relieve their miseries, as the Lord has generously done in the past.

The responsorial psalm also describes the people calling out to God, "With your great power free those doomed to death." The Gospel parable of the weeds growing with the wheat reminds us that we live in a human Church of saints and sinners.

403 WEDNESDAY OF THE SEVENTEENTH WEEK OF THE YEAR

YEAR I

READING I   Exod. 34:29-35   RESP. Ps. 99:5, 6, 7, 9
GOSPEL   Matthew 13:44-46

Today's reading reveals that the Book of Exodus — like other books of the Bible — includes several traditions about a single event, and that sometimes these appear out of sequence in the text. The additional information in this passage about Moses receiving the Ten Commandments should really come *before* the story of the golden calf that we heard at Mass on Monday. However, some Scripture commentators believe the author may have placed this new material about Moses here to show that God renewed his covenant with the Jewish people even after their sin of idolatry. The responsorial psalm retells how God gave the Law to Moses "at his holy mountain." In the Gospel, Jesus tells parables about buried treasure and a valuable pearl. They stress how joyful a man feels when he discovers God's ways to live a happy life and the self-sacrifice he is willing to make to pursue those ways.

YEAR II

READING I   Jer. 15:10, 16-21   RESP. Ps. 59:2-3, 4, 10-11, 17, 18
GOSPEL   Matthew 13:44-46

In today's reading, the young prophet Jeremiah lays bare his heart at a moment of spiritual crisis that nearly leads him to despair. At first he found God's words had sustained him in his difficult preaching of the need to repent. Now he experiences how lonely this vocation is because his condemning prophecies have put a distance between himself and his beloved people. Then the Lord gently rebukes his prophet for feeling sorry for himself and calls him back to God's service. Jeremiah must have confidence that God's presence will protect him. The responsorial psalm becomes Jeremiah's prayer as he calls out in the midst of threats against his life, "Rescue me from my enemies, O my God." The Gospel parables reveal how joyful a man feels when he discovers God's ways to live a happy life and the self-sacrifice he is willing to make to pursue those ways.

READING I Exod. 40:16-21, 34-38 RESP. Ps. 84:3, 4, 5-6, 8, 11
GOSPEL Matthew 13:47-53

The first reading tells about the ark of the covenant, a small portable box made of wood and overlaid with gold that contained the stone tablets of the Ten Commandments. The Jewish priests used for sacrificial worship a flat plate of gold on top of the ark called a propitiatory. Since a sacrifice "propitiates" or softens the wrath of God and makes us one with him, the priests applied this feature of worship to the place of worship itself. The ark, and the tent in which the priests kept it, became the place of God's special presence among his people. The Jews carried the ark at the front of their ranks so God would protect them on their journey to the promised land. The responsorial psalm accents this theme by praising the loveliness of God's dwelling place among men. In the Gospel, the parable of the dragnet points to the judgment at the end of the world.

YEAR II

READING I Jer. 18:1-6 RESP. Ps. 146:1-2, 2-4, 5-6
GOSPEL Matthew 13:47-53

The first reading brings us into the workshop of a pottery-maker on the south side of Jerusalem, where the prophet Jeremiah learns a lesson about God's relationship to the Jewish people. As he watches the craftsman reshape a piece of clay for another turn at his wheel, Jeremiah understands that in the same way God will work with the clay of his people in the land of Judah. The Lord is not an arbitrary craftsman, molding men's lives at his whim, Jeremiah realizes. Rather he is a personal God who shapes his creatures through suffering when they turn away from him. The responsorial psalm also recalls the idea of God as man's creator in the verse, "God made heaven and earth, and the sea and all that is in them." In the Gospel, the parable of the dragnet points to the judgment at the end of the world. This story concludes St. Matthew's special collection of parables about God's kingdom.

405 FRIDAY OF THE SEVENTEENTH WEEK OF THE YEAR

YEAR I

READING I Lev. 23:1, 4-11, 15-16, 27, 34-37 RESP. Ps. 81:3-4, 5-6, 10-11
GOSPEL Matthew 13:54-58

Today's reading describes the most important Jewish religious feasts during the year. Passover and unleavened bread relate to God's delivery of the Jews from Egypt. The feast of Weeks or Pentecost was a harvest festival to thank God for the wheat. On the annual Day of Atonement, the people proclaimed the guilt of the nation before God and fasted in repentance for their sins. Our Lenten season has its roots here. The joyous feast of Booths or Tabernacles recalled primitive life in the Sinai Desert during the Exodus when the Jews lived in temporary shelters called booths. The responsorial psalm is a hymn that the Jews prayed as part of the feast of Tabernacles. In the Gospel, Jesus returns to the town where he grew up. He meets hostile and closed hearts that lock out the kindnesses he wishes to do there.

YEAR II

READING I   Jer. 26:1-9   RESP. Ps. 69:5, 8-10, 14
GOSPEL   Matthew 13:54-58

Today's first reading reveals how the prophet Jeremiah nearly touched off a riot at the temple in Jerusalem in 609 B.C. He warned the crowd of worshipers passing through the courtyard that God would soon deal with the temple "like Shiloh." He was referring to the time when God allowed Israel's enemies to destroy the people's most important religious shrine at Shiloh in central Palestine, about a century before Solomon had built the temple in 931 B.C. Jeremiah's prediction that God would also destroy his own temple was tantamount to blasphemy, and for this reason the crowd flared into anger at the prophet's threat. The liturgy suggests that the responsorial psalm reveals the thoughts of Jeremiah's troubled heart as he faced the menacing crowd and turned to God for help. In the Gospel, Jesus meets, in the town where he grew up, hostile hearts that lock out the good he wishes to do there.

406   SATURDAY OF THE SEVENTEENTH WEEK OF THE YEAR

YEAR I

READING I   Lev. 25:1, 8-17   RESP. Ps. 67:2-3, 5, 7-8
GOSPEL   Matthew 14:1-12

Today's Mass explains the special year of jubilee that God commanded the Jewish people to observe every fifty years. Besides the Sabbath rest for man and beast, God provided a certain "rest" for the land by leaving it uncultivated during this jubilee year. The law of jubilee reflects God's ownership of the land as well as being a practical step to insure the land's fertility. Scripture commentators believe that other aspects of the law — returning property to its owners, resolving debts, and freeing slaves — were more an ideal. Since the Bible records no observance of the jubilee, they may be right. To tie in with the jubilee theme, the responsorial psalm declares, "The earth has yielded its fruits; God, our God, has blessed us." The Gospel narrates the events that led to the beheading of John the Baptist which closed an important phase of our Lord's public life.

YEAR II

READING I   Jer. 26:11-16, 24   RESP. Ps. 69:15-16, 30-31, 33-34
GOSPEL   Matthew 14:1-12

As today's reading begins, the prophet Jeremiah faces death at the hands of an angry crowd in the temple courtyard at Jerusalem in 609 B.C. The people have accused the prophet of showing contempt for God's house of worship by predicting that the Lord himself would destroy the temple and the city as punishment for the nation's sins. Jeremiah defends himself as one whom the Lord had really sent to speak in his name. From this day until the disaster of Judah's exile in 597 B.C. that Jeremiah foretold, his voice in the temple court commands the people's attention, if not their acceptance. In the responsorial psalm we hear Jeremiah turning in prayer to God and asking, "May I be rescued from my foes." The Gospel narrates the events that led to the beheading of John the Baptist which closed an important phase of our Lord's public life.

407   MONDAY OF THE EIGHTEENTH WEEK OF THE YEAR — Cycle A

YEAR I
READING I   Num. 11:4-15   RESP. Ps. 81:12-13, 14-15, 16-17
*GOSPEL   Matthew 14:22-36
  *Use first text in Lectionary for #408, Tuesday of the Eighteenth Week.

Today we begin to read from the Book of Numbers, which gets its name from the census the Jews took during their journey through the Sinai Desert to the promised land. In this passage, we hear how the people tire of eating the bread-like food called manna that God had sent to them. They begin to hound Moses for meat. Moses then turns to God for help. As we listen, we can sense how frustrated Moses feels trying to guide such malcontent people any further. The responsorial psalm underscores the rebellion of the people against God's desire to feed them "with the best of wheat." In the Gospel, Jesus walks on the Sea of Galilee to calm a storm threatening the lives of his disciples. Even today, our Lord comes to us in the midst of our stormy lives and says, "It is I. Do not be afraid."

READING I Jer. 28:1-17 **RESP. Ps.** 119:29, 43, 79, 80, 95, 102
*GOSPEL Matthew 14:22-36
*Use first text in Lectionary for #408, Tuesday of the Eighteenth Week.

The first reading deals with the tragic period after the forces of Babylonia had invaded the land of Judah in 597 B.C. and taken into exile thousands of the people, as well as the temple treasures. In today's dramatic clash between two prophets in the temple at Jerusalem, the one prophet, Hananiah, sees the nation's tragedy ending in two years. To make his point, he walks up to the prophet Jeremiah and smashes a wooden yoke that Jeremiah had worn around his neck to symbolize his people's approaching slavery in Babylon. But God later reassures Jeremiah that *his* prophecy is the one that will come true. The responsorial psalm expresses Jeremiah's desire to learn what was really God's will when, temporarily confused by Hananiah's action, he left the temple. In the Gospel, Jesus walks on the Sea of Galilee to calm a storm threatening the lives of his disciples.

407 MONDAY OF THE EIGHTEENTH WEEK OF THE YEAR — Cycles B & C

YEAR I

READING I Num. 11:4-15 **RESP. Ps.** 81:12-13, 14-15, 16-17
*GOSPEL Matthew 14:13-21
*Use text in Lectionary for today.

Today we begin to read from the Book of Numbers, which gets its name from the census the Jews took during their journey through the Sinai Desert to the promised land. In this passage, we hear how the people tire of eating the bread-like food called manna that God had sent to them. They begin to hound Moses for meat. Moses then turns to God for help. As we listen, we can sense how frustrated Moses feels trying to guide such malcontent people any further. The responsorial psalm underscores the rebellion of the people against God's desire to feed them "with the best of wheat." The Gospel story of Jesus feeding a crowd of five thousand reveals our Lord's tender concern for the human needs of people. He reaches out to others through his disciples, who represent his servant-Church.

YEAR II

READING I Jer. 28:1-17 **RESP. Ps.** 119:29, 43, 79, 80, 95, 102
*GOSPEL Matthew 14:13-21
*Use text in Lectionary for today.

The first reading deals with the tragic period after the forces of

Babylonia had invaded the land of Judah in 597 B.C. and taken into exile thousands of the people, as well as the temple treasures. In today's dramatic clash between two prophets in the temple at Jerusalem, the one prophet, Hananiah, sees the nation's tragedy ending in two years. To make his point, he walks up to the prophet Jeremiah and smashes a wooden yoke that Jeremiah had worn around his neck to symbolize his people's approaching slavery in Babylon. But God later reassures Jeremiah that *his* prophecy is the one that will come true. The responsorial psalm expresses Jeremiah's desire to learn what was really God's will when, temporarily confused by Hananiah's action, he left the temple. The Gospel story of Jesus feeding a crowd of five thousand reveals his tender concern for the human needs of people.

408 TUESDAY OF THE EIGHTEENTH WEEK OF THE YEAR
Cycle A

YEAR I

READING I   Num. 12:1-13   RESP. Ps. 51:3-4, 5-6, 6-7, 12-13
*GOSPEL   Matthew 15:1-2, 10-14
  *Use second text in Lectionary for today.

The first reading shows that Miriam and Aaron, Moses' sister and brother, were dissatisfied with God for revealing himself only through Moses and not through them, too. Miriam apparently felt she had a right to leadership equal to her brother's because she had once acted as a spokesman for God. The Lord's intimate friendship with Moses proves, however, that the authority of Moses is unique and hence superior to Miriam's. God punishes Miriam for her pride with a mild form of leprosy, but at Moses' prayer God heals her — another sign that her brother is superior to her. We hear in the responsorial psalm an echo of Aaron's plea for God to forgive his foolish sin. In the Gospel, Jesus teaches the crowd that religion is not just observing ritual regulations — even as the prophets of old had warned the Jews — but a matter of the heart, too.

YEAR II

READING I   Jer. 30:1-2, 12-15, 18-22   RESP. Ps. 102:16-18, 19-21, 29, 22-23
*GOSPEL   Matthew 15:1-2, 10-14
  *Use second text in Lectionary for today.

Today's first reading deals with the difficult period after the Jewish people had returned in 539 B.C. to the wasteland of Palestine at the end of their Babylonian exile. Like people of our own times who must face the discouraging task of rebuilding their homes after the devastation of a flood, an earthquake, or war, the hearts of the people needed a future to believe in. For this reason, the prophet Jeremiah, after first painting a dismal picture of the wounds that Judah had suffered in her exile, then offers the hope of a new Jerusalem. Once again, he says, crowds will fill the city streets, and a prince will rule who respects God and keeps faith with his covenant. The responsorial psalm accents this theme in the refrain, "The Lord will build up Zion again, and appear in all his glory." In the Gospel, Jesus tells the crowd that in the long run religion is a matter of the heart.

408   TUESDAY OF THE EIGHTEENTH WEEK OF THE   YEAR
Cycles B & C

YEAR I

READING I   Num. 12:1-13   RESP. Ps. 51:3-4, 5-6, 6-7, 12-13
*GOSPEL   Matthew 14:22-36
    *Use first text in Lectionary for today.

The first reading shows that Miriam and Aaron, Moses' sister and brother, were dissatisfied with God for revealing himself only through Moses and not through them, too. Miriam apparently felt she had a right to leadership equal to her brother's because she had once acted as a spokesman for God. The Lord's intimate friendship with Moses proves, however, that the authority of Moses is unique and hence superior to Miriam's. God punishes Miriam for her pride with a mild form of leprosy, but at Moses' prayer God heals her — another sign that her brother is superior to her. We hear in the responsorial psalm an echo of Aaron's plea for God to forgive his foolish sin. In the Gospel, Jesus walks on the Sea of Galilee to calm a storm threatening his disciples. Even today, our Lord will come into our stormy lives and say, "It is I. Do not be afraid" — if we let him.

YEAR II

READING I   Jer. 30:1-2, 12-15, 18-22   RESP. Ps. 102:16-18, 19-21, 29, 22-23
*GOSPEL   Matthew 14:22-36
    *Use first text in Lectionary for today.

Today's first reading deals with the difficult period after the Jewish people had returned in 539 B.C. to the wasteland of Palestine at the end of their Babylonian exile. Like people of our own times who must face the discouraging task of rebuilding their homes after the devastation of a flood, an earthquake, or war, the hearts of the people needed a future to believe in. For this reason, the prophet Jeremiah, after first painting a dismal picture of the wounds that Judah had suffered in her exile, then offers the hope of a new Jerusalem. Once again, he says, crowds will fill the city streets, and a prince will rule who respects

God and keeps faith with his covenant. The responsorial psalm accents this theme in the refrain, "The Lord will build up Zion again, and appear in all his glory." In the Gospel, Jesus walks on the Sea of Galilee to calm a storm threatening his disciples.

409 WEDNESDAY OF THE EIGHTEENTH WEEK OF THE YEAR

YEAR I

READING I Num. 13:1-2, 25—14:1, 26-29, 34-35

RESP. Ps. 106:6-7, 13-14, 21-22, 23

GOSPEL Matthew 15:21-28

In today's Scripture reading, we learn why the Jews spent a generation wandering in the desert wilderness before they reached the promised land. The people were drawing near their destination, and Moses sent men ahead to scout the terrain. When they brought back disconcerting news about the strength of the people who lived in Canaan, the Israelites became so discouraged that they wanted to return to Egypt. In their rebellion, they mistrusted that God could lead them to victory as he had done in the past. As a result, God barred that generation from the land of promise and condemned them to wander for forty years until "the last man" died. The responsorial psalm recounts this rebellion of the people in the desert. The Gospel also teaches us how important faith is. We learn that a Gentile woman — who won't take no for an answer — sees Jesus cure her sick daughter.

YEAR II

READING I Jer. 31:1-7   RESP. Ps. 31:10, 11-12, 13

GOSPEL Matthew 15:21-28

The first reading once again portrays the joyous day when all the scattered peoples of Israel will return to their homeland following periods of exile in foreign lands for their sins. We hear the prophet Jeremiah comfort the exiles by reminding them of God's everlasting patience and mercy. The responsorial psalm takes up Jeremiah's message of hope with additional verses from this same passage. Here, the prophet describes God as the Good Shepherd who gathers his flock together. Once again there are sounds of song and scenes of dancing as the exiles rejoice in their new-found salvation. The Gospel teaches us how important faith is. We learn that a Gentile woman — who won't take no for an answer — sees Jesus cure her sick daughter in response to her great faith. This story points to the day when the Gentiles will share in the rich foods of God's kingdom.

YEAR I

READING I   Num. 20:1-13   RESP. Ps. 95:1-2, 6-7, 8-9
GOSPEL   Matthew 16:13-23

Today's first reading tells about a severe shortage of water that created problems for the Jewish people and their livestock during their journey to the land of promise. We hear God instruct Moses to strike a rock so that the Lord can demonstrate his power and his love for his people, as in the past, by pouring out water for their needs. Instead of using this event as an opportunity for "showing forth God's sanctity before the Israelites," Moses and his brother Aaron rebuke the people for their rebellious hearts. This seems to be one of the reasons why God will not permit Moses and Aaron to lead the people into the promised land. The responsorial psalm recalls how the people hardened their hearts against God at the spring of Meribah. The image of a rock also appears in the Gospel where Jesus changes Peter's name to "Rock" in giving him authority over the Church.

YEAR II

READING I   Jer. 31:31-34   RESP. Ps. 51:12-13, 14-15, 18-19
GOSPEL   Matthew 16:13-23

Today the prophet Jeremiah reveals God's promise of a new covenant with mankind. This promise became a reality six centuries later when Jesus said at the Last Supper, "This is the cup of my blood, the blood of the new and everlasting covenant." Our Lord's death made available to us the rich possibilities for growth into union with God that Jeremiah could only dream about. The quality of our response to this new covenant — which every Mass recalls — depends on how generously we fulfill the responsibilities of our daily lives as Christians. The responsorial psalm emphasizes this inner covenant with God that we entered into with Christ at baptism in the refrain, "Create a clean heart in me, O God." In the Gospel, Jesus changes Peter's name to "Rock" in giving him authority over the Church. Once again we see in the Bible how a change of name denotes a new role in God's service.

411 FRIDAY OF THE EIGHTEENTH WEEK OF THE YEAR

YEAR I

READING I   Deut. 4:32-40   RESP. Ps. 77:12-13, 14-15, 16, 21
GOSPEL   Matthew 16:24-28

In the first reading, Moses appeals to the Israelites to remember how dearly God has loved them and how tenderly he has cared for them throughout their history. As we listen to Moses give his farewell address in the wilderness of Moab and recall the important events of the past, we discover the mystery of God's call of a special people to return his love and obey his laws. At the same time, we realize in wonder that we too are caught up in this mystery today as members of God's *new* chosen people, the Church. The responsorial psalm echoes this theme in the refrain, "I remember the deeds of the Lord." In the Gospel, Jesus reminds us what it will cost if we follow his ideals of taking up our cross daily and practicing self-denial. Our Lord then refers to his coming at the end of the world.

YEAR II

READING I Nahum 2:1, 3; 3:1-3, 6-7   **RESP. Ps.** Deut. 32:35-36, 39, 41
GOSPEL Matthew 16:24-28

Today's reading introduces a contemporary of Jeremiah, the prophet Nahum. His prophecy is a series of poems that rejoice over the fall of Nineveh, capital of the Assyrian empire, in the year 612 B.C. The Jewish people had cause for rejoicing because Assyria had ruthlessly crushed and led into exile the northern tribes of Israel a century before and had nearly conquered Judah as well. As Nahum begins this passage, messengers arrive telling the people of Judah to celebrate a feast because the "scoundrel" of Assyria has met defeat. The prophet then describes in vivid poetic images the enemy forces capturing the city of Nineveh. The responsorial psalm reveals that God is the one who punished Assyria for its violence and wickedness in the verse, "With vengeance I will repay my foes." In the Gospel, Jesus reminds us what it will cost to be one of his followers.

412   SATURDAY OF THE EIGHTEENTH WEEK OF THE YEAR

YEAR I

READING I Deut. 6:4-13   **RESP. Ps.** 18:2-3, 3-4, 47, 51
GOSPEL Matthew 17:14-20

The first Scripture reading contains the great Jewish profession of faith called the Shema from the opening word of Moses' exhortation, "Hear, O Israel!" Jesus quoted this prayer on loving God with every fiber of our being as the greatest commandment. In our Lord's time, many Jews took literally the advice of Moses in this passage. They wore at the time of prayer, and sometimes in public, the words of the Shema and two other biblical texts in little boxes laced to their left arm and forehead. In this way, they constantly remembered the importance of loving God. Even today, all adult orthodox Jews recite the Shema prayer every morning and evening. The responsorial psalm refrain

echoes today's theme on love for God. In the Gospel, Jesus emphasizes that even faith no bigger in size than a mustard seed can move
God to help us solve the mountainous problems of life.

YEAR II

READING I   Hab. 1:12—2:4   RESP. Ps. 9:8-9, 10-11, 12-13
GOSPEL   Matthew 17:14-20

In today's reading, the prophet Habakkuk complains to God that "the
wicked man devours one more just than himself," while the Lord closes
his eyes to this injustice. Habakkuk apparently refers to God's using
the armies of Babylonia to chastise the kingdom of Judah. The prophet
believes that the Jewish people, although sinners, are better than the
pagan Babylonians and deserve kinder treatment. In this regard,
Habakkuk compares Babylonia to a fisherman hauling off the helpless
Jews in his net. The prophet then climbs to his watchtower to await the
Lord's answer. God replies that, come what may, the just man will live
if he remains loyal to the Lord. The responsorial psalm also insists that
God "will never abandon those who seek" him. In the Gospel, Jesus
emphasizes that even faith no bigger in size than a mustard seed can
move God to help us solve the mountainous problems of life.

413 MONDAY OF THE NINETEENTH WEEK OF THE YEAR

YEAR I

READING I   Deut. 10:12-22   RESP. Ps. 147:12-13, 14-15, 19-20
GOSPEL   Matthew 17:22-27

The first Scripture reading for today's Mass continues the address of
Moses to the Jewish people in the Moab wilderness en route to the
promised land of Canaan. In summoning the Israelites to renew in their
hearts their covenant with God, Moses recalls God's special love for
them. He then urges them to reflect in their own lives the compassion
God has for orphans, widows, and foreigners — the neediest classes
of people to whom Jesus himself offered such tender love and devoted
service. Moses reminds the Jews that God had chosen them "in prefer-
ence to all other peoples." The responsorial psalm affirms this by declaring, "He has not done thus for any other nation." In the Gospel,
Jesus makes a second prediction of his approaching death. He then
deals with the problem of paying the annual tax to support the temple.

YEAR II

READING I   Ezek. 1:2-5, 24-28   RESP. Ps. 148:1-2, 11-12, 12-14, 14
GOSPEL   Matthew 17:22-27

The first reading allows us to share in an extraordinary vision that a

Jewish priest named Ezekiel experienced while living in exile in Babylonia with his countrymen about 593 B.C. In the past, God had appeared in all his glory to men whom he had selected for special missions to the Jewish people. Now the Lord reveals himself in this way once more to Ezekiel in the midst of a dark cloud, flashing lightning, and the awesome majesty of God's throne. God was calling Ezekiel to serve as a prophet among the exiles to prepare their hearts for the destruction of Jerusalem and afterwards to keep their hopes alive for a return to their homeland. The responsorial psalm accents this scene when Ezekiel saw "heaven and earth filled with God's glory." In the Gospel, Jesus tells his disciples that even though they are members of God's kingdom, they should still pay the annual temple tax.

414 TUESDAY OF THE NINETEENTH WEEK OF THE YEAR

YEAR I

READING I   Deut. 31:1-8   RESP. Ps. Deut. 32:3-4, 7, 8, 9, 12
GOSPEL   Matthew 18:1-5, 10, 12-14

In the first reading, Moses assures the Israelites that God will be with them as they conquer the pagan land of Canaan in the same way as the Lord led them to victory in the past. Moses then summons his military commander, Joshua, and bestows on him the authority of his leadership because God will not allow Moses to enter the promised land. The responsorial psalm from the Song of Moses recalls in the verse "The Lord alone was their leader" God's role in protecting his people. In the Gospel, Jesus teaches his disciples how to exercise authority in his kingdom. They must make themselves as lowly in the eyes of others as a child is in the view of adults. They must be responsible for every single member of the kingdom as a shepherd takes care of his sheep.

YEAR II

READING I   Ezek. 2:8—3:4   RESP. Ps. 119:14, 24, 72, 103, 111, 131
GOSPEL   Matthew 18:1-5, 10, 12-14

Today we learn that while the prophet Jeremiah was preaching the doom of the nation to the Jews living in the land of Judah, God called another man to act as his spokesman to the Jews living in exile in Babylonia about 593 B.C. This man was one of the exiles, a priest named Ezekiel. In this reading, God gives Ezekiel a scroll — the rolled-up piece of parchment that served as a book in ancient times — and tells him to eat it. This is a symbolical way of showing that Ezekiel has accepted God's call to become a prophet. He must now digest the Lord's words in his heart and then preach to his fellow exiles a sorrowful message. God will soon destroy their homeland because they have turned away from his laws. The responsorial psalm refrain recalls the sweet taste of the scroll. In the Gospel, Jesus tells his disciples that authority in his kingdom means humble diligent service to others.

415 WEDNESDAY OF THE NINETEENTH WEEK OF THE YEAR

YEAR I

READING I Deut. 34:1-12   RESP. Ps. 66:1-3, 5, 8, 16-17
GOSPEL   Matthew 18:15-20

Today's first reading takes us with Moses to the top of Mount Nebo near the Dead Sea. There God gave Moses a panoramic view from north to south of the promised land of Canaan that stretched out far beyond his vision. We can imagine how thrilled Moses felt when he saw the grandeur of this scene — and yet how disappointed at never being able to lead the people into this land that God had promised to Abraham, Isaac, and Jacob. We learn how Moses "had laid his hands" upon Joshua to bestow authority on him as the new leader. This sign of authority also appears today in the ordination of priests. The responsorial psalm proclaims the gratitude of Moses for "what God has done for me." In the Gospel, Jesus gives us guidelines for restoring friendship with those who have hurt us. He then promises that he will be there praying with us whenever we gather with others in his name.

YEAR II

READING I Ezek. 9:1-7; 10:18-22   RESP. Ps. 113:1-2, 3-4, 5-6
GOSPEL   Matthew 18:15-20

In the first reading, the prophet Ezekiel is undergoing an extraordinary religious experience as he sits in a trance at his home in Babylon. God has transported Ezekiel in spirit to the temple in Jerusalem, where the prophet has seen many of the Jews there taking part in pagan religious ceremonies that fill the Lord with disgust. At this point, today's passage begins. We hear God summon six "scourges of the city" to punish with death all who are guilty of profaning the temple with their "abominations," while he spares the innocent. Ezekiel then beholds God's glory fading from the temple as a final sign that the Lord has rejected Jerusalem and its sinful people. The responsorial psalm refrain highlights this theme of God's glory. In the Gospel, Jesus gives us guidelines for restoring friendship with those who have hurt us. He then promises to pray with us when we gather with others in his name.

YEAR I

READING I   Josh. 3:7-10, 11, 13-17   RESP. Ps. 114:1-2, 3-4, 5-6
GOSPEL   Matthew 18:21—19:1

The first reading describes one of the most memorable days in Jewish history when the Israelites crossed the Jordan River into the promised land of Canaan. We find several parallels between this story and the flight of the Jews from Egypt. God's presence in the ark of the covenant at the Jordan recalls his presence in the pillar of cloud and fire at the Red Sea. There is the same miraculous separation of the waters. The Book of Joshua that narrates this historic drama is the first book in "The Prophets" — one of three major divisions of the Old Testament. The responsorial psalm focuses on this event that fulfilled God's promise to Abraham centuries before. The Gospel parable teaches us to forgive people who hurt us, no matter how often they do so. In this way, we pass along to others the same feeling of joy we experience whenever God forgives us.

YEAR II

READING I   Ezek. 12:1-2   RESP. Ps. 78:56-57, 58-59, 61-62
GOSPEL   Matthew 18:21—19:1

Today's first reading makes clear how the Jewish people resisted the preaching of the prophets. God's word comes to the prophet Ezekiel at a time when he was probably discouraged at not being able to reach his countrymen's rebellious hearts. God's message suggests that the Jewish people simply refuse to believe that God will destroy their land and its glory — the temple in Jerusalem. They hope instead that the Babylonian exile they are enduring will be short, and they will soon return home. Six hundred years later, St. Mark's Gospel used this text from Ezekiel to show how our Lord's disciples failed to understand that Jesus came to give people spiritual food rather than bread. The responsorial psalm echoes today's theme in the verse, "They rebelled against God, and kept not his decrees." The Gospel parable tells us to forgive those who hurt us, no matter how often they do so.

417 FRIDAY OF THE NINETEENTH WEEK OF THE YEAR

YEAR I

READING I   Josh. 24:1-13   RESP. Ps. 136:1-3, 16-18, 21-22, 24
GOSPEL   Matthew 19:3-12

As the first reading begins, Joshua has called an assembly of the Israelite tribes at the city of Shechem, a strong fortress in a pass between two mountains in central Palestine. Joshua retells the glorious events of the past from the time of Abraham to the present, when God displayed his power to help his beloved people conquer Canaan. This speech prepares the Israelites to renew their covenant with God. We will hear about it in tomorrow's reading. The first line of each verse in the responsorial psalm tells the story of the Exodus, while the second line repeatedly proclaims God's mercy. In the Gospel, the Pharisees ask Jesus to give his opinion in a dispute between two schools of rabbis over the question of divorce. In reply, our Lord points to the ideal for married life that God planned when he created man and woman.

YEAR II

READING I   **Ezek. 16:1-15, 60, 63**   **RESP. Ps. Is. 12:2-3, 4, 5-6**
GOSPEL   **Matthew 19:3-12**

In today's first reading, the prophet Ezekiel intends his story of an unfaithful wife to remind the Jewish people how deeply their sins have offended God, who has so graciously cared for them in the past. We hear God recall how Jerusalem — a symbol for the nation — was once like an abandoned child whom the Lord rescued and later took as his wife. Then Jerusalem forgot her husband and turned prostitute by adopting the pagan religious practices of other nations. Despite all this, God promises forgiveness and an opportunity for a new covenant. Now that Jerusalem realizes what God's love has done for her, she declares in the responsorial psalm refrain, "You have turned from your anger to comfort me." In the Gospel, the Pharisees ask Jesus for his opinion about divorce. Our Lord points to the ideal for married life that God planned when he created man and woman.

OR:

READING I   **Ezek. 16:59-63**   **RESP. Ps. Is. 12:2-3, 4, 5-6**
GOSPEL   **Matthew 19:3-12**

In today's first reading, God promises the Jewish exiles in Babylon that he will one day make an everlasting covenant with them, even though they have been unfaithful to him. We hear God tell the exiles, "I [will] take your sisters and make them your daughters." The term "sisters" here refers to the sister-territories adjoining the Jewish nation, as well as to all other countries of the world. In the age of God's new covenant, all these lands will be like "daughters" in the new family of God. This passage prompts us to rejoice today that we belong to this family of the Church and that this Mass commemorates the new covenant Jesus began at the Last Supper. The responsorial psalm refrain also shows that God has turned from his anger to comfort his people. In the Gospel, Jesus replies to a question about divorce by pointing to God's ideal for married life when he created man and woman.

YEAR I

READING I   Josh. 24:14-29   RESP. Ps. 16:1-2, 5, 7-8, 11
GOSPEL   Matthew 19:13-15

In today's reading, we hear Joshua challenge the Jewish people to decide whether they will serve God sincerely and faithfully or return to their former worship of pagan gods. The Israelites respond that they will be loyal to the one true God despite the demands God will make on them. Joshua then renews the covenant that extended back to Mount Sinai in the days of Moses. After the conquest of Canaan, Joshua divided the land and assigned portions to every tribe of the Israelites. This theme appears symbolically in the responsorial psalm refrain, "You are my inheritance, O Lord," since the Jews referred to the land as their inheritance from God. In the Gospel, we learn that just as Jesus raised the dignity of women by his teachings on love and marriage, so did he reveal how important children were in God's kingdom by giving them his blessing.

YEAR II

READING I   Ezek. 18:1-10, 13, 30-32   RESP. Ps. 51:12-13, 14-15, 18-19
GOSPEL   Matthew 19:13-15

In today's reading, the prophet Ezekiel stresses that each person must answer for his own life and cannot shift the blame to others when God punishes him for his sins. The Jewish people needed to learn this lesson at the time of the Babylonian exile in 587 B.C. Some blamed their ancestors for what was happening to the nation, instead of taking personal responsibility for whatever ways their own lives had displeased God. Others tended toward despair at suffering a punishment they believed God had sent to them unjustly. Ezekiel invites his countrymen to repent what they have done wrong and to believe that God desires to forgive them rather than punish them. The responsorial psalm also reminds us to return to the Lord when we have sinned. In the Gospel, Jesus reveals how important children are in God's kingdom by giving them his blessing.

419 MONDAY OF THE TWENTIETH WEEK OF THE YEAR

YEAR I

READING I   Judg. 2:11-19   RESP. Ps. 106:34-35, 36-37, 39-40, 43, 44
GOSPEL   Matthew 19:16-22

The first reading casts light on the stormy transitional period of about 150 years when spiritually gifted military commanders called judges ruled the twelve tribes of Israel in Palestine. Between the year 1200 B.C. and the time when the first king took his throne in Israel, about 1020 B.C., the people struggled against the temptations of the pagan culture around them. One strong attraction — as the Jews moved from nomadic to farm life — was the worship of fertility gods to insure good harvests. Today's passage gives the pattern of this struggle — rebellion, punishment, repentance, and then rebellion again after the death of the judge. The responsorial psalm reveals the source of Israel's troubles in the verse, "But they mingled with the nations and learned their works." In the Gospel, Jesus invites a man to seek perfection by giving up all the things he has.

YEAR II

READING I   Ezek. 24:15-24   **RESP.** Ps. Deut. 32:18-19, 20, 21
GOSPEL   Matthew 19:16-22

In the first reading, God warns the prophet Ezekiel that his wife, "the delight of his eyes," will soon die. The Lord then instructs Ezekiel not to weep over his wife's death or practice any of the customary public signs of mourning. By refraining from doing so, Ezekiel will embody a grief too great for the eyes of others to behold. This overwhelming hidden sorrow will be a sign of warning to the Jewish people. They, too, will soon experience a great grief themselves when their enemies destroy the temple in Jerusalem, the delight of Israel's eyes, as God's punishment for their sins. The responsorial psalm echoes the tragic note that the Lord "was filled with loathing and anger toward his sons and daughters." In the Gospel, Jesus invites a man to seek perfection by giving up his possessions. Church tradition has regarded this passage as the basis for God's call to serve him in the religious life.

420 TUESDAY OF THE TWENTIETH WEEK OF THE YEAR

YEAR I

READING I   Judg. 6:11-24   **RESP.** Ps. 85:9, 11-12, 13-14
GOSPEL   Matthew 19:23-30

Today's first reading reveals that at this period in the thirteenth century B.C. the now settled twelve Jewish tribes found their farming threatened by the Midianites — roving bands of camel-riding nomads from the Arabian Desert. For this reason, as the passage begins we find a man named Gideon beating wheat, not on his threshing floor but in a wine press to hide it from the enemy. God then summons Gideon to assume leadership in overthrowing the Midianites and promises to help him. In response to this divine call, Gideon eventually led the

Israelites to victory. The responsorial psalm refrain accents God's desire to rescue the Jews in the words, "The Lord speaks of peace to his people." In the Gospel, Jesus warns of the danger of having too much money and then indicates the reward he will give to those who follow him at some personal cost.

YEAR II

READING I   Ezek. 28:1-10   RESP. Ps. Deut. 32:26-27, 27-28, 30, 35-36
GOSPEL   Matthew 19:23-30

The first reading is a small sample from several chapters that the prophet Ezekiel devotes to warnings against seven neighboring countries of Israel. These lands all face destruction, he says, for the harm they have done in various ways to God's chosen people. Ezekiel addresses himself in today's passage to an imaginary prince who rules over the Phoenician port city of Tyre — an important trading center in the ancient world just above Palestine. Because this prince pretends to play the part of God in his foolish pride, Ezekiel at first mocks his wisdom and riches and then predicts a violent death for him. The responsorial psalm also underscores the fate of all who rebel against God in the verse, "Close at hand is the day of their destruction." In the Gospel, Jesus warns of the danger of having too much money and then indicates the reward for those who follow him at some personal cost.

421   WEDNESDAY OF THE TWENTIETH WEEK OF THE YEAR

YEAR I

READING I   Judg. 9:6-15   RESP. Ps. 21:2-3, 4-5, 6-7
GOSPEL   Matthew 20:1-16

In today's reading, a man named Jotham tells a fable about trees, which represent the people of Shechem, a city in central Palestine. His story reveals that the Jews can find no one among even the leading citizens of Shechem to rule the city — although these citizens are the "cedars of Lebanon" that Jotham refers to at the end of the fable. Therefore, the people have to settle for Abimelech as their king. An appropriate symbol for him is the buckthorn, a shrub that people used for firewood. In this way, Jotham implies that Abimelech may kindle the fires of revolt because a king is not the kind of ruler who will best serve the people at this time. Jotham's fears were correct, since three years later the king destroyed the city in a revolution. The responsorial psalm accents Jotham's concern over the king. The Gospel parable shows how God invites the Gentiles to share in the joys of his kingdom.

READING I   Ezek. 34:1-11   RESP. Ps. 23:1-3, 3-4, 5, 6
GOSPEL   Matthew 20:1-16

Today the prophet Ezekiel compares the Jewish people to a flock of sheep, and her leaders to shepherds. Ezekiel denounces Israel's kings, priests, and prophets for acting as bad shepherds by exploiting the people to their own advantage, neglecting their duties, and even allowing the flock to wander into "the high hills," that is, religious shrines to false gods. For these failures, God will remove Israel's shepherds from office. Then the prophet points to the dawn of better days for the people because God himself will act as their shepherd — a promise that Jesus, the Good Shepherd, has fulfilled. To accent this shepherd theme, the liturgy chooses Psalm 23 — a confident prayer to "the Lord, my shepherd" — as our response to the reading. The Gospel parable refers to God's invitation to the Gentiles to share in the blessings of his kingdom, even though they come at the last hour.

422   THURSDAY OF THE TWENTIETH WEEK OF THE YEAR

READING I   Judg. 11:29-39   RESP. Ps. 40:5, 7-8, 8-9, 10
GOSPEL   Matthew 22:1-14

Today's first reading is a story with overtones from Greek tragedy. The pagan Ammonite tribes had attacked the Jews living in the rich pasture land of Gilead east of the Jordan River. The Israelites called Jephthah, once one of their tribesmen, to lead them in battle. Jephthah schemes to get God to bring him victory. He vows to offer a human sacrifice. His strange bargain dooms him in the end to honor his vow with the life of his only daughter. Scripture commentators see in this event primitive people's ideas about what God wanted from them. Our responsorial psalm recalls Jephthah's obedience to his vow. The Gospel tells how the Jews, though invited guests, refuse to enter the wedding feast of God's kingdom. The Gentiles are those whom the servants round up to bring into the feast.

READING I   Ezek. 36:23-28   RESP. Ps. 51:12-13, 14-15, 18-19
GOSPEL   Matthew 22:1-14

Today's first reading shows how particular Old Testament texts helped the apostles and writers of the Gospels to understand more clearly many events in the life of Jesus and in the early Church. Here the prophet Ezekiel reveals that God will restore to their homeland the

Jewish people then in exile in Babylon. God will give them a "new heart" and "place a new spirit" within them. Six centuries later, St. Peter recalled Ezekiel's prophecy in his first sermon moments after his overwhelming experience on Pentecost. Peter told the Jews that what they heard and saw was the outpouring of the spirit that God had promised long ago through Ezekiel. The responsorial psalm accents this theme in the verse, "A steadfast spirit renew within me." The Gospel tells how the Jews, though invited guests, refuse to enter the wedding feast of God's kingdom. The Gentiles are those whom the servants bring in later.

423 FRIDAY OF THE TWENTIETH WEEK OF THE YEAR

YEAR I

READING I   Ruth 1:1, 3-6, 14-16, 22   RESP. Ps. 146:5-6, 7, 8-9, 9-10
GOSPEL   Matthew 22:34-40

Today's reading tells the story of two heroic women who are devoted to each other — Naomi, a Jewish woman, and her daughter-in-law Ruth, a Gentile from the territory east of the Dead Sea called Moab. Their story teaches us how God protects widows and rewards those who keep faith with him. Ruth sounds the keynote to her important destiny in mankind's salvation when she expresses her wish to become a member of the Israelite community in the words, "Your people shall be my people, and your God my God." The responsorial psalm underscores the theme of the reading in the verse, "The fatherless and the widow he sustains." In the Gospel, Jesus answers in unique fashion a question about the "greatest" commandment. Unlike any rabbi before him, Christ unites into one rule of life separate texts from the Old Testament on love of God and love of neighbor.

YEAR II

READING I   Ezek. 37:1-14   RESP. Ps. 107:2-3, 4-5, 6-7, 8-9
GOSPEL   Matthew 22:34-40

The first reading describes an eerie vision that the prophet Ezekiel had of a battlefield covered with the bones of Jewish soldiers who had died defending Israel's freedom against invaders from Babylon. After the prophet breathes new life into this vast army, God interprets this vision of resurrection for Ezekiel. The bones symbolize "the whole house of Israel." God will raise Israel from the grave of its exile in Babylon and restore its members to the homeland, Palestine. This scene also sums up the mission of Ezekiel to inject new spirit into God's downhearted people through his prophetic preaching. The responsorial psalm recalls today's theme in the verse, "Those whom he has redeemed from the land of the foe" he has "gathered from the lands" of exile. In the Gospel, Jesus answers a question about the "greatest" commandment by uniting into one rule of life separate texts from the Old Testament on love of God and neighbor.

424 SATURDAY OF THE TWENTIETH WEEK OF THE YEAR

YEAR I

READING I Ruth 2:1-3, 8-11; 4:13-17   **RESP. Ps.** 128:1-2, 3, 4, 5
GOSPEL   Matthew 23:1-12

In today's first reading, we learn that God will bestow on Israel through a mixed marriage one of his choicest blessings — their shepherd-king, David. We saw yesterday how Ruth decided to return with her mother-in-law Naomi to Bethlehem at the end of a famine in that area of Palestine. Now we find Naomi's kinsman Boaz taking Ruth as his wife. Their son Obed will be one of the ancestors of King David. The responsorial psalm emphasizes this theme in the verse, "Your wife shall be like a fruitful vine in the recesses of your home." St. Matthew devotes the twenty-third chapter of his Gospel to denunciations Jesus leveled at some Scribes and Pharisees. Today we hear our Lord advise his disciples and the crowd to follow what the Pharisees teach them about God's law but not to imitate the proud and hypocritical way many of the Pharisees behaved.

YEAR II

READING I Ezek. 43:1-7   **RESP. Ps.** 85:9-10, 11-12, 13-14
GOSPEL   Matthew 23:1-12

As the first reading begins, the prophet Ezekiel has experienced another extraordinary vision, this time of the Lord's new temple in the restored land of Israel. The prophet falls to the ground awestruck as he witnesses God's glory returning to the temple. This event reminds Ezekiel of the first time he had seen God's glory when the Lord called him to be his spokesman to the Jews in exile in Babylon. In describing this vision, Ezekiel teaches the exiles that God's presence in the midst of his people will be the basis for life in their community when God restores them to their homeland. The responsorial psalm underscores the theme of God's holy presence in the refrain, "The glory of the Lord will dwell in our land." In the Gospel, Jesus advises his disciples and the crowd to follow what the Pharisees teach but not to imitate the proud and hypocritical way many of them behaved.

425 MONDAY OF THE TWENTY-FIRST WEEK OF THE YEAR

YEAR I

READING I 1 Thess. 1:2-5, 8-10   RESP. Ps. 149:1-2, 3-4, 5-6, 9
GOSPEL   Matthew 23:13-22

In the first reading we note how satisfied St. Paul was with the thriving faith, despite persecution, of the young and enthusiastic community he had founded at Thessalonica about twenty years after Christ ascended to heaven. The city was a strategically located northern Greek seaport at the point where east and west trade routes then crossed. The Holy Spirit had sent Paul to this area of Europe on his second missionary journey to help Christianity take hold in key cities there and win back for Christ a world Alexander the Great once called his own. The responsorial psalm reminds us that Paul's delight with his converts reflects the Lord's own "delight in his people." The Gospel gives three denunciations that Jesus leveled at some Scribes and Pharisees. By legalistic hair-splitting and a false show of religion, they had become false guides — even to their own converts.

YEAR II

READING I 2 Thess. 1:1-5, 11-12   RESP. Ps. 96:1-2, 2-3, 4-5
GOSPEL   Matthew 23:13-22

In today's reading, St. Paul addresses a second letter to the young and enthusiastic community he had founded in Thessalonica about twenty years after Christ ascended to heaven. This was a northern Greek seaport strategically located at the point where east and west trade routes then crossed. We note how, despite the hardships they were going through, the strong faith and sincere love of the Thessalonians provided an encouraging example to other communities of Christians. Since Paul prays that "the name of Jesus may be glorified" in their lives, the responsorial psalm echoes this idea by declaring, "Tell his glory among the nations." The Gospel gives three denunciations that Jesus leveled at many Scribes and Pharisees. By legalistic hair-splitting and a false show of religion, they had become false guides — even to their own converts.

426 TUESDAY OF THE TWENTY-FIRST WEEK OF THE YEAR

YEAR I

READING I 1 Thess. 2:1-8   RESP. Ps. 139:1-3, 4-6
GOSPEL   Matthew 23:23-26

Today's reading recalls St. Paul's visit to the Greek city of Thessalonica during his missionary journey to that part of Europe. Paul had run into such hostile audiences while preaching there that his converts had to smuggle him out of the city. Paul might have had the memory of this harrowing experience in mind when he wrote today's passage expressing how dear the community was to him. In fact, Paul uses the word "brother" more often in his two letters to the Thessalonians than in any other letter he wrote. Because Paul worked "to please God, 'the tester of our hearts,'" the responsorial psalm refrain declares, "You have searched me and you know me, Lord." In the Gospel, Jesus makes some Scribes and Pharisees the target of two more "woes" — a word that expresses our Lord's righteous anger against these blind guides, as well as his sorrow that they stubbornly refuse to admit they are wrong.

YEAR II

READING I   2 Thess. 2:1-3, 14-16   RESP. Ps. 96:10, 11-12, 13
GOSPEL   Matthew 23:23-26

Today's reading points out two areas of concern that were disturbing peace of mind in the Christian community at Thessalonica in northern Greece. Many Thessalonians believed that the final coming of Jesus was about to take place and that the final gathering of God's people for this event was also at hand. Paul tells his readers to put no stock in these rumors, no matter from what source the community has learned them. Instead, the Thessalonians should have strong faith in the teachings they received from Paul when he first preached to them and which he explained in his previous letter to the community. The theme of the Second Coming also appears in the responsorial psalm refrain, "The Lord comes to judge the earth." In the Gospel, Jesus reminds the Scribes and Pharisees of something they had forgotten — that real religion is a matter of the heart, not just an outward show of piety.

427   WEDNESDAY OF THE TWENTY-FIRST WEEK OF THE YEAR

YEAR I

READING I   1 Thess. 2:9-13   RESP. Ps. 139:7-8, 9-10, 11-12
GOSPEL   Matthew 23:27-32

Today's reading implies that St. Paul was proud that he had earned his living as a tentmaker while in Thessalonica and for this reason did not have to live off the community. This was his answer to some critics who claimed that Paul was interested in preaching solely for financial gain. He also points out how he had tried to show the same dedication to the community as a father must show to his children. Because Paul calls on God to witness "how upright, just, and irreproachable" his conduct was among the Thessalonians, the responsorial psalm underscores his words in the refrain, "You have searched me and you know me, Lord." The Gospel contains the last two denunciations Jesus directed at the Scribes and Pharisees for keeping up a show of virtue and for the way they hardened their hearts by not putting into practice what the prophets taught.

YEAR II

READING I   2 Thess. 3:6-10, 16-18   RESP. Ps. 128:1-2, 4-5
GOSPEL   Matthew 23:27-32

In today's reading, St. Paul advises the Thessalonians not to bother with those Christians who were upsetting everyone and even living off the community. Out of a false notion that Christ's Second Coming was near, they had stopped working. Paul then stresses how hard he had worked when he first came to Thessalonica because he wanted to set an example of the Christian life to everyone. Finally, we hear the apostle call attention to his signature at the end of the letter so the community will know these are really his own words. Because Paul declares that "anyone who would not work should not eat," the responsorial psalm echoes his advice by saying, "For you shall eat the fruit of your handiwork." The Gospel contains two denunciations Jesus directed at the Scribes and Pharisees for keeping up a show of virtue and for not practicing what the prophets taught.

428   THURSDAY OF THE TWENTY-FIRST WEEK OF THE YEAR

YEAR I

READING I   1 Thess. 3:7-13   RESP. Ps. 90:3-4, 12-13, 14, 17
GOSPEL   Matthew 24:42-51

As the first reading begins, St. Paul tells the Christian community in Thessalonica that he feels comforted by the report from his co-worker Timothy that his converts in that city have a strong faith. This welcome news strengthens Paul to bear the slanders of his enemies while he is visiting the city of Corinth. He longs for another opportunity to visit his dear friends in Thessalonica, and he asks God to work something out for him so he can return. Paul's request that God may "make you overflow with love for one another" is the focus of the responsorial psalm refrain, "Fill us with your love, O Lord." In the Gospel, Jesus reminds us not to let death catch us unprepared because the Lord may call us in the middle of work, while we're asleep — or whenever we least expect it. We will be ready if we try each day to do *everything* the way we know God expects us to.

READING I 1 Cor. 1:1-9 RESP. Ps. 145:2-3, 4-5, 6-7
GOSPEL Matthew 24:42-51

In today's reading, we begin the first letter that St. Paul wrote some-time between the years 55 and 57 to the Christians living in the seaport of Corinth, a key trading center then in southern Greece. Nearly five years before, Paul had worked in the city for about eighteen months during his second missionary journey. Now the apostle has learned that dissensions and a lack of unity are troubling the Church. Paul seems to have these problems in mind in today's passage. We hear him stress the favors the Corinthians have received from God that should unite them in the fellowship of the Lord and inspire them to seek holiness. Since Paul "continually thanks God" for the Lord's good-ness to the community, the responsorial psalm also declares, "Every day will I bless you." In the Gospel, Jesus reminds us not to let death catch us unprepared because the Lord may call us when we least expect it.

429 FRIDAY OF THE TWENTY-FIRST WEEK OF THE YEAR

YEAR I

READING I 1 Thess. 4:1-8 RESP. Ps. 97:1, 2, 5-6, 10, 11-12
GOSPEL Matthew 25:1-13

In the first reading, St. Paul gives a Christian answer to the rampant sexual immorality of his day, as well as of our times. Paul realizes that his converts had newly come from a pagan society that accepted extra-marital affairs and other forms of sexual license as normal and inevit-able. He bases his argument for a responsible attitude toward sex first on God's summons for men to live pure lives because this is God's will for their happiness. Second, Paul recalls that the indwelling presence of the Holy Spirit in our hearts makes us holy to the very core of our being. Hence we must respect everyone because each human body can become a temple of God. The responsorial psalm reminds us of God's call to holiness. The Gospel parable warns us that if we need to reform our lives we had better do so before it's too late.

YEAR II

READING I 1 Cor. 1:17-25 RESP. Ps. 33:1-2, 4-5, 10, 11
GOSPEL Matthew 25:1-13

In today's reading, St. Paul emphasizes that men learn the real secret of wisdom when they humbly believe that Jesus Christ — "the wisdom of God" — has died for their sins and then build their lives around him. This is the powerful message of the cross that fills all of Paul's preaching, not the mere philosophical speculations about abstract wisdom that occupied the attention of Greek scholars and wise men of his day. The apostle readily admits that God's plan to save the world sounds foolish to many people, especially the Jews who reject a Messiah who suffers and the Greeks who ridicule a God who dies. Nevertheless, Paul continues to preach "Christ crucified." The responsorial psalm highlights "the plan of the Lord" for man's salvation which "stands forever." The Gospel parable warns us that if we need to reform our lives, we had better do so before it's too late.

430   SATURDAY OF THE TWENTY-FIRST WEEK OF THE YEAR

YEAR I

READING I   1 Thess. 4:9-12   RESP. Ps. 98:1, 7-8, 9
GOSPEL   Matthew 25:14-30

In today's reading, St. Paul recalls how he had instructed the Thessalonians to live in such a way that others might develop a respect for the Christian way of life. Some Scripture commentators believe that Paul's advice, "Work with your hands as we directed you to do," may imply that some members of the community had a false idea that the Second Coming of Christ was near at hand, so they gave up their jobs. Today's liturgy seems to apply to this theme because the responsorial psalm looks ahead to the Second Coming in the refrain, "The Lord comes to rule the world with justice." In the Gospel, Jesus aims a parable at the Jewish people's spiritual leaders to whom God had given the responsibility of leading men into the kingdom. God will expect much from those to whom he has entrusted such demanding tasks — especially those who lead his Church today.

YEAR II

READING I   1 Cor. 1:26-31   RESP. Ps. 33:12-13, 18-19, 20-21
GOSPEL   Matthew 25:14-30

In today's first reading, we discover once again the mainspring of St. Paul's teaching about how men find salvation. This time in a context of wisdom, Paul stresses his basic insight that the call to faith depends on the merciful goodness of God and not anything that a man can boast about as deserving of that gift — whether it be intelligence, influence, or nobility. The apostle insists that when we follow Jesus we attain real wisdom because everything the human heart longs for we can find in him — and only in him. Because Paul begins by reminding the Christians at Corinth that "you are among those called," the responsorial psalm accents this theme in the refrain, "Happy the people the Lord has chosen to be his own." In the Gospel, Jesus aims a parable at the Jewish people's spiritual leaders to whom he has given the responsibility of leading men into God's kingdom.

431 MONDAY OF THE TWENTY-SECOND WEEK OF THE YEAR

YEAR I

READING I   1 Thess. 4:13-18   RESP. Ps. 96:1, 3, 4-5, 11-12, 13
GOSPEL   Luke 4:16-30

In the first reading, we learn that some members of the community at Thessalonica were worried that their friends who had already died would not share in the final coming of Jesus. St. Paul explains that the life a Christian enjoys with the risen Jesus on earth continues even in death. For this reason, Paul teaches, the dead will be present with Christ when he comes to take into heaven those still alive at the end of time. Paul urges the Thessalonians to comfort one another with this hope so that despair will not trouble their hearts as it did the pagans. The responsorial psalm accents the Second Coming in the refrain, "The Lord comes to judge the earth." In the Gospel, we begin St. Luke's account of the public ministry of Jesus. Our Lord reveals that he has come to fulfill all that the prophet Isaiah said the Messiah would do.

YEAR II

READING I   1 Cor. 2:1-5   RESP. Ps. 119:97, 98, 99, 100, 101, 102
GOSPEL   Luke 4:16-30

The first Scripture readings for the Masses this week are from a section on the meaning of Christian wisdom in St. Paul's first letter to the Corinthians. In today's passage, Paul reminds his converts of the time when he first preached to them. His words had the conviction and power of the Holy Spirit and not the tones of clever philosophy or oratory. Here, as on other occasions, Paul emphasizes that God reveals his wisdom and power to save men from their sins through Jesus crucified. The responsorial psalm also accents this theme that true wisdom and understanding come from God and not the words of men. From now until the season of Advent, the Gospel readings are from St. Luke. Today's passage describes the beginning of our Lord's public ministry in Galilee. Jesus reveals that he is the servant that God promised will set free the captive hearts of men.

432 TUESDAY OF THE TWENTY-SECOND WEEK OF THE YEAR

YEAR I

READING I   1 Thess. 5:1-6, 9-11   RESP. Ps. 27:1, 4, 13-14
GOSPEL   Luke 4:31-37

In the first reading, St. Paul says that "the day of the Lord is coming like a thief in the night." This expression "the day of the Lord" appears frequently in the Old Testament to describe a time when the world would disappear and a new age come into existence. This "day" would come without warning when the world would be shaken to its foundations and men face their judgment before God. As Paul does in this passage, the New Testament saw this day fulfilled in the final coming of Jesus. Paul says that the Thessalonians will be ready for this "day" if they live in the light of a faithful Christian life. The responsorial psalm refrain expresses our deep longing for our final union with Jesus "in the land of the living." The Gospel gives St. Luke's first story involving demonic possession. It reveals Jesus working "with authority and power."

YEAR II

READING I   1 Cor. 2:10-16   RESP. Ps. 145:8-9, 10-11, 12-13, 13-14
GOSPEL   Luke 4:31-37

In today's first reading, St. Paul describes how the Holy Spirit works in the heart of a Christian. Paul points out that the Holy Spirit reveals all of God's deepest secrets and teaches us about the wonderful gifts of grace. As a result, the spiritual person has an insight into everything in life that baffles the man of the world. Because the reading tells of the Holy Spirit's power at work in us, the responsorial psalm accents this theme by saying that God has "made known to men his might and the glorious splendor of his kingdom." In the Gospel, we see Jesus at the beginning of his ministry in Galilee, healing a man with an unclean spirit. Since even a demon can profess faith in Jesus as the Messiah, we realize that it is not enough for us simply to believe in our Lord. We must back up our faith with a life that is pleasing to God.

433   WEDNESDAY OF THE TWENTY-SECOND WEEK OF THE YEAR

YEAR I

READING I   Col. 1:1-8   RESP. Ps. 52:10, 11
GOSPEL   Luke 4:38-44

Today we begin a letter St. Paul wrote while a prisoner in Rome to the Christians in the small town of Colossae in what is now western Turkey. Paul gives "thanks to God" for sending the gift of faith to the Colossians and inspiring them to share their love with one another. Since Paul had never visited the town himself, he mentions his friend Epaphras, also under arrest with Paul, who was the one who brought the faith to Colossae — a faith that false teachers now threaten. The responsorial psalm underscores Paul's gratitude in the verse, "I will thank you always for what you have done." In the Gospel, Jesus cures Simon Peter's mother-in-law, as well as many other sick people. Our Lord then declares that his mission is to "announce the good news of the reign of God."

READING I 1 Cor. 3:1-9   RESP. Ps. 33:12-13, 14-15, 20-21
GOSPEL   Luke 4:38-44

Today St. Paul tells the Christians at Corinth in plain language that they are acting like babies by quarreling with one another and splitting the community into rival parties — some following Paul, others a man named Apollos. Because they are so spiritually immature, Paul cannot help them advance in the Christian life. The apostle then reminds the community that both he and Apollos are really just instruments God works with in building up the Church at Corinth. New Testament writers often use this image of a building to describe the Church as a united community whose members depend on one another like the integrated parts of a building. The responsorial psalm refrain accents this theme by portraying the Church as "the people the Lord has chosen to be his own." In the Gospel, Jesus lays his hands on the sick to demonstrate his concern for each one's sufferings.

434 THURSDAY OF THE TWENTY-SECOND WEEK OF THE YEAR

YEAR I

READING I Col. 1:9-14   RESP. Ps. 98:2-3, 3-4, 5-6
GOSPEL   Luke 5:1-11

Today's first reading allows us to have a brief look into St. Paul's prayer life as he writes from imprisonment in Rome. We note how the Colossians have been on his mind, rather than his own problems. Paul prays that they will always be sensitive to what God wants them to do in their lives. In this way the Colossians will know how to apply their faith in practical ways to help others grow in the spiritual life, too. Paul also prays that the Colossians may move ahead in their Christian life no matter what trials come along. Because Paul reminds them how in baptism God had given them salvation by rescuing them "from the power of darkness," the responsorial psalm appropriately declares, "The Lord has made his salvation known." In the Gospel, we hear Christ's call to the first apostles. The large catch of fish symbolizes the apostles' missionary vocation to become fishers of men.

YEAR II

READING I 1 Cor. 3:18-23   RESP. Ps. 24:1-2, 3-4, 5-6
GOSPEL   Luke 5:1-11

In the first reading, St. Paul continues to teach the Christians in the Greek city of Corinth about real wisdom. Paul warns them not to let worldly knowledge become an obstacle to knowledge of God. He supports his point by quoting from the Book of Job and one of the psalms. The apostle then reminds the Corinthians that God has given them everything, and they now belong to God through Christ. The responsorial psalm highlights this theme by declaring that "the earth and all that fills it" belong to the Lord. In the Gospel, Jesus selects his first apostles from a group of fishermen in Galilee. Their catch of fish symbolizes the task of bringing all men into God's kingdom that the apostles and their successors will assume. We also note how Jesus designated Peter — from the very first moment of his vocation — as the one responsible for the Church's mission to the world.

435   FRIDAY OF THE TWENTY-SECOND WEEK OF THE YEAR

YEAR I

READING I   Col. 1:15-20   RESP. Ps. 100:1, 2, 3, 4, 5
GOSPEL   Luke 5:33-39

In today's first reading, we find one of St. Paul's most powerful statements about Christ as the creator of the world and founder of the Church. Paul has apparently adapted an early hymn about Christ to teach the Colossians that, no matter what false teachers might tell them, Jesus is the unique Lord and center of the universe, who has existed since before the beginning of the world. Paul's doctrine in earlier letters about the Body of Christ reaches a climax here in the idea of Jesus as Head of the Church — its source of authority and power. The responsorial psalm highlights the theme of Christ as creator, in the verse, "He made us, his we are." The Gospel illustrates with two parables of Jesus the difference between the old spirit of the Jewish religion and our Lord's new outlook. Only St. Luke notes our Lord's sadness that most people prefer the wine of the old ways.

YEAR II

READING I   1 Cor. 4:1-5   RESP. Ps. 37:3-4, 5-6, 27-28, 39-40
GOSPEL   Luke 5:33-39

In the first reading, St. Paul appears to address certain individuals in the Christian community at Corinth who had apparently made unfair judgments about his work. As the passage begins, you will hear Paul explaining the true role of an apostle in the community. An apostle is the servant of others and answerable only to God. What the true apostle thinks of himself or what others think about him does not really matter. The responsorial psalm accents the theme that as far as salvation is concerned, each person has to answer to God alone. In the Gospel, St. Luke tells of a discussion Jesus had with the Scribes and Pharisees about fasting. Our Lord's parable of the wine skins suggests that the

Jews cannot appreciate the new wine of his teaching because they are used to the old wine of their traditions.

436 SATURDAY OF THE TWENTY-SECOND WEEK OF THE YEAR

YEAR I

READING I   Col. 1:21-23   RESP. Ps. 54:3-4, 6, 8
GOSPEL   Luke 6:1-5

The first reading sketches the role the Christians in Colossae played in the drama of salvation. St. Paul assures them that now they are God's friends because Christ has died for them. In response, the Colossians must be loyal to their Christian ideals and persevere no matter what happens. By this time, the appeal of Christianity had reached out to embrace all the great cities of the Roman empire. Paul's awareness of the role he has played in this success as God's servant fills him with joy. Because Paul declares that "Christ has achieved reconciliation for us," the responsorial psalm refrain affirms that "God himself is my help." The Gospel reveals that in the opinion of the Pharisees the disciples of Jesus — by picking grain and eating the kernels — were performing farm work that the Sabbath law forbade.

YEAR II

READING I   1 Cor. 4:6-15   RESP. Ps. 145:17-18, 19-20, 21
GOSPEL   Luke 6:1-5

In the first Scripture reading, St. Paul describes the humiliations that the apostles suffered in preaching the Good News. Paul refers to the familiar scene of the cruel games in the Roman arena. Criminals condemned to die had to stand in line exposed to the mockery and ridicule of the spectators. In much the same way, the apostles had to bear the world's rejection. Paul then draws a contrast between the sufferings the apostles endured and the selfish lives some Christians lived in the community at Corinth. The responsorial psalm also treats this theme of persecution. We pray that the Lord may be near all who call upon him in their trials. In the Gospel, the Pharisees judge that the disciples of Jesus, by picking and eating grain as they walked through a field, are guilty of breaking the law that prohibited harvesting crops on the Sabbath.

437 MONDAY OF THE TWENTY-THIRD WEEK OF THE YEAR

YEAR I

READING I   Col. 1:24—2:3   RESP. Ps. 62:6-7, 9
GOSPEL   Luke 6:6-11

Today we continue St. Paul's letter to the community at Colossae, a small town in what is now western Turkey. We hear Paul talk about the "mystery" — his favorite word for describing God's secret plan to offer salvation to all men. We then discover that the deep force of Christ's love at work in the apostle's heart inspired him to suffer all his hardships as a prisoner in Rome for the benefit of people he had never seen — such as the Colossians themselves and also the Laodiceans, who lived in a city near Colossae. Because Paul says that Christ is "your hope," the responsorial psalm also reminds us, "For from God comes my hope." In the Gospel, St. Luke alone adds the detail that Jesus could read the minds of the Pharisees who were "on the watch" for any violations of the Sabbath by him. Our hearts, too, are always open to the loving gaze of Christ.

YEAR II

READING I   1 Cor. 5:1-8   RESP. Ps. 5:5-6, 7, 12
GOSPEL   Luke 6:6-11

In today's first Scripture reading, St. Paul discusses a case of incest in the Christian community at Corinth. He commands in the name of the Church that the community exclude the sinner because he has impaired its holiness. The Jews were quite familiar with excommunication. Its purpose was always to persuade the sinner to be sorry for his sins. Paul then uses the example of yeast working in dough to teach how the corruptive power of evil works in the human heart. The responsorial psalm after this reading also emphasizes the theme that God rejects the wicked. In the Gospel, Jesus heals a man with a crippled hand on the Sabbath. This incident angers the Pharisees and they begin to plan how to put Jesus to death. Many Jewish religious leaders had become so preoccupied with their ritual laws that they could not recognize Jesus as the Messiah from his good works.

438   TUESDAY OF THE TWENTY-THIRD WEEK OF THE YEAR

YEAR I

READING I   Col. 2:6-15   RESP. Ps. 145:1-2, 8-9, 10-11
GOSPEL   Luke 6:12-19

In the first reading, Paul refutes the claim of false teachers that "cosmic powers" rule the universe. He suggests that Jesus, after the victory of his resurrection, paraded these powers around in shame as a Roman general would lead his captives after a military victory. Paul's idea that God "cancelled the bond that stood against us with all its claims" is like saying today that Jesus tore up every IOU his brothers and sisters owed him when he died for us. The responsorial psalm stresses God's compassion "to all his creatures" by pardoning them from sin. In the Gospel, St. Luke shows how important was our Lord's choice of the twelve apostles by telling how Jesus prepared for this by a night he spent in prayer. In the four lists of the apostles in the New Testament, no two agree on the exact order, but Peter's name always appears first.

YEAR II

READING I   1 Cor. 6:1-11   RESP. Ps. 149:1-2, 3-4, 5-6, 9
GOSPEL   Luke 6:12-19

In the first reading, St. Paul writes to the Church in Corinth about the question of Christians going before the pagan courts in lawsuits against one another. He insists that Christians should not bring each other before these courts about grievances over everyday matters. Paul then asks that the Corinthians patiently bear injustices as Jesus had counseled and refrain from inflicting injury on their fellow Christians. He reminds them that by receiving baptism they have committed themselves to a different way of life from the pagans. The responsorial psalm after this reading invites us to praise the Lord because of his great love for us. In the Gospel, following a night spent in prayer to his Father, Jesus chooses twelve men to be his apostles — a word that St. Luke always uses to show that these men are the leaders of the Church.

439   WEDNESDAY OF THE TWENTY-THIRD WEEK OF THE YEAR

YEAR I

READING I   Col. 3:1-11   RESP. Ps. 145:2-3, 10-11, 12-13
GOSPEL   Luke 6:20-26

In the first reading, St. Paul reminds the Colossians to make the ideals of Jesus their one all-absorbing interest so they can say that Christ is their "life" and really mean it. The apostle translates this ideal into daily practice by sketching those sinful attitudes the Colossians must shed like "the old self" they put aside in receiving baptism. When people become members of the Body of Christ, Paul teaches, then the natural boundaries of race, nationality, and state in life disappear, and all become brothers and sisters of Jesus. Since Paul refers to Jesus "seated at God's right hand," the responsorial psalm confirms this sign of his authority by declaring, "Your dominion endures through all generations." In the Gospel, after teaching the Beatitudes, Jesus gives a series of warnings that a man will not find true happiness in life if he follows paths of selfishness.

YEAR II

READING I   1 Cor. 7:25-31   RESP. Ps. 45:11-12, 14-15, 16-17
GOSPEL   Luke 6:20-26

In today's first Scripture reading, St. Paul discusses questions about the single state of life and the married. He suggests that since time is passing on toward the Second Coming of the Lord, it seems better for everyone to remain in his present state, whether single or married. But Paul teaches that a virgin who marries does not commit sin. He stresses this to correct the error of certain heretics who claimed that marriage was evil. Paul's principal message is that a Christian must keep himself detached from the world. The responsorial psalm also relates to this theme of virginity and marriage. We will pray several verses from Psalm 45 that show us a young woman preparing for her wedding. In the Gospel, Jesus teaches the Beatitudes to his disciples and then gives a series of warnings to those who live selfish lives.

440 THURSDAY OF THE TWENTY-THIRD WEEK OF THE YEAR

YEAR I

READING I   Col. 3:12-17   RESP. Ps. 150:1-2, 3-4, 5-6
GOSPEL   Luke 6:27-38

Today we hear St. Paul remind the Colossians that since they are "God's chosen ones," they must reflect his love in their lives when dealing with one another. Paul then describes those virtues that will help the members of the community to grow into true human maturity. The apostle also stresses the important place that gratitude has in the life of a Christian. The liturgy chooses a responsorial psalm that proclaims God's praise through various musical instruments and dancing. In this way, we fulfill Paul's request that we sing to God "in psalms, hymns, and inspired songs." In St. Luke's account of the Sermon on the Mount, Jesus gives an instruction on love of enemies — his revolutionary teaching that so many of us find difficult to live in practice.

YEAR II

READING I   1 Cor. 8:1-7, 11-13   RESP. Ps. 139:1-3, 13-14, 23-24
GOSPEL   Luke 6:27-38

Today's first Scripture reading treats the question of Christians eating meat that pagan priests have offered to idols in religious ceremonies. The priests first used the meat in these sacrifices, and then vendors sold it in public markets. The pagan Romans often served this meat to their Christian friends when they came to dinner. Some Christians began to develop an uneasy conscience about eating this sacrificial meat because the practice implied that they were taking part in the pagan sacrifices. Paul concludes that a Christian must be careful about doing things that will scandalize his more scrupulous brothers. Since in the reading Paul says that "if anyone loves God, that man is known by him," our response to this passage includes several verses from

Psalm 139 relating to that theme. In the Gospel, Jesus teaches his disciples that they must love their enemies.

441   FRIDAY OF THE TWENTY-THIRD WEEK OF THE YEAR

YEAR I
READING I   1 Tim. 1:1-2, 12-14   **RESP. Ps.** 16:1-2, 5, 7-8, 11
GOSPEL   Luke 6:39-42

Today's first Scripture reading begins a personal letter Paul wrote to Timothy, who joined the apostle during his second missionary journey to the Gentiles about the year 49 and became a devoted co-worker. This letter, another one to Timothy, and one to Titus, another convert who helped Paul, make up what we call the Pastoral Letters. They concern the care that Church leaders must give to our Lord's flock. Paul reminds Timothy, his "own true child in faith," how merciful God was to forgive Paul for persecuting the Church and then to call him to be an apostle. The responsorial psalm echoes several references Paul makes to Christ as "our Lord" in the verse, "I say to the Lord, 'My Lord are you.' " In the Gospel, by an association of ideas, St. Luke joins our Lord's saying on the blind leading the blind with a saying on judging others that also refers to the eyes.

YEAR II
READING I   1 Cor. 9:16-19, 22-27   **RESP. Ps.** 84:3, 4, 5-6, 8, 12
GOSPEL   Luke 6:39-42

In today's first Scripture reading, St. Paul tells the Christian community at Corinth that he regards his preaching of the Gospel as evidence of God's power at work in his life. He explains how he has tried to adapt his ministry to all types of people in order to convert as many as possible to the Lord. Finally, Paul uses two comparisons from sports to illustrate the struggle that a Christian must undergo to save his soul. Paul refers to "a crown that is imperishable" as a symbol for our heavenly goal. The responsorial psalm refrain also directs our hearts to heaven as we pray, "How lovely is your dwelling-place, Lord." In the Gospel, Jesus reminds his followers to correct their own faults before criticizing the faults of others. *Our* faults, even when serious, are harder to admit because they demand that we really be honest with ourselves.

442   SATURDAY OF THE TWENTY-THIRD WEEK OF THE YEAR

YEAR I
READING I   1 Tim. 1:15-17   **RESP. Ps.** 113:1-2, 3-4, 5, 6-7
GOSPEL   Luke 6:43-49

In today's reading, we hear St. Paul remind his co-worker Timothy that "Christ Jesus came into the world to save sinners," and Paul assures him, "You can depend on this." On two other occasions in his letters, Paul uses this formula when he talks about our Lord's role as savior in a context of hope for the Christian community. For this reason, the apostle goes on to explain that anyone can find an encouraging example of God's patience with sinners by looking at Paul's own life before his conversion, when he was actually guilty of persecuting Christ. The responsorial psalm echoes Paul's concluding praise of Jesus by declaring in the refrain, "Blessed be the name of the Lord forever." In the Gospel, Jesus warns his disciples that only by living good lives can they hope to produce good results in God's vineyard and be able to stand firm in times of trial.

YEAR II

READING I   1 Cor. 10:14-22   RESP. Ps. 116:12-13, 17-18
GOSPEL   Luke 6:43-49

In the first reading, St. Paul continues to discuss the problem of Christians eating meat used in sacrifices to pagan gods. His theme today is the danger of idolatry. Paul reminds the community what happened to the Jews in the past when many fell into pagan worship. The apostle teaches that the Eucharist unites the faithful to Christ and to one another. For that reason the Corinthians cannot share in the Eucharist if they are taking part in the sacrificial meals of the pagans. Because the reading refers to sacrifices and "the cup of the Lord," the responsorial psalm also includes verses on these themes. In the Gospel, Jesus reminds us that we must prove our love by actions and not just words if we wish to follow him with a sincere heart. In this way, we build a solid seawall to withstand the storms in our spiritual life.

443   MONDAY OF THE TWENTY-FOURTH WEEK OF THE YEAR

YEAR I

READING I   1 Tim. 2:1-8   RESP. Ps. 28:2, 7, 8-9
GOSPEL   Luke 7:1-10

Today's first reading echoes a note that sounds again and again in the New Testament — that God places no limits on his offer of salvation. First, Paul urges his co-worker Timothy to pray for all men, but especially for those in authority. This request follows logically — as Paul shows — from God's desire that all men receive the grace of salvation because his own Son died to ransom them all from the slavery of sin. The responsorial psalm directs our attention again to the themes of prayer and salvation. In the Gospel, we learn how the deep faith of a Roman centurion wins our Lord's cure of his dying servant. In Luke's version here, the centurion approaches Jesus through "some Jewish elders," while in Matthew's account he meets our Lord on his own.

YEAR II

READING I 1 Cor. 11:17-26, 33   RESP. Ps. 40:7-8, 8-9, 10, 17
GOSPEL   Luke 7:1-10

In the first Scripture reading, St. Paul writes about the proper way to celebrate the Eucharist in the setting of the brotherly meal we call the Lord's Supper. Unfortunately, because disagreements had arisen among the Christians at Corinth, serious abuses of charity in celebrating this Supper had hurt the community. You will hear Paul strongly condemn these abuses. Then he reminds the Corinthians that they should regard the Eucharist as a sacrament of brotherly love. This passage probably contains the earliest record we have in the New Testament of how Jesus instituted the Eucharist. The responsorial psalm refrain repeats Paul's reminder that at each Mass we "proclaim the death of the Lord until he comes again." In the Gospel, we learn that Jesus saves the life of a centurion's servant because the soldier has such great faith in our Lord.

444 TUESDAY OF THE TWENTY-FOURTH WEEK OF THE YEAR

YEAR I

READING I 1 Tim. 3:1-13   RESP. Ps. 101:1-2, 2-3, 5, 6
GOSPEL   Luke 7:11-17

Today's first reading points out the kind of life bishops and deacons should be leading as they serve their brothers and sisters in the early Church. However, the terms "bishop" and "deacon" that Paul uses here are not exactly what we mean by them today. This passage reveals that a married clergy existed then and shows that Christian women worked together with the deacons in serving the community. The responsorial psalm was originally the prayer of a Jewish king testifying to his desire to walk worthily in the service of God. This psalm thus fits in with the theme of the reading. In the Gospel, the tears of a widowed mother move Jesus to restore her son to life — a miracle that only St. Luke tells us about. His is the Gospel that emphasizes the deep feeling Jesus always had for people in distress.

YEAR II

READING I 1 Cor. 12:12-14, 27-31   RESP. Ps. 100:1-2, 3, 4, 5
GOSPEL   Luke 7:11-17

In the first reading, St. Paul compares the oneness of the human body, despite its many parts, with the oneness of the Church, despite its many members. Paul declares that Christ mysteriously identifies the Church with his own body. When we receive baptism, God adopts us as his children in Christ. In the final part of this passage, you will hear Paul describing the various classes of people who make up the Christian community, and the special gift of each one. The responsorial psalm refrain relates to Paul's theme that we enjoy oneness with Christ. The psalm reminds us that "we are his people: the sheep of his flock." In the Gospel, the tears of a widowed mother move Jesus to restore her son to life. The people respond by proclaiming Jesus a prophet. This shows how Jesus fulfilled Moses' promise that God would later send another prophet like himself.

445 WEDNESDAY OF THE TWENTY-FOURTH WEEK OF THE YEAR

YEAR I

READING I   1 Tim. 3:14-16   RESP. Ps. 111:1-2, 3-4, 5-6
GOSPEL   Luke 7:31-35

The first Scripture reading reveals the pastoral concern St. Paul had for his friend Timothy, whom he had placed in charge of the Church at Ephesus in what is now western Turkey. We hear Paul praising the "mystery of our faith" — that is, God's plan for the salvation of all men that he revealed in Christ. Paul then quotes a text from a hymn that people sang in church which extols Jesus reigning in his glory in heaven. The responsorial psalm picks out several themes of this hymn in such verses as, "Majesty and glory are his work." In the Gospel, Jesus tells a parable that suggests the Pharisees act no better than spoiled children in the city squares who always want to play games *their* way. John the Baptist and Jesus upset the Jewish leaders by not playing their games of self-indulgence and looking down on sinners.

YEAR II

READING I   1 Cor. 12:31—13:13   RESP. Ps. 33:2-3, 4-5, 12, 22
GOSPEL   Luke 7:31-35

Of all St. Paul's writings, none is more famous than the passage in today's first reading. It is a brilliant hymn to the virtue of love. Paul begins by pointing out that unless we have love in our hearts, nothing else we do really matters. The apostle then describes the qualities of this self-giving love. All other gifts that a man enjoys on earth will pass away at his death, Paul says, except his ability to love. The apostle's closing statement about faith, hope, and love finds an echo in the responsorial psalm verse, "May your kindness, O Lord, be upon us who have put our hope in you." In the Gospel, Jesus tells a parable which suggests that some Pharisees act no better than spoiled children in the city squares. They always want to play games *their* way. John the Baptist and Jesus upset these Pharisees by not playing their games of selfish living and looking down on sinners.

446 THURSDAY OF THE TWENTY-FOURTH WEEK OF THE YEAR

YEAR I

READING I   1 Tim. 4:12-16   RESP. Ps. 111:7-8, 9, 10
GOSPEL   Luke 7:36-50

In today's first Scripture reading, St. Paul advises Timothy to refute by his exemplary conduct and dedication any who might criticize him as bishop of Ephesus simply because he looked too young for the assignment. We hear Paul mention how Timothy received the grace of ordination when the Church leaders "laid their hands" on him — as bishops do in conferring the sacrament of holy orders to this very day. The responsorial psalm centers on this theme, as well as on two key virtues of a good priest, in the verse, "The works of his hands are faithful and just." The Gospel tells how a sinful woman — most likely a prostitute — anointed our Lord's feet with perfumed oil. The story reveals Jesus as St. Luke knew him — the friend of sinners.

YEAR II

READING I   1 Cor. 15:1-11   RESP. Ps. 118:1-2, 16-17, 28
GOSPEL   Luke 7:36-50

The first reading contains the earliest discussion in the New Testament about the resurrection of the dead. St. Paul writes to answer critics who had questioned Christian teaching about the risen body. Because this belief rests on the certainty that Jesus rose from the dead and appeared afterwards in his risen body, Paul begins by bearing witness to the resurrection. He shows that the risen Christ is the central figure in the preaching of the apostles. We learn about several appearances of our Lord after his resurrection that the Gospels do not mention. The responsorial psalm accents this resurrection theme in the verse, "I shall not die but live." In the Gospel, Jesus forgives the sins of a penitent woman. The discourteous Pharisee we meet here is one more example of a person who thinks he is better than others, yet fails to realize how sinful his own life really is.

183

YEAR I

READING I   1 Tim. 6:2-12   RESP. Ps. 49:6-7, 8-10, 17-18, 19-20
GOSPEL   Luke 8:1-3

In today's first reading, St. Paul instructs Timothy to continue teaching the sound principles that Jesus gave them for a happy life. At the same time, he warns his fellow-worker in God's vineyard that he will meet false teachers who are interested only in building up their egos and making a profit out of religion. This point leads Paul into reflections on the danger of getting too absorbed in making money. To highlight this theme, the liturgy chooses for the responsorial psalm a wisdom verse which warns that when a rich man dies "his wealth shall not follow him down." In the Gospel, St. Luke alone tells us about a small but devoted group of women who accompanied Jesus as he journeyed through the towns and villages of Galilee. Loyal to the very end, they shared our Lord's final hours on Calvary, assisted in his burial, and gave witness to his resurrection.

YEAR II

READING I   1 Cor. 15:12-20   RESP. Ps. 17:1, 6-7, 8, 15
GOSPEL   Luke 8:1-3

Today St. Paul meets head-on the objections of his opponents in the community at Corinth who denied that the body can rise after death. Paul insists that if there is no such thing as the resurrection of the body, then Christ cannot have risen from the dead either. The apostle goes on to show the disastrous effects on the lives of all believers if Christ has not indeed risen. Paul concludes by proclaiming that the risen Christ will one day call us from the sleep of death to eternal life with him. The responsorial psalm turns our hearts to that day of final resurrection as we tell our Lord, "When your glory appears, my joy will be full." In the Gospel, St. Luke alone relates how a small but devoted group of women accompanied Jesus as he journeyed through Galilee. They shared his final hours on Calvary, assisted in his burial, and gave witness to his resurrection.

YEAR I

READING I   1 Tim. 6:13-16   RESP. Ps. 100:2, 3, 4, 5
GOSPEL   Luke 8:4-15

In today's first reading, St. Paul closes his letter to his co-worker Timothy by challenging him to remain faithful to all the teachings he has received. As an example for Timothy to follow, Paul refers to the occasion before Pontius Pilate when Jesus declared that he was a king and had a mission to bear witness to the truth. In the same way, Timothy must bear witness to the truth of the Christian religion until the day when Christ returns. The responsorial psalm is a prayer of praise that accents the praise Paul gives to Jesus at the end of the reading. In the Gospel, Jesus tells the parable of the sower and the seed and then explains to his disciples what it means.

YEAR II

READING I   1 Cor. 15:35-37, 42-49   RESP. Ps. 56:10-12, 13-14
GOSPEL   Luke 8:4-15

In the first reading, St. Paul discusses the question of the kind of bodies people will have when they rise to eternal life. Paul declares that we find an approach to that mystery by observing how a plant grows from a seed. In the same way, he says, God will bring to full spiritual bloom in heaven the seeds of our earthly bodies that we leave here when we die. Paul shows how our spiritual body in heaven will differ from the natural body we have now. Finally, the apostle teaches that we who have a body like Adam's will one day possess glorified bodies like the one Jesus has. This is possible because we share our Lord's divine life. The responsorial psalm accents this theme of resurrection by reminding us that God will rescue us from death, and we will then walk in his presence. The Gospel parable of the sower and the seed recalls Paul's image of the body as a seed.

449   MONDAY OF THE TWENTY-FIFTH WEEK OF THE YEAR

YEAR I

READING I   Ezra 1:1-6   RESP. Ps. 126:1-2, 2-3, 4-5, 6
GOSPEL   Luke 8:16-18

In today's reading, as we lift the curtain on the history of the Jewish people in the sixth century B.C., the Israelites have lived away from their homeland for fifty years as captives in Babylon. Then Cyrus the Great, a man of religious tolerance, conquered Babylon in 539 B.C., and shortly afterwards he issued the edict we hear about in the reading. The exiles could return if they wished and begin the task of rebuilding their homes and the temple, but not all of the now prospering Jews in Babylon wanted to get involved in such a risky venture. As a result, those who first returned were probably few, so that the process of immigration stretched out over several generations. The responsorial psalm refers to this return of "the captives of Zion." In the Gospel,

Jesus tells the crowds that they must radiate to others the light of the truths he has taught them in his parables.

YEAR II

READING I   Prov. 3:27-34   RESP. Ps. 15:2-3, 3-4, 5
GOSPEL   Luke 8:16-18

In the first Scripture reading, we begin a collection of wise sayings about life attributed to the Jewish king Solomon and called the Book of Proverbs. Since the primary purpose of this work of the Old Testament was to teach wisdom, it addressed itself particularly to the young and inexperienced. The wisdom this book teaches covers a wide field of human and divine activity. Today's selection teaches the proper attitudes that a good-living man should have toward his fellowman. The responsorial psalm verses also describe the virtues of a just man. In the Gospel, Jesus tells the parable of the lamp. He then invites the crowds to listen more attentively to the word of God he is proclaiming to them and accept it more generously. In this way, the truths Jesus declares will inspire the people to share what they hear with others.

450   TUESDAY OF THE TWENTY-FIFTH WEEK OF THE YEAR

YEAR I

READING I   Ezra 6:7-8, 12, 14-20   RESP. Ps. 122:1-2, 3-4, 4-5
GOSPEL   Luke 8:19-21

Today's first Scripture reading tells how the Jews who had come back from Babylonia began in 539 B.C. to build a new house of worship on the ruins of Solomon's magnificent temple. The Israelites soon ran into opposition from their neighbors, who did not welcome the return of the exiles. But we learn today that the Persian King Darius I reaffirmed the edict of his predecessor by allowing the Jews to finish their temple. The passage concludes with a description of the ceremony on the day in 515 B.C. when the Jews dedicated their new house of worship. The responsorial psalm was one that the Jews sang when they made their pilgrimages to Jerusalem. The psalm reflects how joyful the people felt when they could once again worship God in their own temple. In the Gospel, Jesus teaches us that we become members of his family when we do God's will.

YEAR II

READING I   Prov. 21:1-6, 10-13   RESP. Ps. 119:1, 27, 30, 34, 35, 44
GOSPEL   Luke 8:19-21

In today's first Scripture reading, you will hear a selection of sayings from the twenty-first chapter of the Book of Proverbs. The general theme of these disconnected proverbs is the malice and foolishness of evil men in contrast to the wise ways of good-living men. The responsorial psalm after this reading is the prayer of a man who wants to please God. His prayer becomes our own as we ask, "Guide me, Lord, in the way of your commands." In the Gospel, we wait patiently with relatives of Jesus on the fringe of a crowd outside a house where Jesus is teaching. Then the news reaches Jesus about his waiting relatives. Our Lord seizes this opportunity to teach that everyone belongs to his family who listens to his words and keeps them.

451 WEDNESDAY OF THE TWENTY-FIFTH WEEK OF THE YEAR

YEAR I

READING I   Ezra 9:5-9   RESP. Ps. Tobit 13:2, 3-4, 6, 7-8, 6
GOSPEL   Luke 9:1-6

In today's reading, we hear the prayer of the Jewish priest named Ezra who confesses the guilt of his people before God. Ezra views the Babylonian captivity, which had just ended in 539 B.C., as God's punishment because the Jews had not kept faith with the Lord's covenant. Ezra then thanks God for sparing Israel through the kindness of the Persian king who had freed the people. In this way, God confirmed that he would always be with his people and lead them to their destiny. Finally, Ezra praises God for overcoming opposition to the rebuilding of the temple. The themes of sinfulness, punishment, and God's mercy appear again in the responsorial psalm. In the Gospel, Jesus sends his apostles on a preaching tour of Galilee to do the things he did — driving out demons and healing the sick — to prepare men's hearts to receive his message of Good News.

YEAR II

READING I   Prov. 30:5-9   RESP. Ps. 119:29, 72, 89, 101, 104, 163
GOSPEL   Luke 9:1-6

Today's first reading contains three different thoughts from the closing chapter of the Book of Proverbs. The first point is a reminder of how trustworthy are God's promises to us. The second is a brief prayer that God may help us avoid being insincere in our dealings with others. The third thought is another plea that God may spare us from the evils of poverty, as well as from excessive wealth. Such riches may turn our hearts away from God. Our response to this reading is a statement of confidence in the way the Holy Spirit guides us in our daily lives. His inspiration serves as a lamp to guide our feet in the darkness of life. In the Gospel, we find our Lord sending the apostles out to preach the

Good News of the kingdom of God to the people. Their mission reminds us that our own faith has come through the preaching of the Gospel.

452   THURSDAY OF THE TWENTY-FIFTH WEEK OF THE YEAR

YEAR I

READING I   Haggai 1:1-8   RESP. Ps. 149:1-2, 3-4, 5-6, 9
GOSPEL   Luke 9:7-9

Today's first reading is a kind of flashback to about five years before the dedication of the temple in Jerusalem in 515 B.C. that we learned about at Tuesday's Mass. The Samaritans, neighbors of the Jews, have successfully held up construction work for the time being. Because the Israelites then cooled off in their fervor for finishing the project, God sent his prophet Haggai to rekindle the people's zeal. Today we hear the prophet give a series of vivid pictures of the economic troubles that God has sent to Israel because the Jews are content to live in "paneled houses" while God's house "lies in ruins." The responsorial psalm refrain also recalls the Lord's desire to take "delight in his people" in the temple once again. In the Gospel, we learn how the fame of Jesus' preaching and healing has reached the ears of Herod, the ruler of Galilee.

YEAR II

READING I   Eccl. 1:2-11   RESP. Ps. 90:3-4, 5-6, 12-13, 14, 17
GOSPEL   Luke 9:7-9

The first Scripture reading is from a collection of books in the Old Testament called the Books of Wisdom because they deal with the theme of wisdom and its role in human life. The Scripture reading for yesterday's Mass was a passage from one of these books — the Book of Proverbs. Today we begin another book in this collection of wisdom literature, the Book of Ecclesiastes. In this reading, you will hear a wisdom teacher named Qoheleth taking a pessimistic view of the works of men. He sees those works as nothing but vanity. The responsorial psalm recalls the verse in the reading that "one generation passes and another comes." The psalm refrain echoes this idea by saying that "in every age, O Lord, you have been our refuge." In the Gospel, we learn how King Herod reacted to the preaching of Christ.

453   FRIDAY OF THE TWENTY-FIFTH WEEK OF THE YEAR

YEAR I

READING I   Haggai 1:15—2:9   RESP. Ps. 43:1, 2, 3, 4
GOSPEL   Luke 9:18-22

In today's first reading, we learn that as some people watched the smaller temple rise on the ruins of Solomon's magnificent house of worship, they felt discouraged at the contrast in splendor between the two places. The prophet Haggai tells them to take courage and continue the work because God is with them, as he promised to be when he delivered them from Egypt centuries before. Haggai then expresses confidence that God "will shake all the nations" and usher in a new period of prosperity for Israel. Apparently, he anticipated the sudden fall of the Persian empire. The responsorial psalm also reminds us of the "dwelling place" of God and our joy in going "to the altar of God." In the Gospel, Peter proclaims Jesus as the Messiah. St. Luke — whose Gospel so often emphasizes prayer — carefully points out that this important event also took place in a setting of prayer.

YEAR II

READING I Eccl. 3:1-11   **RESP. Ps. 144:1-2, 3-4**
GOSPEL Luke 9:18-22

The mystery of time and the way it relates to God's plan for our lives is the subject of the first Scripture reading for today's Mass. This passage is a fine example of the literary beauty of the Bible. You will hear a teacher of wisdom portraying the various times in the life of man. He shows that there is a rhythm to all living things, a cycle of change, an ebb and flow of time. Because the reading tells how God notices every moment of time in a man's life, the responsorial psalm refers to this loving divine attention to man by asking, "Lord, what is man, that you notice him?" In the Gospel, St. Luke declares that Peter acknowledged Jesus as the Messiah. Our Lord then tells the apostles about his forthcoming suffering, rejection, and death. Once again, Luke notes that this important event took place while Jesus and his disciples were at prayer.

454 SATURDAY OF THE TWENTY-FIFTH WEEK OF THE YEAR

YEAR I

READING I Zech. 2:5-9, 14-15   **RESP. Ps. Jer. 31:10, 11-12, 13**
GOSPEL Luke 9:43-45

Today's reading introduces us to Zechariah, another prophet who encouraged the Jews in rebuilding the temple in Jerusalem about 520 B.C. As the passage begins, Zechariah sees a man with a measuring line, who is apparently going out to determine where the Jews should build the walls of their devastated city. An angel appears to inform the man that Jerusalem will not need any walls because the city's population will soon swell to great numbers, and God himself will protect the city with the fire of his presence. To encourage his people in rebuilding the temple, God then promises to return to his dwelling in Zion — a symbol for Jerusalem. The responsorial psalm refrain echoes God's pledge to guard the city. In the Gospel, St. Luke emphasizes that when Jesus warned his disciples how he would suffer they failed to understand him.

YEAR II

READING I Eccl. 11:9—12:8   **RESP.** Ps. 90:3-4, 5-6, 12-13, 14, 17
GOSPEL Luke 9:43-45

In today's first reading, we will hear the wise author of the Book of Ecclesiastes speak about the way young people first develop aspirations and ideals. At the same time, he reminds us that we are all responsible for our actions and that God will bring us to judgment. The passage then vividly describes what the author calls "the evil days" — the period of old age with its burdens. Man completes his life on earth and prepares for eternal life with his Creator. The responsorial psalm is a prayer acknowledging that God's presence abides with us through all the years of our earthly life. In the Gospel, Jesus gives his disciples another warning that someone will soon betray him, but they do not understand what he is talking about.

455 MONDAY OF THE TWENTY-SIXTH WEEK OF THE YEAR

YEAR I

READING I Zech. 8:1-8   **RESP.** Ps. 102:16-18, 19-21, 29, 22-23
GOSPEL Luke 9:46-50

The first reading contains a number of prophecies about the future age of the Messiah when God will shower his blessings on the Jewish people and through them on all nations. We hear Zechariah introduce each prophecy with the formula, "Thus says the Lord of hosts." God speaks first about his anger with Jerusalem's enemies. Then the Lord reassures the Jews who face the discouraging task of rebuilding the city and its temple that God will soon fill the streets with the young and the old — symbols of prosperity and peace. The Jews who are scattered over the earth will return to Jerusalem where God will renew his covenant with them. The responsorial psalm refrain underlines the theme that "the Lord will build up Zion again." In the Gospel, Jesus uses the living parable of a child to teach his disciples that they must become humble servants of others.

YEAR II

READING I Job 1:6-22   **RESP.** Ps. 17:1, 2-3, 6-7
GOSPEL Luke 9:46-50

The first Scripture readings for the Masses this week are from the

Book of Job. He is perhaps one of the most tragic figures in the Bible. Job endures great suffering even though he has served God loyally all his life. He is typical of all good-living people who struggle to understand the mystery of evil and suffering in their own lives. As you listen to today's reading, you will relive the opening scene in the temptation of Job. This is a dialogue between God and Satan concerning Job's life and his fidelity to the Lord. Then you will hear how Job responds to the loss of everything he holds dear in life. Since Job says nothing disrespectful when God tests him, the responsorial psalm relates to this theme by saying, "Though you test my heart, you shall find no malice in me." In the Gospel, Jesus instructs his disciples in the virtue of humility.

456 TUESDAY OF THE TWENTY-SIXTH WEEK OF THE YEAR

YEAR I

READING I   Zech. 8:20-23   RESP. Ps. 87:1-3, 4-5, 6-7
GOSPEL   Luke 9:51-56

The first reading encourages the Jews who were rebuilding the temple in Jerusalem about the year 520 B.C. to keep busy at their task because all nations will one day come to the city to share in Israel's worship and blessings. As the passage begins, we hear the prophet Zechariah describe people coming on pilgrimages to attend festivals in Jerusalem. He portrays other people as eagerly contacting their friends to come with them to the city to receive the favors of the Lord. Some even seek to touch the clothes of the Jews — a sign of the foreigners' desire to embrace the faith of Israel. The responsorial psalm accents the theme that "glorious things are said of you, O city of God." The Gospel begins the "journey narrative" in Luke. This literary technique describes Jesus as heading toward Jerusalem to face his Passion and death — a drama extending over the next ten chapters.

YEAR II

READING I   Job. 3:1-3, 11-17, 20-23   RESP. Ps. 88:2-3, 4-5, 6, 7-8
GOSPEL   Luke 9:51-56

In the first reading, we begin a series of dialogues between Job and his friends that make up most of the Book of Job. We have already learned how Job has lost everything he had and has patiently accepted bodily sufferings. Today's reading finds Job by himself, reflecting on his life and its apparent lack of meaning. The passage is one of the most touching scenes in the Bible. Job pours out his complaint about the aching misery of his existence. We may regard the responsorial psalm as prayers Job offers to the Lord to comfort him in his sufferings. The Gospel passage begins a special section of St. Luke's Gospel called "the journey narrative." From chapters nine through eighteen, Luke portrays the drama of Jesus on his way to Jerusalem where he will suffer and die for the sins of the world.

457 WEDNESDAY OF THE TWENTY-SIXTH WEEK OF THE YEAR

YEAR I

READING I   Neh. 2:1-8
GOSPEL   Luke 9:57-62

RESP. Ps. 137:1-2, 3, 4-5, 6

Today's first reading introduces a deeply religious man of tireless energy, Nehemiah, who organized the effort to restore the dilapidated walls of Jerusalem about the year 440 B.C. We hear Nehemiah — while he is still serving the Persian king — tell his story about the sad state of affairs in his native city. The king eventually grants his request to go and rebuild the walls and city gate so that the people may have protection against their enemies. Later chapters in Nehemiah's book tell how Israel's neighbors did their best to keep him from completing the project. The responsorial psalm expresses Nehemiah's zeal for Jerusalem in the refrain, "Let my tongue be silenced, if I ever forget you!" In the Gospel, Jesus reminds his followers that he demands a spirit of self-sacrifice and total commitment to him — a challenging ideal for our own hearts today.

YEAR II

READING I   Job 9:1-12, 14-16
GOSPEL   Luke 9:57-62

RESP. Ps. 88:10-11, 12-13, 14-15

In today's first Scripture reading, we take up again the dialogue between Job and his friends. As a background for this passage, we need to realize that Job's friends have just reminded him about God's fairness to men. They insist that since God is fair, Job will someday experience happiness in life despite his present sufferings. As today's passage begins, you will hear Job agreeing with his friends. Yet he wonders how a mere man can approach an all-powerful God and ask him for fairer treatment. Job then gives examples of God's power over the forces of nature. From his words, you will perhaps share Job's own sense of helplessness before an all-powerful God. Our responsorial psalm becomes a prayer from Job for the Lord's help in enduring his sufferings. In the Gospel, Jesus warns that he expects his followers to give themselves to him totally.

458 THURSDAY OF THE TWENTY-SIXTH WEEK OF THE YEAR

YEAR I

READING I   Neh. 8:1-4, 5-6, 7-12   RESP. Ps. 19:8, 9, 10, 11
GOSPEL   Luke 10:1-12

In today's first reading, we meet Ezra, a Jewish priest skilled in the Law of Moses. Ezra played a vital role in shaping the religious destiny of the Jewish people after their return from the Babylonian exile. Ezra was among those Jews who did not go back to Palestine soon after the Persian king gave them their freedom in 539 B.C. In time, however, Ezra felt called to shape the life of the people who had returned to Jerusalem according to the ideals of Moses. We find him in today's reading proclaiming the book of the Law to the people of Jerusalem — but the exact contents of this book we do not know. The responsorial psalm refrain accents "the precepts of the Lord" that "give joy to the heart." In the Gospel, Jesus instructs seventy-two disciples who will help preach God's kingdom to the towns of Galilee. After the apostles, these men may be our Lord's first vocations.

YEAR II

READING I   Job 19:21-27   RESP. Ps. 27:7-8, 8-9, 13-14
GOSPEL   Luke 10:1-12

The first Scripture reading continues the story of Job from the Old Testament. Job has undergone severe sufferings. At this point he is utterly alone. Family, friends, everyone — including, it seems, even God himself — has abandoned Job. Yet, despite this depth of loneliness, Job can still make an inspiring act of faith. We hear him say that he knows his Redeemer lives and that after death he will see him. We may hear this passage at the Mass for Christian Burial because it contains a message of hope and suggests a future resurrection. The responsorial psalm also emphasizes this theme of hope. We may think of it as a prayer by which Job places his trust in the Lord. In the Gospel, Jesus instructs his disciples before sending them out to preach in the towns and villages. These men probably are the first Christ called to his service — after the apostles.

459 FRIDAY OF THE TWENTY-SIXTH WEEK OF THE YEAR

YEAR I

READING I   Bar. 1:15-22   RESP. Ps. 79:1-2, 3-5, 8, 9
GOSPEL   Luke 10:13-16

In the first reading, we hear a public confession of sins that expresses the guilt of the whole Jewish nation before God at the time of the Babylonian exile in 587 B.C. This confession appears in a letter the exiled Jews in Babylon reportedly sent to the few countrymen their enemies had left behind in Palestine. The exiles humbly acknowledge that God is punishing his chosen people for their sins. The liturgy finds this confession appropriate for us to consider during this time when we have been hearing about the restoration of the temple in Jerusalem after the exile. The responsorial psalm recalls that tragic time when the foreign nations "defiled your holy temple" and "laid Jerusalem in ruins." In the Gospel, Jesus rebukes the citizens of three towns near the Sea of Galilee for not heeding his call to repent their sinful lives.

YEAR II

READING I   Job 38:1, 12-21; 40:3-5   **RESP. Ps. 139:1-3, 7-8, 9-10, 13-14**
GOSPEL   Luke 10:13-16

In the first reading, we reach the climax of the Book of Job. Up to this point, Job has insisted to his friends that the sufferings which have come into his life find their source in God and not in any evil that Job has done. Now God steps into the picture as we hear him ask Job a series of questions about the world of nature. The Lord has a point in raising these questions. If Job were to pretend to correct God on his mysterious ways of dealing with people's lives, then surely Job would have to know all the secrets of the universe as well. Obviously, Job does not. As a result, at the end of the passage, Job declares that he will no longer question the mystery of suffering and God's ways with men. The responsorial psalm accents God's personal knowledge of everyone's life. In the Gospel, Jesus condemns the people of the lakeside cities of Chorazin and Bethsaida for not repenting their sins.

460 SATURDAY OF THE TWENTY-SIXTH WEEK OF THE YEAR

YEAR I

READING I   Bar. 4:5-12, 27-29   **RESP. Ps. 69:33-35, 36-37**
GOSPEL   Luke 10:17-24

Today's reading centers again on the Jewish people who were suffering the shame of the Babylonian exile after 587 B.C. At first we hear the author of this passage tell the exiles that God does not wish to destroy them but only to punish them for a time because they had taken to worshiping pagan gods. He then introduces the city of Jerusalem, mother of the nation. She speaks to her scattered children, encouraging them to repent so God may bring them home in joy. We know from the readings this week that God did restore his beloved people to Palestine through the kindness of a Persian king. The responsorial psalm underlines today's theme in such verses as, "God's own who are in bonds he spurns not." Although Mark and Matthew tell about a mission the apostles made to preach in the towns of Galilee, only Luke relates, in today's Gospel, their joyful return with good news.

YEAR II

READING I   Job 42:1-3, 5-6, 12-16   RESP. Ps. 119:66, 71, 75, 91, 125, 130
GOSPEL   Luke 10:17-24

The first reading tells how Job repents his pride and then places his life completely in God's hands. In responding to Job's love, God blesses him by not only restoring children and property to him but also by increasing them. The author of this book seems to present the tragic experiences that Job went through in his life to teach his readers how to live with their own sufferings. In the New Testament, we gain the additional insight that God became man to share in the mystery of pain and evil himself and use them as the vehicle for mankind's redemption. The liturgy suggests that in the responsorial psalm we hear Job acknowledging that his afflictions served God's purpose for his life. In the Gospel, the seventy-two disciples return with joy to Jesus after a successful preaching tour of Galilee. Our Lord tells them that they should be grateful they live in the age of the Messiah.

461 MONDAY OF THE TWENTY-SEVENTH WEEK OF THE YEAR

YEAR I

READING I   Jonah 1:1—2:1, 11   RESP. Ps. Jonah 2:2, 3, 4, 5, 8
GOSPEL   Luke 10:25-37

Today we begin the story of Jonah. Most modern Scripture scholars believe this is a parable about the Jewish religious attitudes during the Persian era — from 539 to 333 B.C. — when Israel developed a spirit of exclusive nationalism. This caused many Jews to look with disdain on foreign countries and to reject any notion that these pagans could ever be the object of God's mercy. Hence the story of Jonah — as we shall see — marks a real step forward in religious tolerance at this time. We learn today how Jonah sets out in the opposite direction from Nineveh to avoid the difficult task God has given him. The responsorial psalm accents God's rescue of the prophet. In the Gospel, Jesus teaches us through the parable of the Good Samaritan how we should get involved in helping others whenever we find them in need — no matter what inconvenience this may cost us.

YEAR II

READING I   Gal. 1:6-12   RESP. Ps. 111:1-2, 7-8, 9, 10
GOSPEL   Luke 10:25-37

Today, the cycle of readings from the Bible at the weekday Masses moves on to another epistle of St. Paul. He wrote this letter to the pre-dominantly Gentile Christian communities in Northern Galatia, an area corresponding to present-day Turkey. This letter is similar in theme to Paul's letter to the Romans. Both teach the freedom from the Law of Moses that Christians enjoy through their faith in Christ. In today's passage, Paul insists that we believe in the Good News about Christ and not in the teachings of mere men. The responsorial psalm reminds us that God will always keep his promises to us. In the Gospel, Jesus teaches his great commandment of love through the familiar parable of the Good Samaritan. We learn that we should get involved in helping others whenever we find them in need — no matter how inconvenient it may be for us.

462 TUESDAY OF THE TWENTY-SEVENTH WEEK OF THE YEAR

YEAR I

READING I   Jonah 3:1-10   RESP. Ps. 130:1-2, 3-4, 7-8
GOSPEL   Luke 10:38-42

The first reading tells how God sent Jonah on his way to Nineveh in Assyria after rescuing him from a whale's belly. The wicked people of the city listened to Jonah's message of doom and repented immediately. This moved God to cancel the punishment he had planned. The author used Jonah's story to teach the fifth century Jews that they should be more tolerant toward people who did not share the religious beliefs of Israel. The liturgy suggests that in the responsorial psalm we hear the people of Nineveh cry out in repentance, "If you, O Lord, laid bare our guilt, who could endure it?" In the Gospel story of Martha and Mary, Jesus makes the point that we should avoid getting so absorbed in the problems of daily life that we forget the "one thing required" — the spiritual food we get from listening to him in prayer.

YEAR II

READING I   Gal. 1:13-24   RESP. Ps. 139:1-3, 13-14, 14-15
GOSPEL   Luke 10:38-42

In today's first reading, we continue St. Paul's letter to the Gentile Christians in Galatia. Jewish teachers had visited this country and upset the Christians there by claiming that Paul had no authority to teach them. In this passage, we hear Paul defending his vocation to preach the Good News of salvation. He admits that he had persecuted the Church until at Damascus Christ called him to become an apostle to the Gentiles. Because in the first reading Paul says of himself that God "had set me apart before I was born and called me," the responsorial psalm repeats this theme by proclaiming, "Truly you have formed my inmost being; you knit me in my mother's womb." The Gospel tells how Jesus visited Martha and Mary. We should seek the spiritual food of our Lord's words that Mary heard by prayerfully reading the Bible.

463 WEDNESDAY OF THE TWENTY-SEVENTH WEEK OF THE YEAR

YEAR I

READING I   Jonah 4:1-11   RESP. Ps. 86:3-4, 5-6, 9-10
GOSPEL   Luke 11:1-4

We learn today that Jonah knew the Lord would be merciful if the Ninevites repented — and Jonah didn't *want* to spare them from punishment. That is why we find Jonah angry as this passage begins. Jonah in this way reflects the typical attitude of the Jews toward their pagan neighbors in the fifth century B.C. The incident of the shade tree eaten by worms teaches Jonah a lesson. If he could take pity on a single plant, then God certainly had all the more reason to pity the hundreds of thousands of people in Nineveh eaten by the worms of sin. The heart of this story is that God's mercy reaches out not only to his covenanted people, the Jews, but to the Gentiles as well. The responsorial psalm reinforces this lesson by reminding us that God is "good and forgiving" to "all the nations." In the Gospel, Jesus teaches the model for prayer we call the Our Father.

YEAR II

READING I   Gal. 2:1-2, 7-14   RESP. Ps. 117:1, 2
GOSPEL   Luke 11:1-4

Today's first reading tells about a practical problem that troubled the local Church community at Antioch. We learn that the apostle Peter went back to following the ancient Jewish laws about eating only kosher foods, although this was no longer required. He apparently felt pressure from his Jewish Christian friends who stubbornly insisted on keeping the laws. As a result, Peter would no longer dine with the Gentiles, who did not follow the kosher tradition. Peter's efforts to pacify his strict friends led others to follow his example in not eating with the Gentiles. The danger loomed of a split in the community at Antioch. For this reason, we find Paul correcting Peter about the way he was acting. The responsorial psalm accents the common call to salvation that God gave to Jews and Gentiles alike. In the Gospel, Jesus teaches the model for prayer — the Our Father.

197

464 THURSDAY OF THE TWENTY-SEVENTH WEEK OF THE YEAR

YEAR I

READING I Mal. 3:13-20   RESP. Ps. 1:1-2, 3, 4, 6
GOSPEL   Luke 11:5-13

In today's first reading, we hear the Jews of the fifth century B.C. complain that "evildoers prosper, and even tempt God with impunity" — a dilemma that may at times trouble our hearts, too. The prophet Malachi then observes a record book before the Lord containing the names of those who trust in God despite their sufferings. God reminds his beloved people that he has not forgotten them. The Lord feels compassion for those who keep faith with him, and he assures them that the punishment of the wicked is surely coming. The responsorial psalm also urges us to remain faithful to God's ways and not follow the path of the wicked. In the Gospel, Jesus reminds us how willing God is to give us what we pray for. We must go to him with complete confidence for all our needs, especially the best thing we can ask for — God's gift of the Holy Spirit.

YEAR II

READING I Gal. 3:1-5   RESP. Ps. Luke 1:69-70, 71-72, 73-75
GOSPEL   Luke 11:5-13

In the first reading, St. Paul teaches that a person wins salvation not by observing the Law of Moses but by faith in Christ. You will hear Paul mentioning the experience the Galatians had in receiving the Holy Spirit. He asks them to recall that this gift came not through fulfilling the Jewish laws but through their faith in Christ. The whole tone of this passage should help us appreciate Paul as a man of flesh and blood — a hard-working missionary who could get upset over the spiritual failings of his flock. The responsorial psalm after this reading is a prayer of praise to God for his loving visit to us through Christ and the saving ministry of his Church. In the Gospel, Jesus teaches the key lesson of never ceasing to pray, no matter what. We must seek especially the best thing we can ask for — God's gift of the Holy Spirit.

465 FRIDAY OF THE TWENTY-SEVENTH WEEK OF THE YEAR

YEAR I

READING I Joel 1:13-15; 2:1-2   RESP. Ps. 9:2-3, 6, 16, 8-9
GOSPEL   Luke 11:15-26

In the first reading, the prophet Joel, sometime between 400 and 350 B.C., gives a dramatic call to the Jewish priests to proclaim a time for the people to fast and do penance, so that God will end a devastating locust plague. The plague is so severe that even cereal and wine for the priests' offerings in the temple are no longer available. We hear Joel describe the invading army of locusts — "a people numerous and mighty" — as a sign that "the day of the Lord" was near when God would judge his people. The responsorial psalm also views the plague as a sign of God's judgment on Israel in the refrain, "The Lord will judge the world with justice." In the Gospel, Jesus reveals that his power over the forces of evil is a sign that God's kingdom has come into the world. Our Lord performs exorcisms "by the finger of God," that is, by God's power working in him.

YEAR II

READING I Gal. 3:7-14   RESP. Ps. 111:1-2, 3-4, 5-6
GOSPEL   Luke 11:15-26

The first reading begins by pointing out that Abraham's real children are not his blood descendants but those who put their trust in God's word, as Abraham once did. St. Paul tells the Galatians that through their faith they have received the blessing of salvation God promised to Abraham and the peoples of all nations. Paul then goes on to show that Christ came to free mankind from the impossible burden of the Jewish laws and to offer instead the path of faith. Paul says that because Jesus submitted to the "curse" of dying on a cross, our Lord delivered everyone from "the power of the law's curse." The Holy Spirit that the Galatians now enjoy by the gift of faith is the blessing that God promised long ago to Abraham. The responsorial psalm reminds us that God will keep his solemn promise to bless us. In the Gospel, Jesus insists that his power over evil reveals that God's kingdom has come.

466 SATURDAY OF THE TWENTY-SEVENTH WEEK OF THE YEAR

Year I

READING I Joel 4:12-21   RESP. Ps. 97:1-2, 5-6, 11-12
GOSPEL   Luke 11:27-28

Today we hear God summon all the nations to judgment at the end of time to punish those that inflicted violence on his chosen people. This scene receives the appropriate names, the Valley of Jehoshaphat, meaning "God-shall-judge," and the Valley of Decision, because here God decides for Israel against her enemies. The prophet Joel portrays God's destruction of the wicked nations in terms of harvesting crops and treading grapes. Joel then assures Jerusalem, symbol of the whole nation, of her future blessings — the city will no longer fear attacks from strangers, the land shall be fertile, and God will continue to dwell in his temple on Mount Zion. The responsorial psalm appropriately declares that "judgment" is "the foundation" of God's throne. In the Gospel, Jesus praises all who put God's word into practice in their lives.

YEAR II
READING I   Gal. 3:22-29   RESP. Ps. 105:2-3, 4-5, 6-7
GOSPEL   Luke 11:27-28

In today's first reading, St. Paul describes the laws of the Old Testament as a "monitor" from whom Christ has delivered those who have faith in him. In the Roman society of Paul's day, a monitor was a slave boy who watched over his master's son and guided him until he became a man. Paul was saying that the Law of Moses was like a slave boy guiding the Jewish people until they grew into true manhood through the redemption of Christ. Since in the first reading Paul says of the Galatians, "You are the descendants of Abraham," the responsorial psalm also mentions the descendants of Abraham. In the Gospel, Jesus reminds us how important it is to listen to the Word of God and in our daily lives to honor that Word by trying to put into practice what he asks of us.

467   MONDAY OF THE TWENTY-EIGHTH WEEK OF THE YEAR

Year I
READING I   Rom. 1:1-7   RESP. Ps. 98:1, 2-3, 3-4
GOSPEL   Luke 11:29-32

St. Paul's letter to the Romans that we begin today has influenced Christian thought probably more than any other New Testament writing. Paul apparently wrote from Corinth during the winter years of 57-58 shortly before leaving to deliver a collection for the poor in Jerusalem. In the letter's salutation, we find tightly packed together many key truths of the early Christian faith — the vocation of an apostle, how Jesus fulfills the Old Testament hopes, the Messiah's descent from David, the resurrection, the necessity of faith, God's call of the Gentiles, and God as our Father. The responsorial psalm emphasizes how "the Lord has made known his salvation" to "all the ends of the earth." In the Gospel, Jesus instructs the crowds not to seek wondrous signs. Instead, the people must listen to him and answer his call to repentance because he is greater than Solomon or Jonah.

YEAR II
READING I   Gal. 4:22-24, 26-27, 31—5:1   RESP. Ps. 113:1-2, 3-4, 5, 6-7
GOSPEL   Luke 11:29-32

In today's first Scripture reading, St. Paul continues to explain how Christ has given freedom from the Law of Moses to those who believe in him. To demonstrate his point, Paul refers to the two wives of Abraham and their children. Abraham's slave wife named Hagar represents Jerusalem, the earthly city of the Jews. Her children are enslaved in trying to please God by obeying the Law of Moses. The Galatians, and all Christians, are children of Abraham's freeborn wife and citizens of the heavenly Jerusalem that is not a slave to Jewish laws. The responsorial psalm is a prayer of praise for this gift of freedom. We too enjoy it through our baptism in Christ. In the Gospel, St. Luke sees Jonah as a sign that God wanted the Ninevites to be sorry for their sins. The teaching and good works of Jesus are also a sign that God desires the Jews to repent.

468   TUESDAY OF THE TWENTY-EIGHTH WEEK OF THE YEAR

YEAR I

READING I   Rom. 1:16-25   RESP. Ps. 19:2-3, 4-5
GOSPEL   Luke 11:37-41

The first reading introduces the main theme of St. Paul's letter to the Christians in Rome. The apostle teaches that God offers all men the Gospel, that is, the Good News of salvation "which begins and ends with faith." Paul then demonstrates that the world needs salvation by pointing out how men act when they do not know this Good News. He gives the example first of the pagans who have become caught up in the foolishness of worshiping false gods. Because Paul teaches that men can know about God from the world he has made, the responsorial psalm refrain appropriately declares, "The heavens proclaim the glory of God." In the Gospel, St. Luke puts within the setting of a meal at a Pharisee's home our Lord's criticisms of many of the Jewish religious leaders. Jesus stresses that when a man gives to charity he cleanses his heart — a far greater concern than ritual cleansing of dishes.

YEAR II

READING I   Gal. 5:1-6   RESP. Ps. 119:41, 43, 44, 45, 47, 48
GOSPEL   Luke 11:37-41

In today's first reading, the apostle Paul warns the Galatians not to go back to observing the Law of Moses — for example, in circumcising male children as a religious act signifying salvation. To do so would mean losing the freedom the Galatians have achieved by their faith in Christ. Paul reminds them that this faith must prove itself in action by works of charity. Since Paul says in the reading that "Christ freed us for liberty," the responsorial psalm refers to a just man who declares,

"I will walk at liberty because I seek your precepts." In the Gospel, Jesus denounces many Pharisees for their hypocrisy. They were so excessively concerned about exterior rituals of the Law of Moses that they neglected the spirit of the Law. Our Lord then stresses how valuable in his eyes are the generous offerings we make to care for the needs of others.

469 WEDNESDAY OF THE TWENTY-EIGHTH WEEK OF THE YEAR

YEAR I

READING I   Rom. 2:1-11   RESP. Ps. 62:2-3, 6-7, 9
GOSPEL   Luke 11:42-46

Today we find St. Paul turning to an imaginary reader of his letter. This man appears to be a self-righteous individual who agrees wholeheartedly with Paul that God should condemn the pagans for their idolatry. And yet this person is guilty of so many sins himself. For this reason, Paul warns him not to presume on God's patience and kindness by putting off repenting for his sins. The apostle insists that a day of reckoning will come when God will judge all men without show of favoritism by the way they have lived as individuals. The responsorial psalm also recalls the judgment scene in the refrain, "Lord, you give back to every man according to his works." In the Gospel, Jesus denounces many Jewish religious leaders for their injustice, their hypocrisy, and the countless burdens of the ceremonial laws they created for the people.

YEAR II

READING I   Gal. 5:18-25   RESP. Ps. 1:1-2, 3, 4, 6
GOSPEL   Luke 11:42-46

The following Scripture passage concludes St. Paul's letter to the Galatians that we have been reading at the weekday Masses during the past week. Paul compares the two ways of life open to us as Christians. The first is what Paul calls the life of the flesh. You will hear a catalog of the sins involved in this way of life. Afterwards, Paul gives the contrasting way of the spirit. He describes the virtues that should characterize the life of a true follower of Christ. The responsorial psalm relates to this theme of the two ways of life. The psalm describes the happiness of the man who follows the law of God and the way of the wicked that proves destructive. In the Gospel, Jesus criticizes those Pharisees who seek only the flattery and praise of men and not the things of God.

470 THURSDAY OF THE TWENTY-EIGHTH WEEK OF THE YEAR

YEAR I

READING I   Rom. 3:21-29   RESP. Ps. 130:1-2, 3-4, 5-6
GOSPEL   Luke 11:47-54

The first reading contains two key doctrines of St. Paul. First, Paul teaches that "a man is justified by faith apart from observance of the law." Paul insists in this principle that God grants salvation to Jews and Gentiles alike, not because they perform the works that the Law of Moses commanded but because they have faith in Jesus Christ. Paul's second doctrine emphasizes that faith is a "gift" of God, a grace. No man, Paul says, can "boast" that he earned faith by the good works he did. Since Paul refers to "the redemption wrought in Christ Jesus" as the source of man's salvation, the responsorial psalm refrain also accents this theme of redemption. In the Gospel, we take up again our Lord's denunciation of the Scribes and Pharisees. Jesus accuses them of having the same outlook as those Jews in the past who were guilty of murdering the prophets that God had sent them.

YEAR II

READING I   Eph. 1:1-10   RESP. Ps. 98:1, 2-3, 3-4, 5-6
GOSPEL   Luke 11:47-54

The cycle of readings from the Bible for the weekday Masses continues today with another letter St. Paul wrote while he was a prisoner in Rome. He addresses it to the Christian community in the city of Ephesus, a large seaport at that time on the western coast of what is now Turkey. The main purpose of this letter was to instruct the Christians about God's plan for saving mankind in Christ. The passage for today's Mass describes various blessings that come to us from God. He has adopted us as his children in Jesus Christ, who delivered us from our sins by shedding his precious blood. Because Paul mentions that God "bestowed on us in Christ every spiritual blessing," the responsorial psalm accents this theme in the refrain, "The Lord has made known his salvation." In the Gospel, we learn that many Pharisees become hostile to Jesus because he criticized them.

471 FRIDAY OF THE TWENTY-EIGHTH WEEK OF THE YEAR

YEAR I

READING I   Rom. 4:1-8   RESP. Ps. 32:1-2, 5, 11
GOSPEL   Luke 12:1-7

In today's reading, St. Paul points to the example of Abraham — whom all Jews revered — to show that salvation by faith, and not by works, completely agrees with the teaching of the Old Testament. For

Paul, the key text is the bold statement in the Book of Genesis that "Abraham believed God, and it was credited to him as justice" — which makes no reference at all to the patriarch's works. In this way, Paul refutes the belief then current among the Jews that it was Abraham's *conduct* after receiving God's promise that saved him. Paul bolsters his Scripture argument by quoting Psalm 32, which views forgiveness, like faith, as an unmerited gift from God. For this reason, the liturgy uses this psalm as our response to the reading. In the Gospel, Jesus warns his disciples not to be hypocrites like the Pharisees, and to trust in God's care which should rule out all fears.

YEAR II

READING I   Eph. 1:11-14   RESP. Ps. 33:1-2, 4-5, 12-13
GOSPEL   Luke 12:1-7

In today's first reading, St. Paul continues to discuss the divine plan of salvation for mankind in Christ. He explains how God first chose for himself a special people, the Jews, whom he destined to keep the hope of a Messiah alive in the world. Paul then reminds the Gentiles that they now share in the divine invitation to accept the good tidings of salvation. God has given the Gentiles the Holy Spirit whom the prophets promised. Because Paul begins the passage by saying, "In Christ we were chosen," the responsorial psalm echoes this theme in the refrain, "Happy the people the Lord has chosen to be his own." In the Gospel, Jesus encourages his disciples not to be afraid when enemies persecute them or make life difficult. Our Lord assures all who follow him that God knows each of us personally and always has our best interests at heart.

472   SATURDAY OF THE TWENTY-EIGHTH WEEK OF THE YEAR

YEAR I

READING I   Rom. 4:13, 16-18   RESP. Ps. 105:6-7, 8-9, 42-43
GOSPEL   Luke 12:8-12

In today's first reading, St. Paul denies that God's promise to make Abraham the father of many nations had anything to do with the Law of Moses — as some rabbis believed. Paul teaches instead that God blessed Abraham for his faith because the patriarch took God's word for it when the Lord promised to give him children, even though humanly speaking it seemed impossible. Since Abraham had this strong faith, the Lord gave him "justice," that is, salvation. Paul says that the same thing happens when men take God at his word and believe in Jesus Christ as their Lord and Redeemer. Abraham then becomes their spiritual father because they imitate the same faith he had. The responsorial psalm reminds us that we too are "descendants of Abraham" by our own faith in Jesus. In the Gospel, our Lord exhorts us not to deny him when we face challenges in our Christian life.

YEAR II

READING I Eph. 1:15-23   **RESP. Ps.** 8:2-3, 4-5, 6-7
GOSPEL   Luke 12:8-12

In the first reading, St. Paul tells us about the place of honor Christ enjoys as head of all creation. Paul begins by reminding the Christian community at Ephesus that he constantly prays for them. He hopes that they will continue to understand more deeply who Christ is and what he has done for them. Paul then explains that Christ is the Head of the Church and that the members of the Church make up his body. Our relationship with Christ keeps us alive spiritually, just as the working together of the parts of the human body keeps us alive physically. The responsorial psalm also emphasizes the theme of the authority Christ exercises over all creation. In the Gospel, Jesus reminds us that as Christians we are duty-bound to acknowledge him before men. Our Lord assures us that he will defend us when enemies persecute us.

473   MONDAY OF THE TWENTY-NINTH WEEK OF THE YEAR

YEAR I

READING I Rom. 4:20-25   **RESP. Ps.** Luke 1:69-70, 71-72, 73-75
GOSPEL   Luke 12:13-21

In the first reading, St. Paul calls attention to the faith of Abraham as the model of the Christian life of faith. Abraham believed God's promise to make him the father of many nations even though he and his wife were beyond the age for having children. Because he had a strong faith in this promise, Paul says, Abraham received the grace of salvation. The apostle then reminds the Christians in Rome that because they have faith in Jesus who died and rose for them, they too have received the grace of salvation. The responsorial psalm also recalls God's promise — "the oath he swore to Abraham" — to make his descendants as numerous as the stars of heaven. In the Gospel, Jesus meets a man whose brother wanted to keep their inheritance all for himself. This situation prompts our Lord to tell a parable about a rich man who lived the same way — and died a fool.

YEAR II

READING I Eph. 2:1-10   **RESP. Ps.** 100:2, 3, 4, 5
GOSPEL   Luke 12:13-21

The first reading takes up again St. Paul's letter to the Christian community at Ephesus, a prominent seaport in what is now western Turkey.

Paul begins by reminding the Ephesians how sinful their lives were before they knew Christ. The apostle mentions "the prince of the air" who ruled their lives, because ancient belief held that a world of demons controlled the area between heaven and earth. Paul then draws attention to God's immense power at work in the lives of the Ephesians through his great mercy. He stresses again his favorite theme that the abundant kindness of God, not anything that we can do ourselves, saves us. Because Paul says that "we are truly his handiwork," the responsorial psalm refrain declares that "the Lord made us, we belong to him." In the Gospel, Jesus tells a parable about a rich man who lived only for himself — and died a fool.

474 TUESDAY OF THE TWENTY-NINTH WEEK OF THE YEAR

YEAR I

READING I Rom. 5:12, 15, 17-19, 20-21   RESP. Ps. 40:7-8, 8-9, 10, 17
GOSPEL Luke 12:35-38

The first reading draws a parallel between Adam, the first man, and Christ, the new head of mankind, in terms that presuppose the Christian doctrine of original sin. Paul begins by reminding us what happened to all men when Adam committed the first sin. Paul then shows the contrast between man's sin and God's forgiveness that he revealed in his Son, Jesus. The apostle concludes on the optimistic note that all men now have the opportunity to gain eternal life. Since Paul teaches that "through one man's obedience all shall become just," the responsorial psalm portrays Jesus offering himself in obedience to his Father in the refrain, "Here am I, Lord; I come to do your will." In the Gospel, Jesus reminds us that no man can tell the day or the hour when God will summon him to judgment. For this reason, we must always be ready for that call.

YEAR II

READING I Eph. 2:12-22   RESP. Ps. 85:9-10, 11-12, 13-14
GOSPEL Luke 12:35-38

In the first Scripture reading, St. Paul reveals how the death of Christ broke down the barriers that had kept Jews and Gentiles apart and made it possible for them to share peaceful lives together. After reminding the Gentile converts in the community at Ephesus that they once did not even know about Christ, Paul points out that both Jews and Gentiles have now come together as parts of the risen Body of Christ himself. The apostle then uses the images of a household, a building, and a temple to show that all Christians should be living in

206

harmony because they share the same life of the Holy Spirit. The responsorial psalm highlights Paul's references to peace by declaring in the refrain, "The Lord speaks of peace to his people." In the Gospel, Jesus warns us that we must always be ready for the time when God will summon us to judgment.

475 WEDNESDAY OF THE TWENTY-NINTH WEEK OF THE YEAR

YEAR I

READING I   Rom. 6:12-18   RESP. Ps. 124:1-3, 4-6, 7-8
GOSPEL   Luke 12:39-48

In today's reading, St. Paul makes two powerful comparisons to warn the Christians in Rome against letting sin rule their lives. First, Paul takes the military idea of weapons to show that Christians should not use their bodies as "weapons" to visit "evil" on themselves or others, that is, by committing sin. Second, Paul draws on the familiar scene of slaves and their masters in Roman society and insists that Christians must no longer enslave themselves to sin as their master. Instead, they should serve the teachings of their faith that have cut their bonds to selfishness. The responsorial psalm highlights Paul's closing reference to Christian freedom in the verse, "Broken was the snare, and we were freed." The Gospel parable of a master and his steward reminds the leaders of the Church that God will require much from those to whom he gives so important a trust.

YEAR II

READING I   Eph. 3:2-12   RESP. Ps. Is. 12:2-3, 4, 5-6
GOSPEL   Luke 12:39-48

In the first reading, St. Paul describes his special vocation to preach to the Gentiles what he calls the "great mystery of Christ." This mystery was a special revelation God made to Paul that the men of previous ages had no inkling of. Until God made this revelation, the Jews believed that God had destined them alone for his special love and protection. Paul then explains that through faith in Christ eternal salvation is now available to all mankind. The responsorial psalm emphasizes this theme of universal salvation in Christ by declaring that all men "will draw water joyfully from the springs of salvation" — that is, the Sacred Heart of Jesus. In the Gospel, Jesus exhorts his disciples to be vigilant about his final coming. He then warns the leaders of his Church that they must never treat lightly their duty to serve others.

YEAR I

READING I   Rom. 6:19-23   RESP. Ps. 1:1-2, 3, 4, 6
GOSPEL   Luke 12:49-53

In today's first reading, St. Paul takes up again the familiar image of slavery in the Roman world to show how sin enslaves a man's life to all that makes him less human. The apostle then sums up this section of his letter in the verse, "The wages of sin is death, but the gift of God is eternal life in Christ." The word Paul uses for "wages" refers to the regular pay a Roman soldier received. Paul seems to say that each time a man sins he earns more "death" in his spiritual life. The apostle's term for "gift" means the money that the emperor handed out as gifts to his soldiers on special occasions. In this way, Paul teaches that our sharing in eternal happiness is due to the bounty of God. The responsorial psalm also offers the choice of serving God or following the wicked. In the Gospel, Jesus warns that his way of life does not promise peace.

YEAR II

READING I   Eph. 3:14-21   RESP. Ps. 33:1-2, 4-5, 11-12, 18-19
GOSPEL   Luke 12:49-53

In today's first Scripture reading, you will hear St. Paul earnestly pleading with God to shower an abundance of spiritual gifts on the Ephesians. Paul then uses two figures of speech to describe the love that he prays will become the chief motivation of their lives. He takes the first image from gardening. He asks that the Christians root their lives in charity, as in a rich soil from which they will draw divine strength. In the second figure — from architecture — Paul prays that charity may support their lives like the unshakable foundation of a well-designed building. Because Paul prays that the Ephesians "may attain to the fullness of God," the responsorial psalm declares that "the earth is full of the goodness of the Lord." In the Gospel, Jesus warns that it may be necessary to give up even one's family to follow his ideals.

477   FRIDAY OF THE TWENTY-NINTH WEEK OF THE YEAR

YEAR I

READING I   Rom. 7:18-25   RESP. Ps. 119:66, 68, 76, 77, 93, 94
GOSPEL   Luke 12:54-59

In the first reading, St. Paul describes in his own name a man's struggles with temptation. Scripture commentators in the early Church tended to view this man as everyone who finds his life a battleground on which his desires to do wrong fight against the ideals he knows he should follow — even after he has received his life of grace in baptism. Most modern authorities believe, however, that Paul is talking about a man *before* his experience of God's grace. All the same, we will undoubtedly recognize ourselves in Paul's analysis of these tensions. The responsorial psalm refrain accents Paul's reference to "the law of God." In the Gospel, Jesus reprimands the crowds who know how to read the signs of bad weather but cannot recognize the obvious sign right before their eyes. Our Lord's preaching and healing reveals that God's kingdom has arrived.

YEAR II

READING I   Eph. 4:1-6   RESP. Ps. 24:1-2, 3-4, 5-6
GOSPEL   Luke 12:54-59

Today we discover why it is true to say that St. Paul's letter to the Ephesians accents Christian unity more than any of his other letters. The apostle begins by exhorting the Ephesians to keep faith with all the responsibilities of their life and to love one another. Paul goes on to point out that the single inner source of the community's life is the Holy Spirit, who inspires the individual members to work together in a spirit of peace and harmony. Then Paul states the sevenfold ways in which the Ephesians achieve their unity. The responsorial psalm highlights Paul's summons to holiness of life by giving the example of a man "whose hands are sinless, whose heart is clean." In the Gospel, Jesus reprimands the crowds who know how to read the signs of bad weather but cannot recognize the obvious signs of his preaching and healing that clearly show God's kingdom has arrived.

478 SATURDAY OF THE TWENTY-NINTH WEEK OF THE YEAR

YEAR I

READING I   Rom. 8:1-11   RESP. Ps. 24:1-2, 3-4, 5-6
GOSPEL   Luke 13:1-9

We find in the first reading the heart of St. Paul's understanding of the Christian life. The apostle teaches that Jesus has destroyed sin's control over our lives. Now we live with the strengthening power of the Holy Spirit in our hearts. Paul then contrasts the "flesh" and the "spirit." He suggests that the man of the flesh is man left to himself, man following the "death" of his own self-centered interests. The man of the spirit is man guided by the Holy Spirit, man living at peace with himself and others. The responsorial psalm shows us a man living by the spirit "whose hands are sinless, whose heart is clean." In the Gospel, Jesus recalls two recent tragedies and insists that the victims were not worse sinners than those who escaped — as the Jewish view of morality held. Our Lord's point is that all men need to repent their sinful lives — including ourselves.

YEAR II

READING I Eph. 4:7-16
GOSPEL Luke 13:1-9

RESP. Ps. 122:1-2, 3-4, 4-5

In today's reading, St. Paul takes up again his theme of unity in the Church. Paul explains that within the basic oneness of the Church, gifts and offices vary. Christ gave these gifts so that each member might better equip himself to build up the Church, the Body of Christ, to a position of strength and maturity. The apostle's image of Christ as Head of the Church is a fundamental teaching in his writings. The responsorial psalm also relates to the theme of unity by referring to Jerusalem "built as a city with compact unity." The Church is this new Jerusalem built into unity with Christ. In the Gospel, Jesus recalls two recent tragedies and then insists that the victims were not worse sinners than those who escaped — as the Jewish view of morality held. Our Lord's point is that *all* men need to repent their sinful lives — a lesson we also need to take to heart today.

479 MONDAY OF THE THIRTIETH WEEK OF THE YEAR

YEAR I

READING I Rom. 8:12-17
GOSPEL Luke 13:10-17

RESP. Ps. 68:2, 4, 6-7, 20-21

St. Paul in the first reading explains how a man enters into the family of God by comparing this wondrous event to the process of adopting a child in Graeco-Roman society. To grasp Paul's point of view, we must realize that adoption granted a child full rights and obligations as a member of his new family. For this reason, Paul can say in all truth that when the Holy Spirit enters our hearts at baptism we actually become children of God the Father, brothers and sisters of Jesus Christ, and heirs of our Lord's sufferings and glory. The responsorial psalm also emphasizes our divine adoption as God's children in the verse, "The father of orphans . . . is God in his holy dwelling." In the Gospel, our Lord's healing of a woman crippled for eighteen years with an infirmity reveals that salvation has come to Israel, but some Pharisees are too blind to realize it.

YEAR II

READING I Eph. 4:32—5:8
GOSPEL Luke 13:10-17

RESP. Ps. 1:1-2, 3, 4, 6

Today's first reading continues the letter St. Paul wrote to the Christian community in the city of Ephesus in what is now western Turkey. Paul here instructs his Gentile converts about how each of them relates personally to Christ. He reminds them that Christ calls them every bit as much as he did the Jews to share in God's promise of salvation. Paul tells the Ephesians about the vices that they should avoid if they intend to be real followers of Christ and children of the light. Our response to the reading repeats Paul's exhortation that the Ephesians "behave like God as his very dear children." The psalm also portrays the two ways of living that are open to man — the way of God and the way of sinners. In the Gospel, Jesus heals a woman on the Sabbath, even though the Pharisees object.

480 TUESDAY OF THE THIRTIETH WEEK OF THE YEAR

YEAR I

READING I Rom. 8:18-25   RESP. Ps. 126:1-2, 2-3, 4-5, 6
GOSPEL   Luke 13:18-21

In today's first reading, St. Paul develops two points to demonstrate that the glorious life of eternity that awaits us is not an empty dream. First, he explains how even the universe itself anxiously looks forward to release from its bondage to the consequences of man's sin. Second, we too yearn for "the redemption of our bodies" when God will deliver us from the sufferings and injustices of this life. Paul concludes that we must keep this hope alive in our hearts. The responsorial psalm sums up Paul's theme in the verse, "Those that sow in tears shall reap rejoicing." In the Gospel, St. Luke's version of the parable of the mustard seed emphasizes the full-grown tree with birds in its branches — not the tiny size of the seed as Matthew does. In this way, our Lord's point is that all the nations of the world will one day gather in the shelter of God's kingdom.

YEAR II

READING I Eph. 5:21-33   RESP. Ps. 128:1-2, 3, 4-5
GOSPEL   Luke 13:18-21

In the first Scripture reading, St. Paul gives advice to married people. Paul teaches that a husband and wife should have the same relationship that Christ has to the Church. Husbands and wives should love each other to show that they want to live in their lives the same love that Christ has for his Church. Finally, Paul quotes a verse from the opening pages of the Bible that teaches us about the exclusive and total love of husband and wife. In this passage from the letter to the Ephesians, St. Paul gives the scriptural foundation for Christian marriage as a sacrament. Since the reading deals with married life, the responsorial psalm also refers to the happiness of a husband and wife who truly love God. In the Gospel, Jesus uses the parables of the mustard seed and the yeast in the dough to teach us how the kingdom of God will grow.

481 WEDNESDAY OF THE THIRTIETH WEEK OF THE YEAR

YEAR I

READING I   Rom. 8:26-30   RESP. Ps. 13:4-5, 6
GOSPEL   Luke 13:22-30

The first Scripture reading takes up again St. Paul's vision of man's eternal destiny. He points out how the Holy Spirit helps us in our weakness so that we can continue to pray and persevere in our Christian life. At the same time, God's whole plan for mankind aims at bringing his children into eternal glory with him. From the very beginning of the world, God always wanted us to belong to his Son so that Jesus could become "the first-born of many brothers." The responsorial psalm also directs our eyes to the life that awaits us, in the refrain, "All my hope, O Lord, is in your loving kindness." In the Gospel, St. Luke reminds us again that Jesus is continuing his journey to Jerusalem — a writing technique Luke uses to heighten the drama of our Lord's approaching Passion and death. Jesus warns the crowd that God closes the door of his kingdom to evildoers.

YEAR II

READING I   Eph. 6:1-9   RESP. Ps. 145:10-11, 12-13, 13-14
GOSPEL   Luke 13:22-30

In today's first reading, St. Paul continues to give practical advice on Christian family life. He directs his message to children and parents, to slaves and their masters. The civilization of Paul's day was built on slavery. The apostle did not openly denounce this system. He was satisfied to instill principles that prepared the way for a greater respect among all men for one another. The responsorial psalm echoes Paul's words to the Christian slaves that they should work to manifest God's glory and not to please men. The verses of the responsorial psalm ask that all of man's works give praise and honor to the Lord. In the Gospel, Jesus reveals that when the Jews have rejected him, God will call the Gentiles into his kingdom. Jesus also reminds us to work at saving our souls before the door of death closes on us.

482 THURSDAY OF THE THIRTIETH WEEK OF THE YEAR

YEAR I

READING I Rom. 8:31-39   RESP. Ps. 109:21-22, 26-27, 30-31
GOSPEL Luke 13:31-35

In today's first reading, St. Paul raises three questions that go to the core of our life with God. We hear him ask, "Who can be against us?" "Who can bring any charge against us?" "Who can separate us from Christ's love for us?" Paul replies that because God is "for us" no one can really oppose us, or accuse us, or take us away from God's love — a consoling thought for those moments when we get discouraged. Paul concludes with a hymn in praise of God's love. Because Paul reminds us that Jesus intercedes for us "at the right hand of God" against those who would condemn us, the responsorial psalm echoes this idea by saying, "For he stood at the right hand of the poor man to save him from those who would condemn him." In the Gospel, Jesus reveals by his tears how deeply Jerusalem's rejection has hurt him. The city will soon share our Lord's fate when the Romans destroy it.

YEAR II

READING I Eph. 6:10-20   RESP. Ps. 144:1, 2, 9-10
GOSPEL Luke 13:31-35

The first reading is from the closing section of St. Paul's letter to the Christian community in the city of Ephesus. You will hear Paul giving his converts some advice about the spiritual warfare that they must wage against the forces of evil in the world and how important prayer is in this struggle. Paul describes the equipment that the soul must have to carry out this battle. He compares this equipment to the various pieces of armor that the Roman soldiers wore in combat. Because Paul says to "hold faith up before you as your shield," the responsorial psalm relates to this theme by referring to God as "my shield in whom I trust." In the Gospel, Jesus speaks of his approaching death and weeps at the thought that his chosen people are to reject him.

483 FRIDAY OF THE THIRTIETH WEEK OF THE YEAR

YEAR I

READING I Rom. 9:1-5   RESP. Ps. 147:12-13, 14-15, 19-20
GOSPEL Luke 14:1-6

Today's reading begins St. Paul's attempt to answer the critical question of Israel's place in God's plan of salvation, since the chosen people had rejected the Messiah. The three chapters that Paul devotes to the problem in this letter are the seeds of subsequent Christian efforts to explain and defend the faith in a systematic way. Today's passage gives us only the introduction to Paul's discussion. The apostle reveals how deeply this issue touches his heart as he recalls the privileges Israel has enjoyed in the past. The responsorial psalm accents this theme of God's love for Israel because "he has not done thus for any other nation." St. Luke relates four of the seven miracles that the Gospels tells us Jesus worked on the Sabbath. His final story is the cure of a man suffering from dropsy, whose swollen body caused him embarrassment as well as pain.

YEAR II

READING I   Phil. 1:1-11   RESP. Ps. 111:1-2, 3-4, 5-6
GOSPEL   Luke 14:1-6

Today we begin a letter St. Paul wrote about the year 56 to the Church at Philippi, an important town in northern Greece and the first community the apostle founded in Europe. Paul describes the joy that floods his heart whenever he thinks of the Philippians or prays to God for them. Hs asks that the love of God and neighbor that he finds in the lives of the Philippians may continue to increase. In this way, they will be free from fault and will have grown to resemble Christ through their virtues and good works. The responsorial psalm echoes Paul's giving of thanks by declaring, "I will give thanks to the Lord in the company of the just." St. Luke relates four of the seven miracles that the Gospels tell us Jesus worked on the Sabbath. His final story is our Lord's cure of a man suffering from dropsy, whose swollen body caused him embarrassment as well as pain.

484 SATURDAY OF THE THIRTIETH WEEK OF THE YEAR

YEAR I

READING I   Rom. 11:1-2, 11-12, 25-29   RESP. Ps. 94:12-13, 14-15, 17-18
GOSPEL   Luke 14:1, 7-11

Today the liturgy gives us a digest of the eleventh chapter of St. Paul's letter to the Romans that deals with the problem of Israel's failure to accept Christ as the promised Messiah. We hear Paul explain first that God has certainly not rejected his beloved people. The apostle then declares that Israel's loss is the Gentiles' gain. Looking to the future, Paul states that eventually "all Israel will be saved." The responsorial psalm underlines this theme in the verse, "For the Lord will not cast off his people, nor abandon his inheritance." In the Gospel, Jesus tells a story about guests at a wedding feast to teach the Pharisees — and ourselves — a lesson about God's kingdom. We will be lucky to get even the lowest place in the kingdom as long as we think of ourselves in pride as better than other people.

READING I   Phil. 1:18-26   RESP. Ps. 42:2, 3, 5
GOSPEL   Luke 14:1, 7-11

Today St. Paul gives a vivid insight into the meaning of life and death for a Christian. The apostle shows that death is not something he fears. On the contrary, he looks forward to death, as he writes from a prison cell to the community at Philippi, because death would bring him into the joy of eternal union with Christ. Yet, Paul does not despair of life either, since this offers him the opportunity to preach to men about Christ's love for them. Both life and death come under the influence of Christ, and Paul does not know which one to choose. However, he concludes with the hope that God will allow him to work again at Philippi before long. The responsorial psalm also accents Paul's thirst for union with Christ. The Gospel parable of the wedding feast reminds us that we will be lucky to get even the lowest place in God's kingdom if we think of ourselves as better than others.

485   MONDAY OF THE THIRTY-FIRST WEEK OF THE YEAR

YEAR I

READING I   Rom. 11:29-36   RESP. Ps. 69:30-31, 33-34, 36-37
GOSPEL   Luke 14:12-14

In the first reading, St. Paul continues to talk about Israel's place in God's plan of salvation. Paul begins by declaring that God will never revoke his promises to the Jewish people. Paul then reminds his Gentile readers how God showed his mercy to them when the Jews refused the gift of salvation. But one day, the apostle promises, Israel will return to the Lord and also share in his mercy. Paul then praises God for the inscrutable ways of his love. The responsorial psalm also recalls Paul's theme that God "spurns not" his chosen people who are still "in bonds" through their slavery to the Law of Moses. In the Gospel, Jesus teaches us that when we do things for people we should make them feel we are interested in *them* and not in what they might give us in return for our services. This is what real Christian love is all about.

YEAR II

READING I   Phil. 2:1-4   RESP. Ps. 131:1, 2, 3
GOSPEL   Luke 14:12-14

This week the first readings are from St. Paul's letter to the Church at Philippi, an important town in northern Greece. The apostle had founded this first European Christian community about the year 50 during his second missionary journey. Now, about six years later, Paul is in prison — probably at Ephesus in what is today western Turkey. He begins by telling the Philippians how they can cheer him up in the midst of his loneliness. They will make him happy if they strive to work together as a community and show a sincere interest in one another. Since Paul advises that "all parties think humbly of others," the liturgy chooses for the responsorial psalm the prayer of a man whose "heart is not proud." In the Gospel, Jesus teaches us the proper attitude to have in caring for the needs of others. We should help them whether they can pay us back or not.

486 TUESDAY OF THE THIRTY-FIRST WEEK OF THE YEAR

YEAR I

READING I Rom. 12:5-16   **RESP. Ps. 131:1, 2, 3**
GOSPEL   Luke 14:15-24

St. Paul in the first reading gives advice to the Christians in Rome on how to put their faith into practice every day. Paul begins by stating the basic principle of their community life — they all belong to the Body of Christ, and for this reason they are brothers to one another. Each person must be content with the special gifts God has given to him. The apostle then suggests practical ways of expressing love within the community. Because Paul invites the Romans to "rejoice in hope," the responsorial psalm recalls that theme in the verse, "O Israel, hope in the Lord, both now and forever." In the Gospel, Jesus addresses to his critics a parable about a large feast — a common Jewish symbol for God's kingdom. When the invited guests — the Jews — refuse to come, God then goes into the highways and invites everyone to his feast.

YEAR II

READING I Phil. 2:5-11   **RESP. Ps. 22:26-27, 28-30, 31-32**
GOSPEL   Luke 14:15-24

In today's reading, St. Paul apparently quotes from a hymn about Jesus that the early Church used in her worship services. This hymn tells how the Son of God freely chose to surrender his rightful claim to honor and glory *as God.* He became man to share our common lot of suffering and death — but without giving up his divinity. Because he endured this humiliation, all mankind must now acknowledge Jesus as the Lord. We will hear Paul declare that "at Jesus' name every knee must bend on the earth." For this reason, the liturgy selects a respon-sorial psalm that appropriately refers to the adoration of God in the verse, "All the families of the nations shall bow down before him." In the Gospel, Jesus tells a parable about a large feast — a common Jewish symbol for God's kingdom. When the invited guests, the Jews, refuse to come, God then invites everyone to share in the blessings of the kingdom.

487   WEDNESDAY OF THE THIRTY-FIRST WEEK OF THE YEAR

YEAR I

READING I   Rom. 13:8-10   RESP. Ps. 112:1-2, 4-5, 9
GOSPEL   Luke 14:25-33

In today's reading, St. Paul reminds the Christians in Rome that love must be the keynote of their lives. Paul uses a unique expression to develop his point. He tells them to pay off every debt they owe to people except the debt of love. That debt, Paul stresses, they should never pay off. They must spend the rest of their lives returning the love they have "borrowed" in experiencing love from others. In this way, they will fulfill the purpose of all the commandments. The responsorial psalm highlights the apostle's reference to the commandments, in the verse, "Happy the man who . . . greatly delights in God's commands." Two parables in the Gospel teach us that we cannot take our responsibilities as Christians lightly. Following Jesus will demand denying ourselves — especially those things that interfere with our spiritual growth.

YEAR II

READING I   Phil. 2:12-18   RESP. Ps. 27:1, 4, 13-14
GOSPEL   Luke 14:25-33

In today's reading, St. Paul appeals for the Christians at Philippi to continue walking in the footsteps of Christ as they work out their salvation, even though Paul cannot guide them personally because he is in prison. The apostle stresses that the Philippians should allow the example of their lives to shine forth in the pagan society all around them, particularly by not complaining and arguing. Faced with the possibility of having to die for his faith, Paul joyfully embraces this privilege. Because the reading deals with salvation, the responsorial psalm calls on the Lord as "my light and my salvation." Two parables in the Gospel teach us that we cannot take lightly our responsibilities as Christians. Following Jesus will demand denying ourselves — especially in those areas that interfere with our spiritual growth.

488   THURSDAY OF THE THIRTY-FIRST WEEK OF THE YEAR

YEAR I

READING I   Rom. 14:7-12   RESP. Ps. 27:1, 4, 13-14
GOSPEL   Luke 15:1-10

Today's reading reminds us first of all that "we are the Lord's" —

that is, we belong to Jesus by reason of our baptism — and this relationship with our Lord should influence how we act toward one another. St. Paul then mentions two practical situations where we may fail in this ideal. The apostle's point is that each one of us has enough to do worrying about his own salvation without finding fault with others because one day we will have to answer for our failures — and only our *own* — before God our Judge. The responsorial psalm refrain also raises our hearts to the judgment scene "in the land of the living." The Gospel presents two parables of Jesus with the same message — God not only rejoices when sinners repent, he actually goes out of his way to save those who may otherwise be lost.

YEAR II

READING I   Phil. 3:3-8   RESP. Ps. 105:2-3, 4-5, 6-7
GOSPEL   Luke 15:1-10

St. Paul discusses the question of circumcision in today's first reading. You will hear Paul explain how he was circumcised as a child and that he once lived as a Jew. He says that he could have put his "trust in the flesh" by believing that circumcision assured his salvation. But now he believes otherwise. People find salvation not in a physical act that the Law of Moses commanded but by believing in Jesus Christ. The responsorial psalm suggests how Paul searched for God through his years as a Jew and after his conversion. We pray that our "hearts rejoice who search for the Lord." In the Gospel, Jesus tells the parables of the lost sheep and the lost coin to teach how great is the love of God for sinners and how he rejoices when they are sorry for their sins.

489   FRIDAY OF THE THIRTY-FIRST WEEK OF THE YEAR

YEAR I

READING I   Rom. 15:14-21   RESP. Ps. 98:1, 2-3, 3-4
GOSPEL   Luke 16:1-8

Today St. Paul surveys the long letter he has written to the Christians in Rome. In so doing, he reveals those traits of character that made him the outstanding apostle he was. As a sensitive teacher, Paul softens any misunderstanding of points that needed firm emphasis. His heart is deeply grateful to God for his call "to win the Gentiles" for Christ. Finally, Paul quotes the prophet Isaiah as the key to his own pioneering approach to spreading the gospel of Christ. Paul thus discloses again how rooted in the Scriptures was every aspect of his life. The responsorial psalm refrain accents Paul's work with the Gentiles. In the Gospel, Jesus tells a parable about a man who found a practical solution to a crisis in his life. Our Lord suggests that we too must be practical and *do* something to correct whatever threatens our growth in the Christian life.

YEAR II

READING I Phil. 3:17—4:1   **RESP. Ps. 122:1-2, 3-4, 4-5**
GOSPEL   Luke 16:1-8

In today's first reading, St. Paul urges the community at Philippi not to imitate the example of sinful members whose lives reject the salvation that Jesus gained for them on the cross. Instead, the Philippians should follow the pattern of life that Paul has set for them. They should never forget that their real homeland is in heaven, where one day Jesus will reward them with glorified bodies like his own. Because Paul reminds his brothers that they are his "joy," the responsorial psalm accents this theme. The psalm is a joyful hymn that the Jews sang during their pilgrimages to the temple in Jerusalem. In the Gospel, Jesus tells a parable about a man who found a practical solution to a crisis in his life. Our Lord suggests that we, too, must be practical and *do* something to correct whatever threatens our growth in the Christian life.

490 SATURDAY OF THE THIRTY-FIRST WEEK OF THE YEAR

YEAR I

READING I Rom. 16:3-9, 16, 22-27   **RESP. Ps. 145:2-3, 4-5, 10-11**
GOSPEL   Luke 16:9-15

Today's first reading allows us to draw aside the curtain of centuries that separates us from the early days of the Church to meet by name some of the first Christians who were close friends of St. Paul in the community at Rome. We learn that the home of Prisca and Aquila hosted worship services, even as Christian homes do today. We meet the man who was the first convert in the Roman province of Asia and several other converts who shared Paul's hard work among the Gentiles. We learn, too, that a man named Tertius, Paul's secretary, actually wrote down the apostle's complex ideas about salvation. The responsorial psalm echoes the "glory" and "praise" of Paul's closing hymn to God the Father. In the Gospel, Jesus speaks about honesty even in small matters, the true riches of heaven that God entrusts to us, and how our main priority in life must be God, not money.

YEAR II

READING I Phil. 4:10-19   **RESP. Ps. 112:1-2, 5-6, 8, 9**
GOSPEL   Luke 16:9-15

The first Scripture reading for today's Mass reveals how the early

Christians showed concern for Paul's hardships and helped to support him. Paul thanks the community at Philippi in Greece for its prayerful concern and generosity in providing for his needs. Paul specifically mentions that the Philippians were the only community he allowed to assist him in this way. He singles out a man named Epaphroditus, who brought their generous collection to him while Paul was in prison. The responsorial psalm accents how Christians ought to support generously people who are in need, in such verses as, "Lavishly he gives to the poor; his generosity shall endure forever." In the Gospel, Jesus speaks about honesty even in small matters, the true riches of heaven that God entrusts to us, and how our main priority in life must be God, not money.

491 MONDAY OF THE THIRTY-SECOND WEEK OF THE YEAR

YEAR I

READING I   Wis. 1:1-7   RESP. Ps. 139:1-3, 4-6, 7-8, 9-10
GOSPEL   Luke 17:1-6

As we begin the Book of Wisdom today, we hear the author address the men "who judge the earth," as if he were King Solomon talking to other rulers of his time. In reality, the author was a Jew from the Egyptian city of Alexandria — renowned about the year 50 B.C. as a seat of learning. In ancient times, writers often borrowed the name of a famous man to gain more respect for their works, and none was more famous for wisdom than Solomon. In this passage, the author urges the Jews to continue disposing their hearts for those graces that will make them wise. Since the author declares, "The spirit of the Lord fills the world," the responsorial psalm echoes his idea by saying, "Where can I go from your spirit?" In the Gospel, Jesus urges his disciples to open their hearts by forgiving others without limit and to believe that faith makes all things possible.

YEAR II

READING I   Titus 1:1-9   RESP. Ps. 24:1-2, 3-4, 5-6
GOSPEL   Luke 17:1-6

Today's first reading begins a letter that St. Paul wrote to Titus, his fellow missionary. After they had worked together on the Greek island of Crete, Paul left his friend behind to finish organizing Crete's Christian community and to combat false teachers. Paul first recalls the vocation that God gave him to tell the Good News of salvation to everyone. Paul then instructs Titus on what qualifications the pastors that Titus appoints over the island's local churches should possess. These priests must live blameless lives, be steadfast in faith, and be sensible and fair. The responsorial psalm also stresses the theme of holiness of life that must characterize the ministers of God. In the Gospel, Jesus teaches the need to forgive others no matter how often they hurt us. We must also believe that faith makes all things possible.

492 TUESDAY OF THE THIRTY-SECOND WEEK OF THE YEAR

YEAR I

READING I   Wis. 2:23—3:9   **RESP.** Ps. 34:2-3, 16-17, 18-19
GOSPEL   Luke 17:7-10

The first reading reveals that a happy life with God after death awaits the man who has accepted his sufferings patiently and remained faithful to God. This teaching from the Book of Wisdom on immortality — perhaps the first appearance of this idea in the Old Testament — had an important influence on later Jewish and Christian thought about the afterlife. The consoling words of this passage make it appropriate for Masses of the Dead. We also seem to find here the first biblical text that identifies with "the envy of the devil," the serpent's evil influence on man in the Garden of Eden. The responsorial psalm stresses God's concern when a just man has to suffer, by declaring, "When the just cry out, the Lord hears them." In the Gospel, Jesus reminds his Church leaders that the day should never come when they feel that by doing their duty they have done enough to serve their people.

YEAR II

READING I   Titus 2:1-8, 11-14   **RESP.** Ps. 37:3-4, 18, 23, 27, 29
GOSPEL   Luke 17:7-10

Today's first reading contains counsels and instruction for a bishop named Titus, whom St. Paul had put in charge of the Church on the Greek island of Crete. We note that the early Church insisted that preaching follow the "sound doctrine" which the apostles handed on, because Paul tells Titus to conform his words to this teaching. Paul gives Titus advice about four groups in his community, that is, the older men and women and then the younger men and women. Titus himself must always offer his own life as a good example to them, so that there may be no discredit to the Church. Since Paul refers to the Lord "offering salvation to all men," the responsorial psalm declares that "the salvation of the just comes from the Lord." In the Gospel, Jesus reminds his Church leaders that the day should never come when they feel that by doing their duty they have done enough to serve their people.

493 WEDNESDAY OF THE THIRTY-SECOND WEEK OF THE YEAR

YEAR I

READING I   Wis. 6:2-11   RESP. Ps. 82:3-4, 6-7
GOSPEL   Luke 17:11-19

In the first reading, the author addresses the kings of the earth as if he were King Solomon speaking. His audience, however, was in Alexandria, an Egyptian seat of learning in the century before Christ's birth where the author's fellow Jews resided. They were the largest of several groups of Jews who lived away from Palestine. Their language and their whole outlook came from the exciting new Greek culture all around them. They faced the danger that their pagan environment would erode their Jewish heritage. For this reason, the author moves to counter the force of Greek intellectual attractions on his countrymen by summoning them to seek the true wisdom that God alone can give. The responsorial psalm refrain echoes the theme of judgment in the reading. The Gospel account of the one grateful leper who is a Samaritan contrasts the faith of the Jews and the Gentiles.

YEAR II

READING I   Titus 3:1-7   RESP. Ps. 23:1-3, 3-4, 5, 6
GOSPEL   Luke 17:11-19

The first reading combines practical advice about how to live a Christian life with insights into where that life comes from. St. Paul begins by instructing his former co-worker Titus about important virtues he must teach the community. Titus was then bishop of the Church on the fabled Greek island of Crete. Paul goes on to contrast the sinful lives Christians used to lead before God in his mercy revealed his Son to the world. The apostle points to the sacrament of baptism as the source of the new life that turns the faithful into children of God through Christ and prepares them for eternal happiness with him. Because Paul describes the "kindness and love of God" that appeared in Christ, the responsorial psalm also refers to God's kindness and goodness. In the Gospel story of the ten lepers, only the outcast Samaritan returns to thank Jesus, who praises him for his faith.

494 THURSDAY OF THE THIRTY-SECOND WEEK OF THE YEAR

YEAR I

READING I   Wis. 7:22—8:1   RESP. Ps. 119:89, 90, 91, 130, 135, 175
GOSPEL   Luke 17:20-25

We find in today's reading a eulogy to Wisdom that is the summit of Old Testament reflection on this virtue. The author presents Wisdom as a living person and sketches her many qualities. From ideas in this passage, New Testament writers developed important insights into Christ. One example is the author's description of Wisdom as "the image of God's goodness" — a concept that St. Paul applies to Christ in his letter to the Colossians. Early Christian tradition also identified the Wisdom of this passage with the Son of God. Since the author describes Wisdom as the brilliance of "eternal light," the responsorial psalm accents this idea by saying, "The revelation of your words sheds light." In the Gospel, Jesus tells the Pharisees — who are too blind to realize it — that in his own preaching and healing, God's kingdom has already arrived without fanfare.

YEAR II

READING I Philemon 7-20 RESP. Ps. 146:7, 8-9, 9-10
GOSPEL Luke 17:20-25

In the first reading, St. Paul writes to Philemon, a young well-to-do Christian who is his close friend. The letter concerns Philemon's slave Onesimus, who had fled to Rome after some wrong he had done his master. Paul, while in custody in Rome, happened to meet Onesimus. The two became friends and Paul converted him to Christianity. When Paul learned the truth about Onesimus, he wrote the letter we hear in today's reading to ask that Philemon accept Onesimus back. Paul asks Philemon to receive Onesimus not as a slave, but as a brother in Christ. The responsorial psalm echoes Paul's request by declaring that "the Lord sets captives free." In the Gospel, Jesus explains that God's kingdom has begun on earth. He then refers to his future sufferings and how men will reject him.

495 FRIDAY OF THE THIRTY-SECOND WEEK OF THE YEAR

YEAR I

READING I Wis. 13:1-9 RESP. Ps. 19:2-3, 4-5
GOSPEL Luke 17:26-37

Today's reading is unique in the Old Testament for the sympathy it reveals toward pagans who worshiped false gods — that is, the works of nature. "For these the blame is less," says the author when he considers that these people have at least responded to part of God's creation, rather than such works of men as the idols in pagan temples. The line of reasoning the author adopts in this passage — that all men can discover God exists by studying the world he made — also appears in the opening chapter of St. Paul's letter to the Romans. The responsorial psalm underscores the author's view that "the heavens proclaim the glory of God." In the Gospel, Jesus warns that we must always be ready to meet him when he comes at the end of the world — just as

Noah and Lot prepared themselves for God's judgments on the world in their own times.

YEAR II

READING I   2 John 4-9   RESP. Ps. 119:1, 2, 10, 11, 17, 18
GOSPEL   Luke 17:26-37

Today's first reading is from a brief letter St. John wrote to an un-identified local Christian community for which he felt a special loving concern. You will hear John addressing the Church in personal terms as "my Lady" and its members as her children. Because this Church had to weather false doctrines, some members were in danger of absorbing them. As a result, John encourages his flock to resist these teachings and to walk in the truth of Christ. John's request that the Church "walk according to the commandments" appears again in the responsorial psalm. We pray that "happy are they who walk in the law of the Lord." In the Gospel, Jesus tells of the final days of the world when God will reveal his Son to us. We must prepare ourselves, just as Noah and Lot prepared for God's judgments on the world in their time.

496 SATURDAY OF THE THIRTY-SECOND WEEK OF THE YEAR

YEAR I

READING I   Wis. 18:14-16; 19:6-9   RESP. Ps. 105:2-3, 36-37, 42-43
GOSPEL   Luke 18:1-8

As today's first reading opens, the author of the Book of Wisdom describes how God's messenger of death swooped down from heaven upon every firstborn in Egypt. This was the final plague that prepared for God's delivery of the Israelites from slavery. The author then describes the miracle that allowed the people to cross the Red Sea to freedom. He shows that God by his control over nature brings blessings to those who serve him and punishment to those who rebel against him. The responsorial psalm also recalls "the marvels the Lord has done" for Israel. In the Gospel we find still another parable proper to St. Luke that demonstrates how he tells us more about prayer than the other Gospel writers. Our Lord's point in the parable is that we should never give up on God when we pray, but instead we should keep asking for the things we need.

YEAR II

READING I   3 John 5-8   RESP. Ps. 112:1-2, 3-4, 5-6
GOSPEL   Luke 18:1-8

The first reading gives us an insight into the way the early preachers of the Gospel lived. They depended for their support on what their fellow Christians provided. Today's letter of John describes this support as an opportunity to work in spirit, side by side with Christ's consecrated missionaries. In our day, we also regard what we give to the missions as a way for us, too, to share in the work of the missionaries. That is why the responsorial psalm highlights John's praise of generous support of missionaries. The psalm praises the man who is generous with his wealth and graciously lends what he has. In the Gospel, Jesus tells a parable that reminds us never to give up on prayer. The Church offers us a working model of this kind of persevering prayer in the way she constantly asks for the final coming of Christ in her Advent season, at daily Mass, and in the Our Father.

497 MONDAY OF THE THIRTY-THIRD WEEK OF THE YEAR

YEAR I

READING I   1 Mac. 1:10-15, 41-43, 54-57, 62-63
GOSPEL   Luke 18:35-43   RESP. Ps. 119:53, 61, 134, 150, 155, 158

During this week, the liturgy gives us a digest of key events from the two Books of the Maccabees. These deal with the religious wars the Jewish people fought against the power of Syria from the year 175 to 135 B.C. Today we meet the villain of our story, the newly crowned king of Syria, Antiochus Epiphanes. To unify his kingdom so that all its citizens would conform to the current Greek style of life, Antiochus began to force Greek customs and religious practices on Judea — as we learn in this reading. The king's efforts to exterminate the Jewish religion were a major threat to Israel's continued existence as a distinct people in Greek society. We may regard the responsorial psalm as the prayer of a loyal Jew during this time of religious crisis. In the Gospel, Jesus heals the blind man at Jericho to reward him for his faith.

YEAR II

READING I   Rev. 1:1-4; 2:1-5   RESP. Ps. 1:1-2, 3, 4, 6
GOSPEL   Luke 18:35-43

Today we begin the Book of Revelation, the last in the Bible, that tradition attributes to St. John. This book represents a form of writing popular in the two centuries just prior to the birth of Christ — and in the years immediately after. Such literature claimed to reveal hidden truths that God had imparted to its authors, especially events in the future. John uses this literary form to encourage the persecuted Christians of the first century. He reveals to them the unseen forces of God at work behind all the events that threatened their lives. In today's passage, John presents the first of seven messages that Jesus told him to write to local Church communities in what is now Turkey. The responsorial psalm emphasizes how our Lord rejected the wicked in the community at Ephesus. In the Gospel, Jesus restores sight to the blind man at Jericho in another work of healing our Lord performed as the Messiah.

498 TUESDAY OF THE THIRTY-THIRD WEEK OF THE YEAR

YEAR I

READING I 2 Mac. 6:18-31   **RESP.** Ps. 3:2-3, 4-5, 6-8
GOSPEL Luke 19:1-10

Today's reading shows us how hard many Jews fought against the king of Syria's campaign to get them to behave and worship as the Greeks did. The scene was probably the courtyard of the temple in Jerusalem, where the king had set up an altar for the sacrifice of pigs to the Greek god Zeus. We see how an aged scribe named Eleazar refuses to eat from one of these pagan sacrifices the unclean food that the Law of Moses forbade. Eleazar is willing to give his life to support the claim that the Law must have on every loyal Jewish heart. The liturgy suggests that the responsorial psalm is Eleazar's confident prayer to God as he goes to his death. The Gospel deals with an incident that St. Luke alone tells us about. We learn that the Messiah came to bring into God's kingdom even such people as the tax collector Zacchaeus, who in those days was a social outcast.

YEAR II

READING I Rev. 3:1-6, 14-22   **RESP.** Ps. 15:2-3, 3-4, 5
GOSPEL Luke 19:1-10

Today's first reading presents letters to the Christian communities of Sardis and Laodicea, two ancient cities in what is now Turkey. God rebukes the people of Sardis for leading selfish lives and calls on them to reform. We learn that God records the names of the faithful in "the book of the living," because Jewish belief then held that the Lord kept such books of judgment. God also summons the Laodiceans to repent their spiritually lukewarm lives. Because God tells them, "I will give the victor the right to sit with me on my throne," the responsorial psalm declares, "Him who is victorious I will sit beside me on my throne." The Gospel deals with an incident that St. Luke alone narrates. Jesus shows concern to bring into God's kingdom even such people as the tax collector Zacchaeus, who in those days was a social outcast.

YEAR I

READING 1   2 Mac. 7:1, 20-31   RESP. Ps. 17:1, 5-6, 8, 15
GOSPEL   Luke 19:11-28

In today's reading, we discover that the Books of the Maccabees aim to show how the Jewish people clung to the Law of Moses with loyal hearts in a time of severe testing during the second century B.C. At this time, the Syrian king Antiochus had put an end to all forms of Jewish religion and imposed the worship of Greek gods. Antiochus wished to unify his kingdom under the Greek culture then flourishing everywhere. We learn how a mother and her seven sons heroically undergo cruel tortures and accept death rather than eat the unclean food of pork from pagan sacrifices. The responsorial psalm becomes a prayer of these Jewish martyrs as they face death with confidence in God. The Gospel parable about the king who gives his servants money to invest suggests that a Christian must be willing to take risks rather than settle for a comfortable, mediocre life.

YEAR II

READING I   Rev. 4:1-11   RESP. Ps. 150:1-2, 3-4, 5-6
GOSPEL   Luke 19:11-28

Today St. John describes imaginatively the court of heaven where God rules the universe. Around his throne, four "living creatures" continuously praise God's holiness. Early Church writers regarded these creatures as symbolizing the authors of the Gospels, and we still find these images in contemporary religious art. Mark is the lion. Luke is the ox. Matthew is the man and John is the eagle. John offers this awesome scene to console the Christians who were then enduring persecution. Because God is the loving master of his creation, the suffering Church on earth can look forward in hope to the joys of eternal life with him. The responsorial psalm accents the praise of God's holiness. The Gospel parable about the king who gives his servants money to invest suggests that a Christian must be willing to take risks rather than setle for a comfortable, mediocre life.

YEAR I

READING I   1 Mac. 2:15-29   RESP. Ps. 50:1-2, 5-6, 14-15
GOSPEL   Luke 19:41-44

The first reading reveals how, in the small town of Modein, about fifteen miles northwest of Jerusalem, one determined family resisted the efforts of the king of Syria to impose Greek culture and religious practices on the Jews about 167 B.C. After fleeing into the hill country, Mattathias — a Jewish priest of Modein — and his five sons gathered a number of Jews who wished to remain loyal to God. They soon embarked on three years of fierce guerrilla warfare against the Syrian forces and their traitorous Jewish sympathizers. Since Mattathias and his sons "keep to the covenant," the responsorial psalm shows God's pleasure in "those who have made a covenant" with him and keep it. In the Gospel, when Jesus arrives at the end of his journey to Jerusalem, he weeps as he realizes the approaching fate of this city so dear to God in the long history of his chosen people.

YEAR II

READING I   Rev. 5:1-10   RESP. Ps. 149:1-2, 3-4, 5-6, 9
GOSPEL   Luke 19:41-44

As today's first reading begins, St. John beholds a vision of God on his throne with a sealed scroll in his right hand. John weeps bitterly when he realizes that there is no one important enough to open the scroll and reveal its prophecies about the destiny of the world. John is sad because he knows these prophecies will comfort the Church undergoing persecution at that time. Then one of the twenty-four elders at God's throne comforts John by telling him that Christ — under his titles as Lion of Judah and Root of David — has earned the right to open the scroll. Jesus did that through his victory over death by which he redeemed all men. Christ then takes the scroll and receives the worship of the whole heavenly court. The responsorial psalm accents this praise of the Lamb of God. In the Gospel, Jesus weeps, too, when he perceives that Roman soldiers will destroy his beloved Jerusalem.

501   FRIDAY OF THE THIRTY-THIRD WEEK OF THE YEAR

YEAR I

READING I   1 Mac. 4:36-37, 52-59   RESP. Ps. 1 Chr. 29:10, 11, 11-12, 12
GOSPEL   Luke 19:45-48

As today's reading opens, Judas Maccabaeus and his brothers for the time being have overcome the Syrian army and liberated Jerusalem in 164 B.C. Judas had received the name "Maccabee" — the Jewish word for "hammer" — for a good reason. In the face of overwhelming odds, Judas had led the small Jewish guerrilla force in hard-hitting attacks against the enemy. We hear the concern of Judas to purify the temple where the Syrians had set up an altar for sacrifices to the Greek gods. To this day, in their feast of Hanukkah around Christmas time, the Jews commemorate the rededication of the temple in Jerusalem. The responsorial psalm is an appropriate prayer that the Jews sang when they gave offerings for their first temple. The Gospel reading about Jesus driving the money changers from the temple reflects the zeal of the Maccabees for God's house.

YEAR II

READING I   Rev. 10:8-11   RESP. Ps. 119:14, 24, 72, 103, 111, 131
GOSPEL   Luke 19:45-48

In today's first Scripture reading, an angel gives St. John a small scroll and asks him to eat it. This is John's way of saying that he thoroughly understood the special message he was receiving in a vision. To John the scroll tastes both sweet and bitter. This experience refers to the message on the scroll. The sweet taste is the glorious victory that the faithful will achieve at the end of time. The bitter taste is the suffering that the faithful must endure before their triumph. Since the passage says that the scroll tastes "as sweet as honey," the responsorial psalm echoes this theme in the refrain, "How sweet to my taste is your promise." In the Gospel, Jesus cleanses the temple of the money changers and then begins to teach there.

502 SATURDAY OF THE THIRTY-THIRD WEEK OF THE YEAR

YEAR I

READING I   1 Mac. 6:1-13   RESP. Ps. 9:2-3, 4, 6, 16, 19
GOSPEL   Luke 20:27-40

Today's reading begins with a military expedition that the Syrian king Antiochus led into Persia. He was on the prowl for loot to fill his treasury, which wasteful habits had drained about the year 164 B.C. Antiochus then receives the shattering news that his military forces governing the Jews in Judea have met with defeat. We next learn that his conscience is bothering him because of the savage persecution he had inflicted on the Jewish people. The king will be dead in another year, and the Jewish holy war against Syria will expand into a drive for independence that finally came in the year 142. The responsorial psalm becomes Israel's thanksgiving prayer for its freedom. In the Gospel, some Sadducees question Jesus on the resurrection of the dead. Since they quote Moses, our Lord quotes Moses back to them to prove that the Father is a God of the living.

YEAR II

READING I   Rev. 11:4-12   RESP. Ps. 144:1, 2, 9-10
GOSPEL   Luke 20:27-40

In today's reading, St. John tells about two men who act as witnesses for God in the last days of the world. As the prophet Elijah and Moses once did, these witnesses call the people to repent their sinful lives. Then John relates how a wild beast, symbolizing the forces of evil, comes from an abyss and kills the two witnesses. But God soon restores them to life and takes them to heaven, showing that the Lord is mightier than the world of evil. This prophecy probably refers to trials that John foresaw lay ahead for the Church in the last days. In the responsorial psalm, we hear each witness praising God for delivering him from death, in the verse, "My refuge and my fortress, my stronghold, my deliverer." In the Gospel, some Sadducees question Jesus about the resurrection of the dead. Since they quote Moses, our Lord quotes Moses back to them to prove that the Father is a God of the living.

503 MONDAY OF THE THIRTY-FOURTH, OR LAST, WEEK OF THE YEAR

YEAR I

READING I   Dan. 1:1-6, 8-20   RESP. Ps. Dan. 3:52, 53, 54, 55, 56
GOSPEL   Luke 21:1-4

Today's first reading takes up again the life of the Jewish people under a persecution by Syria in the year 168 B.C. — but from an entirely different viewpoint. An unknown author during this period of crisis for the Jews speaks to his countrymen through his story about Daniel, a devout Jew among the exiles in Babylon almost four hundred years earlier. Daniel's loyalty to his religious beliefs among a foreign people contains a hidden lesson for the persecuted Jews of the second century. For this reason, today's story about Daniel's keeping faith with his Jewish dietary laws would encourage the Jews of the second century to remain loyal also, even at the risk of death from their Syrian oppressors. The responsorial psalm is a hymn of praise from the Book of Daniel. In the Gospel, Jesus points to a poor widow giving a donation to the temple as an example of what loving God is all about.

YEAR II

READING I   Rev. 14:1-3, 4-5   RESP. Ps. 24:1-2, 3-4, 5-6
GOSPEL   Luke 21:1-4

Today's first reading must have encouraged the early Christians who were undergoing a fierce persecution at the hands of their Roman oppressors. St. John portrays the risen Christ as the Lamb who at the end of the world stands in triumph on Mount Zion with those who have remained loyal to him despite their sufferings. These people have marks on their foreheads to show that they belong to God and enjoy his protection. Because they have led holy lives, they can learn the song that the heavenly choirs chant before God's throne. Although this is a symbolic vision, the scene should likewise encourage us to look forward to our destiny in heaven and to prepare for it by the way we live each day. The responsorial psalm underscores the holy life that God requires if we would "ascend the mountain of the Lord." The Gospel reveals a poor widow as an example of what loving God is all about.

504 TUESDAY OF THE THIRTY-FOURTH, OR LAST, WEEK OF THE YEAR

YEAR I

READING I Dan. 2:31-45 RESP. Ps. Dan. 3:57, 58, 59, 60, 61
GOSPEL Luke 21:5-11

In today's first reading, the devout Jew Daniel warns the king of Babylon that the stone of God's kingdom will shatter all earthly kingdoms which oppose the Lord God. In this way, Daniel interprets the king's dream about the statue of a man that a large stone destroys. The author of this story intended that Daniel's words might comfort the Jews whom the Syrian king was persecuting in the middle of the second century B.C. Because this Syrian ruler opposes God's kingdom and worships Greek gods, he will surely suffer a downfall like that of the Babylonian king. The responsorial psalm praises God with a hymn from the Book of Daniel. In the Gospel, St. Luke begins a section dealing with the final days of the world. Jesus warns us not to let premature disasters mislead us into thinking that the end is near.

YEAR II

READING I Rev. 14:14-19 RESP. Ps. 96:10, 11-12, 13
GOSPEL Luke 21:5-11

In the first reading, St. John uses two images to describe the judgment of the world at the end of time. First, he compares the judgment to the season for harvesting the fields. Christ, the Son of Man, reaps the harvest of those who have been faithful to him. The second image is a winepress to crush grapes. An angel gathers the grapes of those whose evil lives will condemn them to the winepress of God's wrath. The responsorial psalm echoes the theme of this reading in the refrain, "The Lord comes to judge the earth." In the Gospel, Jesus tells about the coming destruction of Jerusalem and the end of the world. Our Lord's prediction reveals that the precious stones which adorn the temple will soon be a heap of rubble. God wants instead the living stones of men's hearts that will return the love he offers them.

505 WEDNESDAY OF THE THIRTY-FOURTH, OR LAST, WEEK OF THE YEAR

YEAR I

READING I   Dan. 5:1-6, 13-14, 16-17, 23-28   RESP. Ps. Dan. 3:62, 63, 64, 65, 66, 67
GOSPEL   Luke 21:12-19

In today's first reading, we learn how Daniel warns King Belshazzar that the baffling message which appeared on the walls of his palace in Babylon means that he will lose his kingdom very soon. The story really contains a message for the Jewish people who lived under persecution from the Syrians in the second century B.C. — the period when the author wrote this story about Daniel. The writer wanted his Jewish countrymen to realize that the king whom God condemns in the story is not the one in Babylon but the reigning king of Syria, who is responsible for their sufferings. God will punish him, the author says, because he worships Greek gods. The responsorial psalm continues the hymn of praise from the Book of Daniel. In the Gospel, Jesus explains that there will be persecutions before the end of time, but God will take care of those who remain faithful to him.

YEAR II

READING I   Rev. 15:1-4   RESP. Ps. 98:1, 2-3, 7-8, 9
GOSPEL   Luke 21:12-19

In the first Scripture reading, St. John describes the glory of heaven and the final triumph of all suffering Christians. This passage must have greatly consoled the Christian community of the first century because the Roman authorities were conducting a ruthless persecution at that time. The victorious faithful sing two songs that are almost entirely quotations from the Old Testament. The songs are a burst of praise for the greatness of God. He has shown tender love and care for his people down through the long history of man's journey to salvation. The responsorial psalm echoes the songs that the victorious faithful proclaim at the end of time. In the Gospel, Jesus warns that suffering will come to those who follow him. He urges us to be patient when suffering comes because then the strength of God's grace will comfort us.

506 THURSDAY OF THE THIRTY-FOURTH, OR LAST, WEEK OF THE YEAR

YEAR I

READING I Dan. 6:12-28   RESP. Ps. Dan. 3:68, 69, 70, 71, 72, 73, 74
GOSPEL   Luke 21:20-28

Today's first reading introduces us again to the devout Jew, Daniel, who "three times a day offers his prayer" to God in keeping with the directions of the Torah, the collection of Jewish wisdom and laws. Because Daniel defies the king's edict that his subjects may pray only to him, Babylonian soldiers toss Daniel to the lions. This story served to remind the Jews of another day — the victims of persecution by the king of Syria about 168 B.C. — that God expected them to be as observant of his laws as Daniel was, even if it meant that they must die for it. The responsorial psalm takes up all creation's praise of God from the Book of Daniel. In the Gospel, Jesus first tells his disciples about the coming destruction of the city of Jerusalem. He then looks to the future when the "Son of Man" will return in power and glory at the end of time.

YEAR II

READING I   Rev. 18:1-2, 21-23; 19:1-3, 9   RESP. Ps. 100:2, 3, 4, 5
GOSPEL   Luke 21:20-28

In today's first reading, the apostle John has a vision of the doom of Babylon — a symbol of the city of Rome and its vices. You will hear an angel declaring that Babylon's destruction will be so thorough that there will be no signs of life among the minstrels, craftsmen, mill workers, and other people. The passage concludes with the song of a great assembly in heaven praising God's justice in punishing Rome, which appears as a harlot. The responsorial psalm also mentions how those who are welcome at the wedding feast of the Lamb will celebrate joyfully in heaven at the end of time. The Gospel reading also relates closely to this theme. Jesus tells his disciples about the forthcoming destruction of the city of Jerusalem and the appearance of the Son of Man in glory at the end of the world.

507 FRIDAY OF THE THIRTY-FOURTH, OR LAST, WEEK OF THE YEAR

YEAR I

READING I   Dan. 7:2-14   RESP. Ps. Dan. 3:75, 76, 77, 78, 79, 80, 81
GOSPEL   Luke 21:29-33

In today's reading, we begin the first of four visions in the Book of

Daniel about the final days of the world. Daniel beholds four strange beasts coming out of "the great sea" — a symbol in ancient times for the source of all evil powers that warred against God's creation. We will learn what this vision means in tomorrow's reading. Daniel also sees "one like a son of man coming, on the clouds of heaven" — a figure that Jesus identifies with himself throughout the gospels. The responsorial psalm continues to praise God from the hymn in the Book of Daniel. In the Gospel, Jesus declares that "this generation" — the human race — will surely experience one day all that he has promised about the end of the world. The sign of that day will be as obvious as a budding tree that signals the approach of a new season of the year.

YEAR II

READING I Rev. 20:1-4, 11—21:2   RESP. Ps. 84:3, 4, 5-6, 8
GOSPEL Luke 21:29-33

Today's first Scripture reading speaks of a mysterious thousand-year reign of Christ on earth. From the earliest days of the Church, many Christian writers have understood this passage as meaning that Christ would reign for a thousand years on earth, together with the martyrs and saints, before founding a new world in heaven. This expectation of a millenium has persisted to our own day in certain sects, such as the Jehovah's Witnesses. One common interpretation is that of St. Augustine. He explains that the thousand years stand symbolically for the whole history of the Church from Christ's resurrection until his final coming. The responsorial psalm after this reading expresses our yearning for heaven. In the Gospel, Jesus speaks of the destruction of Jerusalem and the signs that will accompany the final days of the world.

508 SATURDAY OF THE THIRTY-FOURTH, OR LAST, WEEK OF THE YEAR

YEAR I

READING I Dan. 7:15-27   RESP. Ps. Dan. 3:82, 83, 84, 85, 86, 87
GOSPEL Luke 21:34-36

The first reading tells us the meaning of Daniel's vision of the four beasts that we learned about at yesterday's Mass. We must remember that the author of this passage was a Jew who lived during a fierce persecution by the king of Syria between the years 168 and 165 B.C. For this reason, the terrible fourth beast in today's reading is a symbol for the king's domain, where he had set up altars to pagan gods. The angel who explains the vision to Daniel refers to the persecution in his comment that the king "shall speak against the Most High and oppress the holy ones of the Most High" — that is, the Jews. The responsorial psalm calls on all men to praise the Lord. The practical importance of today's Gospel for our lives is a warning to prepare for our meeting with Christ at the moment of death. Then we will surely be with him at his final coming.

YEAR II

READING I   Rev. 22:1-7   RESP. Ps. 95:1-2, 3-5, 6-7
GOSPEL   Luke 21:34-36

The readings for the Church year close today, by design, on the theme of the end of time and the beginning of eternal life with God in paradise. Tomorrow a new year begins for the Church with the season of Advent that also looks to the last days of the world. In the passage for this Mass, St. John describes the interior of the heavenly city, Jerusalem. He suggests that God will restore the lost paradise of Eden with its life-giving river and the tree of life. Those who serve before God's throne enjoy the beatific vision forever. This scene of the new paradise serves to bridge the first and last books of the Bible. Because the reading concludes on the note of Jesus' final coming — "Remember, I am coming soon" — the responsorial psalm refrain contains the ancient Aramaic expression *marana tha*, "Come, Lord Jesus!" St. Luke's Gospel urges us to "be on the watch" for Jesus when he does come.

PROPER OF THE SAINTS

512 January 13 — ST. HILARY, Bishop and Doctor

READING I 1 John 2:18-25   **RESP. Ps.** Common or Season
GOSPEL   Common or Season

A special first Scripture reading for today's Mass applies to the life of St. Hilary. The days of the bloody persecution of the Church had scarcely come to an end early in the fourth century when a dangerous heresy arose which denied the divinity of Christ. Hilary, bishop of Poitiers in France, was one of those who defended the faith, especially through his writing on the Blessed Trinity. The liturgy now invites us to listen to this reading as if Hilary himself were issuing to the Christians of his day, and to all Christians, a warning against antichrists — that is, teachers of heresy.

513 January 17 — ST. ANTHONY, Abbot

READING I Common or Season   **RESP. Ps.** Common or Season
GOSPEL   Matthew 19:16-26

The Gospel reading at today's Mass applies to the life of St. Anthony, father of the monastic way of life. As a young man, he heard the words of the Gospel in church, "If you seek perfection, go, sell your possessions, and give to the poor." To Anthony it seemed that Jesus was giving him a personal command which he must obey. The future saint responded by selling his property and going into the Egyptian desert to lead a life of intense prayer and penance. The liturgy now invites us to listen to that same Gospel passage which inspired Anthony to a life of holiness back in the third century.

519 January 25 — CONVERSION OF ST. PAUL, Apostle

READING I Acts 22:3-16   **RESP. Ps.** 117:1, 2
GOSPEL   Mark 16:15-18

In today's first Scripture reading we hear St. Paul explain to a crowd of Jews in Jerusalem his former life as a Jew and then his awesome meeting with the risen Jesus on the road to Damascus — the event we commemorate in today's Mass. Paul had just returned from his third missionary journey to the Gentiles in what is present-day Turkey. The apostle tells the Jews about his conversion experience so that they may believe Jesus was the promised Messiah and receive baptism to wipe out their sins. The responsorial psalm accents Paul's vocation to preach the Good News of salvation to the Gentiles. The Gospel tells how Jesus appeared to the apostles after his resurrection and commanded them, "Proclaim the good news to all creation." This is the command that Paul, in the wake of his conversion, worked so zealously to carry out.

OR:

READING I   Acts 9:1-22   RESP. Ps. 117:1, 2
GOSPEL   Mark 16:15-18

Today's first Scripture reading tells us about St. Paul's meeting with the risen Jesus on the road to Damascus — an event of supreme significance for the Church and the world. The words of Jesus, "Saul, Saul, why do you persecute me?" made a profound and lasting impact on Saul — who would become the fearless apostle Paul. Through his reflection on this experience of the risen Lord present in his disciples, Paul eventually developed the doctrine that Christians are the Body of Christ and Jesus is the Head of this body. The responsorial psalm accents the apostle's vocation to preach the Good News of salvation to the Gentiles. The Gospel reading tells how Jesus appeared to the apostles after his resurrection and commanded them, "Proclaim the good news to all creation." This is the command that Paul, in the wake of his conversion, worked so zealously to carry out.

520   January 26 — ST. TIMOTHY AND ST. TITUS, Bishops

READING I   2 Tim. 1:1-8   RESP. Ps. Common or Season
GOSPEL   Common or Season

A special first Scripture reading honors St. Timothy, a missionary companion of St. Paul. Timothy became Paul's most beloved spiritual son because the apostle had baptized him and ordained him to the priesthood. Paul appointed him first bishop of the important Christian community of Ephesus in present-day western Turkey. During the loneliness of Paul's imprisonment in Rome, he wrote to Timothy, urging him to come quickly to visit him. You will now hear Paul's message that expresses his deep affection for Timothy. It also reveals how concerned Paul was that Timothy remain faithful to the demands his Christian life made on him.

OR:

READING I   Titus 1:1-5   **RESP. Ps. Common or Season**
GOSPEL   **Common or Season**

A special first Scripture reading honors St. Titus, a missionary companion of St. Paul. A Gentile convert, Titus was a decisive, zealous, and competent man. Paul sent him to trouble spots in the Church, such as Corinth, where Titus restored obedience. Titus accompanied Paul during their mission to the fabled Greek island of Crete. The apostle left Titus there to continue the work of organizing the Church as its bishop. You will hear Paul refer to this appointment in the following reading.

524   February 2 — PRESENTATION OF THE LORD

READING I   Mal. 3:1-4   **RESP. Ps. 24:7, 8, 9, 10**
READING II   Heb. 2:14-18
GOSPEL   Luke 2:22-40 *OR* 22-32

You will hear in the first reading an Old Testament prophecy of the Lord's coming to the temple in Jerusalem. God declares through his prophet Malachi that "there will come to the temple" the Lord whom the people seek as their deliverer. Today we recall how the presentation of Jesus in the temple fulfilled that prophecy. At the end of this reading, we will pray from Psalm 24. The liturgy suggests that these verses dramatically announce the entrance of Christ, the King of Glory, into his temple. In the special second reading, the writer of the letter to the Hebrews emphasizes that Jesus was a man like us in every way except sin. Today's feast shows us one way in which Jesus was truly like us. Our Lord did not exempt himself from the Law of Moses that required every firstborn male to become an offering to God in the temple. The Gospel then gives us St. Luke's account of that event.

528   February   6 — ST.   PAUL   MIKI,   Priest,   AND   COMPANIONS, Martyrs

READING I   Gal. 2:19-20   **RESP. Ps. Common or Season**
GOSPEL   Matthew 28:16-20

Today's Scripture readings direct our attention to the martyrdom of St. Paul Miki and his twenty-five companions. The pagan Japanese crucified them at Nagasaki in 1597. They were the first martyrs of the Far East whom the Church raised to sainthood. They included priests and laymen, European missionaries, and Japanese Christians. The first reading is from a letter of St. Paul. The liturgy suggests, however, that we listen to this passage as if each martyr were speaking to us in Paul's words. Especially appropriate is the verse which applies to the death of each, "I have been crucified with Christ." The Gospel reading is also appropriate because it contains the command of Jesus to his disciples to go forth and preach redemption in his name to all nations — a command these martyrs obeyed at the cost of their lives.

531 February 11 — OUR LADY OF LOURDES

READING I Is. 66:10-14   **RESP. Ps. Common or Season**
GOSPEL Common or Season

The first reading discovers in the motherly figure of Jerusalem an image of the Virgin Mary's own tender care for her spiritual children at her shrine in Lourdes. Christians devoted to Mary "rejoice" with her today and are "glad because of her." Those who come to Lourdes asking Mary to restore them to health proclaim in the words of the reading that their "bodies flourish like the grass." Thousands of others who come on pilgrimages have heard Mary speaking to their hearts and saying, "As a mother comforts her son, so will I comfort you." These favors which Mary grants have as their primary object that "the Lord's power shall be known to his servant."

535 February 22 — CHAIR OF ST. PETER, Apostle

READING I 1 Peter 5:1-4   **RESP. Ps. 23:1-3, 3-4, 5, 6**
GOSPEL Matthew 16:13-19

Today's feast honors the chair or throne from which the Holy Father presides in all his official functions. This chair symbolizes the God-given authority that St. Peter has handed down in the long line of popes to the pope of our own time. The first reading reveals how St. Peter exercised his authority through a letter of pastoral advice to the elders or bishops who were responsible for governing the faithful. He appeals to these shepherds to give their flock an example of generous service in a way that will show they really care for the people's needs. Since Peter refers in this passage to "the chief shepherd" — that is, Christ — the liturgy chooses Psalm 23 for the responsorial psalm. The refrain proclaims, "The Lord is my shepherd; there is nothing I shall want." The Gospel also points to the authority of Peter, as Jesus declares that Peter will be the leader of the Church.

READING I   Rev. 2:8-11   RESP. Ps. Common or Season
GOSPEL   Common or Season

The special first Scripture reading for today's Mass applies to the life of St. Polycarp. In the second century, he was bishop of Smyrna, a most important commercial city in what is now western Turkey. During the persecution of Marcus Aurelius, soldiers of the Roman emperor led Polycarp to the amphitheater in Smyrna and put him to the sword. The liturgy now takes a passage from the New Testament and invites us to listen to these words as if God were sending a consoling message to Polycarp while he waited to meet his martyrdom.

543   March 19 — ST. JOSEPH, Husband of Mary

READING I   2 Sam. 7:4-5, 12-14, 16   RESP. Ps. 89:2-3, 4-5, 27, 29
READING II   Rom. 4:13, 16-18, 22
GOSPEL   Matthew 1:16, 18-21, 24

The Scripture readings for today's Mass apply in a special way to St. Joseph's role as the husband of Mary. The first passage from one of the books in the Old Testament tells us about the future descendants of King David. You will hear God instruct the prophet Nathan to inform David that from the young king's family there would come one day a ruler whose kingdom would last forever. In consenting to become the husband of Mary and foster father of Jesus, Joseph played his part in bringing this prophecy to fulfillment. The responsorial psalm emphasizes this same theme in the words, "The Son of David will live forever." In a special second reading, St. Paul praises the great faith of Abraham — a virtue outstanding also in the life of Joseph. The Gospel shows how an angel of the Lord put to rest Joseph's fears about taking Mary as his wife.

OR:

READING I   2 Sam. 7:4-5, 12-14, 16   RESP. Ps. 89:2-3, 4-5, 27, 29
READING II   Rom. 4:13, 16-18, 22
GOSPEL   Luke 2:41-51

The Scripture readings for today's Mass apply in a special way to St. Joseph's role as the husband of Mary. The first passage from one of the books in the Old Testament tells us about the future descendants of King David. You will hear God instruct the prophet Nathan to inform David that from the young king's family there would come one day a ruler whose kingdom would last forever. In consenting to become the husband of Mary and foster father of Jesus, Joseph played his part in bringing this prophecy to fulfillment. The responsorial psalm emphasizes this same theme in the words, "The Son of David will live forever." In a special second reading, St. Paul praises the great faith of Abraham — a virtue outstanding also in the life of Joseph. The Gospel tells about the finding of Jesus in the temple when Joseph, as Mary's husband, shared her sorrow over their lost child.

545 March 25 — ANNUNCIATION

READING I   Is. 7:10-14   RESP. Ps. 40:7-8, 8-9, 10, 11
READING II Heb. 10:4-10
GOSPEL   Luke 1:26-38

Today's Scripture readings present important themes in the feast of the Annunciation. The first passage from the prophet Isaiah mentions a special sign from God. A virgin will conceive and bear a child whose name will be Immanuel. This word Immanuel means "God is with us" — a perfect way to express the mystery of the incarnation of the Son of God which we commemorate today. The responsorial psalm tells about an obedient servant of the Lord. This psalm expresses clearly the Son of God's complete obedience to his Father's will for mankind's redemption and Mary's faithful service as the handmaid of the Lord. By quoting from this same psalm, the special second reading also helps us understand how these verses apply to our Lord's desire to offer himself for our sins. The Gospel gives us the story of the annunciation, when Mary humbly accepted her vocation to become the Mother of God.

555 April 25 — ST. MARK, Evangelist

READING I   1 Peter 5:5-14   RESP. Ps. 89:2-3, 6-7, 16-17
GOSPEL   Mark 16:15-20

The special Scripture readings for today's Mass apply to St. Mark, one of the writers of the Gospels. While he was still a young man, John Mark assisted his cousin St. Barnabas and St. Paul in preaching the Good News on the island of Cyprus. Later, Mark became the beloved companion and secretary of St. Peter in Rome. Tradition records that Mark set down in writing Peter's sermons about the ministry of Jesus, and that these became the foundation for Mark's Gospel. The reading you will now hear is from the first letter of Peter, who refers to Mark near the end of the passage as "my son." In the responsorial psalm, we seem to hear Mark's intention to write about the life of Jesus in the words, "Forever I will sing the goodness of the Lord." The Gospel is from the closing chapter of Mark where Jesus tells the disciples to proclaim salvation to all men.

557   April 29 — ST. CATHERINE OF SIENA, Virgin and Doctor

READING I   1 John 1:5—2:2   **RESP. Ps. Common or Season**
GOSPEL   Common or Season

The special first Scripture reading for today's Mass applies to St. Catherine of Siena, a great Dominican mystic who died at the dawn of the Renaissance in 1380. As the apostle John had a message for the early Church in the reading we now hear, so Catherine had a message for the people of her troubled age — of peace with God and with one another. The "fellowship" of her followers, to whom she wrote many of her nearly four hundred inspiring letters, lived in the "light" of God's holiness. Catherine "announced" confession of sin for cleansing in "the blood of Jesus." She moved so many sinners to repentance that the Church appointed three Dominican priests to confess her penitents.

559   May 1 — ST. JOSEPH THE WORKER

The Scripture Guide is on p. 264, Labor Day.

560   May 2 — ST. ATHANASIUS, Bishop and Doctor

READING I   1 John 5:1-5   **RESP. Ps. Common or Season**
GOSPEL   Common or Season

The special first Scripture reading for today's Mass applies to St. Athanasius, bishop of Alexandria and a doctor of the Church. We hear St. John stress belief in Jesus Christ as the Son of God. Athanasius devoted himself — at great personal sacrifice and risk of his life — to defending this doctrine as a bishop and in his many writings. He was at the Council of Nicaea in the year 325 when the Church officially proclaimed this teaching on the divinity of Christ in opposition to the Arians who denied it.

OR:

READING I   Common or Season   **RESP. Ps. Common or Season**
GOSPEL   Matthew 10:22-25

The special Gospel for today's Mass applies to St. Athanasius, bishop of Alexandria and a doctor of the Church. A great controversy raged in the early fourth century over belief in Christ as the Son of God. Five times the enemies of Bishop Athanasius forced him into exile from his diocese for defending the divinity of Christ. For this reason, the liturgy finds appropriate today our Lord's words to his disciples that when the people of one town persecute them, they should flee to the next.

OR:

READING I 1 John 5:1-5   RESP. Ps. Common or Season
GOSPEL   Matthew 10:22-25

The Scripture readings for today's Mass apply to the life of St. Athanasius, bishop of Alexandria and a doctor of the Church. The first passage stresses why we must believe that Jesus Christ is the Son of God in order to be saved. Athanasius was at the Council of Nicaea in 325 where the Church defined this doctrine about the divinity of Christ in opposition to the Arians who denied it. For the rest of his life, in his teaching as bishop and in his many writings, Athanasius vigorously defended this doctrine. Five times his enemies forced him into exile from his diocese. For this reason, the liturgy selects an appropriate Gospel passage. In it our Lord advises his disciples that when the people of one town persecute them, they should flee to the next.

561   May 3 — ST. PHILIP AND ST. JAMES, Apostles

READING I 1 Cor. 15:1-8   RESP. Ps. 19:2-3, 4-5
GOSPEL   John 14:6-14

Today's Scripture readings direct our attention to the apostles Philip and James. In the first passage, St. Paul shows that the risen Christ is the central figure in the preaching of the apostles. Paul then mentions how Jesus appeared in the flesh to various individuals and groups of people, including the apostle James — the saint we honor today. The early community in Jerusalem came under his leadership, and James defended the freedom of the Gentiles from the Law of Moses at the Council of Jerusalem. Tradition also attributes one of the twenty-one letters in the New Testament to James. The responsorial psalm refrain — "Their message goes out through all the earth" — reminds us how Philip and James preached salvation at the cost of their lives. The Gospel presents the Last Supper scene where Philip asks Jesus to show God the Father to the apostles.

564   May 14 — ST. MATTHIAS, Apostle

READING I   Acts 1:15-17, 20-26   **RESP. Ps.** 113:1-2, 3-4, 5-6, 7-8
GOSPEL   John 15:9-17

Today's Scripture readings apply to the life of St. Matthias, the man whom the apostles chose to take the place of Judas. The first passage tells us why the apostles wished to select a successor for Judas and then describes how they did it. The responsorial psalm refrain directs our attention to the new responsibilities Matthias assumed as an apostle in the words, "The Lord will give him a seat with the leaders of his people." The liturgy then suggests that our Lord's words in the Gospel, "It was not you who chose me, it was I who chose you," apply to the choice of Matthias by the drawing of lots. This was the ordinary way that the Jews assigned offices and duties in the temple. Matthias teaches us that the real mark of a Christian is the witness he gives to Jesus in his daily life.

566   May 20 — ST. BERNARDINE OF SIENA, Priest

READING I   Acts 4:8-12   **RESP. Ps.** Common or Season
GOSPEL   Common or Season

The special first Scripture reading for today's Mass applies to St. Bernardine of Siena. He was a Franciscan priest who traveled extensively in Italy during the early 1400's, preaching repentance and promoting devotion to the Holy Name of Jesus as an antidote to the vices of his age. Because Bernardine had such zeal for the name of Jesus, the liturgy invites us now to listen to a passage in which St. Peter bears witness to the power of our Lord's name.

572   May 31 — VISITATION

READING I   Zeph. 3:14-18   **RESP. Ps.** Is. 12:2-3, 4, 5-6
GOSPEL   Luke 1:39-56

Special Scripture readings for today's Mass apply to Mary's visit to her kinswoman Elizabeth. In the first passage, the prophet Zephaniah calls on the people of Israel to be glad and exult because the Lord is in their midst as a mighty savior. Today's Gospel reminds us that the presence of the Lord within Mary's womb fulfilled the prophet's words about the coming of the Messiah. Awareness of this hope brings great joy to Elizabeth and to John the Baptist in her womb. St. Luke's account of the visitation concludes with Mary's inspiring song of praise to God. We call it the Magnificat. The verses of the responsorial psalm between these readings also stress this theme of God's saving presence among his people. We find an echo of the prophet Zephaniah's words in the verse, "Shout with exaltation, O city of Zion, for great in your midst is the Holy One of Israel!"

OR:

READING I   Rom. 12:9-16   RESP. Ps. Is. 12:2-3, 4, 5-6
GOSPEL   Luke 1:39-56

The special Scripture readings for today's Mass deal with Mary's visit to her kinswoman Elizabeth. In the first reading, the liturgy invites us to consider how Mary and Elizabeth put into practice the advice of St. Paul in his letter to the Romans. Mary proved her love "sincere" by traveling to Judah to "look on the needs" of her relative "as her own," since Elizabeth, too, was preparing for the birth of her first child. On her part, Elizabeth was "generous in offering hospitality" to Mary. Together they "rejoiced" in the blessings God had bestowed on them. The responsorial psalm refrain accents the theme of this feast in the words, "Among you is the great and Holy One of Israel." The Gospel gives us St. Luke's account of the visitation and concludes with Mary's inspiring song of praise to God. We call it the Magnificat.

168   THURSDAY AFTER TRINITY SUNDAY — Cycle A
CORPUS CHRISTI

READING I   Deut. 8:2-3, 14-16   RESP. Ps. 147:12-13, 14-15, 19-20
READING II   1 Cor. 10:16-17
GOSPEL   John 6:51-58

In the first Scripture reading for today's feast of Corpus Christi, Moses reminds the Jewish people how God once fed them in the Sinai Desert with a bread-like food called manna. The liturgy views this manna as a foreshadowing of the gift of the Body of Christ under the appearance of bread in the Blessed Sacrament. The responsorial psalm accents this eucharistic theme in the verse, "With the best of wheat he fills you." In the special second reading today, St. Paul teaches us that Holy Communion unites us to the Body of Christ and to one another. In the Gospel, Jesus promises that whoever eats his flesh and drinks his blood shall live forever. His words comfort us as we prepare our hearts to receive him at this Eucharistic celebration.

169 THURSDAY AFTER TRINITY SUNDAY — Cycle B
CORPUS CHRISTI

READING I   Exod. 24:3-8   RESP. Ps. 116:12-13, 15-16, 17-18
READING II   Heb. 9:11-15
GOSPEL   Mark 14:12-16, 22-26

The Scripture readings for today's Mass show the contrast between the old covenant that God made with the Jewish people through Moses and his new covenant with all mankind through Jesus. The first reading describes how Moses performed the prescribed ritual of the old covenant ceremony. The responsorial psalm also deals with this theme by saying, "I will take the cup of salvation" and "offer a sacrifice of thanksgiving." A special second reading shows how much more valuable for mankind's redemption is the Blood of Christ. It is in no way comparable with the former offering of the blood of animals. The Gospel tells how Jesus offered the sacrifice of the new covenant at the Last Supper. Our hearts rejoice today as we share once again in this great mystery of faith.

170 THURSDAY AFTER TRINITY SUNDAY — Cycle C
CORPUS CHRISTI

READING I   Gen. 14:18-20   RESP. Ps. 110:1, 2, 3, 4
READING II   1 Cor. 11:23-26
GOSPEL   Luke 9:11-17

We find the central theme for today's Mass in the second Scripture reading where St. Paul tells us about the institution of the Holy Eucharist at the Last Supper. Jesus uses the bread and wine of the Passover meal to symbolize the sacrifice of his body and blood. In the first reading, the liturgy prepares us for our Lord's use of food in this special way as a sign of his offering of himself to his Father. The passage tells how an Old Testament priest named Melchizedek used bread and wine for his offerings to God. The responsorial psalm verses from Psalm 110 also direct our attention to Melchizedek. In the Gospel, Jesus feeds a crowd of five thousand with five loaves and two fishes. The way St.

Luke describes Jesus distributing the bread on this occasion reminds us of our Lord's breaking of the bread at the Last Supper.

171 FRIDAY AFTER THE SECOND SUNDAY AFTER PENTECOST —
Cycle A — SACRED HEART

READING I   Deut. 7:6-11   RESP. Ps. 103:1-2, 3-4, 6-7, 8, 10
READING II 1 John 4:7-16
GOSPEL   Matthew 11:25-30

The first Scripture reading for today's Mass tells how God set his heart on the Jewish people and chose them to receive his revelations and mercies. This special choice of the Jews reminds us how Jesus chose Sister Margaret Mary in the seventeenth century to reveal the love of his Sacred Heart for all men. The responsorial psalm relates to today's feast by emphasizing that the Heart of Jesus is "abounding in kindness." The special second reading tells of God's overwhelming love for us — the core of our Lord's message to Margaret Mary. The Gospel passage also applies to this feast by reminding us that God reveals himself to the childlike heart. Jesus then invites us to find rest from our problems and cares in his gentle and humble heart.

172 FRIDAY AFTER THE SECOND SUNDAY AFTER PENTECOST —
Cycle B — SACRED HEART

READING I   Hos. 11:1, 3-4, 8-9   RESP. Ps. Is. 12:2-3, 4, 5-6
READING II Eph. 3:8-12, 14-19
GOSPEL   John 19:31-37

The first Scripture reading for today's Mass expresses the tender love of God for his children despite their faults. This was the heart of the message Jesus revealed to Sister Margaret Mary in the seventeenth century. The responsorial psalm refrain declares, "You will draw water joyfully from the springs of salvation." The liturgy relates this verse to a statement in today's Gospel. John tells us that after Jesus died, a soldier pierced our Lord's side with a lance and "blood and water flowed out." The Sacred Heart of Jesus becomes in this way the "spring of salvation" from which we may joyfully draw the waters of grace. Many commentators on this passage interpret the water and blood as symbols of baptism and the Eucharist. A special second reading from St. Paul also emphasizes the depths of Christ's love for us.

173 FRIDAY AFTER THE SECOND SUNDAY AFTER PENTECOST — Cycle C — SACRED HEART

READING I   Ezek. 34:11-16   RESP. Ps. 23:1-3, 3-4, 5, 6
READING II   Rom. 5:5-11
GOSPEL   Luke 15:3-7

The first Scripture reading, the responsorial psalm, and the Gospel for today's Mass illustrate God's loving concern for us by comparing that love with the tender care a good shepherd gives to his sheep. This image of the good shepherd was for many centuries in art and prayer a favorite Christian symbol of God's love for mankind. From the Middle Ages, however, men began to use instead the imagery of the heart to portray this love. Jesus also used this image in revealing the love of his Sacred Heart to Sister Margaret Mary in the seventeenth century. These readings under the imagery of the shepherd take us into the special second reading from St. Paul with its message about the divine heart's limitless love. Paul reminds us that the greatest proof of God's love was in his dying for us while we were still sinners — even as a shepherd would lay down his life for his sheep.

573 SATURDAY AFTER THE SECOND SUNDAY AFTER PENTECOST — IMMACULATE HEART OF MARY

READING I   Common or Season   RESP. Ps. Common or Season
GOSPEL   Luke 2:41-51

The special Gospel for today's Mass relates to the feast of the Immaculate Heart of Mary. We learn how Joseph and Mary find the boy Jesus in the temple after he had been lost for three days. The liturgy finds especially appropriate St. Luke's final observation that Mary — in response to the promptings of her woman's heart — "kept all these things in memory" concerning her son.

574 June 1 — ST. JUSTIN, Martyr

READING 1   1 Cor. 1:18-25   RESP. Ps. Common or Season
GOSPEL   Common or Season

A special first Scripture reading for today's Mass applies to the life of the second century martyr St. Justin. Learned in literature and philosophy, Justin became a convert about the year 130. From then on in his writings he brilliantly defended the truths of the faith against the attacks of pagan philosophers. For this reason, the liturgy invites us to listen to a passage from St. Paul defending the faith against teachers of worldly wisdom. We might listen to Paul's words as if Justin himself were uttering them to the men of his day and to our own as well.

580   June 11 — ST. BARNABAS, Apostle

READING I   Acts 11:21-26; 13:1-3   **RESP.** Ps. 98:1, 2-3, 3-4, 5-6
GOSPEL   Matthew 10:7-13

In the special Scripture readings for today's Mass, we learn about the life of St. Barnabas, a missionary companion of St. Paul. The first passage tells how Barnabas went as an official representative of the mother Church in Jerusalem to Antioch to incorporate a large number of converts into its Christian community. We then learn how the Holy Spirit set apart Barnabas and Saul — that is, Paul — to preach the Good News of salvation to the Gentiles. The responsorial psalm refrain accents their mission in the words, "The Lord has revealed to the nations his saving power." The Gospel shows our Lord sending out his disciples to prepare the Jewish people for his teaching. God's plan was and is to continue this work in the great missionary effort of the Church and to do it through such dedicated men as Barnabas.

584   June 22 — ST. PAULINUS OF NOLA, Bishop

READING I   2 Cor. 8:9-15   **RESP.** Ps. Common or Season
GOSPEL   Common or Season

The special first Scripture reading for today's Mass applies to the life of St. Paulinus of Nola, a saintly bishop who lived in the fifth century in France. Paulinus became known and loved for his charity to the poor. This is why the liturgy invites us now to listen to St. Paul instructing the Christians in Corinth about their duty as followers of the poor Christ to care for the poor. The apostle's words are an echo of what Paulinus himself might well have said to the Christians of his own time. They should also inspire us today to care for the needs of the poor in whatever way we can.

586 June 24 — BIRTH OF ST. JOHN THE BAPTIST

VIGIL

READING I	Jer. 1:4-10	RESP. Ps. 71:1-2, 3-4, 5-6, 15, 17
READING II	1 Peter 1:8-12	
GOSPEL	Luke 1:5-17	

The first Scripture reading for today's vigil Mass applies to God's call to John the Baptist to become the herald of the Messiah. For this purpose, the liturgy uses a passage from the prophet Jeremiah, who also received from God a special vocation to the Jewish people. The liturgy suggests that we listen to the words of this first reading as a dialogue between the Lord and John the Baptist. The responsorial psalm also serves as a kind of prayer by which John thanks God for strengthening him in his vocation. In a special second reading, St. Peter reminds the early Christians that they enjoy the fullness of salvation which the prophets, such as John the Baptist, proclaimed. The Gospel tells us how an angel of the Lord revealed to Zechariah that he will have a son who will serve God in the spirit of the prophet Elijah. This child grew up to become the prophet we honor today.

587 June 24 — BIRTH OF ST. JOHN THE BAPTIST

MASS DURING THE DAY

READING I	Is. 49:1-6	RESP. Ps. 139:1-3, 13-14, 14-15
READING II	Acts 13:22-26	
GOSPEL	Luke 1:57-66, 80	

Today's special Scripture readings apply to the life of St. John the Baptist. He was the last of the Old Testament prophets, the spokesmen whom God himself had chosen to remind the Jewish people that they had a special relationship to the Lord. When necessary, these prophets called the people to repentance. The liturgy asks us today to listen to the first reading as if John the Baptist were telling us about his own call from God to prepare the way for the Messiah. We may also regard the responsorial psalm as a prayer of thanks by which John the Baptist acknowledges the graces God has given him. In the special second reading, we hear St. Paul referring to John's career during one of the apostle's sermons to the Jews. The Gospel tells how John received his name and then indicates the great destiny that lay ahead of him.

589 June 28 — ST. IRENAEUS, Bishop and Martyr

READING I	2 Tim. 2:22-26	RESP. Ps. Common or Season
GOSPEL	Common or Season	

The special first Scripture reading for today's Mass applies to the life of St. Irenaeus. A second century bishop of Lyons in France, he won renown for his many writings to correct heretical teachings. His very name — which means peacemaker — sums up his life's work. For this reason, the liturgy selects a passage from St. Paul about a Christian's vocation to seek peace and kindness. We might listen to Paul's words as if they were fatherly advice to Irenaeus from his teacher St. Polycarp.

590 June 29 — ST. PETER AND ST. PAUL, Apostles

VIGIL

READING I Acts 3:1-10	RESP. Ps. 19:2-3, 4-5
READING II Gal. 1:11-20	
GOSPEL John 21:15-19	

We have for today's vigil Mass special Scripture readings that teach us about the lives of Peter and Paul. The first passage describes an incident when the apostles went to the temple for prayer. We learn how Peter called upon the name of Jesus to cure a crippled man. The responsorial psalm refrain reminds us that through the preaching of Peter and Paul and their successors in the Church, the message of man's redemption in Christ "goes out through all the earth." In the special second reading, Paul tells the Galatians about his life before his conversion and then how the Lord called him to be an apostle to the Gentiles. You will also hear Paul refer to his first meeting with Cephas — another name for Peter — at Jerusalem. In the Gospel, Jesus, through the imagery of feeding the sheep, gives Peter the authority to care for the Church.

591 June 29 — ST. PETER AND ST. PAUL, Apostles

MASS DURING THE DAY

READING I Acts 12:1-11	RESP. Ps. 34:2-3, 4-5, 6-7, 8-9
READING II 2 Tim. 4:6-8, 17-18	
GOSPEL Matthew 16:13-19	

Today's readings emphasize that God protected the apostles Peter and Paul when they were in danger and rescued them from their troubles. The first passage points out that King Herod began to persecute the early Church. We note how concerned the Christian community felt about Peter's welfare while he was in prison in Jerusalem. Then an angel appears and sets the apostle free. The responsorial psalm underscores this theme in the refrain, "The angel of the Lord will rescue those who fear him." In a special second reading, Paul informs his friend Timothy that the Lord had saved Paul "from the lion's jaws" — that is, his many enemies who opposed him when he preached to the Gentiles. In the Gospel, Jesus declares that he will build his Church on the Rock of Peter. Once again we observe how our Lord promises to protect Peter and his Church so that "the jaws of death shall not prevail against it."

592 June 30 — FIRST MARTYRS OF THE CHURCH OF ROME

READING I Common or Season   RESP. Ps. Common or Season
GOSPEL   Matthew 24:4-13

A special Gospel reading today applies to the first martyrs of the Church of Rome. During the persecution of the Church under the Emperor Nero, about thirty years after Jesus returned to the Father, these men welcomed a martyr's death and crown in the Vatican Circus. Through sacrificing their lives, these saints fulfilled the words of Jesus to his disciples in today's Gospel. Our Lord warned them that the time will come when men will hate them and deliver them over to torture on his account.

593 July 3 — ST. THOMAS, Apostle

READING I Eph. 2:19-22   RESP. Ps. 117:1, 2
GOSPEL   John 20:24-29

Today's special readings focus on the apostle Thomas and the place of the apostles in the Church. St. Paul, in the first passage, compares the Church to a holy building. The Gentiles and the Jewish Christians are the two walls, and the apostles and New Testament prophets are the foundation. Jesus is the topmost stone who keeps the whole structure together. The apostles provide a firm basis for faith that the members of the Church can count on like the solid foundation of a building. Christ himself has taught them and sent them to bear witness to his resurrection, and they enjoy special gifts of the Spirit. The responsorial psalm recalls this missionary vocation our Lord gave to Thomas as an apostle, and ourselves as well, to tell all men about God's love for them. In the Gospel, we hear how the doubting Thomas became a believer when he saw the wounds in our Lord's risen body.

596   July 6 — ST. MARIA GORETTI, Virgin and Martyr

READING I   1 Cor. 6:13-15, 17-20   RESP. Ps. Common or Season
GOSPEL   Common or Season

The special first Scripture reading for today's Mass applies to the life of St. Maria Goretti. Maria was the daughter of a farm worker on a large estate near Rome. On July 5, 1902, a young man stabbed the eleven-year-old girl when she insisted it was wrong to offend God by committing sin and then repulsed the youth's advances. Maria died the next day. Pope Pius XII canonized her in 1950 as a martyr for purity. Appropriately, the liturgy selects a passage from St. Paul, who teaches that a Christian may not engage in sexual immorality because his body is a member of Christ's body. Paul's words, "You have been purchased, and at what a price," remind us of the price Maria paid — her very life — to bear witness to her love for God.

597   July 11 — ST. BENEDICT, Abbot

READING I   Prov. 2:1-9   RESP. Ps. Common or Season
GOSPEL   Common or Season

The special first Scripture reading for today's Mass applies to the life of St. Benedict, who in the sixth century founded monasticism in the western world. The more gentle guidelines which Benedict laid down in his now famous Rule were a departure from the more rigorous demands of religious life as monks were living it in the East. His Rule is a monument of insight into prayer, community life, work, and penance. It has survived the centuries and made a profound impact on Christian spirituality. The liturgy suggests that we listen to the following passage as if Benedict himself were speaking these words to his monks and inviting them to live according to the wisdom of his holy Rule.

603   July 22 — ST. MARY MAGDALENE

READING I   Song 3:1-4   RESP. Ps. 63:2, 3-4, 5-6, 8-9
GOSPEL   John 20:1-2, 11-18

We have special Scripture readings for today's feast of St. Mary Magdalene. She appears in the eighth chapter of St. Luke's Gospel as one of the women who ministered to Jesus and his disciples. During our Lord's final hours on Calvary, Mary Magdalene stood beneath the cross with the Mother of Jesus and the apostle John and took part in the burial service. Today's Gospel reminds us that she was the first one Jesus appeared to after he rose from the dead. The liturgy suggests that we listen to the first reading as if Mary Magdalene were speaking. We hear her tell how she searched for Jesus after discovering that someone had apparently taken his body from the tomb. The responsorial psalm refrain captures Mary's ardent love in the words, "My soul is thirsting for you, O Lord my God."

OR:

READING 1 2 Cor. 5:14-17 **RESP.** Ps. 63:2, 3-4, 5-6, 8-9
GOSPEL John 20:1-2, 11-18

We have special Scripture readings for today's feast of St. Mary Magdalene. She appears in the eighth chapter of St. Luke's Gospel as one of the women who ministered to Jesus and his disciples. During our Lord's final hours on Calvary, Mary Magdalene stood beneath the cross with the mother of Jesus and the apostle John and took part in the burial service. Today's Gospel reminds us that she was the first one Jesus appeared to after he rose from the dead. Just as St. Paul in the first reading could say, "The love of Christ impels us," so too did this same love for Jesus impel Mary Magdalene to seek him when she found the tomb empty. As a member of the early Church, Mary could see with Paul's eyes of faith that "the old order has passed away; now all is new!" The responsorial psalm refrain capture's Mary's thirst to love the Lord her God.

605 July 25 — ST. JAMES, Apostle

READING I 2 Cor. 4:7-15 **RESP.** Ps. 126:1-2, 2-3, 4-5, 6
GOSPEL Matthew 20:20-28

The liturgy chooses special Scripture readings today for this feast of the apostle James, brother of the apostle John. Throughout the Gospels, James, John, and Peter seem to share a special closeness to Jesus inasmuch as they were the only apostles our Lord took to the place of his transfiguration and the garden of Gethsemane. The act of King Herod Agrippa I in putting James to death about 41 A.D. presumably makes James the first martyr among the apostles. The first reading reminds us that we must endure sufferings and trials in our Christian life, just as surely as James underwent them by his martyrdom. This theme of sorrow and suffering appears again in the responsorial psalm. The Gospel passage also suggests the death of James. Jesus points to the cup of suffering that the apostles, like their Divine Master, will have to drink.

606 July 26 — ST. JOACHIM AND ST. ANN, Parents of Mary

READING I Sir. 44:1, 10-15   **RESP. Ps. 132:11, 13-14, 17-18**
GOSPEL   Matthew 13:16-17

Today's first reading begins by praising "those godly men, our ancestors." The liturgy suggests that as we listen to these words of praise we apply them to Joachim and Ann, the ancestors of Christ, whom we honor today. Their "virtues have not been forgotten," and "their names live on and on." The glory of their descendants — that is, their daughter Mary, and their grandson Jesus — "will never be blotted out." Even today, by our gathering at this Mass, we "proclaim their praise." The responsorial psalm reminds us that Joachim and Ann, as grandparents of Jesus, played their part in God's plan to give "the throne of David" to the Messiah. The liturgy also directs the Gospel passage particularly to Joachim and Ann. They can rejoice because their eyes have seen the Mother of the Messiah, and their ears have heard the Messiah's voice — joys which previous ages had so eagerly looked forward to.

607 July 29 — ST. MARTHA

READING I Common or Season   **RESP. Ps. Common or Season**
GOSPEL   John 11:19-27

A special Gospel for today's Mass applies to St. Martha. Jesus used to go to visit Martha, Mary, and Lazarus at their home in Bethany, a short distance south of Jerusalem. Martha served our Lord and his guests. We now learn how Jesus came to console the sisters over the death of Lazarus — the occasion for one of our Lord's greatest miracles.

OR:

READING I Common or Season   **RESP. Ps. Common or Season**
GOSPEL   Luke 10:38-42

A special Gospel for today's Mass applies to St. Martha. Jesus used to go to visit Martha, Mary, and Lazarus at their home in Bethany, a short distance south of Jerusalem. When Lazarus died, Jesus performed one of his greatest miracles for his friends. Now we learn of a time when Martha welcomed Jesus to her home for something to eat.

609   July 31 — ST. IGNATIUS OF LOYOLA, Priest

READING I   1 Cor. 10:31—11:1   **RESP. Ps.** Common or Season
GOSPEL   Common or Season

A special first Scripture reading for today's Mass applies to the life of St. Ignatius, who founded the Society of Jesus. His followers helped the Church to reorganize and strengthen itself after the Reformation. The motto of the Jesuits has always been "For the greater glory of God." With this in mind, the liturgy selects a passage in which St. Paul tells the Christians of Corinth that everything they do in their daily lives they should do for the glory of God. We might also listen to Paul's words as if Ignatius himself were speaking them to the members of his community today — urging them to imitate the way Ignatius himself followed the teachings of Christ.

610   August 1 — ST. ALPHONSUS LIGUORI, Bishop and Doctor

READING I   Rom. 8:1-4   **RESP. Ps.** Common or Season
GOSPEL   Common or Season

A special first Scripture reading for today's Mass applies to the life of St. Alphonsus Liguori, a renowned spiritual writer and moral theologian. After a brief career as a lawyer, Alphonsus became a priest in 1726. Soon afterward he formed a new religious congregation to care for neglected souls among the Italian peasants. Because he named this community in honor of Jesus, the Most Holy Redeemer — popularly known as the Redemptorists — the liturgy chooses for the first reading a passage that refers to mankind's redemption. We hear St. Paul tell the Romans how Jesus redeemed them "from the law of sin and death."

612   August 4 — ST. JOHN VIANNEY, Priest

READING I   Common or Season   **RESP. Ps.** Common or Season
GOSPEL   Matthew 9:35—10:1

A special Gospel for today's Mass applies to St. John Vianney, who died in 1859. Sinners from all over Europe sought John out as their confessor. In time, thousands of penitent pilgrims each year flocked to him at his little country church in central France. For this reason, the liturgy finds appropriate St. Matthew's observation that the heart of Jesus — like the heart of the Curé of Ars — was moved with pity at the sight of the crowds who followed our Lord.

614   August 6 — TRANSFIGURATION

READING I   Dan. 7:9-10, 13-14   RESP. Ps. 97:1-2, 5-6, 9
READING II   2 Peter 1:16-19
GOSPEL   (Cycle A) Matthew 17:1-9
             (Cycle B) Mark 9:2-10
             (Cycle C) Luke 9:28-36

Today's readings give us insights into what our Lord's transfiguration really means. In the first passage, Daniel's vision of a glorious "son of man" helps us to understand that Jesus, the Son of Man, even before his resurrection, was really the glorious Son of God. The Gospel scene reveals that for one dazzling moment the apostles were able to see behind the veil that hides our Lord's glory — a glory that will come to full revelation only after Jesus' suffering, death, and resurrection. This awesome event followed immediately after Jesus had told his apostles about his coming death. In this way, his transfiguration teaches us that the life of glory follows only after a time of trial on earth — a trial which even Christ himself went through. The responsorial psalm accents today's theme of glory. In the second reading, St. Peter recalls how he saw our Lord's display of glory.

618   August 10 — ST. LAWRENCE, Deacon and Martyr

READING I   2 Cor. 9:6-10   RESP. Ps. 112:1-2, 5-6, 7-8, 9
GOSPEL   John 12:24-26

We have special Scripture readings for today's feast of St. Lawrence. Tradition says that he was one of seven deacons who early in the third century served the Church in Rome. He had the responsibility of caring for the poor. Because he carried out this task with warm generosity, the people came to love and respect him. For this reason, the first reading emphasizes God's love for the man who is generous and cheerful in giving to others. The responsorial psalm accents this same theme in the refrain, "Happy the man who is merciful and lends to those in need," and in the verse, "lavishly he gives to the poor." In the Gospel, Jesus says that if the grain of wheat dies, "it produces much fruit." The body of Lawrence, roasted alive on a gridiron, was the grain of wheat that in dying bore much fruit by strengthening and inspiring others.

621   August 15 — ASSUMPTION
VIGIL

READING I   1 Chr. 15:3-4, 15, 16; 16:1-2   RESP. Ps. 132:6-7, 9-10, 13-14
READING II   1 Cor. 15:54-57
GOSPEL   Luke 11:27-28

Today's first reading tells how King David brought the ark of the covenant — the sacred tabernacle of God's presence among the Jewish people — into a place of honor in Jerusalem. The liturgy discovers in that ceremony an image of what God did in taking Mary's body into a place of honor in heaven — the event we commemorate today. God gave Mary this unique privilege because she had once carried in her own immaculate body not just a symbol of the Lord's presence but the very Son of God himself. For this reason, Mary receives the beautiful title "Ark of the Covenant." The responsorial psalm refrain also recalls David's procession with the "ark of God's holiness." A special second reading reminds us that in Mary's bodily assumption God has given her "the victory through Jesus Christ." In the Gospel, the liturgy shows that Mary's dignity as God's Mother gained for her the honor she enjoys today.

622   August 15 — ASSUMPTION
MASS DURING THE DAY

READING I   Rev. 11:19; 12:1-6, 10   RESP. Ps. 45:10, 11, 12, 16
READING II   1 Cor. 15:20-26
GOSPEL   Luke 1:39-56

In the first reading, St. John describes an unusual vision of a woman "clothed with the sun." Today's liturgy discovers in this woman an image of the Virgin Mary now reigning in heaven, body and soul. We learn that the woman gave birth to a son. His destiny as shepherd of "all the nations" suggests that we may identify him today as Jesus, the Good Shepherd. The woman then flees into a "special place prepared for her by God." This verse also reminds us of the place in heaven God made ready for his Mother. The liturgy applies the responsorial refrain to Mary by describing her as a queen standing at God's right hand. A special second reading refers to the resurrection of the body, which Mary has already experienced. In the Gospel, the liturgy sees Mary singing praise for the "great thing" God has done for her in taking her to heaven. God will one day do the same for us if we keep faith with him.

627   August 22 — QUEENSHIP OF MARY

The readings are from the Common of the Blessed Virgin Mary.

READING I   Is. 61:9-11   RESP. Ps. 45:11-12, 14-15, 16-17
GOSPEL   Luke 1:26-38

The Scripture readings today honor Mary as Queen of the Universe. The first passage begins by reminding us that Mary, as a descendant of the Jewish people, now receives renown "among the nations" because she shares in the privileges of Christ our King. Then we hear Mary describe how God invested her with royal robes in heaven so that as queen of all men she might distribute to them the graces of God's kingdom. In the responsorial psalm, we discover in the king's daughter another image of Mary. Since Mary has shared in her son's work of redeeming the world, "the king desires her beauty." In the familiar Gospel story of the annunciation, the liturgy gives us the reason why Mary deserves honor over all other creatures. As the unique virgin who is "full of grace," Our Lady enjoys a spotless dignity that prepares her to become the Mother of God and eventually queen of the world.

629   August 24 — ST. BARTHOLOMEW, Apostle

READING I   Rev. 21:9-14   RESP. Ps. 145:10-11, 12-13, 17-18
GOSPEL   John 1:45-51

Today's readings focus on the apostle St. Bartholomew and the place the apostles have in the Church. St. John, in the first passage, describes a vision of the heavenly city Jerusalem — a symbol of the Church — shining in splendor. John then sees the names of the apostles written on the twelve foundation stones of the wall around the city. Other New Testament texts help us to understand these ideas. The wall symbolizes the people of God whose faith stands on the firm foundation of the apostles, since Christ himself has taught the apostles. The responsorial psalm refrain praises Bartholomew for preaching the name of Jesus, in the verse, "Your friends tell the glory of your kingship, Lord." The Gospel describes how Nathanael became a disciple of Jesus. Scripture commentators believe he is the same person that we honor today by the name of Bartholomew.

632 August 27 — ST. MONICA

READING I   Common or Season   RESP. Ps. Common or Season
GOSPEL   Luke 7:11-17

A special Gospel reading for today's Mass applies to the life of St. Monica, the mother of St. Augustine. The passage tells how Jesus restored a young man to life and gave him back to his widowed mother. The liturgy finds a parallel to that event in the life of St. Monica. Her son Augustine had been spiritually dead for many years. But the grace of God and Monica's tearful prayers eventually brought Augustine back to life and launched him on the road to sainthood.

633 August 28 — ST. AUGUSTINE, Bishop and Doctor

READING I   1 John 4:7-16   RESP. Ps. Common or Season
GOSPEL   Matthew 23:8-12

Special Scripture readings for today's Mass apply to the life of St. Augustine, the illustrious doctor of the Church who died on this day in the year 430. St. John, in the first reading, describes God's love for us and encourages us to respond by giving our love to God's Son, who came to save us from our sins. In this way, the passage reminds us of Augustine's renowned sermons on God's love for men and his classic work the *Confessions*, which describes his conversion from a sinful life. In the Gospel, Jesus tells his disciples that they must be the servants of others. Augustine fulfilled this ideal in his years of defending the Church against her enemies and by his service as bishop of Hippo in North Africa.

634 August 29 — BEHEADING OF ST. JOHN THE BAPTIST, Martyr

READING I   Jer. 1:17-19   RESP. Ps. 71:1-2, 3-4, 5-6, 15, 17
GOSPEL   Mark 6:17-29

In the first reading, the liturgy discovers in God's command to the prophet Jeremiah a statement that also applies to the life of John the Baptist, whose death we commemorate today. God called Jeremiah to preach to the kings and princes of Judah early in the sixth century and "tell them all that I command you." John the Baptist also answered God's inner call to warn King Herod, "It is not right for you to live with your brother's wife." Both prophets suffered similar fates — the rulers disregarded their preaching and each met a violent death. The liturgy suggests that the responsorial psalm reflects John's prayer while he waited for his death in prison. The Gospel gives an account of the events that led up to the beheading of John. This tragedy closed the career of the last of the prophets who had prepared the way for the Messiah.

559 LABOR DAY (United States)

The readings are from the feast of Joseph the Worker on May 1.

READING I Gen. 1:26—2:3   **RESP. Ps. 90:2, 3-4, 12-13, 14, 16**
GOSPEL Matthew 13:54-58

On this Labor Day national holiday, we celebrate the feast of St. Joseph the Worker. The Scripture readings focus on the dignity and importance of how we earn a living and on how this relates to our personal salvation. The first reading gives an account of the sixth and seventh days when God created the world. We see God at work declaring everything he makes to be good and then resting when he finishes his task. The passage thus points to the meaning of this holiday as a rest from the busy activity of our jobs and as an opportunity to give thanks to God for allowing us to share in his creative power. The responsorial psalm appropriately asks God to "give success to the work of our hands." The Gospel reminds us that Jesus was the son of a carpenter and undoubtedly followed this trade himself before starting his public ministry.

OR:

READING I Col. 3:14-15, 17, 23-24   **RESP. Ps. 90:2, 3-4, 12-13, 14, 16**
GOSPEL Matthew 13:54-58

On this Labor Day national holiday, we celebrate the feast of St. Joseph the Worker. The Scripture readings focus our attention on the proper outlook we as Christians should take toward our jobs. In the first passage, St. Paul tells the Colossians that a spirit of thankfulness should characterize whatever they do in life. He actually addressed his final remarks on work to the Christian slaves in that society, but Paul's words also apply to our lives today. Paul teaches that we should work with all our heart and for the honor of God. The responsorial psalm asks God to "give success to the work of our hands." The Gospel reminds us that Jesus was the son of a carpenter and undoubtedly followed this trade himself before starting his public ministry.

636   September 8 — BIRTH OF MARY

READING I   Micah 5:1-4   **RESP. Ps. 13:6, 6**
GOSPEL   Matthew 1:1-16, 18-23 or 1:18-23

Today's Scripture readings remind us that the birth of Mary heralded the dawn of the long-awaited age of the Messiah. For this reason, the liturgy selects readings that contain prophecies about the promised Messiah. In the first passage, we hear the prophet Micah declaring that the "one who is to be ruler in Israel" will come from Bethlehem. The chief priests quoted this text to King Herod when he inquired where the Messiah would be born. The Gospel gives St. Matthew's account of the birth of Christ, the mystery that Mary's own birth has prepared the way for. Matthew sees our Lord's birth as fulfilling the words of the prophet Isaiah about the coming of a child whose name means "God is with us." The responsorial psalm between these readings expresses Mary's joy at the good things that the Lord has done for her.

OR:

READING I   Rom. 8:28-30   **RESP. Ps. 13:6, 6**
GOSPEL   Matthew 1:1-16, 18-23 or 1:18-23

The Scripture readings for today's Mass apply to this feast of the birth of Mary. The first reading speaks of those whom God knew as his children before the world began. He predestined them to share the image of his Son. In selecting this passage, the liturgy sees Mary among those whom God knew before the dawn of time. But only to Mary did God give a special call to become the Mother of Jesus. Because Mary was so generous in accepting her vocation, we now have the opportunity to belong to Christ and share the joy of his glorified life forever. The responsorial psalm expresses Mary's joy over the good things the Lord has done for her. The psalm also allows us to voice our thanks to God for calling us to become his adopted children. The Gospel gives St. Matthew's account of the birth of Jesus, the mystery that Mary's own birth has prepared the way for.

638   September 14 — TRIUMPH OF THE CROSS

READING I   Num. 21:4-9   **RESP. Ps. 78:1-2, 34-35, 36-37, 38**
READING II   Phil. 2:6-11
GOSPEL   John 3:13-17

Today's Scripture readings apply to this feast of the Triumph of the

Cross. In the first passage, we hear how the Jewish people rebelled against God while they were journeying through the desert to the promised land. Although God at first punished his chosen people, he later healed them in an extraordinary way. God told Moses that anyone who looked at a bronze serpent that Moses had raised on a pole would be saved from his affliction. In the Gospel, Jesus also refers to this incident of the bronze serpent. His words that "the Son of Man must be lifted up" suggest how the Roman soldiers will one day lift him up on the cross, where by his death he will heal our wounded hearts. The responsorial psalm recalls the time when the Jews turned against God in the desert. In a special second reading, St. Paul tells how God exalted Jesus for obediently accepting death on a cross.

639 September 15 — OUR LADY OF SORROWS

READING I Heb. 5:7-9   **RESP.** Ps. 31:2-3, 3-4, 5-6, 15-16, 20
GOSPEL John 19:25-27

Today the Scripture readings apply to the feast of Our Lady of Sorrows. In the first passage, St. Paul draws our attention to the sufferings Christ endured that brought great sorrow to Mary. After this reading, we will pray several verses from Psalm 31. This is an afflicted man's prayer of thanksgiving because God had delivered him from suffering and persecution at the hands of his enemies. The liturgy finds in this psalm many references to the sufferings of Christ in his Passion that caused Mary such grief. For this reason, we may regard this psalm as our Lord's confident prayer to his Father when his enemies gathered around him. The Gospel refers to the Sorrowful Mother standing by the cross on Calvary. At the hour of his death, Jesus gave his own Mother to us.

OR:

READING I Heb. 5:7-9   **RESP.** Ps. 31:2-3, 3-4, 5-6, 15-16, 20
GOSPEL Luke 2:33-35

The Scripture readings for today's Mass apply to the feast of Our Lady of Sorrows. In the first passage, St. Paul draws our attention to the sufferings Christ endured that brought great sorrow to Mary. After this reading, we will pray several verses from Psalm 31. This is an afflicted man's prayer of thanksgiving because God has delivered him from suffering and persecution at the hands of his enemies. The liturgy finds in this psalm many references to the sufferings of Christ in his Passion that caused Mary such grief. For this reason, we may regard this psalm as our Lord's confident prayer to his Father when his enemies gathered around him. The Gospel describes how Joseph and Mary presented the child Jesus in the temple. On that occasion, the holy man Simeon told Mary that a sword of sorrow would one day pierce her heart.

643   September 21 — ST. MATTHEW, Apostle and Evangelist

READING I   Eph. 4:1-7, 11-13   **RESP. Ps. 19:2-3, 4-5**
GOSPEL   Matthew 9:9-13

Today's special Scripture readings apply to the life of the apostle St. Matthew. In the first passage, we hear St. Paul remind the Christian community at Ephesus that there are many roles which God asks people to fill in serving the Church. He ranks the apostles first among those who build up the Church, the Body of Christ, through their service. Today we recall how Matthew, as an apostle, faithfully fulfilled that vocation to give himself to the needs of God's people. The responsorial psalm reminds us that our Lord commanded Matthew and the other apostles to preach the message of salvation throughout the world. In the Gospel that bears his name, we learn how Jesus called Matthew to become his disciple while Matthew was working as a tax collector. Later, in Matthew's house, Jesus reveals that he has come to befriend and save sinners.

647   September 29 — ST. MICHAEL, ST. GABRIEL, AND ST. RAPHAEL, Archangels

READING I   Dan. 7:9-10, 13-14   **RESP. Ps. 138:1-2, 2-3, 4-5**
GOSPEL   John 1:47-51

The Scripture readings today apply to this feast of the three archangels. Michael is the warrior who guards the faithful against the attacks of Satan. Gabriel brought glad tidings to Mary at the annunciation. Raphael guided Tobiah on his unfamiliar journey and healed his father of blindness. In the first passage, the prophet Daniel experiences a vision of God seated on his throne and receiving the worship of countless millions. The liturgy discovers in this scene the presence of the three archangels whom we honor today. In the responsorial psalm, we praise God "in the sight of the angels." In the Gospel, Jesus tells Nathanael that he shall see the sky open and "the angels of God ascending and decending on the Son of Man" — a reference to Christ himself. In this vision, the liturgy finds that even the archangels acknowledge Jesus as their Lord and do his bidding.

OR:

READING I Rev. 12:7-12   RESP. Ps. 138:1-2, 2-3, 4-5
GOSPEL   John 1:47-51

The Scripture readings today apply to this feast of the three archangels. Michael is the warrior who guards the faithful against the attacks of Satan. Gabriel brought glad tidings to Mary at the annunciation. Raphael guided Tobiah on his unfamiliar journey and healed his father of blindness. The first passage describes a battle in heaven between the angelic hosts led by Michael and a dragon — the symbol of Satan. The powers of good prevail. The angels drive Satan from heaven and establish the rule of the Lamb of God. In the responsorial psalm, we praise God "in the sight of the angels." In the Gospel, Jesus tells Nathanael that he shall see the sky open and "the angels of God ascending and decending on the Son of Man" — a reference to Christ himself. In this vision, the liturgy finds that even the archangels acknowledge Jesus as their Lord and do his bidding.

648 September 30 — ST. JEROME, Priest and Doctor

READING I   2 Tim. 3:14-17   RESP. Ps. Common or Season
GOSPEL   Common or Season

Today's special first reading applies to the life of St. Jerome, who is renowned as a biblical scholar. Early in the fifth century, Jerome produced a Latin version of the Bible that has received the name "the Vulgate," a word meaning "common," probably because it found common or widespread use in the Church. No man in Jerome's time, and few men afterwards, could qualify as well as he did to cope with so challenging a task. The liturgy now selects for the first reading St. Paul's words that emphasize the value of the Scriptures for the Christian life — a lesson that Jerome took to heart and which we should appreciate today.

649 October 1 — ST. THERESA OF THE CHILD JESUS, Virgin

READING I   Is. 66:10-14   RESP. Ps. Common or Season
GOSPEL   Matthew 18:1-4

Today's special Scripture readings apply to the life of St. Theresa of the Child Jesus. She was a Carmelite nun, popularly known as the Little Flower, who died in 1897 in France. Both readings center our attention on the saint's childlike relationship to God. In the first reading, the prophet Isaiah says that Jerusalem will be like a mother nourishing and comforting her child Israel. The liturgy suggests today that in this passage Jerusalem represents the Church and Theresa is the little child. She draws nourishment for her contemplative life from the Church and finds comfort there. In the Gospel, Jesus selects a child as a model of the attitude he desires to find among his followers.

650   October 2 — GUARDIAN ANGELS

READING I   Exod. 23:20-23   **RESP. Ps.** 91:1-2, 3-4, 5-6, 10-11
GOSPEL   Matthew 18:1-5, 10

The special Scripture readings for today's Mass apply to the Guardian Angels and how God has appointed them to take care of his children. In the first passage, God is speaking to his servant Moses after giving him the Ten Commandments. The Jewish people still have a long way to travel before they will reach the promised land. That is why, as the reading begins, the Lord assures Moses that he will send an angel to guide the chosen people on their journey. The liturgy suggests that this angel stands for the special Guardian Angel who watches over the life of each of us, as Church tradition teaches. The liturgy also finds in the responsorial psalm another reminder of how God has provided "angels in charge of you, to guard you in all your ways." In the Gospel, Jesus refers to the little ones whose angels in heaven constantly behold his Father's face.

651   October 4 — ST. FRANCIS OF ASSISI

READING I   Gal. 6:14-18   **RESP. Ps.** Common or Season
GOSPEL   Common or Season

The special first reading at today's Mass applies to the life of St. Francis of Assisi, the little poor man who died in 1226. We hear St. Paul asserting that he would "never boast of anything but the cross of our Lord Jesus Christ." This spiritual outlook also characterized the life of St. Francis. He embraced the cross of severe penance and devoted his life to prayerful reflection on the sufferings of Christ. St. Paul also mentions that he bears on his own body "the brand marks of Jesus." His words remind us that the body of Francis bore the wounds of Jesus after a mystical experience near the end of his life while in prayer on Mount La Verna.

657   October 15 — ST. TERESA OF AVILA, Virgin and Doctor

READING I   Rom. 8:22-27   **RESP. Ps.** Common or Season
GOSPEL   Common or Season

The special first reading at today's Mass applies to the life of St. Teresa of Avila, a Carmelite nun who lived four hundred years ago. You will hear St. Paul explain how the Holy Spirit works in the life of a Christian, particularly in his life of prayer. Paul's words remind us how the Holy Spirit guided Teresa in many ways throughout her life — in her contemplative prayer, in her sufferings and ecstasies, in her reform of the Carmelite community, and in her great mystical writings. These works have earned for Teresa the title, doctor of the Church.

660   October 17 — ST. IGNATIUS OF ANTIOCH, Bishop and Martyr

READING I   Phil. 3:17—4:1   **RESP. Ps.** Common or Season
GOSPEL   John 12:24-26

The special Scripture readings for today's Mass apply to the life of St. Ignatius of Antioch. He suffered martyrdom on this day in Rome in the second century. St. Paul actually composed the first reading, but today the liturgy suggests that we listen to his words as if Ignatius himself were speaking them. They closely reflect the saint's own great love for Christ. In the Gospel, Jesus uses the image of a grain of wheat to illustrate how we must die to self in order really to live. The text applies particularly to the way Ignatius died. When his persecutors threw Ignatius to the lions, and he heard the roar of the beasts, he exclaimed, "I am a grain of wheat for Christ. I must be ground by the teeth of beasts to be found bread wholly pure."

661   October 18 — ST. LUKE, Evangelist

READING I   2 Tim. 4:9-17   **RESP. Ps.** 145:10-11, 12-13, 17-18
GOSPEL   Luke 10:1-9

The special Scripture readings for today's Mass apply to the life of St. Luke, author of the third Gospel and the Acts of the Apostles. In the first passage, St. Paul writes to his friend Timothy and asks him to come to Rome. You will hear Paul mention that Luke was with him in the city. Luke had been a companion of Paul during the second and third missionary journeys among the Gentiles. The responsorial psalm refrain declares, "Your friends tell the glory of your kingship, Lord." The liturgy suggests that Luke fulfilled those words in his writings. For the Gospel, the liturgy selects Luke's account of our Lord's appointment of seventy-two disciples to preach the Good News of salvation to men. Tradition once considered Luke to be one of these disciples.

666 October 28 — ST. SIMON AND ST. JUDE, Apostles

READING I   Eph. 2:19-22   RESP. Ps. 19:2-3, 4-5
GOSPEL   Luke 6:12-16

The special Scripture readings for today's feast of the apostles Simon and Jude direct our attention to the role the apostles play in the Church. In the first passage, St. Paul assures his converts in the city of Ephesus that they have every right to belong to God's household by reason of their faith in Christ. He then explains that the apostles and prophets are like a firm foundation that supports God's household, the Church. Simon and Jude proved by sacrificing their lives how much they loved that Church. The responsorial psalm praises the work of the apostles in spreading the message of salvation through all the earth. In the Gospel, you will hear Jesus calling twelve men to be his apostles, including Simon the Zealot and Judas the son of James, the saints we honor today.

667 November 1 — ALL SAINTS

READING I   Rev. 7:2-4, 9-14   RESP. Ps. 24:1-2, 3-4, 5-6
READING II 1 John 3:1-3
GOSPEL   Matthew 5:1-12

Since we honor all the saints in one feast today, the special Scripture readings for this Mass remind us of our own destiny to share the joy of God's presence with the saints. In the first passage, St. John describes a scene from his mystical vision of the last days. We behold the vast numbers from every nation who stand in worship before the throne of God. After this reading, we will pray several verses from Psalm 24 that express our longing as God's people to see his face. In the special second reading, St. John reminds us of the joy that awaits us at the end of time when we shall see God as he is. In the Gospel, the Church recalls to our minds today the message of the beatitudes, because by living them we too will become saints.

671   November 9 — DEDICATION OF ST. JOHN LATERAN

The readings are from the Common of the Dedication of a Church.

READING I   1 Kings 8:22-23, 27-30   RESP. Ps. 95:1-2, 3-5, 6-7
GOSPEL   John 2:13-22

The Scripture readings today apply to the dedication of St. John Lateran, a basilica in Rome that dates back to the Emperor Constantine, about the year 325. To remind us of the occasion when this mother church of Western Christendom received its blessing, the first reading takes us back many centuries earlier to the dedication of another famous house of worship — the temple of Solomon. We hear the king beseech God to hear the requests which the people will offer in that holy place. The responsorial psalm refrain — "Let us come before the Lord and praise him" — suggests the millions of people who have honored God in the several churches that succeeded the original St. John's down to our times. The Gospel tells how Jesus drove the money changers from the temple. We learn that we must be reverent when we come to worship the Lord in our own churches.

673   November 11 — ST. MARTIN OF TOURS, Bishop

READING I   Common or Season   RESP. Ps. Common or Season
GOSPEL   Matthew 25:31-40

The special Gospel reading for today's Mass applies to the life of St. Martin, bishop of Tours, who lived in the fourth century. He was one of the first to receive the honors of a saint without suffering martyrdom. The liturgy finds our Lord's words about clothing the naked fulfilled in a famous incident in Martin's youth. While serving in the Roman army, he met a poor naked beggar who asked for money in the name of Christ. Having nothing with him except his weapons and soldier's mantle, Martin cut the mantle in two and gave half to the beggar. The following night Christ appeared to Martin wearing half a mantle.

679   November 18 — DEDICATION OF THE CHURCHES OF ST. PETER AND ST. PAUL, Apostles

READING I   Acts 28:11-16, 30-31   RESP. Ps. 98:1, 2-3, 3-4, 5-6
GOSPEL   Matthew 14:22-33

The special Scripture readings for today's Mass apply to the lives of the apostles Peter and Paul. The first passage directs our attention to Paul's account of his journey to Rome to appeal his arrest by the Jews. He was eventually released and continued his missionary work until his final imprisonment and martyrdom in Rome in the year 67. The responsorial psalm refrain declares that "the Lord has revealed to the nations his saving power" through the apostles Peter and Paul. The Gospel then centers on St. Peter. Just as the first reading showed Paul on a boat, the Gospel tells how Peter was in a boat when a storm came up on the Sea of Galilee. Jesus comes walking toward the disciples on the waters. When Peter's faith wavers, our Lord rescues him.

684   November 30 — ST. ANDREW, Apostle

READING I   Rom. 10:9-18   RESP. Ps. 19:2-3, 4-5
GOSPEL   Matthew 4:18-22

Today's special readings apply to the life of St. Andrew, an apostle and the brother of Simon Peter. In the first passage, St. Paul writes to the Christians in Rome about faith in Christ. He emphasizes that the Church needs to preach about Christ to all nations. Faith comes through hearing the Good News that Jesus has redeemed all men. Paul's words remind us that Christ chose Andrew to preach this joyous message. The saint's martyrdom should help bring home to us how deep Andrew's faith in Christ really was. The liturgy discovers in the responsorial psalm another echo of Andrew's vocation to preach the Good News to men. The refrain declares that the message of Andrew and his successors in the Church "goes out through all the earth." The Gospel tells how Peter and Andrew abandoned their fishermen's nets and followed Jesus.

689   December 8 — IMMACULATE CONCEPTION

READING I   Gen. 3:9-15, 20   RESP. Ps. 98:1, 2-3, 3-4
READING II   Eph. 1:3-6, 11-12
GOSPEL   Luke 1:26-38

Today's readings focus on Mary's privilege of the Immaculate Conception — the special title under which our Lady is patroness of the United States. In the first passage, we hear God promise a Redeemer after the fall of Adam and Eve. The Church in 1854 explained that God anticipated the merits of Christ, mankind's one Redeemer, by preserving Mary free from sin in the very first moment of her existence. The responsorial psalm refrain invites us to "sing to the Lord a new song, for he has done marvelous deeds" in giving Mary this unique privilege among all God's creatures. In the special second reading, the liturgy applies to Mary today Paul's words that God chose her in Christ "before the world began, to be holy and blameless in his sight, to be full of love." The liturgy discovers in the Gospel passage that Mary's great dignity as the Mother of God was the reason for her Immaculate Conception.

707   December 12 — OUR LADY OF GUADALUPE

The readings are from the Common of the Blessed Virgin Mary.

READING I   Is. 9:1-6   **RESP.** Ps. 113:1-2, 3-4, 5-6, 7-8
GOSPEL   Luke 2:15-19

Today's Scripture readings apply to Mary's apparition to the Indian Juan Diego on a hillside near Mexico City in 1531. In the first passage, we hear that "upon those who dwelt in the land of gloom a light has shone." This reminds us that Mary appeared at a time when the Aztec Indians offered human sacrifices to their gods and labored under the oppression of their conquerors. Mary desired a shrine where people could come and honor her son, whose name is "Prince of Peace." The responsorial psalm suggests that "from the rising to the setting of the sun" the name of the Lord has received praise for over four hundred years at the basilica of our Lady of Guadalupe. The Gospel story of Mary becoming Mother of God recalls her message to Juan Diego. The Queen of the Americas told him that since she was the Mother of all men, they should turn to her in confidence for all their needs.

INDEX OF READINGS

In the columns Proper of Seasons and Proper of Saints, the numbers in italic type refer to readings as numbered in the lectionary and the numbers in roman type refer to pages in this book.

	Proper of Seasons				Proper of Saints	
	Year I		Year II			

OLD TESTAMENT

GENESIS

1:1-19	*329*	82				
20–2:4	*330*	83				
26–2:3					*559*	264
2:5-9, 15-17	*331*	84				
18-25	*332*	85				
3:1-8	*333*	86				
9-15, 20					*689*	273
9-24	*334*	87				
4:1-15, 25	*335*	87				
6:5-8; 7:1-5, 10	*336*	88				
8:6-13, 20-22	*337*	89				
9:1-13	*338*	90				
11:1-9	*339*	91				
12:1-9	*371*	117				
13:2, 5-18	*372*	118				
14:18-20					*170(C)*	249
15:1-12, 17-18	*373*	119				
16:1-12, 15-16	*374*	120				
6-12, 15-16	*374*	120				
17:1, 9-10, 15-22	*375*	121				
3-9	*255*	36	*255*	36		
18:1-15	*376*	122				
16-33	*377*	123				
19:15-29	*378*	123				
21:5, 8-20	*379*	124				
22:1-19	*380*	125				
23:1-4, 19; 24:1-8, 62-67	*381*	126				
27:1-5, 15-29	*382*	127				

	Proper of Seasons				Proper of Saints	
	Year I		Year II			
28:10-22	*383*	128				
32:23-33	*384*	128				
37:3-4, 12-13, 17-28	*235*	27	*235*	**27**		
41:55-57; 42:5-7,						
17-24	*385*	129				
44:18-21, 23-29						
45:1-5	*386*	130				
46:1-7, 28-30	*387*	131				
49:2, 8-10	*194*	9	*194*	9		
29-33; 50:15-24	*388*	132				
EXODUS						
1:8-14, 22	*389*	133				
2:1-15	*390*	134				
3:1-6, 9-12	*391*	134				
11-20	*392*	135				
11:10–12:14	*393*	136				
12:37-42	*394*	137				
14:5-18	*395*	138				
21–15:1	*396*	139				
16:1-5, 9-15	*397*	140				
17:1-7	*237*	28	*237*	28		
19:1-2, 9-11, 16-20	*398*	140				
20:1-7	*399*	141				
23:20-23					*650*	269
24:3-8	*400*	142			*169(B)*	249
32:7-14	*248*	33	*248*	33		
15-24, 30-34	*401*	143				
33:7-11; 34:5-9, 28	*402*	144				
34:29-35	*403*	145				
40:16-21, 34-38	*404*	146				
LEVITICUS						
19:1-2, 11-18	*225*	23	*225*	23		
23:1, 4-11, 15-16, 27						
34-37	*405*	146				
25:1, 8-17	*406*	147				
NUMBERS						
6:22-27	*18*	15	*18*	15		
11:4-15	*407*	148, 149				
12:1-13	*408*	150, 151				
13:1-2, 25–14:1,						
26-29, 34-35	*409*	152				

	Proper of Seasons				Proper of Saints	
	Year I		Year II			
20:1-13	*410*	153				
21:4-9	*253*	35	*253*	35	*638*	265
24:2-7, 15-17	*188*	6	*188*	6		

DEUTERONOMY

4:1, 5-9	*240*	29	*240*	29		
32-40	*411*	153				
6:4-13	*412*	154				
7:6-11					*171(A)*	250
8:2-3, 14-16					*168(A)*	248
10:12-22	*413*	155				
26:16-19	*230*	25	*230*	25		
30:15-20	*221*	21	*221*	21		
31:1-8	*414*	156				
34:1-12	*415*	157				

JOSHUA

3:7-10, 11, 13-17	*416*	158				
24:1-13	*417*	158				
14-29	*418*	160				

JUDGES

2:11-19	*419*	160				
6:11-24	*420*	161				
9:6-15	*421*	162				
11:29-39	*422*	163				
13:2-7, 24-25	*196*	9	*196*	9		

RUTH

1:1, 3-6, 14-16, 22	*423*	164				
2:1-3, 8-11; 4:13-17	*424*	165				

1 SAMUEL

1:1-8			*305*	63		
9-20			*306*	64		
24-28	*199*	11	*199*	11		
3:1-10, 19-20			*307*	65		
4:1-11			*308*	65		
8:4-7, 10-22			*309*	66		
9:1-4, 17-19; 10:1			*310*	67		
15:16-23			*311*	68		
16:1-13			*312*	69		
17:32-33, 37, 40-51			*313*	70		
18:6-9; 19:1-7			*314*	70		
24:3-21			*315*	71		

	Proper of Seasons				Proper of Saints	
	Year I		Year II			

2 SAMUEL

1:1-4, 11-12, 19						
23-27			*316*	72		
5:1-7, 10			*317*	73		
6:12-15, 17-19			*318*	74		
7:1-5, 8-12, 14, 16	*201*	12	*201*	12		
4-5, 12-14, 16					*543*	243
4-17			*319*	75		
18-19, 24-29			*320*	75		
11:1-4, 5-10, 13-17			*321*	76		
12:1-7, 10-17			*322*	77		
15:13-14, 30; 16:5-13			*323*	78		
18:9-10, 14, 24-25,						
30–19:3			*324*	79		
24:2, 9-17			*325*	79		

1 KINGS

2:1-4, 10-12			*326*	80		
3:4-13			*328*	82		
8:1-7, 9-13			*329*	83		
22-23, 27-30			*330*	84	*671*	272
10:1-10			*331*	84		
11:4-13			*332*	85		
29-32; 12:19			*333*	86		
12:26-32; 13:33-34			*334*	87		
17:1-6			*359*	108		
7-16			*360*	109		
18:20-39			*361*	109		
41-46			*362*	110		
19:9, 11-16			*363*	111		
19-21			*364*	112		
21:1-16			*365*	113		
17-29			*366*	114		

2 KINGS

2:1, 6-14			*367*	115		
4:18-21, 32-37	*251*	34	*251*	34		
5:1-15	*238*	28	*238*	28		
11:1-4, 9-18, 20			*369*	116		
17:5-8, 13-15, 18			*371*	118		
19:9-11, 14-21, 31-35,						
36			*372*	119		
22:8-13; 23:1-3			*373*	120		
24:8-17			*374*	120		
25:1-12			*375*	121		

	Proper of Seasons				Proper of Saints
	Year I		Year II		
1 CHRONICLES					
15:3-4, 15, 16; 16:1-2					*621* 261
2 CHRONICLES					
24:17-25			*370*	117	
EZRA					
1:1-6	*449*	185			
6:7-8, 12, 14-20	*450*	186			
9:5-9	*451*	187			
NEHEMIAH					
2:1-8	*457*	192			
8:1-4, 5-6, 7-12	*458*	193			
TOBIT					
1:1, 2; 2:1-9	*353*	102			
2:9-14	*354*	103			
3:1-11, 16	*355*	104			
6:10-11; 7:1, 9-14; 8:4-7	*356*	105			
11:5-15	*357*	106			
12:1, 5-15, 20	*358*	107			
JUDITH					
ESTHER					
C:12, 14-16, 23-25	*228*	24	*228*	24	
1 MACCABEES					
1:10-15, 41-43, 54-57, 62-63	*497*	225			
2:15-29	*500*	227			
4:36-37, 52-59	*501*	228			
6:1-13	*502*	229			
2 MACCABEES					
6:18-31	*498*	226			
7:1, 20-31	*499*	227			

	Proper of Seasons				Proper of Saints	
	Year I		Year II			
JOB						
1:6-22			*455*	190		
3:1-3, 11-17, 20-23			*456*	191		
9:1-12, 14-16			*457*	192		
19:21-27			*458*	193		
38:1, 12-21; 40:3-5			*459*	194		
42:1-3, 5-6, 12-16			*460*	195		
PSALMS						
PROVERBS						
2:1-9					*597*	256
3:27-34			*449*	186		
21:1-6, 10-13			*450*	186		
30:5-9			*451*	187		
ECCLESIASTES						
1:2-11			*452*	188		
3:1-11			*453*	189		
11:9–12:8			*454*	190		
SONG OF SONGS						
2:8-14	*198*	10	*198*	10		
3:1-4					*603*	256
WISDOM						
1:1-7	*491*	220				
2:1, 12-22	*249*	33	*249*	33		
23–3:9	*492*	221				
6:2-11	*493*	222				
7:22–8:1	*494*	222				
13:1-9	*495*	223				
18:14-16; 19:6-9	*496*	224				
SIRACH						
1:1-10	*341*	92				
2:1-11	*342*	93				
4:11-19	*343*	94				
5:1-8	*344*	95				
6:5-17	*345*	96				
17:1-15	*346*	97				

	Proper of Seasons				Proper of Saints	
	Year I		Year II			
19-27	*347*	97				
35:1-12	*348*	98				
36:1, 5-6, 10-17	*349*	99				
42:15-25	*350*	100				
44:1, 9-13	*351*	101				
1, 10-15					*606*	258
47:2-11			*327*	81		
48:1-4, 9-11	*187*	6	*187*	6		
1-14			*368*	*115*		
51:12-20	*352*	102				
ISAIAH						
1:10, 16-20	*232*	26	*232*	26		
10-17			*389*	133		
2:1-5	*176(B, C)*	1	*176(B, C)*	1		
4:2-6	*176(A)*	1	*176(A)*	1		
6:1-8			*388*	132		
7:1-9			*390*	134		
10-14	*197*	10	*197*	10	*545*	244
9:1-6					*707**	274
10:5-7, 13-16	*391*	135				
11:1-10	*177*	1	*177*	1		
25:6-10	*178*	2	*178*	2		
26:1-6	*179*	2	*179*	2		
7-9, 12, 16-19			*392*	136		
29:17-24	*180*	3	*180*	3		
30:19-21, 23-26	*181*	3	*181*	3		
35:1-10	*182*	4	*182*	4		
38:1-6, 21-22, 7-8			*393*	137		
40:1-11	*183*	4	*183*	4		
25-31	*184*	4	*184*	4		
41:13-20	*185*	5	*185*	5		
42:1-7	*258*	37	*258*	37		
45:6-8, 18, 21-25	*190*	7	*190*	7		
48:17-19	*186*	5	*186*	5		
49:1-6	*259*	38	*259*	38	*587*	253
8-15	*247*	32	*247*	32		
50:4-9	*260*	38	*260*	38		
54:1-10	*191*	8	*191*	8		
55:10-11	*226*	23	*226*	23		
56:1-3, 6-8	*192*	8	*192*	8		
58:1-9	*222*	22	*222*	22		
9-14	*223*	22	*223*	22		
61:9-11					*627*	262

*from Commons

	Proper of Seasons				Proper of Saints	
	Year I		Year II			
65:17-21	*245*	31	*245*	31		
66:10-14					*531*	242
					649	268
JEREMIAH						
1:1, 4-10			*397*	140		
4-10					*586*	253
17-19					*634*	263
2:1-3, 7-8, 12-13			*398*	141		
3:14-17			*399*	142		
7:1-11			*400*	143		
23-28	*241*	30	*241*	30		
11:18-20	*250*	33	*250*	33		
13:1-11			*401*	143		
14:17-22			*402*	144		
15:10, 16-21			*403*	145		
17:5-10	*234*	27	*234*	27		
18:1-6			*404*	146		
18-20	*233*	26	*233*	26		
20:10-13	*256*	37	*256*	37		
23:5-8	*195*	9	*195*	9		
26:1-9			*405*	147		
11-16, 24			*406*	148		
28:1-17			*407*	149		
30:1-2, 12-15, 18-22			*408*	150, 151		
31:1-7			*409*	152		
31-34			*410*	153		
LAMENTATIONS						
2:2, 10-14, 18-19			*376*	122		
BARUCH						
1:15-22	*459*	193				
4:5-12, 27-29	*460*	194				
EZEKIEL						
1:2-5, 24-28			*413*	155		
2:8–3:4			*414*	156		
9:1-7; 10:18-22			*415*	157		
12:1-2			*416*	158		
16:1-15, 60, 63			*417*	159		
59-63			*417*	159		
18:1-10, 13, 30-32			*418*	160		
21-28	*229*	24	*229*	24		

	Proper of Seasons				Proper of Saints	
	Year I		Year II			
24:15-24			*419*	161		
28:1-10			*420*	162		
34:1-11			*421*	163		
11-16					*173(C)*	251
36:23-28			*422*	163		
37:1-14			*423*	164		
21-28	*257*	37	*257*	37		
43:1-7			*424*	165		
47:1-9, 12	*246*	32	*246*	32		
DANIEL						
1:1-6, 8-20	*503*	230				
2:31-45	*504*	231				
3:14-20, 91-92, 95	*254*	36	*254*	36		
25, 34-43	*239*	29	*239*	29		
5:1-6, 13-14, 16-17,						
23-28	*505*	232				
6:12-28	*506*	233				
7:2-14	*507*	233				
9-10, 13-14					*614*	260
					647	267
15-27	*508*	234				
9:4-10	*231*	25	*231*	25		
13:1-9, 15-17, 19-30,						
33-62	*252*	34, 35	*252*	34, 35		
41-62	*252*	34, 35	*252*	34, 35		
HOSEA						
2:16, 17-18, 21-22			*383*	128		
6:1-6	*243*	30	*243*	30		
8:4-7, 11-13			*384*	129		
10:1-3, 7-8, 12			*385*	130		
11:1, 3-4, 8-9			*386*	131	*172(B)*	250
14:2-10	*242*	30	*242*	30		
			387	131		
JOEL						
1:13-15; 2:1-2	*465*	198				
2:12-18	*220*	21	*220*	21		
4:12-21	*466*	199				
AMOS						
2:6-10, 13-16			*377*	123		
3:1-8; 4:11-12			*378*	124		
5:14-15, 21-24			*379*	125		

	Proper of Seasons				Proper of Saints	
	Year I		Year II			
7:10-17			*380*	125		
8:4-6, 9-12			*381*	126		
9:11-15			*382*	127		
OBADIAH						
JONAH						
1:1–2:1-11	*461*	195				
3:1-10	462	196				
	227	24	*227*	24		
4:1-11	*463*	197				
MICAH						
2:1-5			*394*	137		
5:1-4					*636*	265
6:1-4, 6-8			395	138		
7:7-9	*244*	31	244	31		
14-15, 18-20	236	27	236	27		
NAHUM						
2:1, 3; 3:1-3, 6-7			*411*	154		
HABAKKUK						
1:12–2:4			*412*	155		
ZEPHANIAH						
3:1-2, 9-13	*189*	7	*189*	7		
14-18	*198*	11	*198*	11	*572*	247
HAGGAI						
1:1, 15–2:9	*453*	188				
1-8	*452*	188				
ZECHARIAH						
2:5-9, 14-15	*454*	189				
8:1-8	455	190				
20-23	*456*	191				
MALACHI						
3:1-4					*524*	241

	Proper of Seasons				Proper of Saints	
	Year I		Year II			
1-4, 23-24	*200*	12	*200*	12		
13-20	*464*	198				

NEW TESTAMENT

MATTHEW

1:1-16, 18-23					*636*	265
1-17	*194*	9	*194*	9		
16, 18-21, 24					*543*	243
18-23					*636*	265
18-24	*195*	9	*195*	9	*636*	265
4:12-17, 23-25	*213*	18	*213*	18		
18-22					*684*	273
5:1-12	*359*	107	*359*	108	*667*	271
13-16	*360*	108	*360*	109		
17-19	*240*	29	*240*	29		
	361	109	*361*	109		
20-26	*229*	24	*229*	24		
	362	110	*362*	110		
27-32	*363*	111	*363*	111		
33-37	*364*	112	*364*	112		
38-42	*365*	112	*365*	113		
43-48	*230*	25	*230*	25		
	366	113	*366*	114		
6:1-6, 16-18	*220*	21	*220*	21		
	367	114	*367*	115		
7-15	*226*	23	*226*	23		
	368	115	*368*	115		
19-23	*369*	116	*369*	116		
24-34	*370*	117	*370*	117		
7:1-5	*371*	117	*371*	118		
6, 12-14	*372*	118	*372*	119		
7-12	*228*	24	*228*	24		
15-20	*373*	119	*373*	120		
21, 24-27	*179*	2	*179*	2		
21-29	*374*	120	*374*	120		
8:1-4	*375*	121	*375*	121		
5-11	*176*	1	*176*	1		
5-17	*376*	122	*376*	122		
18-22	*377*	123	*377*	123		
23-27	*378*	123	*378*	124		
28-34	*379*	124	*379*	125		
9:1-8	*380*	125	*380*	125		
9-13	*381*	126	*381*	126	*643*	267
14-15	*222*	22	*222*	22		
14-17	*382*	127	*382*	127		

	Proper of Seasons				Proper of Saints	
	Year I		Year II			
18-26	*383*	128	*383*	128		
27-31	*180*	3	*180*	3		
32-38	*384*	128	*384*	129		
35–10:1					*612*	259
35–10:1, 6-8	*181*	3	*181*	3		
10:1-7	*385*	129	*385*	130		
7-13					*580*	252
7-15	*386*	130	*386*	131		
16-23	*387*	131	*387*	131		
17-22					*696*	12
22-25					*560*	245, 246
24-33	*388*	132	*388*	132		
34–11:1	*389*	133	*389*	133		
11:11-15	*185*	5	*185*	5		
16-19	*186*	5	*186*	5		
20-24	*390*	134	*390*	134		
25-27	*391*	134	*391*	135		
25-30					*171(A)*	250
28-30	*184*	4	*184*	4		
	392	135	*392*	136		
12:1-8	*393*	136	*393*	137		
14-21	*394*	137	*394*	137		
38-42	*395*	138	*395*	138		
46-50	*396*	139	*396*	139		
13:1-9	*397*	140	*397*	140		
10-17	*398*	140	*398*	141		
16-17					*606*	258
18-23	*399*	141	*399*	142		
24-30	*400*	142	*400*	143		
31-35	*401*	143	*401*	143		
35-43	*402*	144	*402*	144		
44-46	*403*	145	*403*	145		
47-53	*404*	146	*404*	146		
54-58	*405*	146	*405*	147	*559*	264
14:1-12	*406*	147	*406*	148		
13-21	*407*	149	*407*	149		
22-33					*679*	272
22-36	*407*	148	*407*	149		
	408(B,C)	151	*408(B,C)*	151		
15:1-2, 10-14	*408(A)*	150	*408(A)*	150		
21-28	*409*	152	*409*	152		
29-37	*178*	2	*178*	2		
16:13-19					*535*	242
					591	254
13-23	*410*	153	*410*	153		
24-28	*411*	153	*411*	154		

	Proper of Seasons				Proper of Saints	
	Year I		Year II			
17:1-9					*614(A)*	260
10-13	*187*	6	*187*	6		
14-20	*412*	154	*412*	155		
22-27	*413*	155	*413*	155		
18:1-4					*649*	268
1-5, 10					*650*	269
1-5, 10, 12-14	*414*	156	*414*	156		
12-14	*183*	4	*183*	4		
15-20	*415*	157	*415*	157		
21-35	*239*	29	*239*	29		
21–19:1	*416*	158	*416*	158		
19:3-12	*417*	158	*417*	159		
13-15	*418*	160	*418*	160		
16-22	*419*	160	*419*	161		
16-26					*513*	239
23-30	*420*	161	*420*	162		
20:1-16	*421*	162	*421*	163		
17-28	*233*	26	*233*	26		
20-28					*605*	257
21:23-27	*188*	6	*188*	6		
28-32	*189*	7	*189*	7		
33-43, 45-46	*235*	27	*235*	27		
22:1-14	*422*	163	*422*	163		
34-40	*423*	164	*423*	164		
23:1-12	*232*	26	*232*	26		
	424	165	*424*	165		
8-12					*633*	263
13-22	*425*	166	*425*	166		
23-26	*426*	166	*426*	167		
27-32	*427*	167	*427*	168		
24:4-13					*592*	255
42-51	*428*	168	*428*	169		
25:1-13	*429*	169	*429*	169		
14-30	*430*	170	*430*	170		
31-40					*673*	272
31-46	*225*	23	*225*	23		
26:14-25	*260*	38	*260*	38		
28:8-15	*261*	39	*261*	39		
16-20	*59(A)*	54	*59(A)*	54	*528*	241
MARK						
1:7-11	*210*	17	*210*	17		
14-20	*305*	63	*305*	63		
21-28	*306*	63	*306*	64		
29-39	*307*	64	*307*	65		
40-45	*308*	65	*308*	65		

	Proper of Seasons				Proper of Saints	
	Year I		Year II			
2:1-12	309	66	309	66		
13-17	310	67	310	67		
18-22	311	68	311	68		
23-28	312	68	312	69		
3:1-6	313	69	313	70		
7-12	314	70	314	70		
13-19	315	71	315	71		
20-21	316	72	316	72		
22-30	317	73	317	73		
31-35	318	73	318	74		
4:1-20	319	74	319	75		
21-25	320	75	320	75		
26-34	321	76	321	76		
35-41	322	77	322	77		
5:1-20	323	77	323	78		
21-43	324	78	324	79		
6:1-6	325	79	325	79		
7-13	326	80	326	80		
14-29	327	81	327	81		
17-29					634	263
30-34	328	82	328	82		
34-44	214	19	214	19		
45-52	215	19	215	19		
53-56	329	82	329	83		
7:1-13	330	83	330	84		
14-23	331	84	331	84		
24-30	332	85	332	85		
31-37	333	86	333	86		
8:1-10	334	87	334	87		
8, 34–9:1	339	91	339	91		
11-13	335	87	335	88		
14-21	336	88	336	89		
22-26	337	89	337	89		
27-33	338	90	338	90		
9:2-10					614(B)	260
2-13	340	92	340	92		
14-29	341	92	341	93		
30-37	342	93	342	94		
38-40	343	94	343	95		
41-50	344	95	344	95		
10:1-12	345	96	345	96		
13-16	346	97	346	97		
17-27	347	97	347	98		
28-31	348	98	348	99		
32-45	349	99	349	99		
46-52	350	100	350	100		

	Proper of Seasons				Proper of Saints	
	Year I		Year II			
11:11-26	*351*	101	*351*	101		
27-33	*352*	102	*352*	102		
12:1-12	*353*	102	*353*	103		
13-17	*354*	103	*354*	104		
18-27	*355*	104	*355*	104		
28-34	*242*	30	*242*	30		
	356	105	*356*	105		
35-37	*357*	106	*357*	106		
38-44	*358*	107	*358*	107		
14:12-16, 22-26					*169(B)*	249
16:9-15	*266*	41	*266*	41		
15-18					*519*	239, 240
15-20	*59(B)*	55	*59(B)*	55	*555*	244
LUKE						
1:5-17					*586*	253
5-25	*196*	9	*196*	9		
26-38	*197*	10	*197*	10	*545*	244
					627	262
					689	273
39-45	*198*	10, 11	*198*	10, 11		
39-56					*572*	247, 248
					622	261
46-56	*199*	11	*199*	11		
57-66	*200*	12	*200*	12		
57-66, 80					*587*	253
67-79	*201*	12	*201*	12		
2:15-19					*707**	274
16-21	*18*	15	*18*	15		
22-32					*524*	241
22-35	*203*	14	*203*	14		
22-40					*524*	241
33-35					*639*	266
36-40	*204*	14	*204*	14		
41-51					*543*	243
					573	251
4:14-22	*216*	20	*216*	20		
16-30	*431*	171	*431*	171		
24-30	*238*	28	*238*	28		
31-37	*432*	171	*432*	172		
38-44	*433*	172	*433*	173		
5:1-11	*434*	173	*434*	173		
12-16	*217*	20	*217*	20		
17-26	*182*	4	*182*	4		

*from Commons

	Proper of Seasons				Proper of Saints	
	Year I		Year II			
27-32	*223*	22	*223*	22		
33-39	*435*	174	*435*	174		
6:1-5	*436*	175	*436*	175		
6-11	*437*	175	*437*	176		
12-16					*666*	271
12-19	*438*	176	*438*	177		
20-26	*439*	177	*439*	177		
27-38	*440*	178	*440*	178		
36-38	*231*	25	*231*	25		
39-42	*441*	179	*441*	179		
43-49	*442*	179	*442*	180		
7:1-10	*443*	180	*443*	181		
11-17	*444*	181	*444*	181	*632*	263
18-23	*190*	7	*190*	7		
24-30	*191*	8	*191*	8		
31-35	*445*	182	*445*	182		
36-50	*446*	183	*446*	183		
8:1-3	*447*	184	*447*	184		
4-15	*448*	184	*448*	185		
16-18	*449*	185	*449*	186		
19-21	*450*	186	*450*	186		
9:1-6	*451*	187	*451*	187		
7-9	*452*	188	*452*	188		
11-17					*170(C)*	249
18-22	*453*	188	*453*	189		
22-25	*221*	21	*221*	21		
28-36					*614(C)*	260
43-45	*454*	189	*454*	190		
46-50	*455*	190	*455*	190		
51-56	*456*	191	*456*	191		
57-62	*457*	192	*457*	192		
10:1-9					*661*	270
1-12	*458*	193	*458*	193		
13-16	*459*	193	*459*	194		
17-24	*460*	194	*460*	195		
21-24	*177*	1	*177*	1		
25-37	*461*	195	*461*	195		
38-42	*462*	196	*462*	196	*607*	258
11:1-4	*463*	197	*463*	197		
5-13	*464*	198	*464*	198		
14-23	*241*	30	*241*	30		
15-26	*465*	198	*465*	199		
27-28	*466*	199	*466*	200	*621*	261
29-32	*227*	24	*227*	24		
	467	200	*467*	200		
37-41	*468*	201	*468*	201		

	Proper of Seasons				Proper of Saints
	Year I		Year II		
42-46	*469*	202	*469*	202	
47-54	*470*	203	*470*	203	
12:1-7	*471*	203	*471*	204	
8-12	*472*	204	*472*	205	
13-21	*473*	205	*473*	205	
35-38	*474*	206	*474*	206	
39-48	*475*	207	*475*	207	
49-53	*476*	208	*476*	208	
54-59	*477*	208	*477*	209	
13:1-9	*478*	209	*478*	210	
10-17	*479*	210	*479*	210	
18-21	*480*	211	*480*	211	
22-30	*481*	212	*481*	212	
31-35	*482*	213	*482*	213	
14:1, 7-11	*484*	214	*484*	215	
1-6	*483*	213	*483*	214	
12-14	*485*	215	*485*	215	
15-24	*486*	216	*486*	216	
25-33	*487*	217	*487*	217	
15:1-3, 11-32	*236*	27	*236*	27	
1-10	*488*	217	*488*	218	
3-7					*173(C)* 251
16:1-8	*489*	218	*489*	219	
9-15	*490*	219	*490*	219	
19-31	*234*	27	*234*	27	
17:1-6	*491*	220	*491*	220	
7-10	*492*	221	*492*	221	
11-19	*493*	222	*493*	222	
20-25	*494*	222	*494*	223	
26-37	*495*	223	*495*	224	
18:1-8	*496*	224	*496*	224	
9-14	*243*	30	*243*	30	
35-43	*497*	225	*497*	225	
19:1-10	*498*	226	*498*	226	
11-28	*499*	227	*499*	227	
41-44	*500*	227	*500*	228	
45-48	*501*	228	*501*	229	
20:27-40	*502*	229	*502*	229	
21:1-4	*503*	230	*503*	230	
5-11	*504*	231	*504*	231	
12-19	*505*	232	*505*	232	
20-28	*506*	233	*506*	233	
29-33	*507*	233	*507*	234	
34-36	*508*	234	*508*	235	
24:13-35	*263*	40	*263*	40	
35-48	*264*	40	*264*	40	

	Proper of Seasons		Proper of Saints	
	Year I		Year II	
46-53	*59(C)*	55	*59(C)* 55	

	Proper of Seasons Years I and II		Proper of Saints	
JOHN				
1:1-18	*205*	15		
19-28	*206*	15		
29-34	*207*	16		
35-42	*208*	16		
43-51	*209*	17		
45-51			*629*	262
47-51			*647*	267, 268
2:1-12	*211*	18		
13-22			*671*	272
3:1-8	*267*	41		
7-15	*268*	42		
13-17			*638*	265
16-21	*269*	42		
22-30	*218*	20		
31-36	*270*	43		
4:5-42	*237*	28		
43-54	*245*	31		
5:1-3, 5-16	*246*	32		
17-30	*247*	32		
31-47	*248*	33		
33-36	*192*	8		
6:1-15	*271*	43		
16-21	*272*	44		
22-69	*273*	44		
30-35	*274*	45		
35-40	*275*	45		
44-51	*276*	45		
51-58			*168(A)*	248
52-59	*277*	46		
60-69	*278*	46		
7:1-2, 10, 25-30	*249*	33		
40-53	*250*	33		
8:1-11	*252(A,B)*	34		
12-20	*252(C)*	35		
21-30	*253*	35		
31-42	*254*	36		
51-59	*255*	36		
9:1-41	*244*	31		

	Proper of Seasons				Proper of Saints	
	Years I and II					
10:1-10	*279(B,C)*	47				
11-18	*279(A)*	47				
22-30	*280*	48				
31-42	*256*	37				
11:1-45	*251*	34				
19-27					*607*	258
45-57	*257*	37				
12:1-11	*258*	37				
24-26					*618*	260
44-50	*281*	48				
13:16-20	*282*	48				
21-33, 36-38	*259*	38				
14:1-6	*283*	49				
6-14					*561*	246
7-14	*284*	49				
21-26	*285*	50				
27-31	*286*	50				
15:1-8	*287*	51				
9-11	*288*	51				
9-17					*564*	247
12-17	*289*	52				
18-21	*290*	52				
26–16:4	*291*	52				
16:5-11	*292*	53				
12-15	*293*	53				
16-20	*294*	54				
20-23	*295*	56				
23-28	*296*	56				
29-33	*297*	56				
17:1-11	*298*	57				
11-19	*299*	57				
20-26	*300*	58				
19:25-27					*639*	266
31-37					*172(B)*	250
20:1-2, 11-18					*603*	256, 257
2-8					*697*	13
11-18	*264*	39				
24-29					*593*	255
21:1-14	*265*	41				
15-19	*301*	58			*590*	254
20-25	*302*	59				

ACTS OF THE APOSTLES

1:1-11	*59*	54, 55				
15-17, 20-26					*564*	247

	Proper of Seasons			Proper of Saints	
	Years I and II				
2:14, 22-32	*261*	39			
36-41	*262*	39			
3:1-10	*263*	40		*590*	254
11-26	*264*	40			
4:1-12	*265*	41			
8-12				*566*	247
13-21	*266*	41			
23-31	*267*	41			
32-37	*268*	42			
5:17-26	*269*	42			
27-33	*270*	43			
34-42	*271*	43			
6:1-7	*272*	44			
8-10; 7:54-59				*696*	12
8-15	*273*	44			
7:51–8:1	*274*	45			
8:1-8	*275*	45			
26-40	*276*	45			
9:1-20	*277*	46			
1-22				*519*	240
31-42	*278*	46			
11:1-18	*279*	47			
19-26	*280*	48			
21-26; 13:1-3				*580*	252
12:1-11				*591*	254
24–13:5	*281*	48			
13:13-25	*282*	48			
22-26				*587*	253
26-33	*283*	49			
44-52	*284*	49			
14:5-18	*285*	50			
19-28	*286*	50			
15:1-6	*287*	51			
7-21	*288*	51			
22-31	*289*	52			
16:1-10	*290*	52			
11-15	*291*	52			
22-34	*292*	53			
17:15, 22–18:1	*293*	53			
18:1-8	*294*	54			
9-18	*295*	56			
23-28	*296*	56			
19:1-8	*297*	56			
20:17-27	*298*	57			
28-38	*299*	57			
22:3-16				*519*	239

	Proper of Seasons			Proper of Saints	
	Years I and II				
30; 23:6-11	*300*	58			
25:13-21	*301*	58			
28:11-16, 30-31				*679*	272
16-20, 30-31	*302*	59			

	Proper of Seasons			Proper of Saints	
	Year I		Year II		

ROMANS

1:1-7	*467*	200			
16-25	*468*	201			
2:1-11	*469*	202			
3:21-29	*470*	203			
4:1-8	*471*	203			
13, 16-18	*472*	204			
13, 16-18, 22				*543*	243
20-25	*473*	205			
5:5-11				*173(C)*	251
12, 15, 17-19, 20-21	*474*	206			
6:12-18	*475*	207			
19-23	*476*	208			
7:18-25	*477*	208			
8:1-4				*610*	259
1-11	*478*	209			
12-17	*479*	210			
18-25	*480*	211			
22-27				*657*	270
26-30	*481*	212			
28-30				*636*	265
31-39	*482*	213			
9:1-5	*483*	213			
10:9-18				*684*	273
11:1-2, 11-12, 25-29	*484*	214			
29-36	*485*	215			
12:5-16	*486*	216			
9-16				*572*	248
13:8-10	*487*	217			
14:7-12	*488*	217			
15:14-21	*489*	218			
16:3-9, 16, 22-27	*490*	219			

1 CORINTHIANS

1:1-9			*428*	169	

	Proper of Seasons				Proper of Saints	
	Year I		Year II			
17-25			*429*	169		
18-25					*574*	251
26-31			*430*	170		
2:1-5			*431*	171		
10-16			*432*	172		
3:1-9			*433*	173		
18-23			*434*	173		
4:1-5			*435*	174		
6-15			*436*	175		
5:1-8			*437*	176		
6:1-11			*438*	177		
13-15, 17-20					*596*	256
7:25-31			*439*	177		
8:1-7, 11-13			*440*	178		
9:16-19, 22-27			*441*	179		
10:14-22			*442*	180		
16-17					*168(A)*	248
31—11:1					*609*	259
11:17-26, 33			*433*	181		
23-26					*170(C)*	249
12:12-14, 27-31			*444*	181		
31—13:13			*445*	182		
15:1-8					*561*	246
1-11			*446*	183		
12-20			*447*	184		
20-26					*622*	261
35-37, 42-49			*448*	185		
54-57					*621*	261
2 CORINTHIANS						
1:1-7	*359*	107				
18-22	*360*	108				
3:4-11	*361*	109				
15—4:1, 3-6	*362*	110				
4:7-15	*363*	111			*605*	257
5:14-17					*603*	257
14-21	*364*	112				
6:1-10	*365*	112				
8:1-9	*366*	113				
9-15					*584*	252
9:6-10					*618*	260
6-11	*367*	114				
11:1-11	*368*	115				
18, 21-30	*369*	116				
12:1-10	*370*	117				

	Proper of Seasons				Proper of Saints	
	Year I		Year II			
GALATIANS						
1:6-12			*461*	195		
11-20					*590*	254
13-24			*462*	196		
2:1-2, 7-14			*463*	197		
19-20					*528*	241
3:1-5			*464*	198		
7-14			*465*	199		
22-29			*466*	200		
4:4-7	*18*	15	*18*	15		
22-24, 26-27, 31–5:1			*467*	200		
5:1-6			*468*	201		
18-25			*469*	202		
6:14-18					*651*	269
EPHESIANS						
1:1-10			*470*	203		
3-6, 11-12					*689*	273
11-14			*471*	204		
15-23			*472*	205		
17-23	*59*	54, 55	*59*	54, 55		
2:1-10			*473*	205		
12-22			*474*	206		
19-22					*593*	255
3:2-12			*475*	207		
8-12, 14-19					*172(B)*	250
14-21			*476*	208		
4:1-6			*477*	209		
1-7, 11-13					*643*	267
7-16			*478*	210		
32–5:8			*479*	210		
5:21-33			*480*	211		
6:1-9			*481*	212		
10-20			*482*	213		
PHILIPPIANS						
1:1-11			*483*	214		
18-26			*484*	215		
2:1-4			*485*	215		
5-11			*486*	216		
6-11					*638*	265
12-18			*487*	217		

	Proper of Seasons				Proper of Saints	
	Year I		Year II			
3:3-8			488	218		
17–4:1			489	219	660	270
4:10-19			490	219		
COLOSSIANS						
1:1-8	433	172				
9-14	434	173				
15-20	435	174				
21-23	436	175				
24–2:3	437	175				
2:6-15	438	176				
3:1-11	439	177				
12-17	440	178				
14-15, 17, 23-24					559	264
1 THESSALONIANS						
1:2-5, 8-10	425	166				
2:1-8	426	166				
9-13	427	167				
3:7-13	428	168				
4:1-8	429	169				
9-12	430	170				
13-18	431	171				
5:1-6, 9-11	432	171				
2 THESSALONIANS						
1:1-5, 11-12			425	166		
2:1-3, 14-16			426	167		
3:6-10, 16-18			427	168		
1 TIMOTHY						
1:1-2, 12-14	441	179				
15-17	442	179				
2:1-8	443	180				
3:1-13	444	181				
14-16	445	182				
4:12-16	446	183				
6:2-12	447	184				
13-16	448	184				
2 TIMOTHY						
1:1-3, 6-12			355	104		

	Proper of Seasons		Year II		Proper of Saints	
	Year I					
1-8					*520*	240
2:8-15			*356*	105		
22-26					*589*	253
3:10-17			*357*	106		
4:1-8			*358*	107		
6-8, 17-18					*591*	254
9-17					*661*	270
TITUS						
1:1-5					*520*	241
1-9			*491*	220		
2:1-8, 11-14			*492*	221		
3:1-7			*493*	222		
PHILEMON						
7-20			*494*	223		
HEBREWS						
1:1-6	*305*	63				
2:5-12	*306*	63				
14-18	*307*	64			*524*	241
3:7-14	*308*	65				
4:1-5, 11	*309*	66				
12-16	*310*	67				
5:1-10	*311*	68				
7-9					*639*	266
6:10-20	*312*	68				
7:1-3, 15-17	*313*	69				
25–8:6	*314*	70				
8:6-13	*315*	71				
9:2-3, 11-14	*316*	72				
11-15					*169(B)*	249
15, 24-28	*317*	73				
10:1-10	*318*	73				
4-10					*545*	244
11-18	*319*	74				
19-25	*320*	75				
32-39	*321*	76				
11:1-2, 8-19	*322*	77				
1-7	*340*	92				
32-40	*323*	77				
12:1-4	*324*	78				
4-7, 11-15	*325*	79				
18-19, 21-24	*326*	80				

	Proper of Seasons				Proper of Saints	
	Year I		Year II			
13:1-8	*327*	81				
15-17, 20-21	*328*	82				
JAMES						
1:1-11			*335*	88		
12-18			*336*	89		
19-27			*337*	89		
2:1-9			*338*	90		
14-24, 26			*339*	91		
3:1-10			*340*	92		
13-18			*341*	93		
4:1-10			*342*	94		
13-17			*343*	95		
5:1-6			*344*	95		
9-12			*345*	96		
13-20			*346*	97		
1 PETER						
1:3-9			*347*	98		
8-12					*586*	253
10-16			*348*	99		
18-25			*349*	99		
2:2-5, 9-12			*350*	100		
4:7-13			*351*	101		
5:1-4					*535*	242
5-14					*555*	244
2 PETER						
1:1-7			*353*	103		
16-19					*614*	260
3:12-15, 17-18			*354*	104		
1 JOHN						
1:1-4					*697*	13
5–2:2					*698*	13
					557	245
2:3-11	*203*	14	*203*	14		
12-17	*204*	14	*204*	14		
18-21	*205*	15	*205*	15		
18-25					*512*	239
22-28	*206*	15	*206*	15		
29–3:6	*207*	16	*207*	16		
3:1-3					*667*	271